W9-AFS-605

COLLECTED WORKS OF ERASMUS

VOLUME 2

THE CORRESPONDENCE OF ERASMUS

LETTERS 142 TO 297

1501 TO 1514

translated by R.A.B. Mynors and D.F.S. Thomson

annotated by Wallace K. Ferguson

University of Toronto Press

Toronto and Buffalo

The research costs of the Collected Works of Erasmus
have been underwritten by a Killam Senior Research Scholarship
awarded by the Killam Program of the Canada Council.

Toronto and Buffalo
Printed in Canada

Library of Congress Cataloging in Publication Data
Main entry under title:
The correspondence of Erasmus.
(Collected works of Erasmus, v. 1–)
CONTENTS: [1] Letters 1 to 141, 1484 to 1500.–
[2] Letters 142 to 297, 1501 to 1514.
1. Erasmus, Desiderius, d. 1536–Correspondence.
PA8511.A5E55 1974 199'.492 72-97422
ISBN 0-8020-1983-8

The Collected Works of Erasmus

The aim of the Collected Works of Erasmus
is to make available an accurate, readable English text
of Erasmus' correspondence and his
other principal writings. The edition is planned
and directed by an Editorial Board, an Executive Committee,
and an Advisory Committee.

Contents

Illustrations

Preface

This volume contains all that has survived of Erasmus' correspondence from the beginning of 1501 to the summer of 1514. This was a period of crucial importance in the career of the Dutch humanist in which he emerged from the obscurity of his early years to achieve an international reputation. During this time he acquired his hard-won mastery of Greek, adumbrated the basic concepts of his religious thought in the *Enchiridion*, established his scholarly status with the magnificent Aldine edition of the *Adagia*, wrote *The Praise of Folly*, published the *De copia*, edited the Correspondence of St Jerome, and laid the foundations for his edition of the Greek New Testament. Much of the correspondence of this period consists of familiar letters to friends or formal dedications addressed to his patrons, but it also affords occasional revealing glimpses of the intense intellectual activity that filled these years.

It is unfortunate that the surviving letters do not form a continuous record, and especially unfortunate that they afford such meagre evidence of Erasmus' activity in the decade between 1501 and 1511, during which he passed from his middle thirties to his middle forties. There are, indeed, a number of letters from 1501, written mostly to friends in the Netherlands. After fleeing from Paris to avoid the plague in the spring of that year, Erasmus spent some weeks visiting old acquaintances in Holland, then a couple of months with Batt at Tournehem, and the rest of the year nearby in the neighbourhood of Saint-Omer. That so many letters from this year survive, as well as those written to Batt from Orléans the previous year, is probably the result of a request addressed by Erasmus to his servant-pupil Louis urging him to collect and copy as many of his letters as he could find.[1] For the next four years, on the other hand, while Erasmus was busy writing the *Enchiridion* and studying Greek at Saint-Omer or Louvain, finally re-

* * * * *

1 Cf Epp51:24n and 162:16–17.

turning to Paris and London, there are only nineteen letters in all. There are more from 1506, including a group of dedicatory prefaces and four brief notes from Florence and Bologna.[2] The correspondence for the remainder of the all-important Italian visit is, however, disappointingly thin. Only three of Erasmus' letters survive from each of the years 1507 and 1508 and none at all from 1509. Even after his return to England in the summer of 1509 there is a complete blank for nearly two years and Erasmus disappears from view until April 1511. Thereafter, until his departure from England in July 1514, there is a fairly continuous exchange of letters between Erasmus and his friends and patrons in London and Cambridge. Among these are some of the most delightful and familiar letters revealing the maturing character of an Erasmus no longer young but well into middle age.

Most of the letters in this volume were printed during Erasmus' lifetime. As is noted in the headnotes to the letters, many of these were dedicatory prefaces or complimentary letters first published in printed books. Of the remainder all but half a dozen were first printed with Erasmus' consent in the *Farrago nova epistolarum Erasmi* (Basel: Froben 1519). The others are scattered through equally authorized editions.[3] One group of letters written to friends at Steyn and Gouda was first published by Paul Merula in *Vita Erasmi* (Leiden 1607); Merula had evidently come upon a letter-book, probably that put together at Erasmus' request by Franciscus Theodoricus.[4] The source of other letters published after Erasmus' death, mostly from still surviving MSS, is noted in the introduction to the letters.

The dating of letters published under Erasmus' supervision, particularly those written before 1517 or 1518, presents a difficult problem, for which Erasmus himself was largely responsible. Until he began to think seriously of publishing his familiar letters, he seldom bothered to append a year date. Then when preparing them for the press he frequently added year dates from his notoriously faulty memory or allowed his editors to do so. As a result, more than half of the dates printed in the *Farrago*, from which most of the letters in this volume are drawn, are demonstrably

* * * * *

2 These notes, addressed to friends in or near Gouda, were probably preserved because they were part of the collection made by his friend Franciscus Theodoricus (see note 4).

3 Ep 279 was first printed in the *Auctarium selectarum aliquot epistolarum* (Basel: Froben August 1518); Epp 270, 285, and 293 in *Epistolae ad diversos* (Basel: Froben 3 August 1521); Epp 204 and 206 in the *Opus epistolarum* (Basel: Froben August 1529).

4 Cf Ep 186 and Allen I 597f. The letters published by Merula are Epp 171, 172, 176, 178, 185, 186, 189, 190, and 200–3.

wrong.[5] A further confusion is occasionally introduced by the practice, common at this time in parts of Europe and in England, of dating the beginning of the year not from 1 January, but from the feast of the Annunciation or Lady Day, 25 March; thus letters written between 1 January and 25 March are frequently given the date of what according to the modern calendar would be the preceding year. To rectify the errors in dating and in general to establish the chronology of Erasmus' correspondence was one of Allen's major achievements. The editors have with few exceptions accepted Allen's conjectural dates and have followed his practice of placing the date at the head of each letter in square brackets if the letter was undated or if the date added in the printed source has been rejected as false, in which case the erroneous date appended at the foot of the letter has also been placed in square brackets.

The translators of this volume have so divided their work that one has made a draft for each letter on which the other has commented, and the agreed result has then been submitted to the Editorial Board. The drafts for this volume are the work of DFST, but responsibility for their final form must be shared by the Board.

Each volume of the correspondence will contain an index to the persons, places, and works mentioned in that volume. When the correspondence is completed, the reader will also be supplied with an index of topics, and of classical and scriptural references. The index for volume 2 was prepared by James Farge. The footnotes dealing with technical problems of coinage and moneys-of-account have been provided in this volume by John H. Munro.

The editors again wish to record here their personal gratitude to the Killam Program of the Canada Council, the generous patron of this extensive undertaking, and to University of Toronto Press. This volume and the preceding one have been published with assistance from the Publications Fund of University of Toronto Press.

WKF

* * * * *

5 Cf CWE 1 xxff.

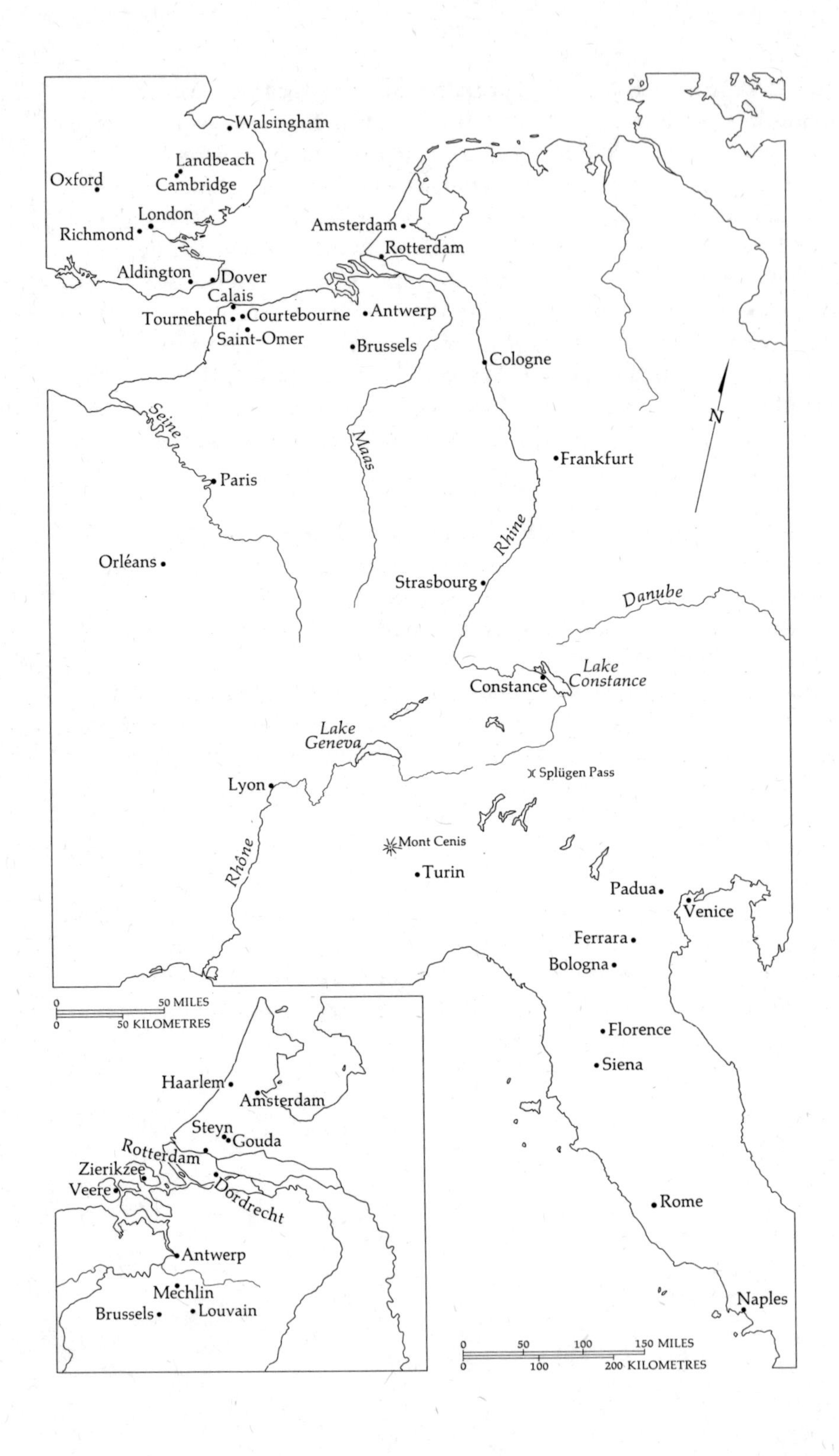
Walsingham
Landbeach
Oxford
Cambridge
London
Richmond
Aldington
Dover
Calais
Tournehem
Courtebourne
Saint-Omer
Antwerp
Brussels
Amsterdam
Rotterdam
Cologne
Seine
Paris
Maas
Frankfurt
N
Rhine
Orléans
Strasbourg
Danube
Lake Constance
Constance
Lake Geneva
Splügen Pass
Lyon
Rhône
Mont Cenis
Turin
Padua
Venice
Ferrara
Bologna
Florence
Siena
Rome
Naples
0 50 MILES
0 50 KILOMETRES
Haarlem
Amsterdam
Steyn
Gouda
Rotterdam
Zierikzee
Veere
Dordrecht
Antwerp
Mechlin
Brussels
Louvain
0 50 100 150 MILES
0 100 200 KILOMETRES

THE CORRESPONDENCE OF ERASMUS

LETTERS 142 TO 297

142 / From Willem Hermans to Servatius Rogerus

[Haarlem]
6 January [1501?]

Willem had evidently moved to a priory in Haarlem, while Servatius remained at Steyn. Just what was the difficulty about the copies of the *Adagia* Erasmus had sent in December (cf Epp 138:176ff and 139:191ff) is not clear. Since they had been sent only some three weeks earlier, they may simply not have arrived, but this does not fully explain Willem's embarrassment. He also seems to have sensed a cooling in Erasmus' attitude toward him, and apparently not without reason (cf Ep 138:173). The only source given for this letter is LB app 492.

WILLEM OF GOUDA TO HIS FRIEND SERVATIUS

Greetings, dear Servatius. Arnold has arrived here, and greeted me on your behalf. You will know whether you so instructed him or whether he pretended that you had in order to curry favour with me. I am ready to believe that he was so instructed, if only because I am pleased when greetings are brought to me from a good friend. After a while, I put several questions to Arnold about your health; he told me what I hoped to hear, and I was very happy at the news that you were well. Of course it would have delighted me still more to have an opportunity to learn this from your own lips and not those of someone else, and I cannot but be surprised at your failure to send me even a brief note; to put it more strongly, if I were not the mildest of men it might seem that I had good reason to be angry with you and to reproach you. I have written to you again and again, assuming, that is, that the letters are being delivered; but I have no doubt that one at least has reached you.

About the copies of Erasmus' *Adagia*, I hardly know what to reply to someone so devoted to me when he tackles me about those books. As you love me, Servatius, I am terrified that the courier from Paris is about to arrive here at any moment, since I have no idea how I can explain myself to our friend Erasmus. I owe a great deal to him indeed, but either through my own negligence or by bad luck I am not returning his favours. So if my name means anything to you at all, advise me about this as soon as possible. Am I to speak, or not? I need not disguise the fact that I am perturbed by the reflection either that 'out of sight is out of mind,' according to the old proverb, or that he has some new friends and I, as the old friend, have given up my place in the sun to those newcomers.

These complaints I have made to you, mostly in your manner but sometimes also in mine. What hope is there left in the affair you mention in your letter? 'Make thy heart strong, and for prosperity reserve thyself.'

* * * * *

24 proverb] *Adagia* II iii 86

28 'Make ... thyself'] Virgil *Aeneid* 1.207

Fortune is fickle; and, though she hurts at random, sometimes she blesses at random too. Perhaps the gods will favour you again sooner than you think. 30
Farewell, sweet companion; may your love prosper. Finally, leave out nothing which I ought to know, or which you think I shall enjoy.

In my library, late at night on the feast of the Epiphany.

143 / To Antoon van Bergen

Paris, 14 January 1501

This is the first of a group of letters (Epp 143, 144, 145) written to patrons in the Tournehem–Saint-Omer circle at Batt's request, but very much against Erasmus' inclination (cf Ep 146:27–9). Antoon van Bergen (1455–1532), abbot of St Bertin at Saint-Omer, was the fourth son of Jan, lord of Glimes and Bergen-op-Zoom cf Ep 42:21n. He had secured the abbey against the will of the monks through the influence which his brother, Hendrik van Bergen, bishop of Cambrai, had with the archduke Philip. He was appointed to the council of the archduke in May or June 1500, and later had a distinguished career as courtier and diplomat. He was a patron from whom Erasmus hoped much, but received little. Erasmus would probably have met him when he was in the service of the bishop of Cambrai in 1493 or 1494 (cf Ep 33 introduction and Allen I app v). But Erasmus' claims were also pressed by Batt, who was himself from Bergen (cf Ep 35 introduction) and had as well close relations with Saint-Omer, which was close to Tournehem. He frequently urged Erasmus to write to the abbot (cf Epp 129:58–9, 130:58ff, 137:77ff.)

TO THE VERY REVEREND THE LORD ABBOT OF ST BERTIN, FROM ERASMUS, GREETINGS

Although your extraordinary kindness, most venerable Father, holds me bound in your debt by such an accumulation of favours that I am in no position to repay the principal, even if I should auction off my very life to do 5
so, yet I should like at least to convey to you somehow in a letter the spontaneous expression of the gratitude I feel, in order that my signature may not deserve to be thought worthless, as it would if I pretended no obligation to recognize my debt by any service whatsoever. For a time I was held back by a degree of hesitation, insofar as I was a little afraid that my 10
unseasonable trifling might interrupt the important and most holy business which, as I am well aware, presses your lordship at home and abroad, in private and in public; also that, whereas I was anxious only to show myself eager to do my duty, I might become a nuisance instead. As the Greek proverb puts it so neatly, 'Good will untimely differs not from hate'; 15
the real meaning of which is that it matters not whether one's tiresome

* * * * *

143:15 Greek proverb] *Adagia* I vii 69

conduct springs from ill will or good, so it be tiresome. Yet on the other hand I thought of your majestic bearing and that splendid health which is equal to the most severe labours, and of the spirit that matches a frame such as yours – a noble spirit, brilliant and well-born, large and lofty, fit for so many great undertakings at once, ready and adaptable for any enterprise, and, as it were, made for all purposes. I reflected that by some wondrous favour on nature's part it had been granted to you scarcely to notice the diverse burden of business so great that even a part thereof might easily crush any other man. This seems almost a hereditary trait in your family, for I have also observed it long since in the bishop, your brother and my patron, when I was one of his household, and often have wondered that a single breast could be equal to so many demands at once. Yet, though that same Herculean strength of heart is something you, my most gracious Lord, share with the rest of your family, still somehow you more than anyone else display a peculiarly engaging charm of character, combined too with the greatest dignity of manner. The result is that you command unrivalled authority in the conduct of public business, while in addition in private life you are the essence of affability, courtesy, and refinement. In the former sphere you are the object of universal admiration; in the latter of universal love; and in both spheres supremely able, so readily can you assume or put aside any role you wish, treating with sceptred monarchs with dignity yet practising a kind of homespun amiability towards small men, like myself, of the lowest class. I can think of nobody who fits better the proverbial Greek line of verse (if your Lordship will bear with me when I perhaps overdo Greek in a letter to the point of absurdity, since I am a recent and keen beginner in that language) – 'An upright man doth all beseem' – which is to say that exceptional persons, such as your Lordship, can do everything gracefully. It was the same versatile kind of intellect that Horace celebrated in Aristippus when he said 'Every hue did Aristippus suit,' whether he strode in royal purple bright, or crept along in dusty Cynic's gown – though you yourself never change, but by a most rare combination of qualities can be kind in dignity, dignified in kindness –

20

25

30

35

40

45

But why, you will say, this long discourse of mine? Your warning is a good one; for the period I have not yet completed must be given shape, and, late though it is, I must put an end to this display of verbosity – a display caused not by natural garrulity but by a sort of agreeable meditation upon your portrait. So, I repeat, when I reflected that your unprecedented physical and mental gifts enabled you to undertake the most exacting tasks with

50

* * * * *

42 'An upright man doth all beseem'] *Adagia* II ix 60

44 Horace] *Epistles* 1.17.23

an effortless ease such as scarcely anyone else could reveal even if he were completely at leisure, and that you found the most weighty business mere sport, I decided that I need not be too anxious in case you were offended by an untimely interruption from the present letter, particularly as I had heard in a letter from my friend Batt with what a kind expression you received my last. Yet I have still very little to say, except that I am forever struggling with Nemesis, yet am eagerly determined, if I cannot attain to scholarship, at least to die among my books like Philemon; and that the remembrance of your kind services to me is very far from dwindling in my sight – a memory which comes back to me every day so strongly that the feeling of your kindness could not be more freshly and pleasantly alive even if I were still enjoying it in person. May I add that I should like nothing better than a pretext afforded by you for serving your Reverence to the utmost extent which such humble talents as I possess and the labours of my studious nights may permit. Later I shall look out in person for such an opportunity; in the meantime, to provide you with a letter of adequate length, I will tell you a tragic tale; quite modern, it is true, but so ghastly that in comparison the story of Medea or Thyestes or any other ancient tragedy would look like a comic theme.

Last year at Meung, a little town near Orléans, a dying sorcerer instructed his wife to hand over all his books of magic, and the other instruments of his cult, to a certain citizen of Orléans who would presently come to ask for them, since he had been his accomplice and partner in crime. This person took all the materials away to Orléans. Now for more than three years the sorcerer had at his own home been practising a wicked ritual, even more abominable than any kind of idolatry, with the connivance of his wife and the active assistance of his maiden daughter; so I shall give a brief account of the rites and ceremonies in which the blasphemous worship consisted, as I have been told them by most reliable informants.

He had placed the sacred body of Jesus our Redeemer in a kind of small wicker box and concealed it under the bedclothes. Oh, divine patience! As I relate this, 'a shudder cold my limbs doth shake.' Three years before he had purchased it from a starveling irreligious priest, a class too numerous hereabouts, for a smaller sum, I believe, than the Jews once paid for Christ,

* * * * *

61 Nemesis] *Rhamnusia illa*: literally 'the famous goddess of Rhamnus' (her shrine in Attica). Erasmus often speaks of Nemesis where we should expect him to say Fortune.

62 Philemon] The Greek comic poet who was found dead with a book in his hand (Apuleius *Florida* 16)

86 shudder ... shake] Virgil *Aeneid* 3.29.30

so that that wicked priest not only brought Judas back again but even outdid him, and it is said that he paid for his impious behaviour by a sudden death. Well then, whenever the sorcerer was about to perform his not holy but diabolical rites, the divine sacrament was brought out by profane hands, dug up from the bedclothes, stripped bare, and exposed to view. The daughter, a girl as yet unmarried, held up a naked sword (it being supposed that only a virgin could properly perform this function) and directed its point towards the sacred body in a threatening gesture. Next there was produced a kind of head, fashioned out of some substance or other, having three faces: of course, this represented the Three in One and One in Three. They swathed it in ninefold wrappings on which were a thousand representations of the letter *tau*, each inscribed with unknown angels' names; followed by as many decorated with the dreadful names of demons. When this had all been put together, the high priest of evil opened his books and, in accursed prayers dictated by Hecate, named first the Holy Trinity and a great number of angels, each in his proper company; and then hundreds of demons' names; and continued until the Devil himself arrived and answered his summons in person.

This abominable being provided, or at least pointed the way to, vast treasures; he had promised mountains of gold to his officiating priest, and even made him some gifts, but so disappointing were these that the latter began to repent of his three years' effort. Accordingly he used the customary formulae to call up the author of the promises made to him, and complained that for some considerable time he had been hoodwinked, and led on by nothing but hopes, without gaining anything worth while. The Devil, in reply, made excuses, saying that it was not his fault that it fell out so, but that there was something amiss in the ritual, for he must have an educated man there; and, if the man could find one, he himself would point the way to treasures richer than anyone hoped for. And when the other asked him whom he could best enlist for this purpose, the Devil urged him to approach the prior of a monastery of the order known as Preachers,

* * * * *

100 the letter *tau*] As Allen points out (IV xxi), the Greek *tau* was regarded as a kind of talisman, 'partly from its resemblance to the Hebrew word of Ezekiel 9.4, used for the sign put on the foreheads of the faithful, and partly from its likeness to a cross.'

108 mountains of gold] Literally 'Persian mountains' (cf *Adagia* I ix 15)

119 Preachers] The Order of Preachers was the official title of the Dominican Order, to which was especially entrusted the prosecution of heresy and blasphemy (cf Ep 290:11).

which is behind the walls of Orléans, and cautiously sound him out. Now, this prior is what is called a *baccalarius formatus*; he has some repute among the vulgar, and is not the worst of preachers, as divines go nowadays at any rate; but, as it seemed to me afterwards and most men of the kind share this weakness, he is excessively hungry for notoriety. Yet I simply cannot even conjecture what the evil one was up to; was he trying to drive straight to ruin that priest of his, who was already thinking of quitting? Or did he seriously entertain the idea that the mind of a theologian could be bribed by the size of the reward offered to him? He was relying, I suppose, on the fact, superbly expressed by Virgil, that

Men's hearts to every ill incites
Th'accursed love of gold,

or again, as is claimed by those who have a closer acquaintance with men of this kind, that, hidden under those hoods, and under the most abject reputation for beggary, there sometimes lurk hearts ablaze with insufferable arrogance and an extraordinary lust for money.

But this is a question I leave undecided. Once he was duly persuaded, our hero went to meet the man. Thereupon, in order that he might gradually try out his attitude, he pretended to have some manuscripts at home that were of no use to him, since he was unlettered, but might be exceedingly serviceable to a man of education, and asked if he would like to purchase any of them. The theologian bade him produce the books, so that he might look at them; and he produced an Old Testament, popularly called the Bible, in a French translation. The theologian having expressed disdain for this book, and asking whether he had any others, the fellow produced, though with a show of unwillingness and reluctance, another one that lay concealed under his coat. When the other had turned the pages and observed that here was a master of illicit practices, he took a closer look – whether intrigued by its novelty, as frequently happens, or on purpose to investigate thoroughly what he began to suspect as an underlying scandal, I do not know. Therefore, asked what his decision was, he answered that it looked to him like a book of witchcraft. The other, pledging him to secrecy, said that he possessed several of the same sort at home but that they needed the help of a scholar. It was possible, however, that they might be worth a

* * * * *

121 *baccalarius formatus*] This term, which is untranslatable, was applied to bachelors who had completed nine months of the *Sentences* (H. Rashdall *Universities of Europe in the Middle Ages* (Oxford 1938) I 478).

129 Virgil] *Aeneid* 3.56–7

fortune. The theologian pricked up his ears at this, and begged him to bring those books also for him to see. He was, he said, deeply interested in the subject. He must certainly not neglect such a marvellous opportunity; and he was absolutely confident that it would come to a happy issue. 155

So they shook hands, and the poor wretch brought the rest of the books. The theologian continued his interrogation until the man, who by now trusted him completely, confessed the whole affair, even finally the matter of the body of Christ. Then the prior, appearing overjoyed, begged him to enact those momentous rites before him, and said he was now all agog to proceed quickly with the business. The man then took him home, and told his wife to bring out the aforesaid sacrament and the other instruments of witchcraft. These were produced and examined. The monk, completely concealing his purpose, as he himself recounts, went directly from the spot to the Official, as they call him – a man of the most unquestionable uprightness of life, with a high reputation for complete proficiency in civil and canon law, and a very good friend of mine. He, thereupon, acting on information laid by the theologian, instructed the royal constables to imprison the man together with his wife and daughter, deeming that an incident of so portentous a nature admitted of no delay. At once the house was forcibly entered, the holy sacrament brought forth with due reverence, and the remainder of that day and all the following night devoted to solemn hymns and prayers by the clergy and monks, who kept night-long vigil. 160 165 170 175

The next day a solemn supplication was decreed; the streets going to and coming from the church were hung with tapestries, and throughout the city the churches resounded with the ringing of holy bells. The entire body of clergy walked in procession, each carrying his relics, the whole city having turned out to view the spectacle; and the eucharist, that had been removed from the house of sin, was conveyed with fitting solemnity to the church of Ste Croix, where, before a larger congregation, they say, than had ever before been seen there, the theologian, not without suspicion of vainglory, gave an account of the whole affair, repeatedly appealing to the body of Christ which lay before him in the open air exactly as it had been brought from the sorcerer's house. He did likewise the following day, and was to have done so on consecutive days to come, announcing to the assembled multitude anything that the prisoners had meantime confessed – I imagine because he thought it presented him with absolutely sure basis for winning immortality – had not the Official, who was no fool, silenced the theologian, 180 185 190

* * * * *

167 Official] The official-principal, a term still in use, is a regular member of a bishop's staff with legal or judicial functions.

already in full flight upon the windy chariot of fame. The prisoners were examined and heard, at some length, by theologians summoned from Paris for the purpose, with the assistance of two legal experts. I was informed by the Official that some amazing revelations were made by the man during the investigations, but that they could not yet be treated as reliable since the 195 man's account was still not free of inconsistency; that the woman was terribly harassed by a demon at night – stabbed and beaten and pulled about until she almost fainted; but the girl was at peace with herself and not at all upset by the fear of punishment, since she stated that every morning at daybreak she was visited by someone or other who consoled her and took 200 all her grief away and bade her be calm in spirit. And at Meung the widow of the sorcerer, whom I mentioned above, is also detained in prison.

We may now proceed to regard the Medea and Thyestes and Nero of the poets as mere trifles, since the impiety of Christians has produced abominations whereof the very names were unknown to the ancients. What 205 name indeed are we to give to such a horror as this? The names of Chaldeans, casters of horoscopes, astrologers, sorcerers, magicians, diviners, soothsayers, augurs, wizards, necromancers, geomancers, fortune-tellers, and enchanters are but trivial in my opinion, and inadequate for such deep-dyed wickedness as this. The augur notes the swift flight aloft of 210 birds, and the favourable omen of the hungry chickens, while the soothsayer probes the configuration of the victim's entrails; the astrologer consults the stars, while the wizard collects herbs under a spell; the enchanter deals in prayers, the magician calls up departed spirits, and the palmist examines the wrinkles of the hand. These are terrible practices, and Christ- 215 ian ears can hardly bear to hear tell of them; but are they not vastly less so than this tragedy at Orléans? Did even Thessaly, that notorious haunt of witches, ever produce the like? Now the Jewish law visits the punishment of death upon those who commune with departed spirits, while the laws of the Roman Empire denounce in the strongest terms the superstitions of 220 soothsaying and augury, referring to those who practise them as strangers to nature and enemies of the human race, worthy of punishment by the retributive sword, or burning, or being thrown to wild beasts (these are Constantine's own words), and prescribing that any who consult them are to be deprived of all their property and banished to an island; this is clear 225 from the Code, in the title 'Of Sorcerers and Astrologers,' where there is an

* * * * *

211 hungry chickens] It was considered a most favourable omen when the sacred fowls ate so ravenously that the grain fell from their beaks to the ground.

226 Code] *Codex Justinianus* ix tit.18

additional gloss that is indeed 'noteworthy' (to use the language of Accorso's school), but deserves to be marked in black, inasmuch as it explains a 'soothsayer' (*haruspex*) as one who watches heavenly movements and birds, and a 'priest' (*sacerdos*) as one who professes necromancy, and 230 some other instances of the kind of which it is hard to say whether their barbarity or their ignorance is greater. What is certain is their complete absurdity; yet I am by no means unfamiliar with such things, since monstrosities of this sort are of such frequent occurrence everywhere in the Digest that now that I am accustomed to them they do not even amuse me 235 any longer, much less annoy me.

But to return to my point. The pontifical decrees, and also the letters known as Decretals, when they mention sorcery and damnable superstitions of the kind, do not even touch upon this kind of witchcraft, either because those bygone ages never suspected that such impiety was possible 240 or because the authors of the written text considered that they had a duty to spare the ears of mankind. This novel and unprecedented abomination was the child, not of Night, mother of the Furies (as the poets' legend has it), but of greed, the parent of every crime; nor was it a single phenomenon, but a fusion of superstition, impiety, idolatry, and blasphemy, like the mingled 245 brood of several different monsters. Are people then surprised if our modern generation is afflicted, now by wars, now by famine, now by pestilence, now by divers other evils, when, over and above those vices which have already well nigh ceased to appear as vices, so common are they, we are guilty of crimes that far outdo either the Giants, whom the thunderbolt 250 confounded, or Lycaon's cruelty, for which the great flood itself hardly atoned? Are we ourselves surprised that new plagues come upon us every day, when each day, by fresh wickedness, we provoke the Lord our God

* * * * *

228 Accorso's] Cf Ep 134:30–1n.

235 Digest] The main body of the code of law (Pandects) of the emperor Justinian; it was adopted in AD 533.

237 pontifical decrees] The bull of Innocent VIII, 1484, *Summis desiderantis affectibus*, for example, condemns sorcery, but makes no mention of the sacrilegious use of the host.

250 Giants] A race of monsters in ancient mythology, sons of Earth and Tartarus, who rebelled against the gods and attempted to storm Olympus. They were smitten with lightning by Jupiter and buried under Mount Aetna.

251 Lycaon] A mythical king of Arcadia, turned into a wolf by Zeus for cruelty and sacrilege. Because of other sins he caused Zeus to bring a deluge upon the earth (cf Ovid *Metamorphoses* 1.222).

and, as Horace says, 'through our crimes will not permit / Heaven to lay its thunderbolts aside'? 255

My gracious Lord, I have sent you a very Iliad; but what ran away with my pen, almost without my realising it, was partly the keen anguish I felt, partly a certain delight I take in conversing with your Lordship; so I beg you to pardon my love, or my grief. Concerning Dismas, I have written to your chaplain Antonius. Should my appeal be successful, I feel quite certain that 260 the day will come, and very soon, when I shall be happy that I gave you the advice, and you will be happier still that you followed it.

Farewell.

Paris, 14 January [1500]

144 / To Nicholas of Burgundy Paris, 26 January [1501]

Nicholas of Burgundy (d 1522) was a natural son of Anthony of Burgundy, 'le Grand Bâtard,' lord of Tournehem (cf Ep 80 introduction). He was thus an uncle of Batt's pupil, Adolph of Veere. In 1498 he was made provost of St Peter's church at Utrecht, and it was as provost that Erasmus frequently mentioned him in letters to Batt (cf Epp 129:55, 130:41, 138:140, 151:15).

ERASMUS TO MASTER NICHOLAS OF BURGUNDY, THE PROVOST

My affection for you is such that any letter is bound to seem excessively short when it is measured against my enthusiasm; yet I am so busy that even the shortest letter must appear unduly long. The ancients used to describe poets and men of eloquence allegorically as swans – with good 5 reason, in my opinion, for the pure white plumage of the latter answers to the former's purity of inner being, while both tribes are sacred to Apollo; both take particular delight in clear streams and well-watered meads; both are tuneful. Yet nowadays each of them seems to have fallen silent, especially in our own country, and not to have a voice even at death's approach. 10 The reason for this I conjecture to be that of which naturalists inform us: that no swan will sing unless the west wind blows – and can we wonder that

* * * * *

254 Horace] *Odes* 1.3.38–40

256 Iliad] *Adagia* IV v 51

259 Dismas] Cf Ep 137:15ff and n.

144:10 at death's approach] Cf *Adagia* I ii 55.

11 naturalists] Cf *Adagia*, where Aelian *De naturis animalium* is cited as authority for the singing of swans in a west wind.

all the swans are silent today, when so many rough breezes blow from north and south, but never a one from the balmy west? I, at least, was so completely deprived of voice, as well as cash, when that British blizzard blew, 15
that no wolf-who-saw-you-first could equal its performance. But it is only in early springtime that the soft westerlies blow. Wherefore if you, my most gracious Provost, should be like spring for the Lady of Veere, my patroness, and from her the west wind should blow upon me, then I in turn shall be such a singing swan to both of you that even later ages will hear the tune. 20
There is no need for me to explain the riddle: for of course I am writing this to an Oedipus and not to a Davus. Only hasten to be that second Batt, whom you promised me you would be, for a little while in the Lady's ear! Farewell.

Paris, 26 January [1497]

145 / To Anna van Borssele Paris, 27 January 1501

TO THE MOST NOBLE LADY, ANNA VAN BORSSELE,
PRINCESS OF VEERE, FROM ERASMUS, GREETINGS

Three Annas there were, on whom ancient literature conferred enduring fame: first, Anna who bore the cognomen Perenna and in ancient days was held to have been allowed to join the heavenly hosts for her extraordinary 5
devotion to her sister Dido; next, Hannah the wife of Elkanah, for whose glory it is enough that in her old age, with the blessing of God, she bore Samuel, yet bore him not for herself only, but that he might be a faithful priest to God and serve the people as an upright judge; and lastly Anna, parent to the Virgin Mother and grandmother to Jesus, who was God and 10
Man, so that she at least has no need of further eulogies. The first is immortalized by the poetic muses of Rome. The second receives high praise in the Hebrew annals. The third is an object of adoration to pious Christ-

* * * * *

15 British blizzard] Cf Ep 119: 9n.

16 wolf-who-saw-you-first] It was believed that, if a wolf saw a man before the man saw the wolf, the man was struck dumb (cf *Adagia* I vii 86).

18 spring] Erasmus seems to be playing with the words 'ver' (spring) and 'Veere.'

22 Davus] A slave who in Terence's *Andria* (194) professes himself unable to interpret a meaning conveyed by hints, saying 'I am Davus, not Oedipus' (cf *Adagia* I iii 36).

145:4 Perenna] Anna Perenna, an old Italian deity, identified with Anna the sister of Dido in Virgil's *Aeneid* by Ovid *Fasti* 3.545–654.

6 Hannah] Cf 1 Samuel 1ff.

ians, celebrated in the eloquent works of Rodolphus Agricola and Baptista Mantuanus. And I would that now my pen too might find skill enough to 15 make posterity aware how devout, how pure, how chaste your soul is, for then it would add you, a fourth Anna, to the former three; which will surely come to pass, if my poor talent should but prove equal to your goodness.

I believe indeed that the name of Anna fell to your lot 'not without heaven's plan, and purposes divine,' as Virgil expresses it, so much do I 20 observe to be alike in you and in those I have mentioned. If they were ladies of high degree, is not your pedigree the most exalted in this realm of ours? And if they were famed for piety, your piety also finds the greatest favour in the sight of Heaven. The patience of those ladies was sorely tried and tested in severe sufferings; and this you have more in common with them than I 25 could wish, for, I do confess, your high sense of honour and maidenly simplicity deserve unbroken happiness. But alas, what can one do? It is ever Fortune's sport to raise aloft the unworthy and hamper the innocent. Yet do thou, my patroness, follow the example of the palm-tree:

> Yield not to troubles, but upon the way 30
> More boldly press, by fortune circumscribed.

And though I myself am full of indignation at your misfortunes, as befits the affection I bear towards you, or loyalty, rather (for I owe my entire well-being to her by whose kindness I am enabled to live a life of learning, without which I cannot live at all), yet I am somewhat consoled by the fact 35 that tempests of this kind are now and again sent by Heaven's favour, not to overwhelm us, but to furnish us with a kind of field and opportunity for the exercise of virtue, only that it may come to shine ever more brightly. It was thus that the courage of Hercules, of Aeneas and Ulysses, was fired, and that the patience of Job was tested. 40

This is why the anguish I feel at your present difficulties is surpassed by the joy I experience at the way in which you endure them. You endure, indeed, as I have more than once observed with admiration, so patiently or rather so cheerfully, that, let me say frankly, I myself now take more encouragement from your example than from any set by the heroes of 45 antiquity – I, a man almost born to misfortune, who indeed for the past year has been sailing continuously against wind and current and bad weather.

* * * * *

14 Agricola] Cf Ep 23:58n.

14–15 Baptista Mantuanus] Battista Spagnuoli of Mantua (cf Ep 48:86n)

20 Virgil] *Aeneid* 5.56

30–1 Yield not ... circumscribed] Virgil *Aeneid* 6.95–6

And also (for why should I not venture to confess this to you?) somehow or other my affection for you becomes especially strong when I observe that Nemesis, who has always been my great enemy, is not as good to you either 50 as she ought to be, just as hardships endured together sometimes constitute a bond of good will among mankind. Yet the resemblance is invalid, for in your case the place you occupy in society can scarcely be touched by Fortune's caprice; thus Fortune only plagues you now and again, whereas she assails me so constantly (only in constancy unlike herself) that it might 55 seem as if she had formed a plot to ruin my scholarship.

As I pen this letter, it occurs to me (and to whom could I more properly reveal my unhappiness than to her who alone is able and willing to cure it?) – it occurs to me, I say, that today's dawn saw the anniversary of the occasion when the little store of money that supported my studies made 60 shipwreck on the English coast; and, as I remember, from that very day to this Fortune has furnished me with an endless series of misfortunes, linked one to the other. For no sooner had that English Charybdis spewed me back upon the world you and I know, than it was succeeded by a raging storm, and hence a dreadfully uncomfortable journey, and thereafter by the sharp 65 points of robbers' poniards at our throats; next by fever, followed by the plague, though this last merely put me to flight and failed to infect me. Besides this, there have been private anxieties, of the sort whereof men's lives produce considerable quantities every day. But I should be ashamed, I swear, to fall into dismay; because, in the first place, I, being a man, am at 70 any rate fortified by the bulwarks of my profession as a scholar and by the precepts of philosophy, whereas you, created a woman by Nature herself, and by Fortune's indulgence born to the highest station and brought up amid the utmost refinement, have something you are obliged to endure, and endure so unlike a woman; and in the second place, no matter how 75 many thunderbolts Fortune aims at me, I see no reason to abandon literature or lose heart so long as you shine, like an immovable pole-star, to guide me on my way. For it does not lie in Fortune's power to rob me of my learning; while the little money that a scholar's leisure requires can easily be supplied from your wealth, inasmuch as this is not inferior to your 80 heart's demands. And, whereas you owe your power to your good fortune, I owe to your goodness of heart the fact that you are willing, and freely

* * * * *

50 Nemesis] Cf Ep 143:61n.

59 anniversary] It was on 27 January 1500 that Erasmus had £20 confiscated by the authorities at Dover (cf Ep 119 introduction and 10–11n).

66 robbers' poniards] Cf Ep 119.

67 plague] Cf Ep 129 introduction.

willing, to foster my literary talents, which undoubtedly depend upon you alone, look to you alone, and are devoted to you alone. Choerilus, bad and (to use Lucilius' word) iron-harsh poet though he was, was adopted by Alexander the Great. The inexhaustible generosity of Maecenas fostered Virgil and Horace, men of slender means. The enthusiasm felt by Vespasian encouraged the labours of Pliny. The emperor Gratian's enlightened patronage rewarded with the consulship itself the half-Greek productions of Ausonius. The noble rank of Paula and Eustochium lent lustre to the pious eloquence of Jerome. Even in latter days Lorenzo de' Medici produced Poliziano, the darling of our present age, brought up as though he were the son of his bosom. And since I would not count the sands, as the Greek proverb has it, suffice it to say that every man of genius has had his Maecenas. 85 90 95

And no contemptible degree of gratitude, as it seems to me, was shown by those writers to their patrons, whose memory they consecrated to eternity in their books. For my part, I would not in my right mind exchange you, my foster parent, for any Maecenas or emperor; while, as to repayment, I too shall endeavour, so far as I may with this small talent, to see that my patroness is also known to later generations, who shall be amazed that at the world's edge there lived one woman who by her generosity was eager to revive the works of sound learning which lay in part corrupted by the ignorance of the untaught, in part languishing through the negligence of princes, in part neglected through the slothfulness of mankind; and who refused to allow the small literary skill of Erasmus to perish from poverty when it had been forsaken by gilded dispensers of promises, robbed by a despotic king, and assailed by every kind of misfortune. May you go on as you have begun; my works, your foster-children, raise their hand to you in supplication, calling upon you both in the name of your own fortune, which you so creditably despise in prosperity and have so bravely borne in adversity, and in that of their own fortunes, which are ever foes to them and against which they cannot stand, save with your help; and for the love of that splendid queen, ancient Theology, whom the divinely inspired psalmist, as he is translated by Jerome, describes as sitting on the right hand of the king eternal, not in dirt or in rags, as she is now to be seen in the lecture halls of the sophists, but in a vesture of gold, wrought about with divers 100 105 110 115

* * * * *

85 Lucilius] Cf Cicero *De finibus* 1.2.5; but, as Allen points out, the name is there given as Licinius or Licinus. Erasmus apparently misremembered. On Alexander and Choerilus see Ep 104:22–4.

93 count the sands] *Adagia* I iv 44

114–15 psalmist] Psalm 44:11 (45:9)

colours; whom to save from squalor and neglect is the earnest endeavour of all the poor fruits of my nightly toil.

And to this very end there are two things I have long perceived to be most necessary: first, that I should visit Italy, in order that from the fame of that country some measure of authority may accrue to my small scholarship; and second, that I should be able to style myself a doctor. Now both of these ambitions are trivial enough; for, as Horace says, men do not all at once 'alter their souls, who cross the main'; and I should not be made one jot more learned for the shadow of a mighty name; yet one has to follow the present-day fashion, since nowadays not only the vulgar but even the most highly reputed scholars are unable to regard anyone as a learned man unless he is styled *magister noster* – though Christ, the prince of theologians, forbids this. In antiquity, on the other hand, no man was reputed to be learned merely because he had purchased a doctorate, but those who in their published books showed clear proof of sound doctrine were alone entitled to the appellation of doctors. But, as I have remarked, it is no use putting on a good performance if everyone hisses it. I must therefore put on the lion's skin, in order that those who judge a man by his title and not by his books, which they cannot understand, may believe that I too have learnt my letters. Men of this kind exist, steeped in foolish lore, trained, at great expense, of course, to know nothing; dull-witted, scarcely gifted with average sense, yet by Heaven how stiff-necked in their arrogance and how disdainful of others! – men who along with the meaningless title have assumed the entirely false notion that they are finished scholars. They remind one of the characters of Philoxenus and Gnatho – horrible gormandizers – in besmirching all departments of learning with the grime of kitchen-jargon and, may I say it, by blowing their noses upon them, so that, after those who possess decently bred minds have felt ill and withdrawn,

120

125

130

135

140

145

* * * * *

121 Italy] Cf Ep 75:15n.

123 doctor] Erasmus had come to Paris in 1495 with the intention of taking a doctorate in theology (cf Ep 48:27–9). Later he set his heart on a degree from Bologna (cf Ep 75:15n). In his discouraged mood in the summer of 1500 he seemed willing to settle for a Parisian doctorate, if even that were not too expensive (cf Ep 129:67n), but the dream of acquiring an Italian degree revived at the slightest encouragement.

124 Horace] *Epistles* 1.11.27

126 shadow of a mighty name] Lucan 1.135

135 the lion's skin] *Adagia* I iii 66

138 dull-witted] 'Crassa Minerva': cf *Adagia* I i 37.

142 Philoxenus and Gnatho] Characters in Plautus' *Bacchides* and Terence's *Eunuchus* respectively

they may have the field to themselves. These then are the monsters I have also to struggle against, with the bearing of a second Hercules: so if you can equip your humble servant to be fit to conduct his fight against such portents as these with as much authority as courage, then not I alone but scholarship itself will owe its life to you. The arms I need, my princess, are those of Glaucus in Homer – those he gave, not those he received. The meaning of this riddle will be explained to you in a letter from my friend Batt, to whom I have revealed my entire situation without reserve. I did it brazenly, contrary to my own habits and natural inclination and also contrary to the maidenly bashfulness of the profession of letters; but necessity is a powerful weapon, as has been remarked. 150 155

I am sending you a version of yourself – another *Anna* – in the shape of a poem, or rather a set of verses which I threw off when I was a mere boy; for ever since my earliest years I have burned with eager devotion to that saint. I send also a few prayers which will enable you to call down from Heaven, as by magic charms (and even against her will, if I may so put it), not the poets' moon but her who brought to birth the sun of righteousness, though indeed the Virgin is wont to be gracious, whenever a virgin calls upon her with virginal prayers. For I reckon you as maiden rather than as widow, since your former marriage, when you were but a young girl, was made partly in resignation to your parents' will, partly to your family's need of offspring, and was a marriage of such a sort that it should be thought of as a source not of pleasure but of trial and endurance. And inasmuch as now in your still blooming youth and well-nigh girlish years you do not allow the importunity of suitors to cause you to give up your determination to remain chaste, and in spite of your ample fortune you indulge yourself not at all – these things spell maidenhood, not widowhood, to me. If you remain true to it, as I am sure you will, then, believe me, I shall boldly count you not among the maidens who are, saith the Scripture, without number, nor among the eighty concubines of Solomon, but, with Jerome himself approving, I hope, among the fifty queens. 160 165 170 175

* * * * *

151 Glaucus] Cf Homer *Iliad* 6.230–6. He gave gold armour in exchange for bronze (cf *Adagia* I ii 1).

155–6 necessity is a powerful weapon] *Adagia* II iii 40

158 poem] 'Rhythmus iambicus in laudem Annae, aviae Jesu Christi,' written probably about 1497 and first printed in the *Epigrammata* (Basel: Froben March 1518) and shortly after in the *Enchiridion* (Basel: Froben July 1518). Cf Reedijk 202ff.

159 earliest years] Literally 'from tender nails': cf *Adagia* I vii 52.

174 Scripture] Song of Songs 6:8. There were three-score queens, not fifty.

For some time now I have been engaged on a work 'On Letters' and also another 'On Variation of Style,' the purpose of which is to assist the studies of your son Adolph. There is also one 'On Literature' which is to be dedicated to you. If these should happen to appear later than could have been wished, please do not blame this on my remissness but on my misfortune, or, if you prefer, on the difficulty of the task; for, while it is sheer madness to publish bad books, it is extremely difficult to publish good ones. Farewell, and think kindly of my muses. 180

Paris, 27 January 1500 185

146 / To Jacob Batt Paris, 27 January [1501]

This letter answers one from Batt which apparently repeated whatever arguments or demands were contained in the letter brought by Louis to Orléans and which annoyed Erasmus so much that he answered it (by Ep 139) only after he had been urged to do so by Jacob Voogd (cf lines 23ff and Ep 139 introduction). Erasmus was now sending the letters Batt had evidently asked for (Epp 143, 144, 145).

ERASMUS TO HIS FRIEND BATT

That sycophant brought me, believe it or not, another letter from you, not a whit less foolish and insulting than your previous one. If I am not mistaken, dear Batt, some evil genius, out of spite at seeing friends who agree so well together, is scheming to sever the link of affectionate good will between us. I shall never be responsible for causing this to happen, and you must see that the same is true of you. 5

In the first place, was it necessary for Louis to hurry back to me as if he had a thousand nobles instead of eight francs? Would it not have been possible to send a small sum like that by someone else? Again, granted you were sending it, why did you suppose you ought to keep something back even out of an amount so tiny? In case, I imagine, I should forget my duty, now that I was rolling in money; or perhaps in order to have a couple of gold 10

* * * * *

146:8 Louis] Erasmus had made the same complaint when Louis was sent to Orléans with a disappointingly small sum of money (cf Ep 139:15). That this refers to a second occasion is shown by line 89, which indicates that Louis has been to Paris and is returning to Batt with the present letter.

9 eight francs] Erasmus is undoubtedly again using the term franc as a popular synonym for the French livre tournois. The sum of £8 0s 0d tournois was then worth, by relative silver values, £1 7s 6d gros Flemish or 18s 11d sterling; by relative gold values, 2.8 gold English angel-nobles, the type of nobles evidently referred to here and in lines 83–5 below. Cf Epp 119:277n; 139:15n; 214:4n; 256:117n; CWE 1318, 325; and tables A and B below, 327–37.

pieces handy as an excuse for sending me yet another ambassador? As for your objections about that letter: believe me, the whole business could have 15 been finished off without it, if only you had shown fight – and you could have asked someone else to fetch the letter anyway. You will never comprehend what a nuisance this rushing back has been to me. Out of the entire year fever leaves me no more than four months to devote to study, and for this reason I must work manfully. I have been trimming, or rather recasting, 20 the work on letters which I sketched out long since. The task I had set myself was both onerous and exacting; just then in came Louis, bearing your letters filled with reproaches, and with even the pittance docked. I was so annoyed at this that I wanted to throw away the work I was engaged on, and would have sent the youth back without a letter if Jacob Voogd had not 25 urged me, at great length, to change my mind.

And I swear I never wrote anything so much against the grain as the nonsense – indeed the Gnathonisms – I have penned to the Lady, the provost, and the abbot. I know you will find fault with my sullen mood but you will not do so, my dear Batt, if you assess my circumstances correctly 30 and also reflect how hard it is to drive oneself to the writing of a major work, and how much crueller still to be distracted by irrelevant trifles when one is already fired with enthusiasm for it. Because you have not tried all this yourself, you imagine that my mind is always fresh and eager, just as yours is, in your life so full of leisure. Cannot you appreciate that there is no 35 burden of weariness greater than that of a mind tired out with writing, and do you not think that I ought to discharge my duty towards those whose generosity I am enjoying here? Lastly you ask me for huge parcels of books, without taking steps to see that I am furnished with the leisure required for producing them. Last of all, it does not satisfy you that I shall in due time 40 make famous both our friendship and the Lady's munificence, when the books are published; but I must also write hundreds of letters every day!

* * * * *

15 letter] This may refer to the letter Batt had apparently asked Erasmus to send to the Lady Anna and which he seems to have neglected to write, since Ep 145 to the lady is of the same date as the present letter. It might also refer to Ep 139, which outlined the arguments Batt should use, but which did not satisfy his desire for a letter to the lady herself.

19 fever] Cf Ep 124:11n.

21 on letters] The *De conscribendis epistolis* (cf Ep 145:177)

23 letters] This must refer to the letters Louis brought to Orléans, since Jacob Voogd who persuaded Erasmus to answer was there.

28 Gnathonisms] Coined from Gnatho, a parasite in the *Eunuchus* of Terence, and type of all such. Erasmus refers to him frequently in that sense (cf Epp 26:6 and 44:22)

42 hundreds of letters] Cf Ep 139:130–1.

A year has now elapsed since the promise of the money and still your letters offer me nothing but vain hopes: 'I am not despairing,' 'I shall look after your interests attentively,' and similar sentiments, which now make me sick, so often have they been dinned into my ears. When you finally express regret for the Lady's misfortunes, it seems to me that you are suffering from another person's illness. If she neglects her own fortune, are you to be distressed about this? If she is wasting her time and trifling with her beloved X, are you to be indignant over this? Has she nothing to give? One thing I can see clearly: if she refuses to give for reasons like these, she never will give anything, for noble patrons never want for such excuses. How little difference it would make, among so much that is completely squandered, if she were to give me two hundred francs! Is she able to feed those fornicators in monkish garb, those worthless rascals (you know whom I mean), and yet unable to afford support for the leisure of one who is able to write books that deserve to live – if I may for once be a shade boastful about myself? Yes, she has certainly met with a great many difficulties, but the fault was her own. She elected to link herself with that conceited little fop, rather than with some responsible and serious husband, appropriate to her sex and age. I myself foresee far worse trials to come if she does not discard this fancy. Yet if I say this it is not from any hostility I have towards her; I am as fond of her as I ought to be, considering how much she has done for me.

But I ask you, what does it matter in terms of her fortune if I am given two hundred francs? Seven hours after they are handed over she will have forgotten about them. The whole problem here is to extract the money, either in cash or by a banker's draft, so that I may draw it here at Paris. You yourself have already sent her numerous letters about this, all containing messages, suggestions, and hints. What could be more useless? What you should have done was to look out for an opportunity (if not ideal, at least reasonably good), and then, after intelligent preparation, you should have gone in determinedly for the kill. As things now stand, this is what you must still do, late though it is. I feel certain that you are bound to get what you are after, provided you go about it courageously. In the interests of a friend it is possible for you to show yourself a little more brazen than is

* * * * *

50 beloved X] This probably refers to Louis Viscount Montfort whom she married some time before September 1502 (cf Ep 172:6–7), at which time she ceased to patronize Erasmus. In Ep 145:169ff Erasmus seems to be urging her not to consider a second marriage, possibly foreseeing the result.

54 two hundred francs] Cf Epp 139:57–8n and 146:8n. This sum of £200 tournois was then worth, by relative silver values, £34 8s 11d gros Flemish, or £23 13s 8d sterling; and by relative gold values, about 70.3 gold English angel-nobles.

usual, so long as you have regard to my own name for modesty. You must decide for yourself how much to tell X. But before you go yourself or send someone, send me the rest of the gold pieces by some reliable messenger, and also, if I can prevail upon you, four or five gold pieces of your own, to save me from destitution meantime. You will get them back when the Lady's money arrives. See how my little hoard has melted away. I was sent eight francs, for that was what your nobles realized when I exchanged them, and out of these the boy took away two, or almost two. Not to mention food for the moment, you say you have two angelets left, and some of this too must be deducted for the messenger's benefit. Jean, whom you sent to England, has absconded, taking some loot with him, I believe; and Augustin has ridden in pursuit of him to Orléans. There will be general confusion here, I can see. Louis will tell you the rest. 80 85

Farewell, dear Batt, and please take in good part what I have said. It was not written in excitement or panic but, as one should do with one's best friend, in perfectly plain-spoken terms. And please treat my boy Louis not like that rascal Adrian, who is so bad that he could not possibly be worse, but as one who has finer instincts and can be very serviceable to you in many ways. He will cheer your loneliness, and you will have someone to read to, to converse with about literature, and lastly to practise your gifts upon. So, though I will not quarrel with you about the coat, still if you give it to him it will be fair, and I shall be much obliged. Farewell. 90 95

Paris, 27 January [1499]

147 / To Antonius of Luxembourg Paris, 27 January [1501]

This letter is essentially a repetition of Ep 137.

ERASMUS TO HIS FRIEND ANTONIUS OF LUXEMBOURG

Despite the fact that we have spent so very few days in each other's

* * * * *

83 your nobles] As the 'angelets' of line 85 below suggest, Erasmus is probably referring to the gold English angel-nobles, worth 6s 8d sterling apiece (1465–1526), rather than to the Henricus or ryal-nobles. Indeed three gold angels should have been worth about £8 10s 8d tournois, before deducting the money-changer's fee. Cf note 9 above and Epp 214:4n; 227:31n; 237:64n; 248:40n; 270:30n; and CWE I 312, 319, 325; tables A–F below, 327–45.

85 angelets] *angelotos*: half-angels (angel-nobles), an English gold coin then worth 3s 4d sterling (1465–1526). Cf Ep 214:4n; CWE I 312, 325; and tables A and B below, 327–37.

86 Jean] Cf Epp 128:1–2n and 133:5n.

93 Adrian] Cf Ep 80:57n.

97 coat] Cf Epp 135:70; and 139:181–2.

company, my dear Antonius, still I must confess I am attracted to you by a kind of natural affection, just as iron is attracted by a magnet. Indeed the affection I entertain for you is so extraordinarily warm that it is not outdone even by my ardent love for Batt himself; and him I cherish more than my very being. And I feel sure, dear Antonius, that my affection is returned, so many were the indications I had, when I was staying in your part of the world, of your kindly disposition and readiness to form friendships.

If you are anxious to be informed of my circumstances, I have left Orléans and moved back to the Paris we knew of old, now that the plague which banished me has died out. About Dismas, I decided to write to you rather than to the abbot, both in order to avoid the appearance of sending him a book instead of a letter and also so that, in the present instance, your authority, which weighs heavily with the abbot, might intercede in favour of rescuing a young man of excellent promise. For whatever you do or do not believe, Antonius, believe me when I say that I shall set down no idle fantasies, but only what I know for certain to be extremely important for Dismas' well-being. So, because I know you have the abbot's interests at heart, I request you to grant an attentive hearing to the case, and to do all you can to help.

In the first place, on the subject of Dismas' character I think I ought to bear witness (not with a view to pleasing, but just because I have found it to be so) that never in my life hitherto have I seen a nobler, more lovable, or better-endowed nature. Truly, in the words of the book of Wisdom, he has been endowed with a good spirit, so that nature appears to have created him for great achievements. He is very intelligent and learns amazingly quickly; his memory is retentive; his disposition is bashful, modest, and charming. He respects learning, and delights in the company of those who always leave him better informed. As a daily companion he has no harsh or irritating qualities at all. I too (for he has been a visitor in our household) took especial delight in his society, and he was almost the only person at Orléans whom I expected to become signally distinguished. Since nature seems to have equipped him with every endowment necessary for great achievements, it would appear to rest with you to ensure that a being so gifted and so well-born may not sink to the common level by infection with vice, or merely through apathy; I see no small danger, since he is spending his youth in what they call a lodging-house, with all the drawbacks that word suggests, eating unclean food, in sordid surroundings, neglected and

* * * * *

147:4 magnet] Cf *Adagia* I vii 56.

13 abbot] Cf Ep 143:259–60. Evidently his letter to the abbot was already too long.

26 a good spirit] Wisdom 8:19

uncared for; surrounded by worthless fellows, lazy, undisciplined, disorderly, who hate nothing more than good learning, the very negation of lawyers, men who prowl the streets at night and drink during the day, and from whom he can learn nothing but wickedness. As you know, Dismas is now entering the dangerous phase of adolescence, and you are aware how easily boys of this age, however virtuous, are attracted to vice. As Seneca remarks, an evil companion rubs off the contagion of his ways upon others; and as a wise Hebrew wrote, 'he that toucheth pitch shall be defiled therewith.' And this is something I would not have written concerning the morals of others, were not the facts so manifest that nobody could stand in doubt about them.

I have described the danger to you, and will now explain how it may be obviated. At Orléans there is a certain Master Jacobus Tutor, of Antwerp, with whom I stayed for the three months I spent there. I solemnly assure you that he is a man of absolute integrity and distinguished learning, filled with zeal for study, and he is a licentiate, as they are called, of long standing in canon law. He is regarded with fraternal affection by the bishop's official, a man, of course, of the highest reputation, as indeed he is by all the best men in the community. He himself loves Dismas just as if he were his son, partly because he was once acquainted with him at Louvain, and is loved by him as a father. It is to him that I think Dismas ought to be attached, and without any delay, to prevent him from being diverted into evil courses by remaining in that lodging-house any longer during his adolescence. My friend Jacob has a number of well-born youths boarding with him; first and foremost two brothers of the house of Breda, also called Nassau, who are young men of excellent character, and a more loving pair of brothers than any I have yet seen. One of the pair holds a benefice in the church at Breda. If Dismas should live in company with them he will neither hear nor see anything unworthy of himself, and will have Jacob to guide his life, who, being most studious, will be delighted to meet someone with whom he can

* * * * *

45 Seneca] Cf *Epistles* 7.7.

47 Hebrew] Ecclesiasticus 13:1

64 brothers] Heinrich (1483–1538) and Wilhelm (1487–1559), sons of Count Johann of Nassau-Dillenburg, whose older brother, Count Engelbert II of Nassau-Breda, had large estates in the Netherlands. On the death of Engelbert in 1504 his lands passed to Johann, thus uniting the holdings of the family. On the death of Johann in 1516, however, they were again divided. Heinrich inherited Nassau-Breda and married the heiress of the principality of Orange. Wilhelm succeeded to Nassau-Dillenburg. In 1544 his eldest son, Wilhelm, inherited Nassau-Breda and the principality of Orange through the will of his cousin René, Heinrich's son and heir. This Wilhelm is better known to history as William the Silent.

freely share his learning. Dismas will have a person with whom he can live 70
just as in a parent's house, and by whose example and friendly exhortation
he can be spurred on to the most honourable achievements.

Partly I am moved to write in this way, dear Antonius, by the character
of the youth himself; partly because, owing everything to his family, I did
not consider that I could abstain from doing so without committing a very 75
grave crime. For the rest I have no axe of my own to grind in this matter.

Farewell, dearest Antonius, and kindly convey my warmest regards to
your most gracious patron. I have dictated, not written, this letter to you,
both for my stomach's sake and also because I am already tired out with
writing. 80

Paris, 27 January [1498]

148 / To Antonius of Luxembourg [Paris, February 1501?]

ERASMUS OF ROTTERDAM TO HIS FRIEND ANTONIUS
OF LUXEMBOURG

I have received the abbot's present, and together with it the small sum of
money sent by Batt. In this connection, if my expression of thanks is rather
cursory for the present, you must not suppose that the reason for this lies in 5
any want of pleasure over the gift, but simply that I was preoccupied with
business and in a most uncertain state of health. However I shall presently
inform both you yourself and the reverend abbot how much obliged I am
for this generosity in return for my deserts, which are non-existent. I bid
you farewell; and may you always stay the same, dear Antonius. 10

[1499]

149 / To Antoon van Bergen [Paris? 16 March? 1501]

This letter is interesting as the first clear enunciation of Erasmus' conviction that a knowledge of Greek is indispensable to the study of the Scriptures and of such Fathers of the church as St Jerome, a conviction that was to furnish the motive for much of his life's work.

TO THE RIGHT HONOURABLE THE LORD ANTOON,
ABBOT OF ST BERTIN

Surely letters from me must remind you, most gracious Father, of the
donkey in Aesop; for now that they have repeatedly experienced your

* * * * *

76 axe ... to grind] *Adagia* I vi 82

148:3 the abbot's present] Evidently Ep 143 had borne fruit.

149:4 Aesop] Fable 133 (the ass who would be his master's playmate)

courtesy and kindness, they have acquired so much extra self-confidence that they are emboldened to face your Lordship quite unprepared, whereas before they lacked courage to do so even after careful grooming. Yet I would not wish you to attribute this informality to carelessness on my part, but to my literary labours, which of course always engage my full attention whenever my health allows, but are now taxing me so violently that they do not even spare my health itself. For I had the good fortune to come upon some Greek books, and am secretly engaged night and day in copying them. One might ask why I find the example of Cato the Censor so attractive as to want Greek at my age. Indeed I should now be the happiest of men if in my boyhood I had formed such an intention, or rather if I had enjoyed more favourable circumstances. But as I see it now, it is better to learn, even somewhat late, the things we ought to grasp first, than never to learn them at all. I did indeed have a taste of this language long ago, but only with the tip of the tongue, as the saying is; but lately, now that I have gone a little deeper into it, I have come to see the truth of a statement one has often read in the most important authors: that Latin scholarship, however elaborate, is maimed and reduced by half without Greek. For whereas we Latins have but a few small streams, a few muddy pools, the Greeks possess crystal-clear springs and rivers that run with gold. I can see what utter madness it is even to put a finger on that part of theology which is specially concerned with the mysteries of the faith unless one is furnished with the equipment of Greek as well, since the translators of Scripture, in their scrupulous manner of construing the text, offer such literal versions of Greek idioms that no one ignorant of that language could grasp even the primary, or, as our own theologians call it, literal, meaning. For example, could anyone understand that phrase in the Psalm *Et peccatum meum contra me est semper* ('And my sin is ever against me'), unless he reads the Greek, which runs to the following effect: 'And my sin is continually before me.' In this passage some theologian will tell me a long story about how the flesh wages an endless war with the spirit – being misled by the ambiguity of the preposition (*contra*), whereas the Greek word for 'before' (ἐνώπιον) has a local, not adversative, meaning, just as if one were to say 'over against,' that is, opposite in one's sight; thus the prophet meant that his guilt displeased him so much that the consciousness thereof never left his mind but was

* * * * *

13 Cato] Marcus Porcius Cato, who held the office of censor in Rome in 184 BC and lived to be eighty-five, devoted his old age to learning Greek, a precedent which Erasmus never forgot.

18 long ago] Cf Allen I 592.

19 tip of the tongue] Cf *Adagia* I ix 93.

31 the Psalm] 50:4 (51:3)

always as it were in his view, as if it were physically present. And then elsewhere, *Bene patientes erunt ut annuncient* ('They shall be ... flourishing; / To show ...'); would not anyone be misled by the deceptiveness of the expression if he had not learned from the Greeks that, just as in common Latin parlance we say that those who confer a benefit on someone 'do well,' similarly the Greeks speak of those who receive a benefit as '*suffering* well' (*bene patientes*)? Consequently the meaning of the phrase *Bene patientes erunt ut annuncient* is 'They shall be well treated, and by my benefits they shall be helped, so that they shall declare my kindness toward them.'

But why need I rehearse a mere handful of trivial examples among so many notable instances, when I am supported by the holy authority of the pontifical council, whose decree is still extant in the decretal letters, to the effect that the leading universities, as they were at that period, should engage persons capable of giving complete instruction in the Hebrew, Greek, and Latin tongues, for as much as they claimed that Scripture could not be understood, much less discussed, without them? This extremely sound and most venerable decree is something we so far disregard nowadays that we are perfectly satisfied with the most elementary rudiments of Latin, no doubt because we are convinced that we can get everything out of Scotus, as a sort of horn of plenty.

With this breed of men I for one will not quarrel: as far as I am concerned, each to his taste, and let ancient groom take ancient bride. My own inclination is to follow the path to which I am beckoned by St Jerome and the glorious choir of all those ancient writers; and, so may Heaven love me, I should prefer to be crazed in their splendid company than to be infinitely rational with the mass of present-day theologians. Besides this I am trying to encompass a difficult achievement, one, if I may so put it, worthy of Phaethon, namely to restore, as well as I can, the works of Jerome, which have partly been corrupted by those half-taught critics, partly blotted out or cut down or mutilated, or at least filled with mistakes and monstrosities, through ignorance of classical antiquity and of Greek. And I intend not only

* * * * *

41 elsewhere] Psalm 91:15–16 (92:14–15)

51 decretal letters] This refers to the constitutions of Clement v, usually called the *Clementinae*, published in 1314 and including the decrees promulgated at the Council of Vienne in 1311–12. Erasmus was wrong in assuming that the three languages referred to were Hebrew, Greek, and Latin (cf Ep 182:205n).

59 horn of plenty] Cf *Adagia* I vi 2.

61 let ancient groom ... bride] Cf *Adagia* I ii 15; I ii 62.

67 Phaethon] The child of the sun who tried and failed to drive his father's chariot

to restore them, but to elucidate them in a commentary, so that every reader in his study may come to recognize that the great Jerome, the only scholar in the church universal who had a perfect command of all learning both sacred and heathen, as they call it, can be read by anyone, but understood only by accomplished scholars. Since I am earnestly engaged in this attempt, for 75 which I recognize knowledge of Greek to be of the first importance, I have decided to spend several months in attendance upon a Greek tutor; and a genuine Greek he is, or perhaps a Greek twice over; for he is always starving, and charges an exorbitant fee for his teaching.

About the sorcerers, all I have to tell you is that a letter from Tutor 80 informs me the man was condemned to imprisonment for life on a diet of bread and water, his wife was punished by imprisonment for three months, and the poor girl was sent away to a convent, where she will be happy if she accepts it willingly; otherwise it will be a worse sentence than that passed on either parent. The books and sword and other reminders of 85 the sorcery are to be burned. But I suppose that punishment by the civil arm was withheld because the entire proceedings against sorcery were initiated by the ecclesiastical judge. My informant tells me that he could find out nothing further from the Official. Farewell.

[Orléans, 1499] 90

150 / To Antonius of Luxembourg

Paris, 16 March [1501]

ERASMUS TO HIS FRIEND ANTONIUS OF LUXEMBOURG

Fond of you as I was before, my delightful Antonius, it was merely as a man of very pleasant address, to whom I owed much; but, as I have come belatedly to recognize from your correspondence with me, I am now to salute you as a man of letters. You must not suppose that I am indulging in 5 flattery. It was your unadorned, natural style that delighted me enormously, the words not borrowed but such as best fit the thoughts expressed; the judgments sound and well based, with nothing unnatural or distorted

* * * * *

72 Jerome] Cf Ep 138:45n.

77 Greek tutor] Probably George Hermonymus of Sparta, who came to Paris in 1476 and lived there for more than thirty years, copying Greek MSS and teaching the language. Erasmus, Budé, and Beatus Rhenanus thought him a mediocre teacher, but Reuchlin had a higher opinion of him (cf Renaudet *Préréforme* 117).

79 starving] Cf Juvenal 3.78.

80 sorcerers] Cf Ep 143:73ff.

or artificial in the language and ideas, nor for that matter anything unduly fine-spun, or grossly elaborated. 10

About Dismas, the situation is as follows. Both in Varro and in Gellius we can find a very ancient adage to the effect that 'bad advice harms the adviser most.' But I am confident that we shall all be happy at the outcome of this good advice: first of all that very cultured man the abbot, your patron and mine if you will allow the expression, who has made excellent arrangements for the dear boy; I, who gave good advice; you, who did your dependable best in a friendly spirit; Dismas, himself, who is now already most grateful to me; and finally Tutor, who has at long last found someone with whom he can freely share his scholarship and in whom his labours will be profitably invested. Take it from me, he is quite the most honest and the most straightforward man under the sun. Please make my excuses to the most reverend lord abbot for the disorder of my letter. Encourage Batt to live up to his name; for there never was a better time to do so. Farewell, dear Antonius. 15 20

Paris, 16 March [1498] 25

151 / To Jacob Batt Paris, 5 April [1501]

ERASMUS TO HIS FRIEND BATT

I hope it was a false rumour about your illness; all the same I am a little anxious, human infirmity being what it is. There is no need for you to feel distress over me, dearest friend; our mutual affection did not begin in the first instance with the pursuit of advantages, and consequently is unlikely to evaporate when they are withdrawn. We ought to bear with composure, and indeed with courage, whatever fate may bring, so long as we ourselves are not at fault. I wish only that Heaven may grant me good health; the rest I can wrestle through for myself. But my health, dear Batt, is in fact rather precarious at the moment. 5 10

The Lady who once protested that she would never behave like a

* * * * *

11 Dismas] Cf Epp 137 and 147.

11 Varro] *Res rusticae* 3.2.1

11 Gellius] Aulus Gellius 4.5.5; cf *Adagia* I ii 14.

22 Batt] In *Adagia* II i 92 Battus is the name of a feeble and repetitive poet.

151:11 Lady] Anna van Borssele. The fulsome flattery in Ep 145 had apparently not been effective. There is no mention in the correspondence of further patronage from the lady, perhaps because of her family's troubles with the ducal government (cf Ep 157:24n) or because of her forthcoming marriage (cf Ep 146:49–50n).

woman, as far as I was concerned, is now behaving in a more than feminine way, which causes me intense surprise. But necessity is a powerful weapon; so we must ignore it all and await better times. About my lord provost, I have always had a foreboding of trouble, but the outcome will be 15 the test. At the moment I am ceasing to complain of my fortune, since I have given up hoping. I am displeased only that the news has got about so widely, not unaccompanied, as I believe, by hostility on the part of many men. My dear fellow, just be sure to get well, and look after your interests as soon as you can attend to them; for you know the kind of waves that seethe 20 about a court.

I have written notes on Cicero's *De officiis*; this work will be printed soon. I had intended to dedicate it to Adolph, but I see no reason to do so now. Please tell Louis on my behalf that I shall be greatly obliged if he makes careful copies of such letters as are in your possession. Farewell, my 25 dear delightful Batt.

Paris, 5 April [1498]

152 / To Jacob Voogd Paris, 28 December [1501]

Having decided not to dedicate his edition of Cicero's *De officiis* to Adolph of Veere (cf Ep 151:23–4), Erasmus wrote this preface for the edition published in Paris by J. Philippi without date but at about this time (there is a copy of this edition in the British Museum). Through some oversight the preface was omitted from this edition, but it was printed, together with a new preface also addressed to Jacob Voogd, dated 10 September 1519 (Allen Ep 1013), in a revised edition (Louvain: Th. Martens s.d. and Basel: Froben August 1520). The *De officiis* was the first annotated edition of a classical work published by Erasmus, and the preface furnishes an interesting account of his critical method.

Jacob Voogd of Antwerp was a young doctor of law whose acquaintance Erasmus made at Orléans in the fall of 1500, when he lodged with him for three months (cf Epp 131 introduction and 133:42ff and n). Erasmus was greatly

* * * * *

13–14 powerful weapon] Cf *Adagia* II iii 40.

14–15 lord provost] *D.P.*: probably Nicholas of Burgundy (cf Ep 144 introduction)

22 *De officiis*] It was dedicated to Jacob Voogd (cf Ep 152). Erasmus' intention to dedicate the *De conscribendis epistolis* and *De copia* to Adolph of Veere (cf Ep 95:37, 39 and nn) was also abandoned.

24 Louis] Cf Ep 167 introduction. It was probably through the copies made by Louis that so many of Erasmus' letters to Batt survived (cf Ep 163:17).

attracted by his personality and learning and worked hard to secure for him young Dismas of Burgundy as a pupil (cf Epp 137, 147, and 150). Their friendship lasted for many years. In this letter Erasmus addresses him as Tutor, and he generally refers to him by this Latinization of Voogd, which means a guardian in Dutch as Tutor does in Latin. In many of his references to Tutor he seems to have this pun in mind (cf especially Ep 157:55).

ERASMUS OF ROTTERDAM TO THE EXCELLENT MASTER JACOBUS TUTOR, MOST LEARNED IN BOTH CIVIL AND CANON LAW, GREETINGS

A great many authors dedicate their works to noblemen, partly in order to obtain from them a reward for their entirely creditable labours of the lamp, 5 partly in order to secure the support of a great man's authority against the dislike attached to novelty. However for my part I have preferred to dedicate the fruits, not of hard work in my case but of leisure – although they are by no means fruits of idleness – to our own friendship, kind and scholarly Voogd; and as I reckoned that this would last for life, inasmuch as it was not 10 bound together with ropes of tow by the usual reasons for liking, but fastened by chains of steel and the so-called knot of Hercules through your association with me in the most honourable pursuits and your sheer goodness, I decided that it would be fitting if some imperishable record of it should be preserved. Now, so far as human affairs are concerned, clearly 15 literature is permanent, if anything is. During recent walks, therefore, such as I often take after meals because of ill-health, as you know, for you were almost the only person to accompany me on them, I have reread with equal pleasure and profit those three truly golden books of Cicero's *De officiis*.

Since Pliny the Elder says these books should never be out of one's 20 hands, I have reduced the bulk of the volume as far as possible to permit its being carried about always as a pocket handbook and, as Pliny also recommended, learnt by heart. Instead of the commentaries by Pietro Marso (how I wish these had been selective rather than exhaustive!), I have appended a large number of brief notes, my intention being that, like little stars, they 25 should conveniently illuminate each obscure passage. As to the headings

* * * * *

12 knot of Hercules] *Adagia* I ix 48

20 Pliny] *Historia naturalis* praef 22

23 Marso] Pietro Marso (c 1430–after 1509), an Italian scholar who published an annotated edition of Cicero's *De officiis, De senectute, De amicitia, Paradoxa* (Venice: Bapt. de Tortis 12 October 1481). Later Erasmus recalled meeting him in Rome when he was about eighty years old and being impressed more by his industry than by his scholarship (cf Allen Ep 1347:258ff).

with which someone or other has cut up, rather than divided, the work, some of these I have removed as superfluous, while some, as irrelevant to their context, I have transposed elsewhere; I have altered them all and replaced them in an enlarged version as brief summaries. And I have 30 worked equally hard at improving the text. I found a great many flaws, as one would expect in such a familiar work; one scribe will throw the order into confusion as he copies, while another will replace a word, which perhaps had eluded him, with an approximation. These flaws are of course not monstrosities, but still they are intolerable in such a great author. I have 35 corrected all of them, partly by collating editions, in which the disagreements are astonishing, partly by informed guesswork based on Cicero's style, so that at least I can promise the reader that no copy is closer to the original text than the present edition.

Wherefore I urge you, my dear Jacob, always to carry about with you 40 this tiny dagger. It is short, but neither Homer's Achilles nor Virgil's Aeneas was better equipped, though their arms were forged by Vulcan himself. For it is more heroic to tackle faults than foemen, and, as the poet truly wrote, 'virtue is mortal man's mightiest weapon,' inasmuch as there is no better panoply for arming men than goodness. And though you are 45 reaping a rich harvest from the spreading plains of legal practice, still this particular field, small as it is, will by itself yield everything you need if you cultivate it with care. From it you will be able to gather herbs, the potent juices whereof may enable you to pass through the midst of monsters and reach the Golden Fleece; and in no other place can you find that herb, 50 mentioned in Homer, called *moly*, which is hard indeed to find but a most effective antidote to all the poisons of Circe. From this place too you may pluck either the sprig of bay which can bring success to your enterprises or the golden bough that will enable you to reach even Hades' realm unharmed. Here too is that divine fountain of honour which is divided into 55 four channels; to drink of it makes a man not only eloquent, like the famed Aonian spring, but also immortal. If from time to time you dip the limbs of

* * * * *

41 dagger] *pugiunculus*: the Greek equivalent is *enchiridion*, which has another sense ('pocket handbook') in which it appears in line 22 above. Erasmus plays on the double meaning of the Greek word.

43 poet] Menander *Monosticha* 433

51 Homer] Cf *Odyssey* 10.305. The *moly* was given by Hermes to Ulysses.

53 sprig of bay] *Adagia* I i 79

54 golden bough] It was given by the Sibyl to Aeneas to enable him to enter the kingdom of the dead (cf *Aeneid* 6.130ff).

your mind in its waters, you will emerge like another Achilles, invulnerable to all the arrows of Fortune. Farewell.

Paris, 28 April [1498] 60

153 / To Jacob Anthoniszoon

Tournehem, 12 July [1501]

In the spring of 1501 plague again broke out in Paris and Erasmus fled to the Netherlands some time after the end of April. His movements during the next two months are difficult to trace, but it can be inferred from the following letters that he probably went directly to Holland, where he spent a month or more visiting friends at Steyn and Willem Hermans at Haarlem. At Dordrecht his servant pupil fell ill of a fever and he set sail on 9 June (cf Ep 157:16–17) to Zierikzee where the boy's mother lived (cf Ep 155:18–19). After spending several days there he went on to Brussels to visit the bishop of Cambrai, thence to Antwerp, Veere, and Tournehem. There he remained with Batt for a couple of months. Epp 153–161 form a group written from Tournehem or Saint-Omer in July.

Jacob Anthoniszoon of Middelburg was a doctor of canon law and vicar-general to the bishop of Cambrai. He was an old friend of Erasmus, probably from the days of his service with the bishop. Erasmus sent him greetings in July 1497 (cf Ep 60:11), and stayed with him as his guest in Brussels in July 1498 (cf Ep 77:5), as he did again on his recent visit to Brussels. Cf P. Lefèvre 'Deux amis d'Erasme, membres du grand collège canonial à Bruxelles' *Scrinium* (Fribourg) 1 (1950) 25–7.

TO THE HONOURABLE MASTER JACOB, VICAR TO THE LORD BISHOP OF CAMBRAI, FROM ERASMUS, GREETINGS

Since I had as yet done you no service whatever, kindest of men, or most learned, I know not which, but in any case highly distinguished, while you for your part have so behaved towards my lowly self that out of your 5 well-nigh incredible goodness you have as it were loaded me down with enormous favours, I was extremely happy that at last I had found an opportunity, such as it was, not perhaps of returning your favours but at any rate of signifying, by some tiny act of good will, the grateful and devoted feelings of my heart. Accordingly I could not help being pro- 10 foundly distressed that my servant, after repeated and careful instructions, left your distinguished book behind at your house, and I did not realize it

* * * * *

12 book] Antoniszoon had composed a treatise *De precellentia potestatis imperatoriae* which he had asked Erasmus to take with him, possibly to assist in securing a publisher. It was published by Martens at Antwerp, 1 April 1503 (NK 120), with a complimentary letter from Erasmus (Ep 173).

until we had already reached Antwerp. But I beseech your most gracious Reverence, by your kind services to me and by my own gratitude to you, to hand the volume to the bearer of this letter, to be delivered to me – I intend 15 to reside here for several months. The bearer is a member of the following and household of the illustrious prince, Anthony 'le Bâtard'; he is a youth of proven reliability and conscientiousness and extremely devoted to me, and you can entrust it to him as safely as to myself. Merely let him understand that this is a matter of great importance, which cannot be neglected save at 20 his peril. I shall make sure that it comes back to you either in my own charge or at least by the hand of a thoroughly dependable messenger.

When you are with my most noble father and patron, the bishop of Cambrai, pray do as you have always done: either make me more pleasing to him if the good will he used to have for me still exists, or restore me to 25 favour if he has grown cold. As God, who sees deep into the recesses of every human heart, is my witness, my affection for him is as ardent now as in those earliest months when he treated me with a kind of fatherly devotion and I in return was unbounded in my admiration and love for him. I am all the more anxious to play my part as well as I can in the matter of your 30 book; because I know well that the honour it will win, or rather the valuable services it will render, belong in common to you, my kind host and friend, and to him, my patron and the promoter of those studies which to me are life itself.

Farewell, distinguished teacher, and pray keep up the affection you 35 always have for your humble dependant, who is entirely and wholeheartedly devoted to you. I only heard at nine o'clock in the evening that the present messenger was to leave, and he is preparing to set out before cock-crow; I have had to write three letters late at night, after a heavy dinner, and they are all addressed to people to whom it is a perilous 40 undertaking to send even the most careful letter. But please explain my audacity as the result of your own kindness.

Tournehem, 12 July [1499]

154 / To Hendrik van Bergen — Tournehem, 12 July [1501]

ERASMUS TO HIS LORDSHIP THE BISHOP OF CAMBRAI, HIS PATRON

May I incur the wrath of the Lord God if Fortune, which else has been my bitter foe, has ever wounded my heart more grievously than in the sugges-

* * * * *

17 Anthony] Anthony 'le Grand Bâtard' of Burgundy was the proprietor of Tournehem castle (cf Ep 80 introduction).

tions of ingratitude with which your most gracious Reverence reproached me when last we met – whether because I would rather win your approval alone than that of myriads of other men, or because, not only by upbringing but by natural inclination, I have always felt an especial abhorrence of that sin, and held that there is nothing in the world more unpleasant or disgraceful or deserving of public execration than failure to repay, at least by good will and remembrance, a favour one has received. For myself, I bore your reproach not as the injurious act of an enemy, but as a reprimand administered by a loving father or physician. It remains for me to beseech you that, as 'my refuge and sweet glory,' both by your forgiving gentle heart and for my misfortunes' sake, if hitherto any fault has been committed, or rather because a fault has been committed, you should pardon it as due to my simplicity or inexperience; for I am certainly not aware that I have been guilty of any ill will. I do recognize my foolishness and inexperience, in this matter and also in many others. I invoke every kind of curse on my own head if I have not always received your generosity in the spirit in which an honest and grateful dependant should. I have loved you unreservedly, looked up to you, reverenced you, sung your praises, and not forgotten you. To this very day I have not once said a mass without beseeching immortal God to repay you with ample interest, since he alone can, for all that you have given me.

And what can I do more than this? If you still cannot be induced to believe what I have said, I ask only this: permit me to assure you that I do now entertain those sentiments and shall do so until my poor soul deserts my body. It is not in our power to command Fortune; but I promise that in devotion to you I will not yield first place, even to your friends. Even if the fates should be merciless to me, though they may make me very unhappy, they neither will, nor can, make me ungrateful. But if, my kind lord, you of your goodness now deem sufficient what you have hitherto so generously bestowed on me, I shall even consider it the fulness of generosity since you have afforded me so much, freely and out of great kindness, whereas I deserved nothing. And I am not so boorishly ungrateful that I keep in mind what my necessity hopes to receive rather than what your goodness has lavished upon me beyond any merit of my own. Lastly I would have you reflect that in the beginning it was not as a man of power or riches or high birth (for none bestows this on himself), but as an enthusiast for studies,

* * * * *

4 ingratitude] The bishop had reason for his reproaches if some of Erasmus' comments on his inadequacy as a patron had been repeated to him (cf, eg, Epp 48:30–2; 75:23–7; 80:75–7; 81:14f; and especially 135:19–21).

13 'refuge and sweet glory] Horace *Odes* 1.1.2

that I was commended to your indulgence. This is still my mind, much more ardently so than ever before. This mind I dedicate and consecrate entirely to you. How infinitely happy I shall be, if ever I have a chance to show that I was not ungrateful but most grateful! If in this regard I ever shun any study or labour or nightly task, then I shall think myself deserving of your most severe censure. Meanwhile I beg you to look indulgently on your humble servant. If I do not gain this wish, still I shall not cease to love and venerate even a patron who frowns, and I shall pray for suitable retribution to fall on those mischief-makers who are trying to separate us. 40 45

I have stayed for more than a month with my brethren in Holland. They have decided that I ought to spend a year longer on my studies; they think it will be discreditable to themselves as well as to me if I return after all those years without acquiring any qualification at all. Farewell, my gracious and right eminent Lord. 50

Tournehem, 12 July [1499]

155 / To Jan of Brussels — Tournehem, 12 July [1501]

Jan of Brussels was another old friend from the bishop of Cambrai's entourage (cf Ep 60).

ERASMUS TO HIS MOST VALUED FRIEND MASTER JAN OF BRUSSELS

I beseech you for your fortune's sake, Jan, my very kind friend, to offer my apologies to my very kind host and patron the reverend vicar for leaving his book behind because of my servant's forgetfulness. I swear that for many years past there is nothing I have regretted more. If you have any news about our friend Augustin or Bensrott or my patron the bishop, or finally 5

* * * * *

45 censure] Literally 'a black mark'; cf *Adagia* I v 54.

49 Holland] It is odd that, if Erasmus had seen the bishop after his visit to Holland (cf Ep 157:20f), he should have mentioned it here. Since this is one of the three letters written in haste late at night (cf Ep 153:39ff, 155:24), Erasmus may simply have forgotten whether he had mentioned it to the bishop at an interview which this letter suggests may have been stormy. Perhaps he wished to remind the bishop that he was not absent from his monastery without leave, and that the authorities at Steyn were willing to permit him to continue his studies abroad.

155:5 book] Cf Ep 153:12n.

7 Augustin] Vincent (cf Ep 156). Jan's acquaintance with Augustin probably dated from at least 1497, since Ep 60 shows him familiar with Erasmus' situation at Paris when he went to live with Augustin (cf Ep 58).

7 Bensrott] Cf Ep 158 introduction.

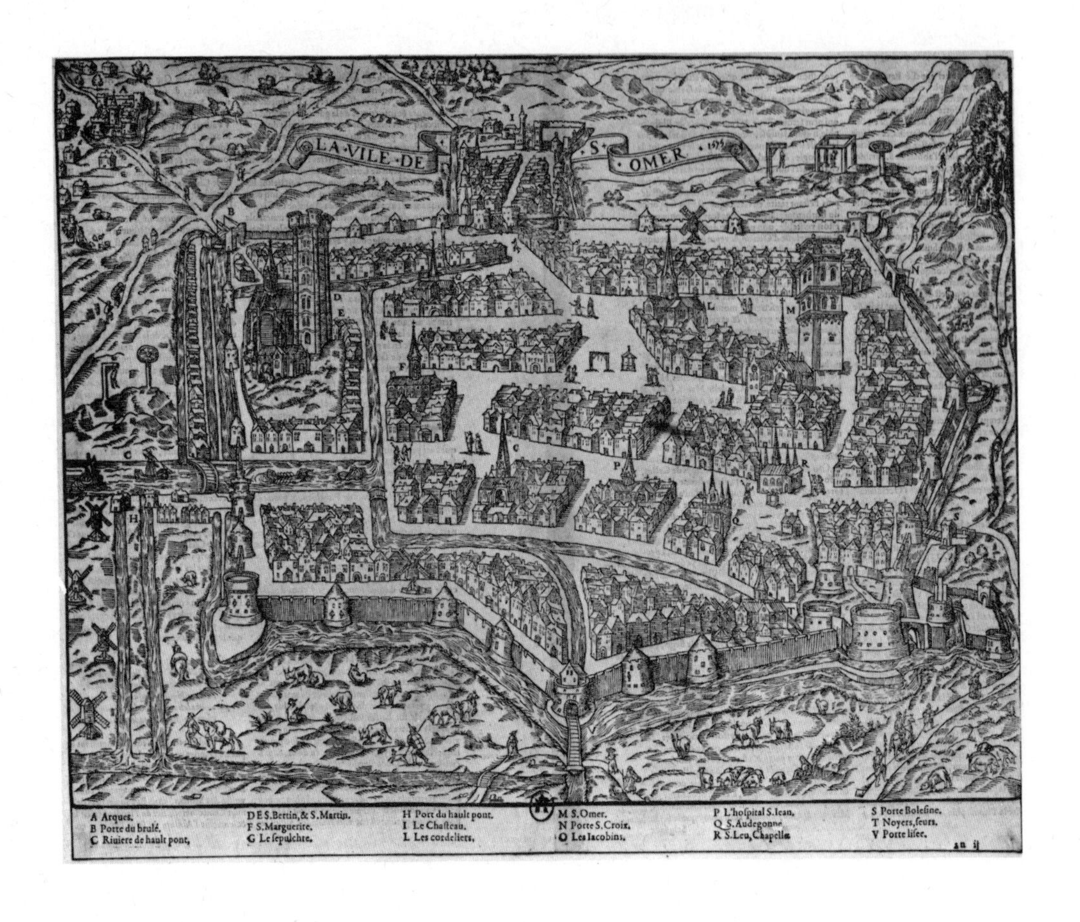

A bird's-eye view of Saint-Omer
Woodcut of 1575
Département des Estampes, Bibliothèque Nationale, Paris

about Louis, who was sent your way with instructions to fetch me, I implore you earnestly, by our friendship, to write and tell me of it. It would oblige me as much as any of the numerous kindnesses you have done for me before. In a member of the household of Anthony 'le Bâtard' you will find a reliable messenger to whom you can safely entrust anything you like. 10

At Veere I found everything to be just as you had predicted. By a lucky chance I encountered the Lady in the street, and she held out her hand to me with a friendly enough expression; but on the advice of certain people who did not, I think, wish me ill, I refrained from entering into a conversation. My boy caught a fever at Dordrecht, a tertian fever too. This worried me a great deal, and caused me for his sake to go by boat to Zierikzee, since that is his mother's home. I myself am well thus far, but have no other reason to rejoice in my luck. Batt is well, and sends his warm greetings; he is a friend to anyone whom your humble servant loves. Look after yourself well, my dear obliging Jan; and please do not lose your affection for your utterly devoted friend, or rather humble client, Erasmus. 15 20

Tournehem, late at night in the greatest of haste, 12 July [1499]

156 / To Augustin Vincent

Saint-Omer at St Bertin's abbey, [about 15 July 1501]

Erasmus was uncertain of Augustin's movements at this time (cf Epp 155:7, 157:61, 160:11). This letter was therefore dispatched in care of Bensrott (cf Ep 158:15). The fact that it was written from St Bertin's in Saint-Omer probably means that Erasmus had gone there for a brief visit, since it is only about eleven miles from Tournehem.

ERASMUS OF ROTTERDAM TO HIS FRIEND AUGUSTIN

From the letter I left there you can gather how I feel towards you. I have been travelling for almost two months and have only just settled down with my friend Batt. There are persistent rumours here that the plague is making havoc in your vicinity. If you deem it advisable to move here, as you suggested in your letter, you will discover for yourself that I have told the truth. You must not suppose that my departure had anything to do with ill 5

* * * * *

8 Louis] Louis had been sent to fetch Erasmus by the abbot of St Bertin (cf Ep 157:35ff).

12 messenger] Cf Ep 153:16ff.

14 Lady] Cf Ep 157:21ff and 24n.

156:2 left] Presumably in Paris

will or deceit. I swear that never before have I been so reluctant to leave Paris, but I was terrified by the number of deaths. And if you are entertaining some suspicion of me because of our old quarrels, then put me to the test, and I shall ensure that you will understand that my affection for you is such as to make my former feelings appear cold in comparison. 10

Nowhere on my travels could I find out anything about your return; I was both sorry and surprised at this. At long last a man named Antonius told a tale of having heard somebody claim that he had seen you and spoken with you in Lübeck, adding as evidence that he had handed over to you a copy of Valla's *Elegantiae* in the abridged version I once compiled. But to this very day there has been no report, dependable or otherwise, to the effect that you were back in Paris; so I have written this brief and hastily penned note, to avoid the risk of embarking on a more elaborate work. If you have already returned, please at least draft as long a letter as you can manage, about all your travels and whatever else has happened to you. 15 20

I should like you, for many reasons, to give my kindest remembrances to your friend Rodolf; and please give greetings for me to Nikolaus and your other pupils who have done a great deal for me. Look after yourself. If you should rush here, though this I hardly dare hope, then, though I shall not make any explicit promises, I shall in practice do everything that ought to be done by anyone who is full of gratitude and affection. 25

St Bertin's, [1498]

157 / To Jacob Voogd [Tournehem, 17 July 1501]

For Tutor as the Latin name for Jacob Voogd, which Erasmus uses throughout this letter, see Ep 152 introduction.

ERASMUS TO HIS FRIEND VOOGD

I had intended to come straight back to you, dear Voogd, after I left Paris; for to whom would I rather go? I had already scraped together a small sum of money, so that I should not burden your resources; but, when I heard that the plague was beginning to break out among you as well, I was obliged to 5

* * * * *

10 quarrels] Cf, eg, Ep 133: 8ff.

14 Antonius] Possibly the courier mentioned in Ep 161:15 who was in Saint-Omer at this time

17 *Elegantiae*] Cf Ep 23:108n.

24 Rodolf] Probably Rodolf von Langen (cf Ep 70:52n)

24 Nikolaus] Bensrott (cf Ep 158 introduction)

change my course hither. In Antwerp I paid a visit to your excellent parents, who naturally resemble you so deeply. I was in Holland for almost two months, not sitting still indeed, but running to and fro and drinking, just as the dogs do in Egypt; for my part, I would even prefer to live among the Phaeacians. As for my good Willem, that pleasant fellow, no inducements sufficed to prompt him to studious activity; and so I took my leave of him on such bad terms that I do not miss him even now. For your sake, at any rate, I gave him such a scolding that when he said goodbye we scarcely parted as friends. If Epicurus were to be born again and see that pattern of living, he would regard himself (by comparison) as an austere Stoic.

At considerable risk I sailed from Dordrecht on the eve of Corpus Christi. While I tarried for several days at Zierikzee for the sake of the boy, who since the voyage had begun to be feverish, I nearly fell ill myself, and should have, had I not fled away as speedily as I could from Zeeland – that is, from the nether regions. I paid my respects to our bishop; as usual, he is thinking up new excuses for giving nothing. In relation to the Lady of the town of Veere, the situation there was such that I could neither enter into a conversation with her without extreme danger, nor take my leave without incurring grave suspicion. You are aware of the provost's case; just as he is now in prison, so the Lady is under surveillance. Freed from such expectations as these (I say freed, for in my view it is a wretched business to remain in useless suspense), I have made my way straight to Batt, who is my greatest delight. Here I am practising Greek, but alone, for Batt has too little

* * * * *

6 change my course] Literally 'turn my sails'; cf *Adagia* I ix 60.

9 dogs in Egypt] Dogs in Egypt drank only while running for fear of being snapped up by crocodiles; cf *Adagia* I ix 80.

10 Willem] Hermans. Erasmus' feeling for his old friend had been cooling for some time (cf Ep 138: 173n); he had been disappointed by Willem's failure to continue his studies (cf Ep 138:182ff). The estrangement did not last long (cf Epp 172, 186:16).

10 Phaeacians] A people visited by Ulysses in the sixth and seventh books of the *Odyssey* whose famous hospitality to strangers included a great deal of drinking

16–17 Corpus Christi] 10 June in 1501

24 provost] Nicholas of Burgundy (cf Ep 144 introduction) had evidently been implicated in the suspicion of disloyalty to the duke of Burgundy incurred by his father Anthony 'le Grand Bâtard' (cf Ep 80 introduction). This situation also accounts for the surveillance of the Lady Anna, Anthony's daughter-in-law, and for Erasmus' fear that it would be unsafe to enter into conversation with her (cf below, lines 41ff and Ep 155:13ff).

time, and moreover is fonder of Latin. My plan is to anchor myself in this spot for a couple of months, and then I shall set my course according to the winds. 30

You have been waiting too long to hear whether my lord abbot bids me welcome graciously, now that I am close at hand. There is nothing I could say on that point in this letter, dear Voogd; his feelings ebb and flow more often than the tides of the Euripus itself. Shortly before I arrived here he was so hot for me that he despatched that noisy fellow Louis to Holland in order to fetch me, throwing in a generous present of two gold pieces for my expenses on the journey. But when I turned up in person his coldness was such that one might describe it as inhuman; from which I conclude that I ought not to depend on admiration of this sort, which comes and goes with the tide. The Lady, whom I met by chance in the street, held out her hand and clearly showed, by the very kind look she gave me, that she still retained her former good will; still, I dare hardly hope for anything, so alert are those watchdogs who now do double duty also as wolves. So for the present your Erasmus is living on his own resources and clothing himself in his own feathers. I have gone as far as Haarlem (and whether it cost me more in expense or effort or danger I cannot yet tell) on purpose to visit my friend Willem, or rather to make a Greek out of him, taking a huge bundle of books with me; but all my trouble and all my money were wasted. By making the journey I lost twelve couronnes, and one friend along with them; for I have come to realise what his character is, and that previously I was deluding myself about him. But I shall come to my senses, like a boy chastised by a whipping, and learn for my own rather than others' benefit. 35 40 45 50

I have now told you, dearest Voogd, almost all the news of your Erasmus; for I could not decently allow my Voogd to be unaware of a single Erasmian item. I have the fullest confidence that you are doing your duty by Dismas, and therefore I am making bold to entertain high prospects for 55

* * * * *

32 lord abbot] Antoon van Bergen

35 Euripus] The strait between the island of Euboea and the Greek mainland, proverbial for the speed with which its tidal currents reversed their flow; cf *Adagia* I ix 80.

36 Louis] The abbot had sent Louis to look for Erasmus in the neighbourhood of Brussels (cf Ep 155:8) as well as in Holland. He apparently desired his services in composing Ep 162.

50 couronnes] See CWE I 315.

53 learn ... benefit] *Adagia* I vi 20

55 my Voogd] Erasmus is here clearly punning on the meaning (guardian) of Voogd or Tutor.

57 Dismas] Now established as a pupil with Voogd (cf Ep 150)

your sake and his. It remains for you to tell me about your whole situation: how the brothers from Breda are faring, for I myself believe they ought to be restrained with bit and bridle from excessive application to study; what news there is of our friend Augustin, about whom I have not yet been able to learn anything, and also how my friend Bensrott is. In a word, please be sure to write and tell me about everything that concerns either of us. My dear Batt is as ardently fond of you as he is even of me. You must not take this as a fib, dear Voogd; nothing could in fact be truer. I have thoughts, or rather dreams, for I see not a ray of hope anywhere, of making my way to Italy this autumn. I hear that Jérôme, brother to the bishop of Besançon, is planning to go there, and that he is one who values aspiring scholars and has not too poor an opinion of my intellectual gifts. If I had not been so totally inept when I was in your part of the world, I should surely have found some loophole through which I could penetrate the defences of his friendship. Farewell. 60 65 70

[Paris, 1498]

158 / To Nikolaus Bensrott Tournehem, [17 July 1501]

Nikolaus Bensrott was one of Augustin Vincent's pupils (cf Epp 136:56 and 156:24), whom Erasmus also taught either at Orléans or Paris. He was a native of Ueffeln in the province of Osnabrück and had been brought up in the household of the count of Virneburg. Before coming to France he had studied law in Bologna. Later he returned to Germany and became secretary to Count Dietrich of Virneburg. He was evidently fairly affluent and occasionally made gifts or loans to Erasmus.

ERASMUS TO NIKOLAUS BENSROTT

A great many reports of the most trustworthy sort are being received here every day to the effect that the plague is raging fiercely where you are and not sparing anything. So, since I was afraid you might already have fled

* * * * *

59 brothers] Cf Ep 147:64n.

67 Italy] Cf Ep 75:15n.

67 Jérôme] de Busleyden (cf Ep 205 introduction)

67 bishop] François de Busleyden was tutor to Archduke Philip and later became his chancellor and one of his most trusted advisers. He was rewarded with several benefices, including the archbishopric of Besançon.

70 inept] Cf Virgil *Eclogues* i.16; *Adagia* III viii 15.

71 loophole] Cf *Adagia* III ii 75.

158:3 where you are] *istic*: probably Paris

elsewhere for safety, I did not think I ought to write a very long letter or send 5
you any considerable quantity of material for fear I should waste a great deal
of labour, should you be away. I will, then, merely touch on the principal
points.

The present messenger is the earliest by whom I have been able to
write to you, dear Bensrott. I am sending you Euripides and Isocrates; other 10
things are being got ready, and will follow. I shall take care to see that the
speech in defence of Milo conforms to your wishes, as soon as I can get hold
of the speech and of the books I need for the purpose. If anything has
cropped up there which you think I ought to know about, please tell me. If
Augustin is back yet, kindly give him the letter which I enclose. May I 15
commend to your particular attention the literary trifles I left with you. If
you have worked out a method of co-operation between us, you will find
me all readiness for it, and I believe you take my meaning. I shall not easily
convince you, my very kind Nikolaus, how much I long for this, but as I
scarcely dare hope, so I dare not in any way try to influence you. What gives 20
me acute pain is that even now I am hardly yet on terms of understanding
with that irreproachable and philosophic spirit of yours, and, whereas I
have always thought, and spoken, highly of it, yet either because we were
both of us modest almost to a fault, or through other men's influence, it
somehow never occurred to me to promise myself that I should become 25

* * * * *

10 Euripides and Isocrates] It is not clear whether these were copies of the Greek or of translations. Erasmus was at this time urging Bensrott to send him any Greek books that came on the market in Paris (cf Ep 160). He may have been sending copies of Greek works to Bensrott in return. In any case the copies Erasmus mentions could scarcely have been the translations he later dedicated to Archbishop Warham in 1506 (cf Epp 188, 198, and 208), as H.W. Garrod suggests in 'Erasmus and his English Patrons' *The Library* 5th series 4, 1 (June 1949) 2. The *Hecuba* was translated when Erasmus was a guest of Jean Desmarez in Louvain in 1503 or 1504, the *Iphigenia* in London in 1506 (cf Allen I 4–5). Moreover Erasmus could scarcely have made the translation before the publication of Euripides by Aldus in February 1503 (cf J.H. Waszink in ASD I i 195). The *Isocrates* was probably a copy of Agricola's translation of the *Paraenesis ad demonicum* which Erasmus later published with his edition of Cato (cf Allen Epp 298 and 677).

12 speech in defence of Milo] Erasmus had apparently promised a copy of Cicero's defence of Milo with explanatory notes.

15 letter] Ep 156

18 take my meaning] Apparently there was some plan for literary collaboration or studying together, possibly Greek in which Erasmus himself was not yet far advanced (cf Ep 160:5).

your close friend. I am as shy about making new friendships as I am tireless in keeping them up once they are made.

If any new Greek books have arrived, load the bearer of this with a bundle of them – and myself with kindness at the same time. And do not be afraid, Nikolaus, that I may prove unresponsive to your kindnesses; trust me, I shall not grow weary, nor shall I rest, until I have paid the last farthing of the debt, as far as I am able. When I say debt, I do not mean only the little sum I have received from you as a loan – that is the least part of the indebtedness I feel towards you – but much more your good will, and the great kindness which I shall remember with undiminished gratitude all my life. 30 35

Please accept this message for the time being, dear Bensrott; when I know for sure that you are there, I shall see to it that something is sent to you forthwith as concrete evidence of my studious activity. As for the letter addressed to Jacob Voogd, will you kindly ensure that it is forwarded to Orléans by a reliable messenger. Farewell. 40

Tournehem castle, [1498]

159 / To Jacob Voogd Tournehem, [18 July 1501]

This letter is largely a recapitulation of Ep 157, written for fear the former letter might go astray. Erasmus had now found a more trustworthy messenger in Saint-Omer (cf Ep 161:14f).

ERASMUS TO JACOB VOOGD

The day before I wrote this letter I gave somebody else a letter addressed to you; but I have decided I should make certain by sending another, not in precisely the same terms, of course, but roughly to the same effect, by the present bearer, just in case anything chanced to go wrong. 5

I have wasted over a month and a half very expensively in Holland – wasted, I say, for never was time so lost. Again I was delayed for several days in Zeeland by my boy's illness; and not only was this a great annoyance, since I was in a hurry to move on, but it was also no small danger to my health. I have never before experienced a climate that was harsher and more unkind to my poor body. As for the rest, it has turned out, my dear Voogd, just as your friend's affairs usually do. The bishop of Cambrai is very much his accustomed self, while the Lady of Veere is so hard pressed by fate that one would say she ought to be relieved of her own burdens rather than laden with others. 10 15

At present I am resting in the welcoming arms of Batt and in the study of letters – yet not altogether deprived of your presence, since we very often mention your name in conversation; and there is no topic more agreeable to me nor any sweeter to the ears of Batt. He is already very fond of you, eager and longing to meet you. If you believe anything in the world, believe this: I find so much deceit and perfidy in men's friendships, and not only those of the common sort but even what are called Pyladean friendships, that I am no longer disposed to risk making new ones. In Batt, and in him alone of mankind, I have experienced true good will, as staunch as it is genuine. This is one friend I do not owe to Fortune, inasmuch as virtue and virtue alone brought us together; and for the same reason I have no fear that Fortune may rob me of him, for what should make him cease to love me in trouble when he began to love me in deepest trouble? This is the man whom you, my greatly learned Jacob, resemble not only in name but also in frankness and wonderful simplicity. My own opinion of you both is accordingly so high that if I lost confidence in you, which Heaven forbid, I should lose faith in faithfulness itself.

I am, Heaven be praised, in fairly good health, a little better than when I was with you. I have almost abandoned the Roman for the Greek muses, and will not rest until I have obtained a reasonable command of the language. I was indescribably eager to get back to your household, for I could see that without causing you any expense I should be able to enjoy your company, which is the most agreeable in the world, and in turn put myself at your disposal; but what deterred me was the same plague that banished me from Paris and thrust me hither into exile. For what could ever hold any charms for me here, except Batt? Even so, I cannot enjoy him all to myself, since he is obliged to give a large share of his attention to the slavery of a court.

I recommend Dismas to you, though I know he has already been warmly commended to you on a number of grounds, not only because his intelligence and character are highly congenial to you, but because you are bound to reap enormous gratitude if you are wholly successful in training his youthful years and making him worthy of the hopes reposed in him by everyone. For almost all the family of Bergen have declared their hopes of him; yet I should like him to have a little extra affection and attention for my sake. You have got splendid material; it is for you to make sure you play the clever sculptor. If it should ever be necessary, please defend the reputation of your Erasmus there with your accustomed vigour, dear Jacob, and scare away that wolf with your loudest and boldest bark. I have been searching

* * * * *

22 Pyladean] Alluding to the affection between Pylades and Orestes

very hard for a Greek grammar, so as to buy one and send it to you; but both Constantine's, as it is called, and Urban's are sold out, as I have heard on the absolutely reliable testimony of Nikolaus Bensrott, whom one may safely believe even when he is not under oath. 55

Now I shall tell you of my plans for the future. Sometimes I contemplate returning to England in order to spend a month or two studying divinity with my friend Colet, as I am well aware how profitable this might be for me; but I am still terrified of those ill-famed cliffs on which I once was wrecked. As for a visit to Italy, I am as eager as ever to go there, but, as Plautus remarks, it is not easy to fly without wings. The plague bars me from France, while in Holland I find the climate agrees with me but I cannot stomach those Epicurean banquets; besides, the people are mean and uncultivated, humane studies are most actively despised, there is no money to be made in scholarship, and it is heartily disliked. The worst thing is that all my friends there appear to insist, without saying so, that I should fortify myself with higher academic status before I return – that I might be thus in a sense protected from the arrogance of the unlearned. Therefore I have not made up my mind, and am still waiting in suspense, with the intention of setting my course whichever way a fair wind favours me. Give me the benefit of your advice if you have unusual perspicuity or particularly wise foresight where your friend's interests are involved; and do be sure to write to me about anything in your household that you think I ought to know. 60 65 70 75

Farewell to you all. Please give greetings for me to that fine, and charming, pair of young men from Breda.

Tournehem castle, [1499] 80

* * * * *

56 Constantine's] The Greek grammar of Constantine Lascaris was first published in Milan in 1476 and again by Aldus in Venice in 1495. Lascaris (1434–1501) was a Greek scholar of the imperial family who came to Italy after the fall of Constantinople and taught at Milan and Naples.

56 Urban's] The *Institutiones graecae grammatices* (Venice: Aldus January 1497) of Urbano Bolzani of Belluno (1443–1524), a Franciscan who had travelled widely in the Near East. He taught Greek to the future pope Leo x. In 1496 he settled in Venice and assisted Aldus in preparing many books for the press. In the adage 'Festina lente' (*Adagia* II i 1) Erasmus mentioned him as one of the scholars who had generously contributed manuscripts for the Aldine edition of the *Adagia* (cf Renaudet *Erasme et l'Italie* 84).

62 ill-famed cliffs] A quotation from Horace *Odes* 1.3.20. The reference is to Dover and the confiscation of Erasmus' money there (cf Ep 119:9n).

64 Plautus] *Poenulus* 871; cf *Adagia* III v 84.

160 / To Nikolaus Bensrott — Tournehem, 18 July [1501]

This is a recapitulation of Ep 158, sent, like Ep 159, because Erasmus had found a more reliable messenger.

ERASMUS TO HIS FRIEND BENSROTT

I sent you a letter yesterday with all my news, my kind and learned Bensrott, but now that I have a second messenger I shall give merely a summary of its contents. I am back from Holland, and living with Batt, and spending all my time on studies, especially Greek. I have sent you Euripides and Isocrates, and would have sent more, but was afraid the plague might already have chased you away somewhere. If any new Greek books have come upon the scene, I would rather pawn my coat than fail to obtain them, especially any Christian works, for example, the Psalms or Gospels. Please look after my precious possessions left in your care. I have written to Augustin also, and would like to know how he is, for I have not heard anything yet. I wish, dear Bensrott, we might combine our literary efforts – but you can write to me at length on this and all the other topics. You have been very good to me, dear Nikolaus, and I shall never forget or conceal my debt. As far as in me lies, I shall try, if I am not able to earn a reputation for gratitude, at least to avoid the opprobrium of ingratitude. Farewell.

Your devoted friend Batt sends you his cordial greetings.

Tournehem, 18 July [1499]

161 / To Antonius of Luxembourg — Tournehem, 18 July [1501]

This letter, like Epp 137, 147, 148, and 150, was intended to reach the abbot of St Bertin through his chaplain, to whom it was addressed.

ERASMUS OF ROTTERDAM TO MASTER ANTONIUS OF LUXEMBOURG

As if it had not been enough for me to trouble you so relentlessly while I was with you, I propose to do the same at a distance. This, however, my most amiable Antonius, you must not put down to my effrontery, but rather to your own unequalled willingness to oblige. I have written a letter to Jacob Voogd, partly as a gift to thank my former host for his hospitality, partly to spur him on, as it were, to exert himself further, with all possible vigour, zeal, intelligence, and conscientiousness, in looking after the young man,

* * * * *

161:5 letter] Ep 159

8 young man] Dismas

so that he may return here fitted by his education and character to increase the renown of the house of Bergen, uniquely distinguished as it is. While I have no doubt that Voogd is freely disposed to put his best foot forward in attending to this, I still feel it to be my duty, and also consonant with my affection for your family, and with its services to me, that I should take pains now and then to spur the willing horse, as the saying goes. Please be sure to give the letter in question to Antonius the courier, and specially instruct him to deliver it, with his usual conscientious care, in Orléans, for I hear he is about to start.

For the rest, my dear obliging Antonius, if you would like to know how I am at this moment, life is at least happy and pleasant. Not only do I enjoy the company of Batt, from whose sound and straightforward nature I derive such delight and such food for thought that I would not exchange this one source of pleasure for all the treasures of Arabia, but I am, besides, completely absorbed in literature – lying hidden, as it were, in the innermost retreats of the muses, far from the noisy world's affairs. Had I but a few more books, it would be a life perfectly fit for the gods. So, dear Antonius, since I owe this state of mind to my poor literary efforts, do you not think it would be extremely ungrateful of me to regret my studies on the grounds that they have brought me no profit? Even though other men should be decorated with gold, raised to high positions, and elected to public offices, whereas my muses win me only wakeful nights and ill will, still I shall not repent of them so long as this heart of mine remains capable of despising Fortune's wheel. I am not unaware that the kind of study I have pursued appears to some men uncongenial, to others interminable or unprofitable, while to others again even impious – I am thinking of the generality of our present-day literary men. Yet this merely increases my ardour for it, since I am convinced of two things: first, that what was best never yet pleased the mob, and second, that, although very few men entirely approve of this kind of study, they are nevertheless quite the best educated of all. If Jerome was mad, if he was ignorant, I am happy to be foolish in such company as his – and happy to be enrolled in a company of ignorant men like him, rather than in their heavenly choirs. And if I should happen never to reach the end of this race I run, it will not have been dishonourable to strive for the fairest prizes of all. If mankind refuses to endorse my purpose, I believe that God will both approve it and aid it. If Fortune's breezes are contrary, he will send his wind as heretofore. And some day mankind too, or posterity at any rate, will give me its approval.

* * * * *

14 spur the willing horse] Pliny *Epistles* 1.8.1; *Adagia* I ii 47

15 Antonius] Cf Epp 156:14 and 167:25.

But how inordinately I am drawing out my letter while, revelling in your friendship as in a kind of delightful frenzy, I am carried away and forget myself – such is the impression I have of conversing with you, rather than writing a letter. My failure to write to that eminent and gracious 50 prelate who is your patron was not because of sloth or lack of leisure, but because I could not find a topic worthy of that great man, and I was at the same time diffident about assailing the ears of a father (kindly indeed as he is, but undoubtedly fully occupied by numerous important tasks) with academic trivialities, such as are most of my things. For the rest, dear 55 Antonius, I must tell you that I should like nothing better than to give pleasure to his lordship by some service; but it is one thing to write off-hand to a close friend, and quite another to indite a letter addressing the proud natures of the great – natures that, as Pliny has told us, have to be approached with careful circumspection even when you say good morning. 60 So in the meantime will you please act on my behalf as a letter to the reverend father? Next, please be sure to give my greetings and Batt's to that extremely agreeable man, Prior Georges, and also give kindest regards from both of us to the physician and to Canon Jacques Plumion. To these very distinguished men both of us owe a great deal. 65

Farewell, dear Antonius.

Tournehem, 18 July [1499]

162 / From Antoon van Bergen to Giovanni de' Medici Saint-Omer 30 July 1501

Cardinal Giovanni de' Medici, the future pope Leo X, had been entertained by the abbot of St Bertin during travels in northern Europe from which he returned to Rome in May 1500. This letter, composed by Erasmus for the abbot, answers one from the cardinal thanking him for his hospitality.

ANTOON VAN BERGEN, ABBOT OF ST BERTIN, TO HIS EMINENCE CARDINAL GIOVANNI DE' MEDICI, WRITTEN BY ERASMUS

I regard the greetings contained in your Eminence's letter as a great present indeed, and now return them with generous interest. Your letter was full of learning, yet also of modesty; it pleasantly reflected for me that gracious- 5

* * * * *

58 off-hand] Literally 'whatever comes into your mouth'; cf *Adagia* I v 72.

59 Pliny] Cf *Historia naturalis* praef 11.

63 Georges] Georges de Bourbourg (d 1505) was prior of the abbey of St Bertin.

64 physician] Ghisbert (cf Ep 95:13n).

ness in your character which is so truly worthy of the family of the Medici, as I found when of late you visited us. Inasmuch as you not only remember the modest entertainment we furnished but take such pains to thank us for it, and inasmuch as you so kindly offer your service in return, while I gladly and joyfully accept your proffered friendship, yet still I do not recognize any merit in my own action. For in so far as we received you in our modest fashion with such attentions as we might when, in the pursuit of knowledge, like Ulysses in Homer or Solon in Herodotus, your travels brought you to our quarter of the world, in this there is no kindness worthy of mention upon our part; rather we should have shown extreme rudeness and unkindness had we not done so. And I would that we had done it in a manner adequate to your rank or indeed to our own wishes. For myself, it is many a year since a more distinguished or welcome guest has entered my house; and upon this account, accordingly, I hold that, if a benefit exists, I am rather your debtor than your creditor. I would add that, should the occasion ever arise, I shall make use of your assistance with a readiness fully equal to the kindness that leads you to offer it.

In the meantime I have taken a fancy to revive, in this same connection, the old custom whereby I should send some small token more to your Eminence, not only a letter from your host but also a souvenir of your visit. And so I am sending two little songs set to music; and I trust that this gift, extremely small as it is and slighter than the *levidensia* of which Cicero speaks, may yet be not unwelcome, both because you yourself are deeply versed in this ancient and, by universal agreement, godlike art, as you are in all arts besides, and also because the song is quite new-born and freshly invented, the child of one who proclaims that he was once brought up in the household of that distinguished family of the Medici which seems to me to have been sent by Heaven for the express purpose of awakening talents and promoting studies. This man is the chief musician in our city.

I have given the reverend provost of Watten your greetings, as you asked. He was extremely pleased to receive them, and cordially bade me return his to you. May Heaven keep your Eminence in health and wealth.

Saint-Omer, 30 July 1501

* * * * *

27 Cicero] *Epistulae ad familiares* 9.12.2; cf *Adagia* III v 22.

34 chief musician] It has not been possible to identify this composer. This was the great period of Franco-Netherlandish music when composers and singers from the Netherlands were in great demand in Italy. Giovanni de' Medici's interest in music was well known. He had been a pupil of Isaac, one of the greatest of the Netherlandish composers. Cf G. Reese *Music in the Renaissance* (New York 1954) 169, 212 et passim.

35 provost] The provost or abbot of an Augustinian abbey in the village of Watten near Saint-Omer

163 / To Jacob Batt Saint-Omer, [August 1501]

After spending a month or two with Batt at Tournehem Erasmus moved to Saint-Omer where he planned to spend the winter months either at the abbey of St Bertin or at the Franciscan convent. This is the last surviving letter to Batt, possibly because Louis, who had been charged with copying Erasmus' letters and thus preserved many of those addressed to Batt (cf Ep 151:24n), was expelled from Tournehem shortly after this (cf Ep 166). Batt's health was already failing and he died early in the following year (cf Ep 170:12).

ERASMUS TO BATT. A LETTER WRITTEN IN JEST

I need not tell you to be cheerful, when I know well that you already have reason enough for rejoicing since you have thrown off your shoulders such a galling burden as I am! At this very moment Adrian invites me to stay with him. The warden is openly advising me rather to take up residence 5 with the abbot if I conveniently can, while the physician on the other hand recommends going to Adrian's. Really I believe that both of them are behaving exactly like dogs who refuse to share the kitchen. I have an underlying doubt whether the warden is quite as disinterested as he might be, for I detect in him a certain latent arrogance. And he never said a word in 10 your presence about Adrian, although this business ought rather to have been negotiated through him. I shall await the final result courageously, whatever it turns out to be.

Look after your health, dear Batt. As soon as you have a suitable opportunity, send me all my things, including all my *Dialogues*, just in case 15 I take it into my head to finish them off. Keep pressing Louis to copy out all my letters, as far as he is able. Farewell.

I will not detain Louis – the doctor's advice is against it – in case those monks should gossip even more at my expense.

Saint-Omer, [1499] 20

* * * * *

4 Adrian] Cf Ep 166 introduction.

5 warden] Jean Vitrier was warden (*gardianus*) of the Franciscan convent at Saint-Omer. Erasmus soon acquired a great and lasting admiration for him. Years later he wrote a joint biographical sketch of Vitrier and Colet, two men who, he felt, had much in common; Ep Allen 1211, trans J.H. Lupton *The Lives of Jehan Vitrier and John Colet* (London 1883). At the end of his life Erasmus also cited Vitrier as an example of proper preaching and of disregard for merely formal observances in the *Ecclesiastes* (LB V 987C; cf Allen Ep 1211:62n).

6 physician] Ghisbert (cf Epp 95:13n and Allen 1211:120)

15 *Dialogues*] Probably the *Familiarium colloquiorum formulae* (cf Ep 130:108–9)

17 letters] Cf Ep 151:24n.

164 / To Johann Poppenruyter — Saint-Omer, [autumn] 1501

While at Tournehem Erasmus began writing the *Enchiridion militis christiani* (the title can mean either the 'dagger' or 'handbook' of a Christian knight), the work in which he first developed fully his conception of the *philosophia Christi* and outlined the themes to which he returned again and again for the rest of his life. He completed a first draft at Saint-Omer in the form of a long letter of which the present letter forms the introduction (lines 1–16) and conclusion (lines 17–62) which were retained in the printed edition. After showing the work to Jean Vitrier and others he revised it for publication at Louvain (cf Allen I 19f). It was first published in the *Lucubratiunculae* (Antwerp: Th. Martens 15 February 1503; NK 835); cf Ep 93 introduction. It was reprinted by Martens 6 November 1509 (NK 836) and in the *Lucubrationes* supervised by Nikolas Gerbell (Strasbourg: M. Schürer 1515). Erasmus himself published a new edition with Froben at Basel in 1518, moving the *Enchiridion* to the front of the book and putting it on the title page. For this edition he wrote a new preface addressed to Paul Volz (Allen Ep 858). The *Enchiridion* did not attract much attention for some time, but after 1515 it was frequently reprinted and translated into nearly every European language. See the list of editions in *Biblioteca Belgica* nos. E 1000ff. It is most conveniently found in LB V 1ff or in H. Holborn and A. Holborn, eds *Erasmus: Ausgewählte Werke* (Munich 1933). For full analysis of its content see E.W. Kohls *Die Theologie des Erasmus* (Basel 1966) 169–175.

As Erasmus later recalled, the *Enchiridion* was written originally at the request of a pious lady whose husband, a friend of both Batt and Erasmus, was much in need of some spiritual inspiration (cf Allen I 20). The friend to whom it was addressed was not mentioned by name in the first edition, nor in any other supervised by Erasmus, but in the Schürer edition of 1515 he was called Johannes Germanus (cf Nichols I 341). Erasmus himself addressed him as Johannes in a letter of November 1517 (Allen Ep 698), and in 1525 he sent greetings to one Johannes whom he described as a gun-founder and an old friend, with whom he had long ago exchanged arms as a symbol of friendship, giving the *Enchiridion* and receiving a dagger in return, weapons of which neither made any use (cf Allen Ep 1556:42ff and n). On the strength of this and his connection with Nürnberg Allen identified the friend with Johann Poppenruyter (d 1534) of a Nürnberg family, who established a gun foundry at Mechlin before 1510 and was later appointed gun-founder to Charles V (cf Allen Ep 1556:42n; also O. Schottenloher 'Erasmus, Johan Poppenreuter und die Entstehung des *Enchiridion Militis Christiani*' ARG 45:1 (1954) 109–16).

ERASMUS, CANON OF THE AUGUSTINIAN ORDER,
TO A FRIEND AT COURT

You have urgently entreated me, most beloved brother in the Lord, to set down for you a kind of summary guide to living, so that, equipped with it, you might attain to a state of mind worthy of Christ. For you say that you have for some time past grown weary of a courtier's life, and are wondering how you may escape from Egypt, with her sins and allurements, and successfully gird yourself to follow Moses on the road to virtue. Holding you especially dear, as I do, I rejoice more heartily in this your most worthy purpose; I hope that, apart from any help of mine, he who vouchsafed to awaken it within you shall prosper and advance it. Yet I very willingly obey a good friend who makes a request so Christian as this. Only you must try not to appear to have insisted on my help without good cause or make me seem to have acceded to your request unprofitably; let us, on the contrary, unite our prayers and beseech Our Lord's gracious Spirit to give me good counsel as I write, and to render my words profitable for you ...

Though I have no doubt that the reading of Scripture will bring you all these things in abundance, yet brotherly love inspired me to forward and assist your holy enterprise as well as I could by means of this small extempore treatise. I did so with all the more alacrity because I was somewhat afraid you might fall into the hands of that superstitious fraternity among the religious, who, partly pursuing their own personal interests, and partly out of great zeal but not according to knowledge scour land and sea, and, whenever they find anyone abandoning wicked courses and returning to a saner and better life, immediately attempt to thrust him into a monastic order by means of the most impudent urging and threats and cajoleries, as if Christianity did not exist outside the monk's cowl; and then, after filling his mind with mere quibbles and thorny problems that nobody could solve, they bind him to some petty observances, of human, not divine, origin, and plunge the poor fellow into a kind of Judaism, teaching him how to tremble, not how to love. Being a monk is not a state of holiness but a way of life, which may be beneficial or not according to each person's physical and mental constitution. I personally do not urge you to adopt it, nor yet do I urge you against it. I merely advise you to identify piety not with diet, or dress, or any visible thing, but with what I have taught here. Associate with those in whom you have seen Christ's true image; otherwise, where there are none whose society can improve you, then withdraw from human intercourse as far as you can, and take for company the holy prophets and Christ and the apostles. Above all make Paul your special friend; him you

* * * * *

23 zeal ... knowledge] Cf Romans 10:2.

should keep always in your pocket and 'ply with nightly and with daily hand,' and finally learn by heart. I have been carefully preparing an interpretation of him for some time. Certainly it is a bold venture. Nonetheless, relying on Heaven's help, I shall earnestly try to ensure that, even after Origen and Ambrose and Augustine and all the commentators of more recent date, I may not appear to have undertaken this task without any justification or profit. Second, I shall try to cause certain malicious critics, who think it the height of piety to be ignorant of sound learning, to realize that, when in my youth I embraced the finer literature of the ancients and acquired, not without much midnight labour, a reasonable knowledge of the Greek as well as the Latin language, I did not aim at vain glory or childish self-gratification, but had long ago determined to adorn the Lord's temple, badly desecrated as it has been by the ignorance and barbarism of some, with treasures from other realms, as far as in me lay; treasures that could, moreover, inspire even men of superior intellect to love the Scriptures. But, putting aside this vast enterprise for just a few days, I have taken upon myself the task of pointing out to you, as with my finger, a short way to Christ. And I pray Jesus, who is the author, I trust, of this your purpose, that he may of his goodness vouchsafe to bless your virtuous undertaking; or rather may increase and fulfil his own good gift in converting you, that you may swiftly grow up in him and come to perfect manhood. Farewell in him, my brother and friend; you have always been beloved of my heart, but now are far dearer and more delightful to me than ever before.

Monastery of St Bertin, at Saint-Omer, 1501

165 / To Edmond Courtebourne, [autumn 1501]

Some time during the fall of 1501 Erasmus accepted an invitation to spend the winter at the castle of Florent de Calonne, Baron de Courtebourne, some ten kilometres west of Tournehem and nearly thirty from Saint-Omer (cf J. Hadot 'Erasme à Tournehem et à Courtebourne' *Colloquia Turonensia* (Toronto 1972) I 94f). Edmond was evidently a member of the Franciscan convent at Saint-Omer of which Jean Vitrier was warden.

ERASMUS TO THE EXCELLENT FATHER EDMOND

I have hidden myself away at the country seat of the gracious prince of Courtebourne, intending to brood in silence over holy writ during the winter months to come. How I wish you could have joined me, dear

* * * * *

40–1 'ply with nightly and with daily hand'] Horace *Ars poetica* 269

41–2 interpretation] Cf Epp 123:25, 165:12ff, 181:35ff, 296:166ff.

Edmond, with the warden's permission! Still, here as elsewhere, we must be content to follow the familiar proverb 'He who cannot do what he likes, must like what he does.' For the rest, will you kindly urge Adrian to furnish me with some books? I request him to send me Augustine and Ambrose on St Paul. He might obtain a temporary loan of Origen from St Bertin, and he may with perfect confidence offer a guarantee in my name, without risk of default. Over and above this I should be immensely glad to have Origen's homilies sent at the same time; they are in the warden's keeping. Also I should like to receive Nicholas of Lyra, or anyone else who has written a commentary on Paul. On Saturday a vehicle will be sent to convey all this to me here; meanwhile will you please see that the books are ready to go on that day? We shall be delighted to see either Adrian or the warden whenever either of them is disposed to honour us with a visit. Farewell, my dear Edmond; I beg you to give careful attention to my request.

Courtebourne castle, [1500]

166 / To Adrian of Saint-Omer Courtebourne, [autumn 1501]

Nothing is known about this Adrian except that he seems to have been closely associated with Vitrier, possibly resident in the convent, and to have had something to do with books. Nichols (I 338) suggests he may have been a transcriber or seller of books. A possibility more in keeping with his association with Vitrier is that he was the librarian of the convent.

ERASMUS TO MASTER ADRIAN, HIS DEAR FRIEND IN CHRIST

The bearer, Louis, is a boy whom Jacob Batt has up to the present, out of regard for me, maintained at Tournehem. However those who now hold despotic power there have been pleased to send him elsewhere. They have also driven out Batt's brother, and even tried to dismiss Batt himself. Accordingly I have counselled the youth to call upon you first of all; if you take him into your household you will do me a great personal favour,

* * * * *

6 proverb] Terence *Andria* 305–6; *Adagia* I viii 43

7 Adrian] Cf Ep 166 introduction.

13 Nicholas of Lyra] Scholastic theologian (c 1270–1349) and one of the best-equipped biblical scholars of the Middle Ages. His *Commentaria in universa Biblica*, which stressed the literal sense of the Scriptures, was highly respected by later scholars and was printed in Rome in 1471–2.

166:4 despotic power] Anthony of Burgundy, 'le Grand Bâtard,' was now more than eighty years old and seems to have fallen under the influence of a clique of clerical advisers who were inimical to Batt (cf Nichols I 339). His patroness, the lady Anna, had been absent from Tournehem for some time (cf Ep 155:14).

besides helping the youth and also honouring God; and lastly you will do no disservice to your own interests. He is a fairly well-educated young man, a very good copyist, and completely upright and honest, as you can easily 10 discover for yourself, and I would not hesitate to assert this on my own responsibility. Farewell.

I am grateful for the loan of the books; and God, who repays pious deeds with generous interest, will reward you.

Courtebourne castle, [1500] 15

167 / To Louis [Courtebourne, winter 1501]

Louis was a young servant, mentioned frequently in the preceding letters, who had entered Erasmus' service before November 1500, when he was sent to Batt at Tournehem, possibly because Erasmus could no longer afford to keep him (cf Ep 135:39ff). He was maintained by Batt for a year until he was forced to leave Tournehem when Batt fell out of favour (cf Ep 166). Thereafter he was for some time in the service of Adrian of Saint-Omer, but was free, as he had been earlier at Tournehem, to do a good deal of copying for Erasmus (cf Bierlaire 47f). Erasmus apparently kept in touch with him for many years (cf Allen Epp 651, 666, 790).

ERASMUS TO HIS DEAR LOUIS

I am sending you three prayers: one to Jesus, Son of the Virgin, and two to the Virgin Mother; see that you write them out as carefully as you can. The first of them is a little disarranged, but you cannot go wrong if you follow the lines as a guide. I should like them all to be written out in a single copy 5 as soon as possible, because the person to whom I propose to present them intends to go to Paris within four days, or perhaps even sooner; as to the rest, we shall arrange about this when you come to see me. Or, if you have time to make more than one copy, use the best paper you can get, ruled with very neat lines, with broader margins than I leave, and rather wide spaces 10 between the verses. Write as elegantly as you can. You will not be doing it for nothing. If you have no time for Franciscus' book, let him know how to procure another scribe; for you will never lack something to write for me from now on, provided that you have the time.

If your people allow you, in two or three days time, once you have 15 made a first copy, come to see me for a talk. I should like you to bring my

* * * * *

167:2 prayers] Cf Ep 93:112–18n.

12 Franciscus'] Cf Ep 168:7. This may be Erasmus' old friend Franciscus Theodericus of Gouda with whom he still kept in touch (cf Ep 186).

cap, since Adrian's, which I have here, is in fresh condition and unused; from the day it reached me I have never worn it. Also go to X and find out the price of a linen kerchief of the kind that was lost at St Bertin, so that either I may buy one and replace his, or, if he prefers, he may have the money to 20 buy it. Go to him and ask which he prefers; or rather, buy it yourself, if he so instructs you, to his complete satisfaction, and I shall repay you when you come here. Give my very best wishes to your gracious patron Master Adrian, and also to Master Edmond, whom I love as a brother. Farewell.

If there is any news from Paris by Antonius, tell me about it. Give my 25 warm greetings to the physician, whenever it is convenient, and to the warden, if he has already returned.

[1499]

168 / To Edmond [Courtebourne, beginning of 1502]

ERASMUS TO EDMOND, WHOM HE LOVES AS A BROTHER

I should like to hear from you whether our friend the warden has returned yet, or how soon his arrival is looked for. Please ask Adrian, on my behalf, to be patient about his books, for I shall be off elsewhere in a few days, but not before I have sent the books back with my best thanks. I am very pleased 5 with myself for undertaking this task, for I trust I shall in future dedicate myself wholeheartedly to the study of holy writ. My Franciscus is to return home in a week or so, so Louis will do well to send any pages of Lorenzo Valla that are in his possession, and payment will not be delayed. Also will he please inform me whether he has learnt anything from the messenger, 10 and what he has done about the lost kerchief. Ask him to send back the master-copy of my prayers if he has finished with it. I have long been expecting a visit from all of you, but in vain. Please give my greetings to Master Adrian, that pattern of devoutness, for whom on several grounds I have a high regard. My best greetings to yourself; and please answer with 15 your love the great love I feel for you; and let us, for our mutual charity's sake, support each other in our prayers to God.

In haste, from the castle where I am sojourning, [1500]

169 / To Pierre le Bâtard de Courtebourne [Saint-Omer, about March 1502]

Pierre, who apparently lived at Courtebourne, was probably the bastard son

* * * * *

25 Antonius] The messenger who frequently went to Paris and Orléans (cf Ep 161:15).

168:7 Franciscus] Cf Ep 167:12n.

of the then baron's father. Erasmus may have ridden over to Saint-Omer for a short visit, intending to return to Courtebourne before Easter, but see line 6n.

ERASMUS OF ROTTERDAM TO HIS FRIEND PIERRE LE BÂTARD OF COURTEBOURNE

My most affectionate and grateful thanks to you, kind Pierre, for your devoted attention to my interests. You would have seen me there long ago had not the abbot of St Bertin delayed me as I was booted and spurred and 5 on the point of leaving. Be sure to buy the psalter so long as it is complete and has a sound text and is reasonably legible. I shall certainly be there to join you before Easter. I intended to send the money, but at the moment, as I write this letter, the boy is not yet sure whether he will be going in your direction. So I ask you not to be anxious about the money. Farewell, and 10 hold me in affection.

[1499]

170 / To Jacob Voogd

Saint-Omer, 2 July [1502]

ERASMUS TO HIS FRIEND JACOB VOOGD

The abbot is disposed to bar Dismas and Antoon from any contact with our mother-tongue. Your situation, however, is such that you are not prepared to dispense with the society of fellow countrymen: thus, at the instance of your good friend and well-wisher, Antonius of Luxembourg, as well as of 5 myself, he is giving them orders to move back into the household of Master Jacques Daniel. But will you, dear Jacob, please be as conscientious as ever

* * * * *

6 psalter] From the way Erasmus speaks of this psalter it was almost certainly a manuscript and, in view of his current interests, probably in Greek (cf Ep 160:7f). The lack of a definite or indefinite article in Latin leaves it uncertain whether Erasmus is referring to *the* psalter, which Pierre may have mentioned to him in a letter, or simply *a* psalter. In either case the unlikelihood of such a MS turning up at Courtebourne suggests that Pierre may have been in Paris and that the letter was addressed to him there. In that case we must assume that Erasmus had planned to return to Paris before Easter. There is some evidence that he did return to Paris later in the year (cf Ep 171 introduction).

170:2 Dismas] Erasmus had worked hard to secure Dismas (cf Ep 137:15n) as a pupil for his friend Voogd in Orléans (cf Epp 137 and 147). He had been with Voogd since March 1501 (cf Ep 150). Erasmus had foreseen the objection that Dismas would not learn French living with Voogd and had attempted to counter it (cf Ep 137:61–5).

2 Antoon] Probably Antoon, third son of Jan, sixth lord of Bergen, the abbot's eldest brother

7 Daniel] It would seem that Dismas was being returned to the household of which Erasmus had painted such a dark picture in Ep 137.

in seeing that these young men are placed as satisfactorily as possible, and as far as possible according to the abbot's wishes, of which you are aware. I am sure Augustin will do likewise. By doing this you will both earn the 10 gratitude of that distinguished and most civilized prelate.

I have written to Augustin, by Cornelius the courier, about my misfortunes. Now Batt is dead, who can doubt that Erasmus has died as well? And more than this, my other circumstances could not be worse. My one remaining hope of salvation lies in courage. Farewell; and my greetings to Augus- 15 tin, who I hear is going to live with you.

Saint-Omer, 2 July [1498]

171 / To Nicolaas Werner [Louvain, September 1502]

During the late summer of 1502 Erasmus may have returned to Paris (cf Allen I 20 11f), but if so he very soon left again to avoid another outbreak of the plague and took up residence in Louvain, where he remained except for occasional intervals for two years. Nicolaas was a monk at Steyn and its seventh prior, an old and sympathetic friend of Erasmus (cf Ep 48 introduction). The letter which Erasmus feared had offended him has not survived. In it he had evidently complained of slanderous attacks by one of the monks under Werner's authority.

ERASMUS OF ROTTERDAM TO FATHER NICOLAAS WERNER

If what I hear is true, it seems you were somewhat offended at my letter; perhaps because, though perfectly true, it was more outspoken than it need have been. Yet a person of your understanding temperament ought to have put this down to my quite justifiable distress, or else reflected that one may 5 sometimes be freer than usual in a letter, which should always be a safe repository of confidences. For how can I be indignant enough at a man who has poured out, or rather spewed out, against me expressions like those he used? There are about you some who despise me, stupid and uneducated people who deem the sum of holiness to consist in a monkish cowl and a 10 long face, but it is the easiest thing in the world, and the most foolish, to despise other men's values.

Hardly had I reached Louvain when the town magistrates offered me the responsibility of lecturing publicly – a charge I had neither sought nor expected – and this, too, on a recommendation volunteered by Master 15

* * * * *

10 Augustin] Vincent (cf Ep 131 introduction). He had evidently returned to Orléans, having taken up the study of law (cf Ep 172:8f).

Adrian of Utrecht, dean of Louvain. I have rejected this offer for specific reasons, one of them being that I am so close to these Dutch tongues, which know how to inflict deep wounds and have never learnt how to be helpful to anybody. Farewell.

172 / To Willem Hermans [Louvain, September 1502]

Erasmus had apparently become friendly with Willem again after their brief estrangement (cf Ep 157:10n).

ERASMUS OF ROTTERDAM TO WILLEM OF GOUDA, HIS MOST LEARNED FRIEND

The plague, which drove me to Louvain, still keeps me there; Fortune has had a glorious fling at my expense this year! Death – or poison rather – has taken Batt, and besides him the bishop of Besançon also, in whom I had 5 placed great hopes. The Lady of Veere has been snatched away from us by a marriage that is worse than slavery; I am cut off by the sea from the count in England; and Augustin has been called away by his legal studies; and the plague puts France, England, and Germany all at once beyond my reach. Everything suits me at Louvain, except that the food is coarse and dear to 10 buy, and besides there is no way of earning a living. I was offered a lectureship by the magistrates, but turned it down. The study of Greek absorbs me completely, and I have not wholly wasted my efforts, for I have made such good progress that I am capable of expressing my meaning in Greek with reasonable proficiency and, what is more, extempore. I hear 15 that your *Apologi* have been published, so please send me some copies; also please send back those Greek fables now that you need them no longer,

* * * * *

16 Adrian] Adrian of Utrecht (1459–1523), the future pope Adrian VI, was at this time professor of philosophy at the University of Louvain and dean of the cathedral. His friendship for Erasmus proved lasting. After his election to the papacy he wrote a cordial letter inviting Erasmus to come to Rome (Allen Ep 1324).

172:5 bishop] Cf Ep 157:67n.

7 marriage] To Louis de Montfort (cf Ep 146:50n)

7 count] Mountjoy

9 Germany] When forced by the plague to flee Paris, Erasmus had thought of going to Cologne, but, since the plague was raging there also, he took refuge in Louvain (cf Allen Ep 1175:37f).

16 *Apologi*] A prose version of Avianus' fables, of which no copies are known to exist

since we are very hard up for Greek books here. Augustin writes to me in abusive terms on the subject of his copies of the *Adagia*; you, on the other hand, merely laugh. 20

Please write and tell me of any news at your end that you think I ought to know. I am surprised you have sent no letter, for, even if you disliked me, you would surely write to one who could do your reputation some good; you see, not only do I meet many people, I even run across some good scholars from time to time. In spite of all this your name is often on my lips, 25 and I have not forgotten you as yet, though I see your attitude to me is very nearly hostile. But it is in affection that I shall gladly compete, not in scorn or dislike especially with you whom I have so loved. Farewell, my dear Willem, and please love me, if you can.

173 / To Jacob Anthoniszoon — Louvain, 13 February 1503

This complimentary letter was prefixed to Anthoniszoon's treatise *De precellentia potestatis imperatorie* (Antwerp: Martens 1 April 1503; NK 120), the manuscript of which had been given to Erasmus at Brussels in July 1501 (cf Ep 153: 12). The volume also contained one of the three Latin epitaphs composed by Erasmus on the death of the bishop of Cambrai, 7 October 1502 (cf Ep 178:54n).

ERASMUS, A CANON OF THE ORDER OF ST AUGUSTINE, TO THE HONOURABLE MASTER JACOB OF MIDDELBURG, MOST LEARNED IN CANON LAW, AND VICAR-GENERAL TO THE BISHOP OF CAMBRAI, GREETINGS

I am deeply surprised that you should need further support from anyone, 5 let alone from me, when you have so great a sponsor as Hendrik van Bergen, bishop of Cambrai, both for undertaking and for publishing your work. Not only did he appoint you his vicar-general (that is, his second self, so to speak, in all matters), but he also deeply loved you as a second self. Moreover he esteemed and praised and welcomed this *Apologia* of yours as 10 warmly as he did its author, regarding it as the first fruits of that genius of yours which filled him with such pleasure. And obviously he was as right to praise your book as to conceive an affection for you. I know that the poets depict their Love as blind, but that is surely the son of the earthly Venus; for the other Love, whom Plato described as the offspring of a heavenly 15

* * * * *

19 *Adagia*] Cf Ep 139:192n.

173:10 *Apologia*] See below, line 115n.

15 Plato] Cf *Symposium* 180D.

mother, has of course the best pair of eyes and the sharpest sight in existence. So one must not therefore suppose that the bishop's sight was imperfect because he bestowed this extraordinary affection upon you. On the contrary, he lavished his affection on you for the very reason that he had turned upon your good qualities the accurate and penetrating gaze of eyes 20 as keen as Lynceus'; for besides being, as you are aware, a man who undoubtedly in all things else had a keen nose, as Horace puts it, he was also, in the matter of judging men's talents, by no means what the Greeks call 'a white line on white marble,' in fact a perfect touchstone. And so, though you have a champion who possesses so much authority and such 25 learning, and ought to be worth thousands of others in your eyes, still your unbelievable modesty leads you, like a modern Apelles, to seek even my verdict, which is that of the man in the street, and so to ask the cobbler to venture beyond his last – something Apelles could not abide. And though I can see how foolish it would be for me to take up the censor's rod, as it were, 30 on a subject that is at once complicated and unrelated to my own studies, yet now that you, to whom I can deny nothing, have said you desire it I will up and don the lion's skin, in Plato's proverbial phrase, and utter my opinion with my usual freedom – though it will in no respect differ from the bishop's, except that his more acute perceptions led him to be more vigor- 35 ous in complimenting you. There are some things I shall all but carp at, though these are few indeed, which itself may serve as evidence to assure you that I liked the rest exceedingly.

To begin with, then, had you chosen for yourself so splendid a subject to write about, you would have deserved praise for your good sense and no 40 more; but as it is you have deftly seized upon one that chance put in your way, and so I think I ought to congratulate you on your good fortune as well. For what task could possibly have come your way that was either more glorious or more pious than to take up your pen in defence of imperial majesty, which itself takes up arms in defence of us all, and to use the shield 45 of your intellect to protect from the darts of calumny that power which

* * * * *

21 Lynceus] Cf *Adagia* II i 54.

22 Horace] *Satires* 1.4.8; cf *Adagia* II viii 59.

24 'a white line on white marble'] A metaphor signifying a person without discrimination; cf *Adagia* I v 87–8.

27 Apelles] The great Greek painter who exposed his pictures to secure the opinion of members of the public with special knowledge, but told a cobbler who presumed to criticize the drawing of a man's leg that he should 'stick to his last': Pliny, *Historia naturalis* 35.84–5; cf *Adagia* I vi 16.

33 Plato] *Cratylus* 411A; cf *Adagia* I iii 66.

protects the peace of Christendom from the calamity of war? Again, mighty as is the task you have undertaken, you have not only risen to its demands but clearly gone beyond them. For you were not satisfied to defend that most invincible power from calumny by adducing proofs equally invincible, but seized the opportunity thus afforded for conceiving a still greater enterprise, that of employing your work to raise a kind of everlasting monument to the glory of the emperor's power. I know that my own experience has been this: though I have always had the highest regard for the prestige of that power which God has decreed should, next to his own, be mightiest of all in the affairs of states, yet the moment I read your defence it began to appear marvellously greater and more imposing in my eyes. And I think you show especial wisdom in those areas where issues of partisan emotion come to the fore; these you either skilfully sail past or, if this proves impossible, steer (so to speak) between the Cyanean rocks, and direct the course of your writing so expertly in these dangerous questions that without any concealment of the truth you manage to keep clear of any commitment to a faction.

And nobody, I believe, could fail to wonder at the eagerness and freshness of your intellect, for all your advanced age; or fail to observe how tireless your industry is, for all your distinguished position; how alert your mind, and how attentive to the very smallest details, for all your preoccupation with such important business; or fail to marvel that one single person could possess a memory of such extent, able to retain such huge quantities of information at once, so that in a work not merely small in size, but written almost in haste, there is to be found such an abundance of learning of every sort, such knowledge of civil and canon law, theology, history, and ancient and modern literature in all its branches. And thus, like a busy bee that flies about everywhere, you seem to me with the most amazing persistence to have overlooked no book that could yield you some honey, though I would that you had exercised more choice and also a little restraint. Sometimes when you crowd a vast quantity of supporting evidence into an issue of no great moment which has long since been settled, you would have done well to guard against the ancient sneer 'a lamp lit at midday'; not that these passages are without profit or pleasure in the reading, but that they

* * * * *

60 Cyanean rocks] The Sympleades, two rocky islands in the Euxine sea, which floated and clashed together. The Argonauts had to pass between them in great danger of being crushed.

79 'a lamp lit at midday'] *Adagia* II v 6

will appear to have been added to satisfy the author's enthusiasm rather than the requirements of the project. Another consequence is that even though you have planned the work exceedingly well, the design is so heavily concealed, by the very abundance of the material, that sometimes it may elude even an alert reader blessed with a good memory. However, since in all mankind's history nothing has ever been finished with such skill and originality and devoted labour that the carping critic, whom the Greeks call Momus, could not find something to censure, there could be no more honourable criticism than to say that you overflow with a superfluity of good things. The fertile exuberance of your mind is indeed a ground for praise rather than a fault. I would add that the simplicity of your style is so far from being reprehensible, in my view, that I consider it deserving of special commendation that you have not even attempted the showy rhetoric, which the very nature of the subject repudiated – with the purpose, to be sure, of avoiding either perfume on lentils or a monkey in fine clothes.

But why touch here on points of which, in more than one passage, you make so elegant a defence? The upshot is that you will be thought guilty of unbecoming conduct if you suppress and blot out a work approved by the votes of the whole learned world, which everyone interested should read and listen to, which deserves publicity and a great future, and which is worthy, in short, either of the memory of the bishop who was so dear to you, or of the glory of the imperial majesty itself – and particularly a work on which you have expended so much toil and study. Come then – enough of modesty; accede from now on to the wishes of your friends, or the verdict of scholars, or the wish of your beloved bishop, and do not rob him, when he is dead, of what you dedicated to him in his lifetime. At long last allow it to be shaken from your grasp; let it see the light; let it be published with good omens and so make its way where men gather together; and thus, though envious death has taken from you a friend so dear, and from me the patron of my studies, yet with your book to console us we may at any rate assuage our grief. My heart foresees that this work will bring fame to you, profit to the studious, and pleasure and honour to the whole of Germany.

* * * * *

88 Momus] The patron deity of carping critics; cf *Adagia* I v 74.

95 perfume on lentils] *Adagia* I vii 23

95–6 a monkey in fine clothes] *Adagia* I vii 10. This and the preceding proverb are in Greek.

100 votes of the whole] Cf *Adagia* I v 60.

108–9 good omens] *bonis avibus: Adagia* I i 75

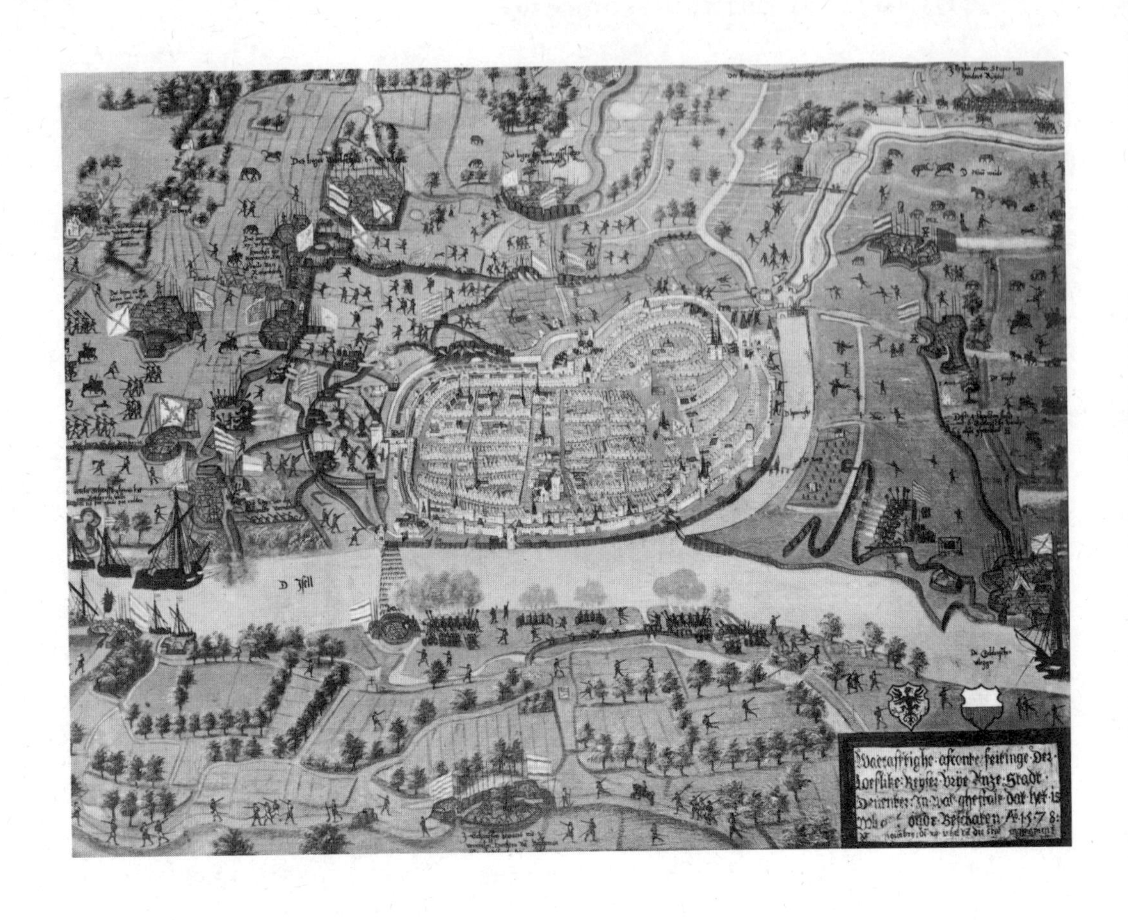

Deventer / Count Kennenberg besieging the town in 1578
By an unknown artist
Museum 'De Waag,' Deventer

I shall end after one caution: the letter which you have undertaken to combat is falsely ascribed to Leonardo Aretino; it is easy to see, both from more reliable copies and from the style, very different from Leonardo's, that it originates with a quite different Aretino, though their common surname gave rise to possible error. Farewell my greatly respected master and right good friend; and return the love of your devoted humble servant. 115

At the celebrated University of Louvain, 13 February 1502 120

174 / From Jacob Faber

Deventer, 9 July 1503

Jacob Faber (1473–after 1517) was a pupil of Alexander Hegius (cf Ep 23:59n) at Deventer, though not at the same time as Erasmus who left the school shortly after the arrival of Hegius. Most of Faber's life was spent at Deventer as a master in St Lebuin's school, but he had some reputation at large as a scholar proficient in Greek as well as in Latin. Cornelis Gerard dedicated the first ten books of his *Mariad* to him. He was still corresponding with Erasmus as late as 1517 (cf Allen Ep 719:9–11). This letter is the preface to his edition of *Alexandri Hegii ... Carmina et gravia et elegantia cum ceteris eius opusculis* (Deventer: R. Paffraet 29 July 1503; NK 1041). Despite the general title only the *Carmina* were printed in this volume, as Faber apparently wished to test the market before publishing the longer *opuscula* (cf lines 69ff and 110ff). These were published later under the title *Alexandri Hegii ... dialogi* (Deventer: R. Paffraet 31 December 1503; NK 1042).

JACOB TO HIS FRIEND ERASMUS, AN ACCOMPLISHED SCHOLAR IN LATIN AND IN GREEK AND A CANON REGULAR, GREETINGS

The writings of that excellent scholar, your teacher and mine, dearest Erasmus, are well worth my editing with your blessing; and I shall take every possible care to see that as far as in me lies they are reproduced in elegant characters. I could justifiably be held guilty of disloyalty, indeed of malice, towards studious youth, if, observing as I do that none of his close friends is undertaking this charge and that they shrink from the toil it involves, I were to fail to rescue those products of his pen, filthy with dust 5

* * * * *

115 Leonardo] Leonardo Bruni of Arezzo, hence called Aretino (1374–1444), one of the most distinguished Italian humanists and historian of Florence. Anthoniszoon's treatise had as subtitle *Apologeticon contra Aretinum quendam*. It was a defence of imperial authority against aspersions in one of Bruni's letters (Aretino *Epistolae* vi 9). There seems to be no justification for Erasmus' statement that it was falsely ascribed to Bruni. It was in fact quite in keeping with his strong anti-imperial feeling. The letter, moreover, was printed in both the 1472 and 1495 editions of Bruni's correspondence.

and buried in darkness, from the devouring worm; for they are works that deserve to be preserved by the cedar oil of Pallas Athene, drawn by our Hercules from an inner shrine. I recognize how much I am indebted to the teacher under whom you and I served, though at different times. Who has ever responded worthily to all he did for us? I have even more for which to be grateful, inasmuch as he was closer to me personally. How loyal you yourself have been to him the Greek adages which you translated some time ago show very clearly; for, near the beginning of that work, in the adage called, as I remember, 'Quid canis in balneo,' you did not forget to mention him in these terms: Rodolphus Agricola, 'whom I name to the general honour of the entire German nation; and name all the more gladly because as a boy I had for my own teacher his pupil Alexander of Westphalia, so that I owe to the latter filial duty, to the former as it were a grandson's affection. But, in case I as a German should arouse resentment by singing the praises of my fellow-countryman Rodolphus, I shall add the epitaph composed by Ermolao Barbaro, whom everyone, I think, must agree to have occupied the pre-eminent place among Italians, both for personal honour and for scholarship:

In this cold tomb hath envious fate sealed up
The hope and glory of the Frisian name;
Whate'er of praise to Rome or Greece belong,
He, living, won for Germany that same.'

How highly Agricola himself respected Hegius is made clear by the following: he was convinced that by virtue of his intense enthusiasm for study and his sincere good will, such as he himself longed to possess, our master was most effective in evoking, prompting, and assisting others' studies. With him he loved to share whatever he had discovered by reflection, or created in writing, or learned by reading, or marked as deserving either praise or censure. And these things he poured into our master's ears, just as Hegius did into his. He always made some relevant point, or expressed reluctance or hesitation, or debated the matter, sometimes chiding carelessness with an outspoken rebuke and sometimes encouraging an attempt with kindly words of praise, but always both able and

* * * * *

11 cedar oil] Cf *Adagia* IV i 54.

18 *Quid canis in balneo*] Faber is quoting no. 25 from Erasmus' *Adagiorum collectanea* (cf Ep 126) in the unrevised version of 1500. Revised and enlarged, it eventually appeared in the *Adagiorum chiliades* I iv 39.

19 Agricola] Cf Ep 23:58n.

21 Alexander] Hegius

25 Barbaro] Cf Ep 126:150n.

willing to speak and to listen. And therefore there was nobody with whom he would have preferred to spend his life than with our master; and he was very sorry that their circumstances made it impossible. 45

Who could easily chronicle all our master's good qualities? Though he surpassed others in rank and authority, he showed exceptional affability in condescending to men of low estate. He was extremely energetic, and always preferred a busy life to a quiet and restful one; he was extraordinarily anxious to find the best way of serving the interests of studious youth, 50 and his life-story shows that he regarded it as his destined task to educate youth well. He took infinite pains to achieve what would be most permanent without calculating what struggles it would cost him; for, in order to deserve well of youth and win its affection, he thought no kind of fatigue was of any consequence, and when he sought hard work, he did so not 55 under the spell of foolish Midas' hidden gold, but out of a longing to do good. In fairness he would not allow those who were obviously poor to be disappointed by others who claimed the same benefits in return for fees, and was very ready to admit them, regarding Heaven as his recompense; and he taught the liberal arts to them with the same careful attention as to 60 the rich. Thus while he was alive he did all that one could do to live a virtuous and unselfish life; he relied on God, and did not hope in vain; indeed he lived up to his own hopes in generous measure, for he was filled with goodness and made perfect in goodness. He was most assiduous in encouraging the pursuit of virtue, to the exercise of which he earnestly 65 called his pupils; he preached and praised virtue, exhorting them to abandon vice, which he hated. The extent of his hostility to it is shown with perfect clarity in the many deeply serious poems he published each year, as was his custom; these I have deliberately decided to issue in advance of his other productions, even though the latter were far more accomplished, for I 70 shall thereby come to know what reception they can expect. When I perceive that they have won approval (and they are sure to receive a warm welcome from every educated person with any taste for literature, both for their profound learning and for their restrained moral exhortations), I shall then be more ready, without suffering the printer's importunate insistence 75 as I do now, to send his other works to the press to be printed. They consist of the following:

An enquiry in the form of a dialogue on the true method of determin-

* * * * *

77 the following] Only the poems were actually published in the volume to which this letter serves as preface. The other works here enumerated were published later in the same year by R. Paffraet, 13 December 1503, as *Alexandri Hegii ... dialogi* (cf lines 110ff).

ing the date of Easter, which depends upon the Bible; this he evidently derived from the Greek, Isaac Argyros; together with a lengthy treatment of 80 the mystery of the incarnation

On knowledge and the known; against the philosophers of the academic school

On philosophy

On the tripartite soul: vegetable, sensory, and rational 85

On ability and its absence

On rhetoric

On morals

On sensation and its object; also several other writings

And thus, as treasures of the mind are finer than transitory and 90 ephemeral possessions, so may his glory ever grow greater from his enduring achievements; for by his teaching he deserved excellently well of his pupils, whom he never teased with circumlocutions, obscurities, or vain and petty cleverness of no relevance to the subject; who never learned the art of adding light to the sun; who did not wrap up in thick veils matters that 95 were clearer than daylight, blunting the understanding with useless additions. On the contrary, he set whatever was obscure in the clearest possible light, in such a way that anyone save he whose 'blood within his breast did coldly run' could understand it with the greatest of ease. For this reason he deserves to enjoy eternal remembrance among posterity through the liter- 100 ary memorials he has left.

Enough on this subject. For the rest, dearest Erasmus, I fail to comprehend why you have not given me, as we agreed, the Greek oration of Libanius when you have done it into Latin; I am waiting for it. I can glimpse your intention; you have decided to add to my Libanius the books you are 105 now engaged upon: on famous metaphors, on ecclesiastical allegories, on allusions in classical authors, and on witty sayings and replies. This is the one thought I console myself with that I may bear patiently the rather long delay. So now accept our teacher's most important poems, to which will also be added, when I see that it would please you and my other kindly 110 readers, his enquiries into a variety of topics, composed in dialogue form;

* * * * *

80 Argyros] A Byzantine monk, theologian, and astronomer (d c 1372). His chief scientific works concerned the sun and moon cycles and included a treatise on the date of Easter.

95 adding light to the sun] *Adagia* II v 7

98–9 'blood … run'] Cf Virgil *Georgics* 2.484.

105 Libanius] Cf Ep 177 introduction.

in this respect he follows the example of Plato, who was most intimately known to him. Finally I shall see to it that any of Rodolphus Agricola's works that come to hand here are sent on to you, except those that have been published in previous years and are now in the booksellers' shops. Also I thought it not inappropriate to add a rough-and-ready dirge that I composed in honour of our departed friend, which touches on certain admirable qualities in him, which may ever serve to commend him to your friends. Farewell. 115

Deventer, 9 July 1503 120

175 / To Robert de Keyzere — Louvain, [September 1503]

This letter was printed for the first time in a now rare edition of Erasmus' *Concio de puero Jesu a puero in schola Coletica nuper Londini instituta pronuncianda* (LB V 599ff). Though without place or date, the type and printer's mark identify it as printed by Robert de Keyzere at Ghent, probably on 1 September 1511 (NK 2887; cf Reedijk 291f), since Colet's school was opened only in 1510. It was reprinted by Schürer at Strasbourg in July 1512 and there were later editions. The date of the letter itself is fixed by the reference to the panegyric for the archduke Philip (cf Epp 176:6, 178:10f, 179 introduction). Its inclusion in the edition of the *De puero Jesu* may be explained by the fact that Keyzere had preserved the letter from Erasmus, and, being proud of it, chose this opportunity to publish it, even though it had no connection with the rest of the book.

Robert de Keyzere (Caesar) was evidently a schoolmaster at Ghent when this letter was written. Later he became a printer and published a number of editions. Erasmus remained acquainted with him for many years. He seems to have been prone to leaving his friends suddenly in a huff, since Erasmus commented on a similar incident in April 1518 (cf Allen Ep 841:3f).

DESIDERIUS ERASMUS TO ROBERT DE KEYZERE

Pray continue, dear Robert, in that endeavour which, as I for one believe, is the noblest of all and most acceptable in the sight of God; that is, to prepare the youth of Ghent for the mastery of the highest forms of learning, by inculcating a pure Latin style. The babbling of the spiteful should trouble you no more than a gnat troubles an elephant; rather their barking ought to inspire you to greater heights. It is good that there are people whom you 5

* * * * *

117 touches on] *prestringuntur*

175:6 gnat troubles an elephant] *Adagia* III i 27

enrage by your virtue. What surprises and grieves me is that you departed from us so suddenly. My host was even more distressed, for he is second to none in his admiration for men like yourself. I have shown your pupils' compositions to my friends here, and could hardly manage to convince them that they were the work of children. I had intended to write to Antonius, but am working night and day, getting something ready for the prince's arrival. Presently I shall send you a few things which will make you admit that your kindness has been well and truly repaid.

Farewell, my dearest Robert, and love your friend Erasmus in proportion to his affection for you, which is very great indeed.

Louvain

176 / To Jacob Mauritszoon — Louvain, 28 September [1503]

Jacob Mauritszoon was a distinguished citizen of Gouda who was appointed to membership in the Council of Holland in 1519. From the address of this and other letters (cf Epp 190 and 202) it appears that he held a degree in civil and canon law. Erasmus was still sending greetings to him as late as 1521 (cf Allen Epp 1092:15, 1188:42). No indication of the nature of Mauritszoon's request or of what Erasmus may have written in response to it has been discovered.

ERASMUS OF ROTTERDAM TO MASTER JACOB MAURITSZOON, A MOST LEARNED LICENTIATE IN CIVIL AND CANON LAW

Though I am long since well nigh exhausted from the endless drudgery of writing (and writing, especially for publication, is the hardest task on earth); and though I could not be busier than I am now, putting the final touches to the last part of my *Panegyricus*; and though this task you have asked me to undertake is tiresome in the extreme and yet quite useless (for what is more tiresome than using one's pen to express other men's anger, or more useless than writing stuff that requires one to forget how to write well?), all the same my affection for you made it seem in my eyes neither

* * * * *

9 my host] Jean Desmarez (cf Ep 180 introduction)

13 Antonius] Antonius Clava, a citizen of Ghent and a patron of letters. Erasmus maintained friendly relations and corresponded with him throughout his life. In 1514 he met him in Louvain when Clava was a member of the Council of Flanders (cf Allen Ep 301:37). He died 31 May 1529 (cf Allen Ep 2197:60f) and Erasmus published an epitaph in the form of a letter to Pieter Gillis appended to his translation of Xenophon's *Hieron* (Basel: Froben 1530); cf Allen Ep 2260.

176:6 *Panegyricus*] Cf Ep 179 introduction.

tiresome nor useless, once I had decided to oblige my dear friend in every way, not only from a sense of duty, but even gladly.

Farewell. Louvain, 28 September

177 / To Nicolas Ruistre — Louvain, 17 November 1503

This is the dedicatory preface to three declamations of Libanius with Greek text and translation which were first published by Martens at Louvain in July 1519 (NK 1367; critical edition by R.A.B. Mynors in ASD I 1 175–92). The delay in publication may have been partly due to the fact that it made only a small book of sixteen quarto pages and also to the fact that Martens could not yet print Greek. The presentation copy, in Erasmus' autograph with professional illumination, survives at Trinity College, Cambridge (MS R.9.26).

Nicolas Ruistre of Luxembourg (c 1442–1509) served four successive Burgundian dukes as secretary and councillor. He held a number of ecclesiastical preferments, was chancellor of the University of Louvain from 1487 and bishop of Arras in 1501. As chancellor he founded the College of Arras (Collegium Atrobatense). From the rather broad hints about his reputed generosity to scholars (lines 52ff) it is evident that Erasmus hoped for patronage from him.

TO THE REVEREND FATHER IN CHRIST, NICOLAS RUISTRE,
BISHOP OF ARRAS, CHANCELLOR OF THE RENOWNED AND MOST
FLOURISHING UNIVERSITY OF LOUVAIN, COUNCILLOR OF
HIS HIGHNESS THE ARCHDUKE PHILIP OF AUSTRIA,
FROM ERASMUS DESIDERIUS OF ROTTERDAM, GREETINGS 5

I have recently come into possession of certain Greek declamations, illustrious prelate, and have resolved to translate these into Latin with the object of determining how far I have made any considerable progress in the knowledge of both these tongues. Accordingly, when I looked about for the person to whom I might most fitly dedicate this my apprentice work, yours 10 was the first and indeed the only name that came to mind. For, all else apart, to whom could I better pay tribute with the fruits of my studies than the chancellor of this flourishing university, who is the governor of all its scholarly pursuits, and its permanent head? Coming to Louvain as I have, by choice, I received much encouragement and inspiration, not only from 15 the universal report of your good qualities 'current on the lips of humankind,' but also in a pronounced degree from the almost daily eulogies

* * * * *

16–17 lips of humankind] A fragment of Ennius, cited by Cicero *Tusculanae disputationes* 1.15.34

pronounced by my friend and host Jean Desmarez, a man of the highest personal as well as scholarly attainments; for he presented me with such a clear picture in words, so to speak, of your whole character that no Apelles 20 could have drawn a more lifelike portrait with the brush. Furthermore one especially notable instance of the countless honours you have won is that, whereas few men indeed have ever held for long the favour of a single prince, your own rare combination of exceptional wisdom and agreeable manners has already earned, and continues to earn, for you the unbroken 25 good will of four succeeding dukes of Burgundy; to such a degree that not a single nobleman at court has been so highly regarded, so influential, so sagacious in policy, or so valued for his counsel, as you are. At the same time for all your long acquaintance with the court you have never been in any way corrupted by it; indeed you yourself have steadily improved its 30 moral tone. There is another fact which does you as much honour as the famous praise that Homer concedes to Nestor alone: your irreproachable behaviour and straightforward frankness of address have always been more welcome, to rulers and subjects alike, than the obsequious flattery of other men. Nor need I now mention the embassies you have so often undertaken 35 with the greatest distinction, so that your fame and reputation have spread abroad in other countries everywhere like the sun. Or again the high honours, earned by your own qualities rather than by any endowment of fortune, all of which you have borne, and continue to bear, in such a way that you yourself dignify those honours far more than you acquire dignity 40 from them, and appear to bless them by your tenure rather than be blest by them.

All this, however, might have deterred me, just because you are so eminently distinguished, had I not on the other hand been attracted by what I heard: that you are not merely unusually well versed in literature and 45 religion, but always cherish a particular affection for such men as exhibit outstanding signs of high moral character or scholarship, and that you make a practice of affording such persons extremely generous help; further that more than anyone else for many generations past you have protected the high estate and fortunes of the church and of learning by your zeal and 50 outspokenness, your combative spirit, and scorn for unpopularity. Moreover you are happy to contribute, for the support, assistance, and

* * * * *

18 Desmarez] Actually Erasmus wrote 'Paludanus,' a Latin translation of 'Desmarez,' i.e., of the marshes (cf Ep 180 introduction).

26 dukes] Philip the Good, Charles the Bold, Maximilian, and Philip the Handsome

32 Nestor] Cf Homer *Iliad* 1.247–52, etc.

encouragement of good and scholarly men, all the means that Fortune has lavished upon you, or your own labours created. It was in the knowledge of these and many other facts, most gracious Father, that my heart had long been fired with eagerness to oblige your Highness in some way or other, and the exhortations of my host as it were spurred on the willing horse. My confidence was increased, moreover, when I recollected that in ancient days, as Plutarch relates, a certain humble man of the people earned the warm gratitude of King Artaxerxes by the gift of a pomegranate of exceptional size; while Virgil, again, secured the favour of Augustus by a single couplet, and on many other occasions the greatest of men have been highly delighted with tiny presents; and lastly that, as Pliny so charmingly puts it, those who have no frankincense can propitiate even the gods with salted meal.

It is in reliance upon these facts that by way of a keepsake I have ventured to present your Excellency with these three flowerets, so to call them, plucked from the rose garden of the Greeks; albeit the gardens of the muses outdo the sweets of Paestum itself, forasmuch as they bloom the whole year round. The first of them, and the fairest and most fragrant of them all by far, has been transplanted into Latin from the well-tilled flower-beds of the sophist Libanius, to whom the verdict of scholarship awards a leading place among the practitioners of Attic style. He has taken its seed-bed, that is, its theme, from the fields of Homer that bear all crops, to be exact, from Antenor's speech in the third book of the *Iliad*, where he relates how Menelaus and Ulysses stayed at his house when they came to Troy to demand restitution, and describes and compares the appearance and manner of speaking of the pair, which he had carefully noted. The dialect used is Attic. Though he preserves everywhere the charm of Attic, he has managed remarkably well to retain an appropriate atmosphere in the character of Menelaus by cleverly suggesting the famous Spartan, or 'laconic,' plainness and outspokenness in speech, which has in fact given rise to a proverb. Again, as if he were drawing from the Homeric original,

* * * * *

57 spurred on] *Adagia* I ii 47

59 Plutarch] *Life of Artaxerxes* 4.4

61 Virgil] According to an apocryphal story inserted in the life of Virgil ascribed to Donatus, para 69

63 Pliny *Historia naturalis* praef 11

69 Paestum] The roses of Paestum in Lucania bloomed twice a year; cf Virgil *Georgics* 4.119.

81 Menelaus] Cf Cicero *De republica* 5.9.11; Quintilian 12.10.64; Aulus Gellius 12.2.7.

83 proverb] Cf *Adagia* II x 49.

he has endowed the king with the attributes of supreme magnanimity, combined however with enormous self-control and good humour: for Menelaus goes so far as to praise Priam, while he diverts all the odium attaching to the crime from the Trojans at large to Paris alone; and even against him he does not say a word that is ill-natured or vindictive. Also he speaks against the war in such a way that he appears to be personally confident of victory and only to have the interests of the others at heart. Lastly the author has even represented his brevity of utterance in express terms: which not only is, as it were, the heritage of all Spartans, but, as the evidence of Cicero and Quintilian and Gellius shows, in Menelaus was specially associated with subtlety, elegance, and gaiety; but all of them follow a single source, namely Homer, whose words, in the passage I have quoted, are the following:

> Ἀλλ' ὅτε δὴ μύθους καὶ μήδεα πᾶσιν ὕφαινον
> Ἦ τοι μὲν Μενέλαος ἐπιτροχάδην ἀγόρευε
> Παῦρα μέν, ἀλλὰ μάλα λιγέως, ἐπεὶ οὐ πολύμυθος
> Οὐδ' ἀφαμαρτοεπής, εἰ καὶ γένει ὕστερος ἦεν.

This I have roughly translated as follows:

> But when they speech and counsel 'gan to weave
> In all men's sight and Menelaus spoke,
> Few were his words, and quick, but clear withal;
> For much to say inclined he not, nor yet
> Wandered in talk, though of more youthful age.

The second declamation is taken from a tragedy; the third from the last book of the *Iliad*, where Andromache utters almost the same kind of lamentation in bewailing Hector. Both of these are of uncertain authorship and of much inferior quality as well. Of course the whole exercise is somewhat trivial; yet I thought it might be suitable for attempting my first ventures in this kind of work, in order, of course, to avoid 'learning the potter's art on a great jar,' as the Greek proverb has it, but rather to 'to take a risk with a Carian.' I have followed Cicero's old rule: in translating I thought it my duty to weigh the meaning, not count the words. However, as an apprentice-translator I have preferred to err on the side of accuracy rather than of boldness. But others must judge how far my efforts have been successful. I

* * * * *

95 Homer] *Iliad* 3.312–15
107 tragedy] Euripides *Medea*
112–13 'learning ... jar'] *Adagia* I vi 15
113–14 'to take ... Carian'] *Adagia* I vi 14
114 Cicero] *De optimo genere dicendi* 14; cf Ep 188:64ff.

can testify to one fact which I have learned by trying: nothing is harder than to turn good Greek into good Latin. If, however, I find that these my preliminary essays and first fruits, so to call them, have not displeased you, 120 then I shall go on with confidence to greater tasks, relying upon your verdict and the support of your authority; and I shall take the liberty of sending you, not mere flowerets, but harvests gathered from the fields of learning.

Farewell, illustrious prelate and father in God; I beg that you may vouchsafe to enrol me, and my studies likewise, in the ranks of your devoted 125 humble servants.

Louvain, 17 November 1503

178 / To Willem Hermans Louvain, 27 September [1503]

ERASMUS OF ROTTERDAM TO HIS BEST OF FRIENDS, WILLEM OF GOUDA

A thousand greetings, sweetest Willem. I have lately translated a few declamations: one by the sophist Libanius, and two of undetermined authorship. These I dedicated and presented to my lord Nicolas Ruistre, 5 bishop of Arras and chancellor of this university. He was much pleased with my little gift, tiny though it was, invited me to dinner, and offered his services if he could do anything to oblige either me or my friends. When he left, he sent me ten gold pieces through the dean of Mechlin. Before Christmas I am also to appear before our Duke Philip with a panegyric upon 10 his voyage to Spain and successful return home; I should have delivered this long since, were it not that I was inadequately informed of the facts. I have made a friend of Jérôme de Busleyden, archdeacon of Cambrai; or rather he has made himself a friend to me. He is brother to the bishop, and has a profound knowledge of both Latin and Greek. From time to time he 15 repeats that, had that great man got back safe, my fortune would have been secure; certainly I reposed all my hopes in him.

I have presented to Busleyden your *Apologi* with a letter commending

* * * * *

178:9 ten gold pieces] In all likelihood Burgundian-Hapsburg florins of St Philip (1500–21), the chief domestic gold coin then circulating in the Low Countries. At a current official value of 4s 2d gros apiece, this sum was worth £2 1s 8d gros Flemish = £1 10s 0d sterling = £12 5s 0d tournois. Cf CWE I 316–18, 321, 336–9; and table A below, 327–33.

9 dean of Mechlin] Jan Robyns (d 1532) was elected dean of Mechlin about the beginning of 1502.

13 Busleyden] Cf Ep 205 introduction.

14 bishop] François de Busleyden, archbishop of Besançon (cf Ep 157:76n)

18 *Apologi*] Cf Ep 172:16n.

your talents and character. Indeed I never cease to sing your praises among my friends everywhere, although I have observed for a while now that you are content with a Dutch reputation. All these years, when I was travelling in France, England, Artois, and Brabant, you have never once sent me any of your writings in order to give me a proper excuse for celebrating your talent, and never even write me a letter to show off to my scholarly friends. Yet in the matter of your *Odes* you had clear evidence of my friendly feelings; and, even if Holland despises me, I am at any rate not invariably despised here, whether among noblemen or clerics or scholars. Perhaps at this point you will remark, 'Plenty of glory, yes, but what about a little more money?' This, however, is just where I am completely at odds with your view, though it is not uncommon for glory to give rise to profits. I have often been surprised at the position you adopt in this matter, my dear Willem, but have not wished to offend a bosom friend by treating him to repeated doses of advice. I suppose you are possibly backing away from close association with me in order to avoid being called to share in my unpopularity. If this guess is right, it does not matter to me how obligingly you do it, when you cannot afford to despise the prattlings of a few manikins in monkish cowls or foolish women for the sake of a very old comrade and to say the least of it, friendly rival in literary studies: with such people you should bother no more than an elephant bothers about a fly, if you have any regard to the calibre of your intelligence and scholarship. And no one can be more fully aware than I am how much you are putting yourself at a disadvantage by such scruples as these.

But enough of this. My host, Jean Desmarez, orator of this University, who has a good knowledge of both languages, is most eagerly awaiting a visit from you. I am surprised at your failure to keep your promise to come. My neighbour the provost of Utrecht mentions you frequently and with pleasure. Come now, would it cost you so much trouble to encourage the friendly attitudes of men like those with a short letter? Floris van Egmont

* * * * *

19 your praises] There is a flattering allusion to Hermans in the *Panegyricus* (LB IV 512D); cf Ep 179 introduction.

25 *Odes*] Cf Ep 49 introduction.

39 elephant ... fly] Cf *Adagia* I ix 69.

46 provost of Utrecht] Philibert Naturel (d 1529), a member of the Privy Council of the Netherlands, became provost of the cathedral of Utrecht in 1500. In 1504 he was made chancellor of the Order of the Golden Fleece. He was thus a person of some wealth and influence.

48 Egmont] Floris van Egmont (1469–1539) was a son of Frederic van Egmont, lord of Ysselstein near Gouda. He accompanied the archduke to Spain in 1501. He is not mentioned, despite Erasmus' stated intention, in the printed version of the *Panegyricus*.

has won all his battles, and returned victorious from Spain, Savoy, France, and Germany with such credit that he has, by himself alone, not merely 50 eclipsed but positively extinguished the renown won by all his ancestors; I shall include a passage in praise of him in my panegyric. You would do well to congratulate him in a letter or, as I should prefer, a poem; I shall see that he receives it, and at my own hands too. I have written three Latin epitaphs, and one Greek one, in honour of the bishop of Cambrai; for which they sent 55 me only six florins, so as to keep up in death the character he had in life! If you condescend to write even a brief letter to my host, you will give much pleasure both to him and to me, and possibly do yourself a good turn as well, for he is more disposed towards friendly admiration for men of letters – and assistance to them – than anyone alive. Farewell, my learned Willem. 60

Louvain, 27 November

179 / To Nicolas Ruistre [Antwerp, February 1504]

Erasmus was working hard during September 1503 on a panegyric to be presented to Archduke Philip on his return from Spain (cf Epp 175:13–14, 176:5–6, 178:51–2). It was delivered before the ducal court at Brussels on 6 January 1504, and was printed by Martens at Antwerp the following month (NK 837) with this letter as preface (see text in LB IV 507–50). A revised edition was printed by Bade in Paris, 1506–7, and one with further revisions by Froben in the *Institutio principis christiani* in 1516 and later editions.

TO THE MOST REVEREND FATHER, NICOLAS RUISTRE, BISHOP OF ARRAS, FROM DESIDERIUS ERASMUS, GREETINGS

There were a great many reasons, most distinguished prelate, why it seemed to me appropriate that the panegyric which I have recently presented to Prince Philip on his return from Spain should be published under 5 the authority and blessing of your name rather than any other. First, you are our nation's most open-hearted patron of literature, and are well accustomed to act as in some sense a Maecenas, or more properly a father, to all

* * * * *

54 Latin epitaphs] One was published in the book of Jacob Anthoniszoon (cf Ep 173 introduction), the other two in Erasmus' *Epigrammata* (Paris: Bade 8 January 1507). See critical edition in Reedijk 262ff. The Greek epitaph has been lost.

56 six florins] Most likely the Burgundian-Hapsburg gold florins of St Philip, as in 178:9n above. If so, this sum would have been worth £1 5s od gros Flemish = 18s od sterling = £7 7s od tournois. Possibly, however, Erasmus was referring instead to the florin-gulden money-of-account, or 'livre de 40 gros,' one of several such systems then used in Brabant. By that reckoning this sum would have been worth £1 os od gros Flemish. Cf CWE I 316–18, 323.

men of learning. Second, there is no one who has more regard for the dignity of the prince than you, and it may be that this labour of mine may do something to shed lustre on his reputation; while, if its effect is rather to encourage him, you have ever adhered to the single purpose – which you have kept in view from Philip to Philip, from great-grandsire to great-grandson – of directing the minds of our rulers towards honourable ends by useful and frank advice. Lastly, my address of congratulation might thus be commended to men of good will by the same person who had beforehand caused it to find favour with the prince. That it did so he showed, not only by his look and expression – his brow serene, as they say – but also by a very generous reward, the pledge as it were, of his verdict. And he promised me the earth if I were willing to come to court as a member of his household. Had it not been for this, there were many reasons that moved me to conceal and suppress it as much as possible. On one hand I reflected how small and limited was the talent I possessed, while on the other it occurred to me how great a business it is to hold forth adequately upon the majesty of the greatest princes, and what a crime it is, as Horace remarks, such majesty 'by lack of talent to impair.' Indeed it is not any and every painter's brush that can worthily limn the features of divine beings. Moreover, in addition to being unequal to the task for other reasons, I was, as you are aware, prevented from doing justice to it by lack of time.

Since the idea occurred to me late and I knew nothing of the subject save what general gossip had conveyed to me, as a person with no interest at all in such things and always brooding over his books, I went to work in a hurry at the outset, and quickly heaped up a kind of log-pile of words; then, so to speak, with the first strokes of the chisel (as they say), I roughed out a kind of approximate likeness of the future panegyric. In the next stage, when I had gleaned very little fresh information about the topic even after probing into it for a long time, since some persons would take no trouble, while others deliberately concealed their knowledge, and since enthusiasts in all quarters were by now clamouring for publication, and I had no stomach to weave the whole fabric of the work over again, I put in certain things to prop up many passages; which makes me apprehensive that experienced critics, running a fingernail over the finished work, will detect unevennesses in the style, and here and there a gaping joint. Further, while the eyes are the sole authorities for good narrative, I was myself unable even

* * * * *

13 Philip to Philip] Philip the Good to Philip the Handsome (cf Ep 177:26n)

18 brow] Cf *Adagia* I viii 48.

25 Horace] *Odes* 1.6.12

42 fingernail] Cf *Adagia* I v 91.

to hear any but a very few reports, and these unconfirmed; so that this whole narrative section had to be skipped through on tiptoe, so to speak. For it is a kind of sacrilege to write about a prince what one does not really know. 45

To this there was added another factor. My own straightforward nature, if truth be told, had some degree of aversion to this whole species of composition, to which above all, it seemed to me, one might apply Plato's description 'the fourth part of flattery.' Yet the thing is not so much praise as precept; and there is surely no more effective method of reforming princes than to present them with a pattern of the good prince under the guise of praising them, so long as you credit them with virtues, and absolve them from vices, in such a way as to be evidently exhorting them to the former and warning them away from the latter. Physicians, similarly, do not treat all their patients alike, but choose the method of cure best adapted to each. I could have kept myself safely within the limits prescribed by this rule, had I not happened to encounter a prince so good that it was not at all necessary to add any false embroidery in praising him, and in this one respect I was fortunate; yet more fortunate still will those be who will describe this same prince in his old age; and I pray that God, of his goodness, may for our sake ever increasingly prosper his counsels. Farewell. 50 55 60

180 / To Jean Desmarez — Antwerp, [February 1504]

While Erasmus was in Antwerp seeing the *Panegyricus* through the press (cf Ep 179 introduction), he wrote this letter and inserted it at the end of the book. Jean Desmarez (called Paludanus; cf Ep 177:18n) of Cassel near Saint-Omer (d 1526; cf Allen Ep 1099) had been Erasmus' host at Louvain during the time when the *Panegyricus* was being written, and indeed seems to have been responsible for suggesting the idea to Erasmus and urging him to carry it out (cf lines 143ff and 194ff). Desmarez was at this time public orator at the University of Louvain and a canon of St Peter's church. Two years later Erasmus repaid his hospitality by dedicating to him his translation of Lucian's *De mercede conductis* (cf Ep 197). Erasmus stayed with him again in 1517 (cf Epp Allen 597:42, 637:9).

ERASMUS TO MASTER JEAN DESMAREZ,
HIS LEARNED AND MOST KINDLY HOST, GREETINGS

Your letter, Jean Desmarez, the muses' delight and mine, tells me what I

* * * * *

46 on tiptoe] *Adagia* IV iii 66

51 Plato] *Gorgias* 463 B–C

could easily guess even without a letter (so much more intent upon my reputation are you than I am myself), that you have for some time waited and thirsted to see what fortune, or guardian sprite perhaps, will attend my *Panegyricus*, as it is born, so to speak, and comes into the daylight. The moment that first fresh page, still damp from the press, began to be shown about and passed from hand to hand, as novelties usually are, your friend Erasmus cocked up his ears (for you know how much delight he always took in that story about Apelles hiding behind his paintings), catching at every indication, not how many readers approved of it, since for me at least one single man's verdict would fully suffice to bolster my self-esteem, provided that man were like you or Valascus, but where it failed to win approval. For your encomiast is positively a nuisance unless his qualifications are exceptional, whereas the hostile critic, even if he is no expert, either reminds one of something one has forgotten, or provokes one to defend what is well expressed, and so either improves the author's knowledge or at least increases his alertness; thus I am quite sure that I should in my right mind prefer a single mocking Momus to ten Polyhymnias.

But no need of words; I should say, on the whole, if it could appear to be said with as much modesty as truth, that there will be many more to find fault with the piece than to understand it. Now there are three kinds of fault-finders: the first kind (and I am not certain whether it excites my pity or derision more) consists of those who think themselves exceptionally well educated when in fact they are nothing of the kind; these men declare that I have made a slip on the very threshold of my *Panegyricus* and run aground, as the saying goes, while I was still in harbour, for they reckon as mistaken everything they fail to comprehend in it. Great God, what do they understand? So they perish like shrews given away by their squeaking; hard on the trail of other men's ignorance, they exhibit their own. But I would rather tell you the whole story in person. I am sure you will thoroughly enjoy it. At the same time I have a considerable respect for the two remaining classes of

* * * * *

10 cocked up his ears] Cf *Adagia* III ii 56.

11 Apelles] Cf Ep 173:27n.

14 Valascus] In the second edition only he is given the cognomen 'Lusitani' suggesting that he was Portuguese. Allen tentatively identifies him with a certain Ferdinandus Valascus who was an ambassador for John II of Portugal.

18–19 improves … alertness] Cf Cicero *De inventione* 1.15.20.

20 Momus] In Greek myth the son of Night and personification of mockery

20 Polyhymnia] The muse of oratory and sacred poetry

27–8 run aground … harbour] *Adagia* I v 76

30 shrews … squeaking] *Adagia* I iii 65

my attackers; they consist of those who naively and foolishly describe all this enthusiasm of mine for celebrating the prince as flattery, and those who have a smattering of letters and seem to find some things objectionable, or rather perhaps a few things missing, in a work which is virtually unfinished as yet. Of these two criticisms the first has hurt me rather keenly because it seeks to cast an aspersion on my character; the other has less effect, because it assails only my intelligence and does not stain my reputation as well. Consequently I have to appease the latter critics as best I can, while the former must be answered more sharply.

First of all, those who believe panegyrics are nothing but flattery seem to be unaware of the purpose and aim of the extremely far-sighted men who invented this kind of composition, which consists in presenting princes with a pattern of goodness, in such a way as to reform bad rulers, improve the good, educate the boorish, reprove the erring, arouse the indolent, and cause even the hopelessly vicious to feel some inward stirrings of shame. Else can we believe that the great philosopher Callisthenes, who praised Alexander, or Lysias and Isocrates, or Pliny, and countless others, had any aim in writing works of this sort other than to exhort rulers to honourable actions under the cover of compliment? Do you really believe that one could present kings, born in the purple and brought up as they are, with the repellent teachings of Stoicism and the barking of the Cynics? Just to make them laugh, I suppose: or even to increase their irritation! How much easier it is to lead a generous spirit than to compel it, and how much better to improve matters by compliments rather than abuse. And what method of exhortation is more effective, or rather, what other method has in fact become habitual to men of wisdom, than to credit people with possessing already in large measure the attractive qualities they urge them to cultivate? Surely 'virtue, when praised, grows great; and boundless is the spur of fame.'

And did not the apostle Paul himself often use this device of correcting while praising (a sort of holy adulation)? Again, how could one reproach a wicked ruler for his cruelty more safely, yet more severely, than by proclaiming his mildness; or for his greed and violence and lust, than by celebrating his generosity, self-control, and chastity, 'that he may see fair virtue's face, and pine with grief that he has left her.'

But, it is objected, Augustine confesses that he uttered many falsehoods in singing the emperor's praises. How relevant it is that the writer

* * * * *

61–2 'virtue ... fame'] Ovid *Epistulae ex Ponto* 4.2.35–6

67–8 'that he may see ... her'] Persius 3.38

69 Augustine] Cf *Confessions* 6.6.9.

was an implacable enemy of falsehood, we need not now discuss. Plato and the Stoics, at least, will permit the wise man to tell a lie in order to do good. Are we not right sometimes to inspire children to enthusiasm for goodness by means of false praise? Do not the best physicians tell their patients that they find their appearance and colour satisfactory, rather in order to make 75 them so than because they are so? Besides, it is a sign of a generous disposition even to be slightly deluded in one's admiration for one's sovereign, and to forget the bounds of moderation in praising him to whom one's loyalty should be unbounded. It is, moreover, in the interest of the commonwealth that the subjects of any prince, even if he be not the best, 80 should nevertheless have an exceedingly high regard for him; indeed, if the ruler should be undeserving of praise, it is for their benefit rather than his that the panegyric is written, for it is not offered merely to him who is its occasion, but also to the multitude in whose hearing it is pronounced. You must therefore adapt it largely to their ears, just as is done in sermons; and 85 the resemblance of a panegyric to these is brought home to us by its very name, which the Greek derives from a meeting of the multitude at large. For the same reason Quintilian is of the opinion that no kind of oratory enjoys such freedom as panegyrics, and that in them it is permissible to show off all the tricks and preciosities of rhetoric in order to solicit the hearer's 90 attention. Finally, this kind of thing is written for posterity and for the world; from this point of view it does not matter much under whose name a pattern of the good prince is publicly set forth, provided it is done cleverly, so that it may appear to men of intelligence that you were not currying favour but uttering a warning. 95

But those who press the charge of adulation apparently fail in the first place to notice that it is not so much me as the prince that they criticize; nor, in the second place, do they realize that the charge recoils upon themselves as the greatest flatterers of all. Is this just one more example of Hesiod's saying, 'potter with potter competes, and joiner is jealous of joiner'? No: 100 there is a huge gap between their deplorable kind of adulation and this kind, which is not my own but rather that of all scholars: for they praise even disgraceful deeds and for their own advantage slavishly cozen the ears of fools, whereas we offer to the gaze of the public what may be called the lovely aspect of goodness, and that too in the name of the man whom virtue 105 best beseems and under whose auspices it may most easily be commended to the populace. And to any who complain that the whole business of paying compliments is foolishness, I might reply in Pliny's words that they

* * * * *

88 Quintilian] Cf 3.10–11.

99–100 Hesiod's saying] *Works and Days* 25

108 Pliny] *Epistles* 3.21.3

only hold this view because they themselves have ceased to deserve them. But let them be as censorious as they like, only let us for our part write 110 foolishness in company with Ambrose and Jerome, who composed many personal tributes of praise; for may I not have the same licence, in this popular and well-nigh theatrical kind of writing, as those holy men enjoyed in their personal correspondence? I do believe that this defence would seem creditable enough in the eyes of sensible critics, even if I had written my 115 *Panegyricus* in praise of someone like Phalaris or Sardanapalus or Heliogabalus; but as it is, in case I should be suspected of insisting that any of the above considerations should protect me from the charge of flattery, the prince I portrayed as best I could was one who, for all his youth, in addition to his surely unparalleled advantages of fortune, is already a 120 shining example of great virtues, while every virtue may be looked for in him in the future. From such a prince I should not so much expect gratitude for my devotion in writing his encomium, as stand in awe of his displeasure, which God forbid: and this because of his own extraordinary modesty, which makes any praise at all seem to him excessive. 125

Again I shall be indicted by others, who are more familiar with the glories of our prince than I, for representing all these glories as smaller and fewer than they are. Whether I have done so I do not know; but I have certainly attempted to arrange the scope and tenor of the whole panegyric in such a way as to seem, in the eyes of informed and attentive critics, to aim at 130 anything but flattery: indeed, as you know better almost than anyone, I have always been so averse to this vice that I could not flatter anyone if I would, nor would if I could. So I have no fear that that charge against my character may be made good in the sight of those who, like yourself, know your Erasmus 'inwardly and 'neath the skin.' Just as it is in your power to 135 witness to, or defend, my sincerity against them, so too, as regards the slur on my abilities, none knows better than you, since it was in your sight that the whole enterprise began and ended, that three essential ingredients were missing: subject-matter, emotion, and time. The first of these is so important that without it you have no means even of beginning your 140 speech; for what could Cicero himself achieve without a brief? The second has so much to contribute that according to Quintilian it will make men full of eloquence even without learning – and you know how hard you found it to extract it from me, how much difficulty I had in forcing myself to

* * * * *

116–17 Phalaris ... Heliogabalus] Phalaris, tyrant of Agrigentum (cf Ep 109:104n), the Assyrian king Sardanapalus, and the third-century Roman emperor Heliogabalus were notorious examples of cruel and despotic rulers.

135 'inwardly ... skin'] Persius 3.30; cf *Adagia* I ix 89.

142 Quintilian] 6.2.26

undertake the task, how disinclined I was for it, in a word how little 145
appetite I had for writing it. The third ingredient, again, is of such consequence that not even the best of scholars can turn out anything fully polished until it has been licked into shape by 'many a day, and many an erasure.' The prince had already reached the frontiers of his realm before the idea occured to you, and it would have been tasteless to congratulate 150
him on his return at a time when the news of that event had turned stale, for what is out of season is never to one's taste.

Accordingly what I may call a heap of words was raked together in great haste. What else could I do, in my ignorance of the whole subject? Now a speech without facts is like a body without bones. The orator, 155
however, is given certain facts; he does not invent them for himself. Considering how little time there was, I did not fall short in readiness to ask questions; but some persons answered me with details about splendid banquets and suchlike trifles, while others gave me reports too unreliable for me to venture to print them. But, if they had been as attentive to the 160
prince's reputation in this respect as some are to their personal interest, I can see how dazzling the speech might be: however I should have to weave the whole fabric afresh; and it was still less encouraging to me that I had been deprived of all prospect of obtaining preliminary information. So I did the only thing I could and would do; I abandoned my former procedure 165
and, as it were, stitched in new material at many places, extempore at that, in such a way that it should not clash with the rest of the fabric like badly sewn patches.

In this way I have undoubtedly made my *Panegyricus* longer; whether better, I know not. It was also necessary sometimes to insert commonplaces 170
as interludes and sometimes to add rather difficult digressions, and yet these themselves had sometimes to be altered to fit the subject matter of the prince's voyage. How enviable indeed, compared to my situation, was that of the younger Pliny! Not only was his a more fluent pen; not only had he a congenial emperor, who was already elderly and done with all his civil and 175
military duties; even more important, most of the achievements he praised he had witnessed himself. For men give excellent accounts of what they know best; and we know nothing better than the events we have seen with our own eyes. For these reasons, then, Pliny dared to write a letter in which he stimulated the bored reader to observe with some care the figures of 180
speech, the modes of transition, and the order. My duty is rather to ask my readers, who are lynx-eyed, to wink at many things. I can see for myself some gaps that still remain, some things far-fetched, some additions and

* * * * *

148–9 'many a day ... erasure'] Horace *Ars poetica* 293

179 letter] Pliny *Epistles* 3.13.3

disturbance of the natural order, some over-ripe language, and the absence of anything really finished or polished. Yet reasonably fair critics will not blame me for these drawbacks, but rather the disadvantages I have just described. 185

I have written all this at somewhat unusual length to you, my learned Desmarez (and to whom better than you?), since it seems to be your part above all to defend me against every accusation; not only because, through the kind of overflowing affection you entertain for me, you are generally as much affected by my fortunes as by your own, but also because it is on you that a great part of the blame, if reproof is what I deserve, or praise, if any praise is due to me, seems to fall. For it was you, if it was anyone, who urged me to undertake this task, reluctant and unwilling as I was, and you always spurred me tirelessly on to continue at it; you gave me the notion of offering it to our mighty prince, and helped me to do so; finally it was you again who refused to be satisfied until you had persuaded me to publish it. Even as the work progressed you made, among other suggestions, the following in particular, which I gladly accepted: that by an honourable mention in the speech I should as far as possible rescue from oblivion and obscurity the memory of that notable father in God, François de Busleyden, lord archbishop of Besançon, a man beyond all praise. I have added a poem, cut from the same cloth; that is to say, extemporaneous, as you will easily perceive without any need for me to tell you so. Farewell, glory of literature; and be stout-hearted in defence of me, as you above all other men both can be and should. 190 195 200 205

Antwerp, at the printing house

181 / To John Colet

Paris, [about December] 1504

After his visit to Antwerp in February 1504, Erasmus returned to Louvain. He was still there in October, when he received a gift of ten livres from Archduke Philip. By December, however, he was back in Paris after nearly four years in the Netherlands.

ERASMUS TO HIS FRIEND JOHN COLET

If our friendship, most learned Colet, had arisen from commonplace causes, or if your character had ever appeared to me to have a tinge of the common

* * * * *

202 Busleyden] Cf Ep 157:67n. For mention of him in the *Panegyricus*, see LB IV 528F.

203 poem] 'Illustrissimo principi Philippo feliciter in patriam redeunti gratulatorium carmen Erasmi sub persona patriae' (Reedijk 272–6). The poem was placed at the end of the *Panegyricus*, following Ep 180.

about it, I should be somewhat anxious in case it might have, not died perhaps, but at least cooled off, when we were so far and so long apart in place and time. As it is, since it was admiration for your extraordinary learning and love of your piety that drew me to you and since you too were perhaps attracted to me by hopes of finding similar qualities in me, or a fancy that I had them, I do not think we need fear that, as generally seems to happen, I have been out of sight, out of mind. If I have not received a line from you for many years past, I would rather think that this was due to your busy life, or your lack of information about my precise whereabouts, or in a word anything other than forgetfulness of a dear friend. But though I ought not to reproach you for your silence, nor should I wish to do so, still I beg and beseech you all the more earnestly sometimes to steal from your studies and public concerns just the tiny amount of spare time required to write me a letter. I am astonished that none of your commentaries on Paul and the Gospels has yet been published. Though I know your modesty well, yet you must sooner or later overcome even this, and shed it out of consideration for the general good. My congratulations on your doctorate, on attaining the office of dean, and certain other honours with which I hear your distinguished qualities have been rewarded without any effort on your part; congratulations not so much for you who will, I am certain, claim nothing for yourself except the work involved, as for those for whose sake you propose to shoulder those responsibilities; congratulations indeed to the very honours you have won, which do not become honours in fact as well as name, until they are bestowed on one who deserves, yet does not court them.

I am now eager, dear Colet, to approach sacred literature full sail, full gallop; I have an extreme distaste for anything that distracts me from it, or even delays me. But the ill will of Fortune, which has ever regarded me with steadfast hostility, is the reason why I have not been able to free myself from these vexations; and so it was in order to shake them off as best I could, even if I proved unable to abolish them altogether, that I withdrew to France. Hereafter I intend to address myself to the Scriptures and to spend all the rest of my life upon them. Three years ago, indeed, I ventured to do something on Paul's Epistle to the Romans, and at one rush, as it were, finished four volumes; and would have gone on, but for certain distrac-

* * * * *

17 commentaries on Paul] Cf Ep 108:76n.

20 doctorate] Colet received his doctor's degree in 1504 (cf Emden BRUO 143).

21 dean] Colet did not actually become dean of St Paul's until May 1505, but he had been administering the office for an absent incumbent since 1503.

30–1 full sail, full gallop] *Adagia* I iv 17

37 Romans] Cf Ep 164:39–40n.

tions, of which the most important was that I needed the Greek at every point. Therefore for nearly the past three years I have been wholly absorbed by Greek; and I do not think my efforts have been altogether wasted. I began to take up Hebrew as well, but stopped because I was put off by the strangeness of the language, and at the same time the shortness of life and the limitations of human nature will not allow a man to master too many things at once. I have gone through a good part of Origen's works; under his guidance I think I have achieved worthwhile results, for he reveals some of the well-springs, as it were, and demonstrates some of the basic principles, of the science of theology. 40 45

I am sending you a small literary gift, consisting of a few of my minor works, including that same debate on the fear of Christ in which we once confronted each other in England, though it is so much altered that you would hardly recognize it. (I may add that your answers, and my rejoinders, could not be reconstructed.) The *Enchiridion* I composed not in order to show off my cleverness or my style, but solely in order to counteract the error of those who make religion in general consist in rituals and observances of an almost more than Jewish formality, but who are astonishingly indifferent to matters that have to do with true goodness. What I have tried to do, in fact, is to teach a method of morals, as it were, in the manner of those who have originated fixed procedures in the various branches of learning; as for all the rest, I wrote them almost against the grain, especially the *Paean* and *Obsecratio*; this task was discharged in deference to the wishes of my friend Batt and the sentiments of Anna, princess of Veere. I was so reluctant to compose the *Panegyricus* that I do not remember ever doing anything more unwillingly; for I saw that this kind of thing could not be handled without some flattery. However I employed a novel strategem; I was completely frank while I flattered and also very flattering in my frankness. 50 55 60 65

If you would like to have any of your works printed, merely send me the manuscript and for the rest I will see to it that the printed version is quite accurate. Lately I sent a letter, as I believe you recall, about the 70

* * * * *

49–50 minor works]. The *Lucubratiunculae* (Antwerp: Martens February 1503; NK 836); cf Epp 93 introduction and 108 introduction. It included the debate between Erasmus and Colet concerning Christ's agony in the garden of Gethsemane (Epp 108–111). At the time Colet's replies were not available, but one was found and printed in later editions (cf Ep 110 introduction). It also included the first edition of the *Enchiridion* (cf Ep 164 introduction) and the *Paean* and *Obsecratio* written for Adolph of Veere (cf lines 59–60 and Ep 93:113n).

56 Jewish formality] Cf Epp 164:28 and 296:87.

63 *Panegyricus*] Cf Ep 179 introduction.

hundred copies of the *Adagia* sent to England at my own expense, and three years ago at that. Grocyn had written to me, saying that he would take the utmost pains to see that they were sold as I wished; and I have no doubt he kept his promise, for he is the most upright, excellent man now living in England. So will you please oblige me by lending me your help in this 75 matter, admonishing and goading into action those by whom you think the business ought to be concluded; for it must be that over such a long period all the books have been sold and the purchase price paid to someone; and it would be more useful to me to have the money now than ever before, since I have somehow to provide myself with several months' complete leisure in 80 order to discharge the commitments I have entered into with respect to secular literature; I hoped it might be possible to do so this winter, and so it would have been had not so many of my prospects proved false. But I can still purchase this liberty not too expensively – for a few months at any rate.

So I beseech you to help me as far as you can in my burning zeal for 85 sacred studies by releasing me from the kind of literature which has now ceased to give me pleasure. I cannot ask my friend the count, William Mountjoy; all the same there would be some point and sense in his action, if of his kindness he were to afford me some help, either because he has always encouraged my studies in this way, or because the subject was one I 90 undertook on his initiative and dedicated to himself, namely the *Adagia*. I regret the first edition, both because it is so full of printers' errors that it looks as if it had been deliberately spoiled, and because some people encouraged me to hurry the work, which now begins to seem to me thin and poor, when I have at last read the Greek authors through. I have decided 95 therefore to publish a second edition to repair the printers' mistakes as well as my own, and at the same time to be of service to scholars by treating a most useful theme. Now, though for the present I am concerned with what may be a rather mundane subject, still while I linger within the garden of the Greeks I am gathering by the way many flowers that will be useful for 100 the future, even in sacred studies; for experience teaches me this, at any rate, that we can do nothing in any field of literature without a knowledge of Greek, since it is one thing to guess, another to judge; one thing to trust

* * * * *

71 *Adagia*] The copies sent from Paris in 1500. The young man, Jean, who carried them apparently never returned to give an account of his handling of the matter (cf Epp 128:2n, 133:5n).

72 Grocyn] Cf Ep 118:26n.

88 Mountjoy] William Blount, Lord Mountjoy (cf Ep 79 introduction). For the dedication of the *Adagia* see Ep 126.

96 second edition] Published, with twenty adages added, by Bade in Paris in 1506 (cf Ep 126 introduction)

your own eyes, and another again to trust those of others. See how long my letter has grown! But it is affection, not a fault of character, that makes me so talkative. Farewell, Colet, my learned and good friend. 105

I am anxious to know what has become of our friend Sixtinus; also how your great friend Prior Richard Charnock is. To ensure that what you are about to write and send me may be safely delivered to me, please give instructions that it is to be handed to Master Christopher Fisher, who is devoted to you and a great patron of all scholars; I am staying in his household. 110

Paris, 1504

182 / To Christopher Fisher — Paris, [about March] 1505

When Erasmus returned to Paris late in 1504 he lodged with Christopher Fisher (d by October 1512; cf Emden BRUO II 687), an Englishman in the service of the papacy as protonotary apostolic. He repaid his host's hospitality by dedicating a book to him, his edition of Valla's notes on the New Testament, *Laurentii Vallensis ... in Latinam Novi Testamenti interpretationem ex collatione Graecorum exemplarium adnotationes* (Paris: Bade 13 April 1505). Erasmus had found the MS in the Praemonstratensian abbey of Parc outside Louvain. It exerted a considerable influence on Erasmus' own notes on the New Testament.

TO THE ILLUSTRIOUS AND HONOURABLE CHRISTOPHER FISHER, PROTONOTARY APOSTOLIC AND DOCTOR OF CANON LAW, FROM ERASMUS OF ROTTERDAM, GREETINGS

As I was hunting last summer in an ancient library, for those coverts offer by far the most enjoyable sport, luck brought into my toils a prey of no ordinary importance: Lorenzo Valla's notes on the New Testament. At once I was eager to share it with the world of scholarship, for it seemed to me ungenerous to devour the prize of my chase in solitude and silence. But I was a little put off, not only by the entrenched unpopularity of Valla's name, but by his subject as well, a subject which on the face of it is singularly apt to generate antagonism. You, however, not only lent your weighty support to my decision the moment you had read the book but also began to urge me, and even to deafen me with importunities, not to cheat the author of the credit he deserved or deprive countless students of such an enormous advantage just because of the angry snarls of a few critics; for you said you 5 10 15

* * * * *

107 Sixtinus] Cf Ep 112 introduction.

108 Charnock] Cf Ep 106:10n.

110 Fisher] Cf Ep 182 introduction.

had no doubt that the work was destined to be extremely useful, and most welcome, to any sensible and fair-minded person, and that anyone else was of unsound judgment and should be firmly ignored. You also offered your services as patron and defender; let it only be published even though you alone underwrote the risk. For my part, honoured sir, I believe that, despite 20 the vigorous personal disregard for unpopularity which your Valla always exhibited, he will go forth to the fray armed with a trifle more confidence if he has the support of a stout and tireless champion like yourself, and also has this preamble, like the shield of Ajax, to protect his front. In it I shall discuss, as you think I should, the purpose and value of the present work, 25 but only after I have first attempted, in a few words, to dispel the widespread dislike of Valla's name.

First of all then: if those to whom we owe not only good will but also gratitude received from us the same fair treatment as we require from others, surely the name of Valla would enjoy not unpopularity but gratitude 30 and respect from all lovers of sound learning, inasmuch as he quite deliberately adopted a most invidious role out of eagerness to reform the state of scholarship. Being an intelligent man, he did not fail to see that a disease so deeply established could not be cured by anything short of harsh medicines, cautery, and surgery, and that this must inevitably involve 35 great suffering for many people. He was well aware that the ears of mankind are so sensitive that even among good men one can hardly find anyone who is willing to listen to the truth, and that there would be an outcry not only from those whose sore spots he had touched but even from those who, seeing others in difficulties, imagined themselves to be threatened as well. 40 In spite of which, fired by a kind of blazing devotion, he undertook to face extreme hardship and unpopularity so long as he might establish his contribution in the eyes of those few who would be grateful, as indeed everyone should have been. But as things are, men's perversity brings it about that by flattery are friends won, by truth dislike. 45

But, they say, he has hay on his horns and savages everyone. Indeed? Is savage the word one applies to literary disagreement; to scoffing at a few things, while praising a great many, out of a desire to instruct? Yet if, as Quintilian says, the most effective method of teaching is to demonstrate by

* * * * *

30 Valla] Compare his similar defence of Valla in 1489 (Ep 26).

45 by flattery ... dislike] Terence *Andria* 68; cf *Adagia* II ix 53.

46 hay on his horns] A handful of hay tied to his horns was said to have been in antiquity the sign of a bad-tempered ox (Horace *Satires* 1.4.34; cf *Adagia* I i 81).

49 Quintilian] 2.5 and 10.2

examples from the texts of the masters not only what should be imitated but what should be avoided, surely the same method ought to be pursued in teaching men to unlearn? Now Valla had the temerity to blame certain eminent authors for using some small expression. Outrageous! As though Aristotle did not object to practically everything in all authors, Cicero was not despised for his entire style by Brutus, Virgil and Livy by Caligula, Seneca by Quintilian and Aulus Gellius, Augustine and Rufinus by Jerome, and finally Quintilian himself by Filelfo! And Pliny, too, cannot believe that his own book has pleased a friend unless he hears that some things in it displeased him. Not only must we decline to regard as reprehensible that disagreement in men's tastes, the strife which Hesiod considered so serviceable to mankind; we should even welcome it warmly, so long as it does not result in ugly passions and stops short of abusive language. Personally, in my sensible moments, I would not be any more pleased at compliments from a friend than at being censured, even by an enemy, so long as it was obviously not a matter of the cobbler not sticking to his last; for compliments are nearly always harmful, while adverse criticism is always beneficial. If it is justified I learn from it, while if it should be wrong still I am sharpened, aroused, awakened, rendered more alert and cautious, and emboldened to defend the truth. Men are indeed spurred on less keenly by the longing for fame than by the fear of disgrace.

As for the fact that he has wholly condemned certain authors: what, I ask, was more urgent than to divest fools of their authority, that is, the ass of his lion's skin, in order to prevent the uninstructed multitude from following the worst of guides in the belief that they were the best? If our hero ever seems to show too much heat, the fault should not be imputed to him but to the authors of the corruptions. Moreover it would have been far wiser to put up with another's weakness than to turn one's back on so many good things because of a single blemish. There are undoubtedly some necessary evils,

* * * * *

54–7 Cicero ... Quintilian] See the similar, though not identical, group in much the same context in Ep 26:57–8n.

55 Brutus] Tacitus *Dialogus de oratoribus* 18

55 Caligula] Suetonius *Caligula* 34; cf Ep 26:57–8.

56 Quintilian] 10.1.126–31

56 Aulus Gellius] *Noctes Atticae* 12.2.1

57 Filelfo] Francesco Filelfo (cf Ep 23:77n)

57 Pliny] *Epistles* 3.13.5

60 Hesiod] Cf *Works and Days* 19.

65 cobbler ... last] Cf Ep 173:27n.

72–3 ass ... lion's skin] Cf *Adagia* I iii 66.

78 necessary evils] *Adagia* I v 26

which sensible men habitually tolerate for their own good, if for no other reason. In this way literature so deeply spoiled and corrupted needed a 80 Zoïlus, a scourge of the barbarians, rather than a Parthenias – in other words it called for a severe censor, indeed a kind of Momus; even, if you like, an insulting one, one who might dare to 'fart against the thunder,' as the old comedy puts it, and would apply a tough wedge to a tough knot. So Valla's spite, if that is what they prefer to call it, has done much more for the 85 art of letters than the foolish benevolence of most critics, who indiscriminately admire all the works of all writers, and applaud each other in turn, scratching one another's back, as the saying goes. But if one reflects upon the squalid confusion brought into every branch of learning by those Goths, the arrogance with which they advertise their own lack of knowl- 90 edge, and the stupidity and stubbornness with which they defend their own ignorance while they pour scorn on other men's scholarship, he will perhaps regard Valla's resentment as very restrained, his indignation as righteous, and his censure as necessary rather than insolent. This same censure earned the approval of scholars for the very reason that it was for 95 our benefit that Valla undertook to wield it, in spite of the hostility to which it exposes its user.

But see how positively unfair we are in this connection; indeed how we act against our own interests. Poggio, a petty clerk so uneducated that even if he were not indecent he would still not be worth reading, and so 100 indecent that he would deserve to be rejected by good men however learned he was, is, despite this character, universally read and translated into every language as an honourable man, that is, one who makes no enemies; while Valla, who is not indecent and is a hundred times more scholarly, is tagged with a reputation for spitefulness and avoided like a dangerous bull, even 105 by those who have never read the poor man's writings. For there are some people who, quite ridiculously, know nothing about him except that he is spiteful, and in this respect, and this alone, they imitate him, or rather surpass him, for they are spiteful towards a man they do not even know. And indeed these wise gentlemen prefer to be barbarous for ever, just 110

* * * * *

81 Zoïlus] *Adagia* II v 8

81 Parthenias] A nickname, said to have been given to Virgil in youth, indicating maidenly shyness and modesty

82 Momus] Cf Ep 173:88n.

84 comedy] Aristophanes *Clouds* 293–4; cf *Adagia* I vii 76.

84 tough wedge ... knot] *Adagia* I ii 5

88 scratching ... back] *Adagia* I vii 96

99 Poggio] Cf Epp 24:34ff and n; 26:49ff.

because Valla is spiteful. Why do we not rather follow Epictetus' splendid rule and take everyone by the handle that lets us hold him conveniently, exactly as Virgil took Ennius, Cyprian took Tertullian, Jerome took Origen among others, and Augustine took Ticonius? And when Valla has so many points from which he might profitably be approached, why do we seize only upon his reputation for spite? Why should we not rather balance this slight fault against his many virtues? Or rather, why must we ungratefully slander his unavoidable frankness by calling it 'scurrility'? 115

But enough of this: now I must come to matters more germane to my subject. I foresee that there may be some who, having barely read the title of my work and before they learn what it is about, will immediately cry 'O heaven and earth!' in the approved tragic fashion, in spite of Aristophanes' witty advice in the *Plutus* 'not to yell and make a fuss before you know the facts.' And I am inclined to believe that the most unpleasantly hostile demonstrations of all will be made by those who stand most to profit, that is, the theologians. They will say it is intolerable presumption in a grammarian, who has upset every department of learning, to let his impertinent pen loose on Holy Scripture itself. Yet if we listen to Nicholas of Lyra, who is, I will not say unscholarly, but undoubtedly modern, who patronizes Jerome as a dotard and carps at a number of things now hallowed by the consensus of many ages, using moreover the Hebrew texts (and even if we allow these to be the source of our current version, still I suspect them of deliberate corruption), tell me what is so shocking about Valla's action in making a few annotations on the New Testament after comparing several old and good Greek manuscripts. After all it is from Greek sources that our text undoubtedly comes; and Valla's notes had to do with internal disagreements, or a nodding translator's plainly inadequate renderings of the meaning, or things that are more intelligibly expressed in Greek, or, finally, anything that is clearly corrupt in our texts. Will they maintain that Valla, the grammarian, has not the same privileges as Nicholas the theologian? Not to mention further that Valla is, in fact, included among the 120 125 130 135 140

* * * * *

120 foresee] Erasmus' forecast of the objections that would be made to Valla's notes was borne out equally in the controversy aroused by his own notes on the New Testament.

122 Aristophanes] *Plutus* 477

128 Nicholas of Lyra] A Franciscan (c 1270–1349) who taught for a time at the University of Paris and was the best known biblical commentator of the later Middle Ages. His *Postilla litteralis* on the Bible had already been printed twenty-eight times by the date of this letter in several folio volumes. Erasmus regarded him as modern in comparison with the church Fathers.

philosophers and theologians by many leading authorities; and conversely when Lyra discusses the meaning of a word he is surely acting as a grammarian rather than a theologian. Indeed this whole business of translating the Holy Scriptures is manifestly a grammarian's function. Nor indeed is it 145 absurd if in certain spheres Jethro has greater competence than Moses.

But I do not really believe that Theology herself, the queen of all the sciences, will be offended if some share is claimed in her and due deference shown to her by her humble attendant Grammar; for, though Grammar is of less consequence in some men's eyes, no help is more indispensable than 150 hers. She is concerned with small details, but details such as have always been indispensable for the attainment of greatness. Perhaps she discusses trivial questions, but these have important corollaries. If they protest that a theologian is too grand to be bound by the rules of grammar, and that the whole business of interpretation depends on the inspiration of the Holy 155 Spirit, what a novel distinction is offered to theologians, who are to have the exclusive privilege of expressing themselves ungrammatically! But I should like them then to explain the meaning of Jerome's remark to his friend Desiderius that 'it is one thing to be a prophet, another to be a translator. In the one case the Holy Ghost prophesies the future; in the other 160 scholarship, together with the resources of language, conveys the meaning it apprehends.' Again what point would there be in advice from Jerome himself on the proper method of translating the Scriptures if the power to do so is bestowed by divine inspiration? Lastly, why has Paul been called more eloquent in the Hebrew tongue than in the Greek? But if it were possible for 165 the translators of the Old Testament to make mistakes occasionally, especially where the faith is not impugned, could not the translators have done likewise in the New Testament? For Jerome indeed did not translate the latter so much as emend it, though moderately, leaving (as he himself testifies), the words of the text; and it is the words that Valla discusses with 170 particular care. Now surely we cannot attribute the mistakes we make to the

* * * * *

145 Jethro] Jethro, Moses' father-in-law, gave him good practical advice in Exodus 18 without having any of Moses' inspiration.

147 some share ... her] Cf *Adagia* IV iii 35.

152 trivial questions] Horace *Ars poetica* 4.51

157 Jerome] *Apologia adversus libros Rufini* col 449C

161 Jerome] At the instigation of Pope Damasus (cf line 185) Jerome revised the Old Latin translation of the New Testament, correcting it by comparison with the Greek. He says in his preface to the Vulgate version of the Gospels that he left the wording as he found it, except where an error affected the sense.

Holy Spirit! Suppose the translators' version to be correct, yet a correct rendering can be perverted; and if Jerome made improvements, still what has been corrected can be corrupted once again – unless we are to suppose that in the world of today the self-confidence of the half-educated is less, or command of languages greater, than before; or that the spread of corruption is not facilitated by the art of printing, which all at once expands an isolated error into a thousand copies. 175

But, it will be said, it is sinful to change anything in the Holy Scriptures; for no jot and tittle therein is without some special import. On the contrary: the sin of corruption is greater, and the need for careful revision by scholars greater also, where the source of corruption was ignorance: but it must be done with the caution and restraint with which all books, and particularly the Holy Scriptures, deserve to be treated. But, it is again objected, it was wrong of Valla to volunteer to undertake a task that was imposed on Jerome by Pope Damasus. Yet even the purpose was different; Jerome replaced an old edition with a new one, whereas Valla confines his annotations to separate comments and does not require the reader to make any alteration in the text before him as a result of the notes, in spite of the fact that the very discrepancies in our current texts prove clearly that they are not free from errors. Moreover 'just as the reliability of the Old Testament books must be tested by the Hebrew texts, so too the accuracy of those of the New must be checked by the rules of Greek usage,' according to Augustine in the passage cited from him in the *Decreta* distinctio 9. On this passage, indeed, I do not think anyone could be so hard-hearted as not to pity, or so lacking in humour as not to laugh at, the extremely foolish gloss by someone or other who fancied Jerome had stated in his letter to Desiderius that the Latin texts were more correct than the Greek, and the Greek than the Hebrew. He failed to see what Jerome was doing, which was to prove his statement by drawing a manifestly absurd inference from its contrary, and that the words 'it is another matter if' had exactly the same force as if one should say 'unless we are to suppose that.' Otherwise it would have been madness to translate one testament from the Hebrew and revise another from the Greek if our Latin version was in fact better in both. What point, then, would there have been in the careful enactment of the 180 185 190 195 200 205

* * * * *

193 Augustine] The sentence quoted from Jerome *Epistles* 71.5.3 is attributed to Augustine in Gratian's *Decreta* part 1 distinctio 9.

196 Jerome] The passage misunderstood by the glossator is from Jerome's preface to his version of the Pentateuch addressed to Desiderius.

church at the Council of Vienne, recorded in the *Clementinae* book two, in the title 'De magistris,' that teachers should be provided for the three languages? In this connection I also wonder afresh why they deleted Greek.

I think, however, that it is enough merely to have brought all this to the attention of scholars. Some, as I understand, are of the opinion that the 210 ancient commentators who knew the three languages gave adequate explanations whenever they were needed. But, in the first place, I should prefer to see with my own eyes rather than another man's; second, much as they did explain, they certainly also left many things for later generations to add. There is also the fact that in order to understand the commentators one 215 has to be reasonably proficient in the languages. Lastly, where is one to turn when one finds the ancient texts in all the languages corrupt, as in fact they are? So, most learned Christopher, you are absolutely right when you remark, as you frequently do, that those who venture to write, not merely on the Scriptures, but on any ancient books at all, are devoid of both 220 intelligence and modesty if they do not possess a reasonable command of both Greek and Latin; for what happens is that when people like that are trying with might and main to show off their learning, this is precisely when they become most ridiculous in the eyes of those who really know the languages, and all the fuss they make is reduced to absurdity when a Greek 225 word is introduced. Even so, those who have no time to gain a perfect knowledge of Greek will be considerably helped by Valla's devoted labours; for he has, with admirable judgment, scrutinized the entire New Testament, incidentally making a great number of comments on the Psalms, of which the version we use has its source in the Greek, not the 230 Hebrew. Students will therefore be enormously in his debt, and he in yours, since it was you who brought him to public notice. Your favourable

* * * * *

205 *Clementinae*] The constitutions of Clement v, generally called the *Clementinae*, published after the Council of Vienne in 1314, ordained that, for the better conversion of the heathen, teachers of the three languages Hebrew, Arabic, and Chaldean should be established at five universities. Greek had originally been included in the list, but was removed presumably because the Greeks were not infidels, though schismatic. Erasmus in an earlier reference to the constitutions seems to have thought that the three languages referred to were Hebrew, Greek, and Latin (cf Ep 149:53–4).

229 Psalms] Valla may have used the *Psalterium Romanum*, Jerome's first revision of the Old Latin translation, corrected against the Greek of the Septuagint. It seems more likely, however, that the current version referred to here is Jerome's second, the so-called *Psalterium Gallicanum*, corrected against the Greek of Origen's *Hexapla*, since this is the version which survives in the Vulgate. Jerome's third version is a translation directly from the Hebrew.

verdict will do much to recommend him to intelligent people, and your support will provide him with a stronger defence against his detractors. Farewell. 235

Paris, 1505

183 / From Josse Bade

[Paris], 7 March 1505

This letter was inserted after Ep 182 in Erasmus' edition of Valla's *Annotationes* which Bade printed.

Josse Bade (1462–1535) of Assche in Brabant, hence called Ascensius, was one of the most distinguished scholar-printers of the Renaissance. He had been educated in the school of the Brethren of the Common Life at Ghent and later studied in Italy, He then worked for several years with the printer Johann Trechsel at Lyon. In 1499 he moved to Paris where he set up a press and also became professor of letters at the university. He remained for years in close relations with Erasmus and published many of his books. Cf P. Renouard *Bibliographie des impressions et des œuvres de Josse Badius Ascensius, imprimeur et humaniste* (Paris 1908) 3 vols.

JOSSE BADE OF ASSCHE TO DESIDERIUS ERASMUS OF ROTTERDAM

Of course, most eloquent Erasmus, I cannot fail to agree with your authoritative opinion, frankly expressed, about our Valla; no fair-minded person could take exception to him, and all students already owe him a considerable debt of gratitude and good will. For it is true that, as St Augustine 5 rightly observes in his *De doctrina christiana*, matters which are somewhat obscure and unintelligible in one tongue become luminous and explicit when they can be compared with a version in another; and so it should not be held against him if he directs attention to passages where the Latin texts sometimes disagree with the Greek original, and sometimes are ill- 10 expressed, unless indeed we resent the fact that he relieves us of so much hard work! But I will not be angry: for my hope is that your hunting will be as pleasant as it is welcome to all students of divinity. Farewell.

7 March 1505

184 / To Pieter Gillis

Paris, [about March 1505]

This letter introduces into the correspondence Pieter Gillis (1486/7–1533) of Antwerp, who remained throughout his lifetime one of Erasmus' closest

* * * * *

183:5 Augustine] *De doctrina christiana* 2.11.16

friends. Erasmus had met him in February 1504, if not earlier, as Gillis was a corrector in Martens' press at the time when Erasmus was supervising the printing of the *Panegyricus* (cf Ep 179 introduction). Gillis was appointed chief secretary of the town of Antwerp in 1510, but he continued to work as a corrector and editor for Martens for several years. He is best known as one of the interlocutors in the *Utopia*, the first edition of which More dedicated to him. There seems to be no evidence that Gillis actually came to Paris to visit Erasmus as he had evidently intended to do.

ERASMUS TO PIETER GILLIS

I was about to write to you, dear Pieter, for I had decided to do so, but some business or other got in the way to make me forget this intention. The Valla is in a safe place together with some other papers you had assembled, and would have been sent back to you before now if I had not disagreed with 5 what you proposed. For if you mean to come here at Easter, as you say in your letter, there is no point in asking for the return of your books; whereas if you are not coming, I will send them whenever it seems convenient. There is no danger that anything may be lost, especially as I am standing guard over them. When I was last in Antwerp your father came to me 10 intending to say something important and serious, but I had to go. I wondered whether it had to do with entrusting you to my care? Personally I should neither advise this, lest I might appear to be seeking to do it for profit, nor yet advise against it, since I am most eager to be of service to you; and I am aware how much I could do if you were to stay with me for several 15 months. If only the notion had occurred to your father before I left your part of the world!

Farewell: get together (from any source you can) the minor works of Rodolphus Agricola, and bring them with you. Master Jan of Gorkum asks me to send you his cordial greetings. 20

Paris, [1503]

185 / To Servatius Rogerus London, [end of 1505?]

Erasmus' indirect approach to Mountjoy through Colet (cf Ep 181:84ff) evi-

* * * * *

6 Easter] 23 March 1505

10 father] Nicolaas Gillis

19 Rodolphus Agricola] Cf Ep 23:58n.

19 Jan] Possibly the Jan Dirk Harius, canon of Gorkum, to whom Cornelis Gerard dedicated his metrical version of the Psalms (cf Ep 17 introduction)

dently bore fruit in an invitation to come to England, and before the end of the year he had been with Mountjoy, though not always living with him, for several months. He remained in England till June 1506, mostly in London, but possibly with a visit to Cambridge (cf E&C 25f).

ERASMUS OF ROTTERDAM TO HIS FRIEND SERVATIUS

Long before I left Paris I wrote you a letter which will, I think, have been delivered to you; but because messengers are so careless I am a little anxious in case it has gone astray. So if I have accidentally offended, I will make amends by taking care to write often. To explain what had induced me to go back to England would be tedious, especially since I have been stripped of my money here before, while opportunities not to be overlooked seemed to await me at home; please believe, however, that I had solid reasons for returning to England, and did so on the advice of men of sense. The further success of my enterprise depends on Heaven's good will; but I have come so that scholarship may profit, and not to make my own fortune.

For the last few months I have been staying with my friend Lord Mountjoy, who pressingly invited me to come back to England. In this he was seconded by the entire scholarly community. There are indeed five or six men in London profoundly versed in Latin and Greek, and I doubt if Italy itself contains such good ones at this moment; yet, without flattering myself, I do believe there is not one of them who does not pay high tribute to my talents and learning. Were it proper for me to boast, I should feel complacent on this score at least, that those whose good opinion I enjoy are men whom no one, however envious or hostile, could refuse to recognize as pre-eminent in those branches of literature. Yet I cannot regard myself as

* * * * *

7 money] Cf Ep 119:9n.

7 opportunities] It is not clear what opportunities Erasmus had in mind. There is no record of a renewal of the offer from Louvain which he had refused three years before (cf Epp 177:14ff and 172:11–12), nor was there any promise of future aid from the archduke (cf Epp 179:19ff and 181 introduction). Perhaps he was simply trying to impress Servatius with his importance, since Servatius had become prior of Steyn in 1504 and was apparently attempting to recall him.

15 men in London] There was a remarkable group of scholars trained in Greek in London at this time. Erasmus later mentioned Thomas Linacre (cf Ep 118:27n), William Grocyn (cf Ep 118:26n), William Latimer (cf Ep 207:24–5n), and Cuthbert Tunstall (cf Ep 207:25n) as scholars to whom he had submitted his translations from Euripides for approval while in London (cf Ep 207:25n). William Lily (cf Allen Ep 341:18n) and Thomas More might have been added to the list of Greek scholars.

successful unless I have the approval of Christ also: and my true happiness depends upon His verdict. Farewell.

London, from the bishop's palace

186 / To Franciscus Theodericus London, [end of 1505?]

Franciscus Theodericus was one of Erasmus' early friends from his first years at Steyn (cf Ep 10 introduction).

ERASMUS OF ROTTERDAM TO HIS FRIEND FRANCISCUS

You will do me a very great favour, my dear friend, if you will arrange for the collection, as far as possible, of the letters which I have written with more than ordinary care to this person and that; for I have a plan to publish a single volume of letters, especially those written in some quantity to Cornelis of Gouda, in very large numbers to my friend Willem, and a few to Servatius. Scrape together all you can, from anywhere you can, but do not send them except by a messenger named by me. 5

I beg you, dear Franciscus, by the affection we entertain for each other and for your happiness' sake, which is as precious to me as my own, to devote yourself entirely to the Holy Scriptures. Go through the ancient commentators. Believe me, either the road to blessedness lies this way for us or we shall never attain to it. However I am sure you are already doing what I am now recommending. Farewell, and commend me continually to Christ in your prayers. 10 15

Please give my greetings to my friend Willem; I have not been writing to him because I have been very busy and also because I was in poor health. Try to make him write as good a letter as he can manage to my friend the count; for the sun never shone on a truer friend of scholars.

London, from the bishop's palace 20

* * * * *

24 bishop's palace] This probably does not refer to the palace of the bishop of London, William Barnes, who is never mentioned as a friend or patron of Erasmus. It is more likely that at the time of writing he was lodged with either Bishop Foxe (cf Ep 187 introduction) or Bishop Fisher (cf Allen I app VI), both of whom had residences in London. The story of his visit to Archbishop Warham at Lambeth (cf Allen I 5) seems to preclude the possibility of his having been Erasmus' host at this time.

186:3 letters] It is to this request that we owe the preservation of a score or so of Erasmus' early letters (cf Allen I app VII and IX).

5–6 Cornelis] Gerard (cf Ep 17 introduction)

6 Willem] Hermans (cf Ep 33 introduction)

7 Servatius] Rogerus (cf Ep 4 introduction)

19 count] Mountjoy

187 / To Richard Foxe London, 1 January 1506

During his stay in London common interests drew Erasmus and Thomas More closer together. As both were still striving to perfect their Greek, the two friends undertook to translate a number of the dialogues of Lucian. The results were published as *Luciani opuscula ... ab Erasmo Roterodamo et Thoma Moro ... in Latinorum linguam traducta* (Paris: J. Bade 13 November 1506). There were several later editions. See edition with introduction by C. Robinson in ASD I 1 361–627. This letter is the preface to the *Toxaris*, the first dialogue in the collection. Cf C.R. Thompson *The Translations of Lucian Toxaris by Erasmus and St. Thomas More* (Ithaca, NY 1940).

Richard Foxe (1448?–1528), bishop of Winchester since 1501, was a statesman-prelate who had a long career in the royal service to which he owed his ecclesiastical preferment. He was lord privy seal 1485–1516, and had held three bishoprics before his translation to Winchester. He was also a patron of learning: he was chancellor of Cambridge 1498–1500, second master of Pembroke 1507–19; and at Oxford he founded Corpus Christi College in 1515–16 to advance the study of the three biblical languages in keeping with Erasmus' programme for the reform of theology.

TO THE RIGHT REVEREND RICHARD, LORD BISHOP OF WINCHESTER, FROM ERASMUS OF ROTTERDAM, GREETINGS

There is a custom which has been handed down from the ages of antiquity to our own times, my lord Bishop, of sending little presents on the calends of January, the first day of the New Year. Such presents are thought to bring 5 some kind of good luck both to the recipients and also to those donors who receive an answering gift. Accordingly I tried to determine what possible gift I might send to so great a patron and so powerful a friend as yourself, but found nothing among my possessions save poor sheets of paper. I was obliged, therefore, to send a paper present; yet after all what gift could be 10 more suitable from a man of studies to a prelate who, though he has been richly endowed with every advantage in Fortune's gift, infinitely prefers virtue, and virtue's companion, good letters; who accepts the gifts of Fortune with a kind of disdain, and, I might almost say, unwillingly, yet in the things of the mind, rich as he is in these already, is ever eager to increase 15 his wealth?

* * * * *

187:4 presents] The practice of presenting the MS of a new book to a prospective patron as a New Year's gift seems to have been fairly common in the sixteenth century. Cf H.W. Garrod 'Erasmus and his English Patrons' *The Library* 5th series 4 (1949) 11f.

CLARVS WYNTONIÆ PRÆSVL COGNOĪE FOXVS
QVI PIVS HOC OLIM NOBILE STRVXIT OPVS
TALIS ERAT FORMA TALIS DVM VIXIT AMICTV
QVALEM SPECTANTI PICTA TABELLA REFERT ·

Richard Foxe, bishop of Winchester
Posthumous portrait by Joannes Corvus,
probably Jehan Raf/John Raven, fl c 1512–c 1544
By permission of the President and Fellows of
Corpus Christi College, Oxford
(Thomas Photos, Oxford)

In favour of this little gift of mine I may further say (if I can say nothing else) what was remarked of Parmeno's in Terence, that it came not from Ethiopia but all the way from Samosata, a city of Greece. It is in fact a dialogue by Lucian, named *Toxaris*, or *On Friendship*. In the last few days I have turned it into Latin. I hope that it may be not altogether unacceptable to your Excellency: for it preaches friendship, an institution so holy that it was formerly held in reverence even by the most savage tribes, whereas nowadays it has among Christians fallen into such deep neglect that its very name has vanished, not to mention the signs of its existence; yet Christianity itself is only that true and perfect kind of friendship which consists in dying with Christ, living in Christ, and forming one body and one soul with Christ; it is indeed a communion between men, like the communion of limbs in the body, one with another. And this dialogue is sure to be no less pleasant than profitable, if the reader only observes the appropriate way in which its characters are treated. How very Greek in flavour, agreeable, witty, and gay, is the conversation of Mnesippus the Greek! On the other hand, the speech of Toxaris the Scythian is wholly Scythian in atmosphere, direct, unsophisticated, rough, earnest, serious, and manly. I have tried as far as possible to reproduce the difference in their styles of address, the different textures, as it were, which Lucian deliberately tries to distinguish.

I beg you then, my Lord, graciously to accept the trivial New Year's gift offered by your humble dependent. May your Lordship continue to cherish, succour, and help Erasmus, as you have done for so long. Farewell.

London, 1 January 1506

187A / From Julius II Rome, 4 January 1506

This brief was unknown until it was discovered in the Vatican archives by the director of the Dutch Historical Institute in Rome who published an abstract in *Archivalia in Italië* in 1909. Allen first published it as 'A Dispensation of Julius II for Erasmus' EHR 25 (1910) 123–5, and then reprinted it among the addenda to volume III (xxix). It is a dispensation freeing Erasmus from any canonical impediment to his accepting ecclesiastical benefices on account of his illegitimate birth. Erasmus had undoubtedly begun negotiations for such a dispensation at this time because he had hopes of receiving a benefice in England (cf *Compendium vitae* Allen I 51, 11, 120ff). He seems, in fact, to have

* * * * *

18 Parmeno] The young man in Terence *Eunuchus* 165 who has gone to great pains to secure a negro slave-girl for his mistress

Julius II
Cartoon for a portrait of Julius II, attributed to Raphael
Galleria Corsini, Florence (Photo Alinari)

been promised one by Henry VII (cf Ep 189:5f). His hopes, however, were for the time being disappointed, and he had no occasion to use the dispensation until 1512 when he was given the rectory of Aldington (cf Ep 255 introduction), although there is no record in the correspondence that it was actually used at that time. Later, when he was promised a canonry at Courtrai in 1516 (cf Allen Ep 436) and when there was also some suggestion of his being given a bishopric (cf Allen Ep 475:4), he secured a fuller dispensation from Leo X, dated 26 January 1517 (cf Allen Epp 517, 518, and 447 introduction). The dispensation granted by Julius II was inadequate in that it did not fully protect Erasmus from charges arising from his 'defect of birth,' since in the brief he is quoted as affirming that he was 'sprung of an unmarried father and a widow' (cf lines 9–10). This may have been literally true, but it was not the whole truth, for in the brief of Leo X he is said to fear that his birth was not only illicit but also sacrilegious and condemned, which can only mean that he feared his father was already a priest at the time of his birth. Erasmus may conceivably have been unaware of this circumstance when he requested the dispensation from Julius and may have heard rumours to that effect in the meantime, while still remaining uncertain about the actual date of his father's ordination. This, however, seems unlikely. It seems more probable that he felt it necessary to be completely protected from the effect of any local gossip about his being the son of an already ordained priest when he was accepting a canonry in the Netherlands than when he merely hoped for a living in England. The brief of Leo X, incidentally, also freed him from the necessity of wearing the garb of his order and, most important of all in view of the persistent efforts of the prior of Steyn to recall him (cf Epp 185, 189, 200, 203, 296), it freed him from the obligation of residence in his home monastery, which at this stage in his career would have been a major disaster.

JULIUS ETC TO OUR BELOVED SON DESIDERIUS ERASMUS, CANON OF THE MONASTERY OF STEYN IN HOLLAND OF THE ORDER OF ST AUGUSTINE IN THE DIOCESE OF UTRECHT, GREETING ETC

The zeal for religion the integrity of your life and character and other estimable evidence of your uprightness and virtue, in respect of which you 5 have been recommended to us by credible witnesses, incline us to visit you with special grace and favour. Hence it is that we, wishing out of consideration for your merits aforesaid to show gracious favour to you who suffer (as you affirm) from a defect of birth being the offspring of an unmarried father and a widow, and absolving you by the terms of this letter and declaring 10 you absolved for the future from each and every the ecclesiastical sentences censures and penalties of excommunication suspension and interdict and any others which may have been imposed upon you by the law or by man for any occasion or cause (if you are held bound in any way by any such), as far as is necessary for the effectiveness of these presents and no farther, do now assent to your prayers in this respect and in virtue of our Apostolic authority by the tenor of these presents and as a gift of special grace give you dispensation as follows: to accept and (as aforesaid) to hold any ecclesiastical benefice whatsoever with or without cure of souls customarily held by secular clerks, even if it be a parish church or the perpetual vicarage thereof or a chantry free chapel hospital or annual duty normally assigned to the same clerks by way of perpetual ecclesiastical benefice and by right of lay patrons or ..., of whatsoever valuation or annual value the fruits revenues and proceeds thereof may be, provided they be conferred upon you lawfully in other respects or you be presented or otherwise appointed to it and instituted thereto, and whether simply or by way of exchange to resign this as often as you wish and in place of that resigned to receive in like manner and to retain as aforesaid freely and lawfully another ecclesiastical benefice be it similar or dissimilar with or without cure of souls with the qualifications hereinbefore specified: the defect aforesaid and the constitutions and ordinances general and special of the Council of Poitiers or any other such of Apostolic authority and those of Otto and Ottoboni of blessed memory formerly legates of the Apostolic See in the realm of England and any others promulgated in Councils provincial and synodical together with the statutes and customs of the monastery of Steyn in Holland of the Order of Saint Augustine in the diocese of Utrecht, whereof you are a canon and as you further assert have expressly taken the vows of the said Order, whether they be ratified by the oath of the said Order by Apostolic confirmation or by endorsement of any other kind, and all other things to the contrary notwithstanding. Let no man therefore etc infringe our grant of absolution and dispensation etc. And if anyone etc.

Given at Rome at Saint Peter's in the year of Our Lord's Incarnation one thousand five hundred and five, the fourth day of January in our third year.

A. Colozzi

* * * * *

32 Otto and Ottoboni] Otto le Blanc and Ottoboni Fieschi were papal legates in England in 1237 and 1268 respectively. The dispensation from their constitutions is evidence that it was in fact an English benefice that Erasmus was at this time hoping to receive.

188 / To William Warham London, 24 January [1506]

This is the preface to the *Hecuba* in *Euripidis ... Hecuba et Iphigenia, Latinae factae Erasmo Roterodamo interprete* (Paris: J. Bade 13 September 1506; critical edition by J.H. Waszink in ASD I 1 193–359). Erasmus' own copy of the Greek Euripides (Venice: Aldus 1503) from which this translation was evidently made is now at Lincoln College, Oxford. Cf N.G. Wilson 'Erasmus as a Translator of Euripides' *Antike und Abendland* 18 (1973) 87. While in London Erasmus was taken by Grocyn to pay a visit to Warham at Lambeth and to present to him the translation of the *Hecuba* of Euripides which he had begun at Louvain. Warham responded by giving him a present of money. On the way home Erasmus indicated to Grocyn that it had been only a small sum, and Grocyn jestingly replied that Warham probably thought he was in the habit of dedicating the same work to several patrons. Erasmus was nettled and, to demonstrate the falsity of the charge, on his return to Paris he added the *Iphigenia* which he had translated in England, dedicating it also (though actually not until the second edition; cf Epp 198 and 208) to Warham although he had no expectation of further favours from him or even of returning to England (cf *Catalogus Lucubrationum* Allen I 5n).

William Warham (1456?–1532), archbishop of Canterbury since 1503, was, like Foxe, a statesman-prelate with an interest in learning. He was lord chancellor from 1504–15 and chancellor of Oxford University from 1506 until his death. He became one of Erasmus' most important patrons, giving him the rectory of Aldington in 1512 (cf Ep 255 introduction). Erasmus always held him in high regard and paid warm tribute to him after his death (cf Allen Ep 2758 and *Ecclesiastes* (Basel: Froben 1535), LB V 810–12).

TO THE MOST REVEREND FATHER IN CHRIST, WILLIAM, ARCHBISHOP OF CANTERBURY, PRIMATE OF ENGLAND, FROM ERASMUS OF ROTTERDAM, A CANON OF THE ORDER OF ST AUGUSTINE, GREETINGS

Having resolved, most illustrious prelate, to translate Greek authorities in 5
order to restore or promote, as far as I could, the science of theology which
had fallen into a most shameful condition through scholastic trifling, but
wishing to avoid risking my potter's skill all at once on a great jar, as the

* * * * *

8 risking ... great jar] *Adagia* I vi 15

Greek adage has it, or rushing into such a large enterprise with feet as yet unwashed, as the saying goes, I determined first to test whether the labour I had spent on Greek and Latin had been wasted by experimenting on a subject which, though very taxing, was secular in nature; one that was hard enough to afford me good practice, while any mistake I made would be at the cost of my intellectual reputation alone, causing no harm to Holy Writ. Accordingly I took in hand the translation of two tragedies by Euripides – *Hecuba* and *Iphigenia in Aulis* – to see whether a favouring breeze might perchance blow from Heaven to forward so bold an endeavour. Presently I observed that a sample of my proposed work did not displease certain persons well versed in both tongues – and England of course now contains several who, if one may speak the truth without giving offence, deserve everyone's admiration, even throughout Italy, in all branches of scholarship. Thus with the muses' favour I finished it in a very few months. How much sweat this cost me, only those who have stepped into the same wrestling-ring can understand.

For, considering that the very task of turning good Greek into good Latin is one that demands exceptional skill, and not only the richest and readiest vocabulary in both languages but also an extremely sharp and alert intelligence, so that for several generations past nobody who has undertaken it has earned approval by the votes of the learned world – you may quite easily guess how painful a task it was to render verse metrically, especially when its metres are so various and so unfamiliar, the work of an author who is not only of great antiquity, and a tragedian at that, but remarkably succinct, delicate, and exquisite in his style; in whom there is not a spare word or anything one could subtract or alter without doing him great violence; who, moreover, is so fond of, and clever at, handling rhetorical themes that he seems to be for ever making declamatory speeches. Besides this there are the choruses, which are so obscure, because of some sort of deliberate artifice, that they need an Oedipus, or Delian prophet, rather than a commentator. These difficulties are increased by poor texts, shortage of manuscripts, and a lack of commentators to whom we may have recourse; so that I am not really surprised if even in the present fortunate age no Italian has ventured to embark on the task of translating any tragedy or any comedy, whereas several have attempted Homer (and,

* * * * *

9–10 feet ... unwashed] *Adagia* I ix 54

22 finished it] Cf *Adagia* I ii 32.

29 by the ... world] *Adagia* I v 60; cf Ep 173:100.

among those, Poliziano himself was dissatisfied with his own work); and a certain translator has tried Hesiod, though here too with unhappy results; 45 while another has attacked Theocritus, still more unsuccessfully; and Francesco Filelfo in one of his funeral orations translated (I discovered after I had begun my own version) the first scene of the *Hecuba*, but did so in such a fashion that I, usually bashful to a fault, was considerably encouraged by this great scholar's performance. 50

For my part, then, I was not deterred, either by these distinguished examples or by the work's many difficulties, but rather attracted by the more than honeyed sweetness of this poet's style (a sweetness conceded to him even by hostile critics). Accordingly I did not hesitate to embark on a task unattempted hitherto, in the hope that, even if I produced little in the 55 way of a result, yet kindly readers might still deem that this attempt of mine deserved some praise, while those of a less friendly disposition should at least be indulgent to a novice's version of a work so hard, especially since I had deliberately added considerably to the other difficulties by my scrupulous accuracy in translation, attempting as far as possible to reproduce the 60 shape and, as it were, the contours of the Greek poems, striving to render verse for verse and almost word for word, and everywhere trying zealously to adapt the force and effect of the meaning to Latin ears, with all fidelity. This I did, perhaps because I do not fully share the freedom in translating authors that Cicero both allows others and (I should almost say excessively) 65 practises himself, or perhaps because as a novice in translation I preferred to err in seeming to keep too close rather than be too free, or in other words to run aground occasionally through hugging the shore, rather than to suffer shipwreck and be left swimming in the ocean; and I thought it better that scholars should perhaps find me wanting in grace, let us say, and 70 elegance of poetic style than in accuracy. Lastly, I did not wish to announce that I was but paraphrasing, and so provide myself with the refuge wherein many translators excuse their ignorance and, like the cuttlefish, spread an

* * * * *

44 Poliziano] Angelo Poliziano (cf Ep 126:150n). In 1470, when only sixteen, he began translating the *Iliad* into Latin verse. As book I had already been translated by Carlo Marsuppini, he began with book II and ended with book V unless later parts have been lost. The translation was dedicated to Lorenzo de' Medici (cf Rossi 360f).

46–7 Francesco Filelfo] Cf Ep 23:77n. For Erasmus' comment on his translation of the first scene of the *Hecuba* see also Allen 14 lines 31ff.

62 verse for verse] In the *Iphigenia* he adopted a freer translation (cf Epp 198 and 208).

73 cuttlefish] Cf Horace *Satires* 1.4.100.

inky obscurity round themselves to escape detection. And if my critics fail to find in my work the elevated language of Latin tragedy, the bombast and words of giant size that Horace speaks of, they should not reckon it a fault in me that, as a translator, I have chosen to reproduce the concise clarity and neatness of my original rather than a pomposity that does not belong to it and in which I take little pleasure in any case. 75

I am accordingly prompted to be full of confidence that my present efforts may be both immune to unfair disparagement and likely to earn the good will of fair-minded and friendly readers, if, most worshipful Father, they have also gained the seal of your approval. It was indeed easy for me to choose you, out of a multitude of eminent princes, to receive the dedication of these fruits of my nightly labours, for besides the supreme eminence of your position I perceived you to be so endowed, adorned, and abundantly furnished with learning, eloquence, prudence, piety, humility, uprightness, and, lastly, unparalleled benevolence towards all who cultivate good letters, that the name of primate suits none better than yourself; for you take the primacy not only in rank and office but much more still in every kind of virtue, and are at one and the same time the chief adornment of the court and the pinnacle of eminence in the church. And if it should be my fortune to win for my work the esteem of one who is so highly esteemed, certainly I shall neither regret that I endured my labours so far, nor be reluctant in future to assist theology by some greater undertaking. 80 85 90 95

Farewell: and pray regard your humble servant as one of those who are most sincerely devoted to your fatherhood.

London, 24 January

189 / To Servatius Rogerus — London, 1 April [1506]

ERASMUS OF ROTTERDAM TO HIS FRIEND MASTER SERVATIUS

I have sent you several letters already, and am most surprised at your failure even to set pen to paper in reply. I am still staying in London, in high favour, it seems, with the greatest men and finest scholars in all England. The king has promised me a benefice, but the arrival of the prince in England has obliged him to put aside the idea. 5

* * * * *

76 Horace] *Ars poetica* 97; cf *Adagia* II ii 52.

90–1 every kind of virtue] Reading *omni* for *omnium*

189:5 prince] On the death of Queen Isabella of Castile in November 1504 Philip, duke of Burgundy, claimed the kingdom of Castile by virtue of his marriage to Isabella's daughter Joanna. With the support of Henry VII, who financed the voyage with a loan, he set sail for Spain on 10 January 1506, but

For myself, I am deeply preoccupied with pondering how I can wholly devote to religion and to Christ whatever life remains to me. How much this may be, I do not know. I am conscious how fleeting and insubstantial is the life of man, even the longest; and I can see also that my own health is frail, 10 and has been further weakened to a considerable degree by my laborious studies, and to some extent also by misfortune. I can see that those studies have no end, and every day I seem to begin all over again. Therefore I have made up my mind to be content with my present undistinguished fortune, especially when I have acquired as much Greek as I need, and to pay 15 attention to the contemplation of my death and the state of my soul. I should have done this long ago; I ought to have been sparing with my years, the most precious possession of all, when that possession was at its best. But, though 'too late to spare when the bottom is bare,' still I must husband it all the more carefully now that it is shorter and poorer. Farewell. 20

London, 1 April

190 / To Jacob Mauritszoon London, 2 April [1506]

Since Jacob Mauritszoon was a citizen of Gouda (cf Ep 176 introduction), this letter was probably sent by the same messenger as Ep 189.

ERASMUS OF ROTTERDAM TO MASTER JACOB MAURITSZOON, A MOST ACCOMPLISHED LICENTIATE IN CIVIL AND CANON LAW

If you are well, my very good friend, I have every reason to rejoice. For my part I am in pretty good health, and ever mindful of you 'so long as life my limbs doth move.' I hope to see you this summer; when I do I shall tell you 5 everything in person, including the secrets of the nether world, for when one is in Pluto's kingdom it is wise to plan for one's return and act carefully in all respects.

I am heartily sorry for the accident that brought our prince to these shores, for many reasons. He has not yet sailed, and it has cost me a pretty 10 penny. My patron has to wait upon him by the king's command and at his

* * * * *

was driven ashore at Melcombe Regis by a violent storm. He remained in England until 23 April, engaged in the negotiations for a political alliance and a commercial treaty, the so-called *intercursus malus* (cf Mackie 183ff). The intensive diplomatic activity during the duke's stay might well have occupied the king's attention to the exclusion of less important matters, but it is not clear why the promise of a benefice to Erasmus should have been permanently set aside.

19 'too late to spare'] Cf *Adagia* II ii 64.

190:4–5 'so long ... move'] Virgil *Aeneid* 4.336

11 patron] Mountjoy

own expense; meanwhile I am rapidly exhausting my small reserve of money. I have written at greater length to our friend Willem. Give my greetings to Master Reyner, that physician who is the second ornament of learning in Holland; and to that amusing person, Master Hendrik, and to 15 my other good friends. I wish all good fortune and happiness to your charming wife and delightful children. Farewell.

London, 2 April

191 / To Richard Whitford — From the country, 1 May 1506

This preface to Erasmus' declamation in reply to Lucian's *Tyrannicida* is one of a series of similar dedications published in the *Luciani opuscula* (cf Ep 187 introduction). By dedicating each dialogue separately Erasmus was able to pay off debts or win the favour of potential patrons. Others in the series are Epp 187, 192, 197, 199, 205.

Richard Whitford was an intimate friend of both Erasmus and More, and at this time chaplain to Bishop Foxe (cf Ep 89 introduction).

ERASMUS OF ROTTERDAM TO HIS DELIGHTFUL FRIEND, THE ENGLISH SCHOLAR RICHARD WHITFORD

After being quite immersed in Greek literature for some years now, my dear Richard, I have recently turned to writing Latin declamations, just for the sake of getting on familiar terms again with that language. This I did at the 5 suggestion of Thomas More, who is, as you are aware, so full of eloquence that he could not fail to carry any argument, even with an enemy, and whom I regard with such affection that, even if he ordered me to join the rope-circle and dance, I should obey him without hesitation. He himself tackles the same theme, with such thoroughness too that there is not a 10

* * * * *

13 Willem] Hermans. The letter has not survived.

14 Reyner] Reyner Snoy of Gouda (c 1477–1537) was a physician with a strong interest in humanist literature. He had studied medicine at Bologna where he took a doctor's degree, and on his return became physician to Adolph of Veere. In 1513 he published a collection of Erasmus' early poems, together with the 'Apologia Herasmi et Cornelii' (cf Ep 19:5n) and Willem Hermans' 'Proposopoeia Hollandiae,' under the title *Herasmi Silva Carminum antehac nunquam impressorum* (cf Reedijk 205ff and *Opuscula* 8ff).

15 Hendrik] Cf Ep 83:87n.

191:8–9 join the … dance] Terence *Adelphoe* 752

10 same theme] More also wrote a declamation in reply to Lucian's *Tyrannicida*, which was printed in the second section of the *Luciani opuscula*.

single point he fails to investigate and account for. And I believe (unless I am deluded by the intensity of the love I bear him) that nature never created a livelier mind, or one quicker, more discerning, or clearer – in short, more perfectly endowed with all the talents – than his; and his intelligence is matched by his power of expression. Moreover, he has an exceptionally 15 charming disposition and a great deal of wit; yet the wit is good-natured; so you could not find him lacking in a single one of the qualities needed by the perfect barrister.

Consequently it was not my intention, when I undertook to write this, either to rival or to outdo such a skilful practitioner, but merely to wrestle, 20 as it were, in this contest of wits with the most congenial of all my friends, in whose company I enjoy combining jest and earnest; and I have done so all the more willingly because I am most anxious that this sort of exercise, which I regard as the most profitable of all, should some day be revived in our schools. The lack of it is, I believe, the sole reason why in this age of 25 ours, in spite of the myriads who peruse the pages of the most eloquent authors, there are nevertheless so few who do not seem totally inarticulate when the occasion calls for an orator. But if we were to follow the precepts of Cicero and Quintilian, and also the general practice of antiquity, and carefully train ourselves from boyhood onwards in exercises of this kind, I 30 believe there would be less of the poverty of expression, the pitiful lack of style, and the disgraceful stammering we see even among public professors of the art of oratory.

Please bear in mind, as you read my declamation, that I did not compose it but merely threw it off as a recreation within a very few days. At 35 the same time I request you also to compare it with More's, and in this way judge if there be any difference in style between two authors whom you used to describe as so similar in mind, character, outlook and pursuits that, you said, no pair of twins on earth could be more alike. One thing is sure; as you love both of them equally, so you in turn are equally beloved of them 40 both. Farewell, my sweet and most charming Richard.

In the country, 1 May 1506

192 / To Thomas Ruthall London, [beginning of June 1506]

This is the preface to *Timon* in the *Luciani opuscula* (cf Ep 187 introduction). More also dedicated the dialogues he contributed to the *Luciani opuscula* to Ruthall. See E.F. Rogers *The Correspondence of Sir Thomas More* (Princeton 1947) 10–14.

Thomas Ruthall (d 1523) was at this time dean of Salisbury. He owed his ecclesiastical preferment to his service as secretary to the king, 1500–16. He was chancellor of Cambridge University in 1503. In 1509 he was made bishop of Durham and in 1516 was appointed to the Privy Council (cf Emden BRUO). Erasmus sought his patronage again on his return from Italy (cf Epp 236:39n and 243:46).

TO THE HONOURABLE DOCTOR RUTHALL, DOCTOR OF CIVIL AND CANON LAW AND SECRETARY TO THE KING, FROM ERASMUS, GREETINGS

See what liberties I am inspired to take by the marvellous affability of your mind and character alike, dear Ruthall. For, fully conscious though I am of 5 your pre-eminence among the leading men at court, whether for authority or influence, for high position or learning, I am not ashamed to send your Excellency my trifles when they are still unfinished and have but now undergone the first correction. But what was I to do? The skipper was impatient already, dinning in my ears that wind and tide wait for no man. 10 So, to avoid leaving no memento of myself in the possession of one who has treated me so kindly, I now send what I happened at that moment to have by me, namely *Timon* the misanthrope; what a present for the most philanthropic of men! It is a dialogue by Lucian; and there is hardly any of them that is more useful or pleasant to read. Long ago somebody translated it, but 15 so badly that it appears that the translator's intention was to prove by doing so that he knew neither Greek nor Latin; indeed it would not be absurd to suppose that he was hired as a translator by Lucian's enemies! Pray take my liberties in good part, and include your humble servant among those who are sincerely devoted to you. 20

Farewell.

London, [1504]

193 / To Christopher Urswick — Hammes, [beginning of June 1506]

After nearly a year in England, and although he had made many influential friends, Erasmus had not received a benefice or any other satisfactory endowment. Then he was suddenly presented with the opportunity to travel to Italy which he had so long hoped for (cf Ep 75:15n). He was invited by a wealthy Italian, Giovanni Battista Boerio, to accompany his two sons to Italy and to supervise their studies (cf Ep 194:33n). He left London with his com-

* * * * *

15 somebody] The *Timon* was included in a volume of translations of Lucian published in Venice in 1494 and 1500 without the name of the translator.

panions at the beginning of June (cf Ep 192). The first leg of the journey took them from Dover to Calais, a rough crossing lasting four days (cf Epp 194:3ff, 196:10ff), and from there to the nearby castle of Hammes to visit Erasmus' patron Lord Mountjoy, who was now its commander (cf Ep 120:46n). Here he apparently stayed long enough to polish his translation of *Gallus* for inclusion in the *Luciani opuscula* (cf Ep 187 introduction) with this letter as dedicatory preface. It was probably during this visit that he wrote the verses 'Arx vulgo dicta Hammensis,' printed in the *Epigrammata* (Paris: Bade 8 January 1507). Cf Reedijk 280.

Christopher Urswick (1448–1522) was a cleric who received numerous benefices through royal favour. He was warden of King's Hall, Cambridge, 1485; dean of York, 1488; dean of Windsor, 1496; and in 1502 he was given the living of Hackney. He also served on many embassies (cf Emden BRUO).

TO THE HONOURABLE DR CHRISTOPHER URSWICK,
FROM ERASMUS, GREETINGS

I have always thought, dear and honoured Christopher, that ingratitude was the meanest of vices and held that anyone who could ever forget what another person had done for him ceased to deserve the name of human 5 being. Again I have always regarded as truly happy those to whom Fortune's favour has given the means of making an adequate return for other men's kindnesses, and happiest of all those she allows to repay with interest a benefit received. Accordingly I have often heretofore reflected how much your generosity has done for me, all undeserving (for I reckon as 10 a gift whatsoever was offered me in such a way that it was my fortune, or my own fault, that prevented me from accepting it, and certainly no fault of yours), and then looked about me to see by what means I could at least prove to you the remembrance and gratitude I felt; yet in my modest circumstances I could find nothing at all to suit, I will not say your deserts, 15 but even my own feelings. In the last resort it occurred to me that I should at least try to imitate certain well-bred persons whose way it is to send some choice nosegay, or other similar token, to express their warm good will and the devotion of a willing heart; more especially if they are poor themselves and direct their generosity to such as stand in no need, by fortune or by 20 temperament, of gifts from anyone else.

And so I went into the precinct of the Greek muses, whose gardens bloom even in the depth of winter, and there at once, among the many flowerets that commended themselves in a number of pleasant ways, this one of Lucian's took my fancy most. So I send it to you, plucked by the pen 25 and not by the hand. It pleases me, not only for the sake of its novelty and its rich colouring, beautiful shape, and fragrant scent, but also because it secretes a juice of sovereign potency for health; and, as Horace has written

He who mingles use with pleasure
Every prize doth bear away. 30

Nobody, in my opinion, has succeeded so well at this as our Lucian. Recalling the outspokenness of the Old Comedy, but lacking its acerbity, he satirizes everything with inexpressible skill and grace, ridicules everything, and submits everything to the chastisement of his superb wit. Nothing that arises even in passing fails to become the target of some jest or 35 other. Philosophers are a special butt, especially the Pythagoreans, the Platonists also because of the marvels they recount, and the Stoics because of their insufferable airs of superiority. He attacks some by deft stabs and cuts, others with any weapon that is handy; quite rightly, too, for what is more detestable or intolerable than rascality which publicly masquerades 40 as virtue? It is for this reason that men have labelled him slanderer, that is to say, one who speaks ill of others; but of course it was those whose sore spots he had touched who did so. He likewise laughs and rails at the gods, and with no less freedom; for which he has been given the nickname of atheist, which naturally acquires positive credit because those who seek to attach it 45 to him are irreligious and superstitious men. He is thought to have flourished about the time of Trajan, but I swear he does not deserve to be classed with the Sophists. He possesses such grace of style, such felicity of invention, such a charming sense of humour, and such pointedness in satire; his sallies arouse such interest; and by his mixture of fun and 50 earnest, gaiety and accurate observation, he so effectively portrays the manners, emotions, and pursuits of men, as if with a painter's vivid brush, not so much inviting us to read about them as to see them with our own eyes, that whether you look for pleasure or edification there is not a comedy, or a satire, that challenges comparison with his dialogues. 55

Yet if you were to ask me what exactly the subject of this dialogue is, the author proceeds according to his usual custom. He censures Pythagoras as an impostor and charlatan and laughs at the pomposity and sage's beard affected by the Stoics; he explains how subject to anxieties are the lives of rich men and kings, and conversely how carefree are those of the cheerful 60 and contented poor. I earnestly beg you to read him with great care

* * * * *

28 Horace] *Ars poetica* 343; cf *Adagia* I v 60.

33 ridicules] *naso suspendit*: *Adagia* I viii 22; II iii 52

38–9 stabs and cuts] Livy 22.46.5

whenever business permits you to relax your furrowed brow. You will hear the voice of the cock, talking with his master the shoemaker, in a more amusing fashion than any jester could achieve, and yet also with a wisdom exceeding that which divines and philosophers commonly attain in the schools when they dispute with immense arrogance over portentous trifles. 65

Farewell, my dear and kindly Christopher; please include myself among your humble clients, for I will be second to none in affection, devotion and service to you.

Hammes castle, [1503] 70

194 / To Thomas Linacre

Paris, [c 12 June] 1506

This and the two following letters were written immediately after Erasmus arrived in Paris. He was delayed there for two months by arrangements for printing the translations of Lucian and Euripides (cf Epp 187 and 188) and also revised and somewhat enlarged editions of the *Adagia*, published after his departure, 27 December 1506 (cf Ep 126 introduction), and the *Epigrammata*, published 8 January 1507. All four were printed by Bade.

DESIDERIUS ERASMUS OF ROTTERDAM TO HIS FRIEND THOMAS LINACRE

I have arrived in Paris quite safely, except that in the course of the four days at sea I contracted a troublesome illness after catching cold, and as a result even now I am racked with pain in the front of my head. The glands under my ears on both sides are swollen, my temples throb, and I have a ringing noise in both ears: and no Linacre here either, to give me relief with his skill! So much has my Italian contract cost up to this moment. I have resolved, more firmly than ever before, never to entrust myself to wind and wave so long as a route by land is possible. 5 10

In France I have come to life again; for a persistent and widespread story had been in circulation, that Erasmus had departed this life. I suppose this rumour sprang up by mistake because of the death of that Frenchman Milo, since he too had left France and joined Mountjoy's household, and a few days later caught the plague and died. Though as an omen it does not disturb me, at least I owe one thing to this mistake: I now have a foretaste, while I am still alive, of what those who survive me will say about me when I am dead! France pleases me so much, now that I have returned to it, that I 15

* * * * *

62 relax ... brow] *Adagia* I viii 48

194:8 skill] Linacre was a physician, practising in London (cf Ep 118:27n).

am not sure which country holds the greater charm for me – England, which has made me so many good friends, or France, which is sweet to me for old acquaintance' sake, and because she it was who gave me my freedom, and lastly because of the pronounced favour and encouragement she has accorded me. As a result I am luxuriating in a kind of double pleasure: it gives me equal joy to remember my stay in England, especially since I hope I may repeat it soon, and to revisit my friends in France.

You would not be able to keep from laughing if you knew how greedily my Greek friend is waiting for the present I promised him in return for the reed-pens from Cyprus. How often he has reminded me of this present, and reproached me for failing to send it! What fun it is to tease a crow when its beak is so very wide open! But the foolish fellow does not notice that what I wrote was to the following effect: 'I shall send a gift worthy of you,' meaning a worthless one.

I am hopeful that the charge of educating Battista's sons, which I have undertaken, will turn out well. I see that they are talented, modest, and manageable, and even now they are intellectually in advance of their years. Their tutor, Clyfton, is the most agreeable and friendly, as well as helpful, of men.

Farewell, my most learned and very kind teacher; write to me often, even briefly, so long as you write something.

Paris, 1506

* * * * *

27 Greek friend] Perhaps George Hermonymus (cf Ep 149:77n).

30 crow] Horace *Satires* 2.5.56

33 Battista's sons] Giovanni Battista Boerio, the king's physician, was the wealthy Italian who employed Erasmus to accompany his sons Giovanni and Bernardo to Italy (cf Ep 267 introduction). The boys returned to England in 1513, but then the family seems to have moved permanently to Italy. The two brothers were living in Rome in 1518 (cf Allen Epp 865: 63f and 905:25), but later retired to their native Genoa. Erasmus remained on friendly terms with them and corresponded at intervals till 1531 (cf Allen Epp 2255 and 2481).

36 Clyfton] Clyfton was the tutor of the two Boerio boys, Erasmus being responsible only for directing their studies. A violent brawl in which Clyfton became involved on the way to Italy made Erasmus take an unfavourable view of him (cf Allen I 4 lines 9ff). Many years later he was still bitter about the trouble Clyfton had caused during the year in which they shared responsibility for the two boys (cf Allen Epp 2255:12 and 2481:34ff). Allen suggests that Clyfton may have been the English friend who, according to Beatus Rhenanus, took a doctorate in theology with Erasmus at Turin (cf Allen I 59 line 109). Allen also ventures the suggestion that he may possibly be identified with a Dr William Clifton (d 1548) who supplicated for the degree of Bachelor

195 / To John Colet

Paris, 12 June 1506

ERASMUS TO HIS HIGHLY ESTEEMED FRIEND JOHN COLET

I find it hard to express the mingled feelings with which I left England and came back to France; and indeed I could not easily make up my mind whether the joy I felt at seeing again friends long since left behind in France outweighed my sadness at leaving behind new-made friends in England. 5 What I can truly say is this: there is no land on earth which, even over its whole extent, has brought me so many friends, or such true, scholarly, helpful, and distinguished ones, graced by every kind of good quality, as the single city of London. And those same friends have so rivalled one another in affection and helpfulness towards me that I should be unable to 10 give any one of them preference over any other, and deem it proper to love them all equally in return. I cannot but be sharply hurt by the pangs of separation from such friends as these; yet again I find solace in remembering them, since my ever-present thought of them brings as it were their presence back to me, while I hope to visit them again quite soon, and never 15 more to leave them afterwards until death, and death alone, divides us. I am confident that you, dear Colet, whose love and devotion to me are so strong, will endeavour in company with the rest of my friends to bring this about as soon, and as satisfactorily, as possible.

I am inexpressibly pleased with the characters of Boerio's boys; they 20 are the most modest and tractable and hard-working students one could wish for. As a result I feel confident that they will answer their father's hopes and my exertions, and some day be a great credit to England. Farewell.

Paris, on the morrow of Corpus Christi 1506 25

* * * * *

of Canon and Civil Law at Oxford in March 1506 and was licenced Doctor of Civil Law in 1517. He held numerous ecclesiastical preferments, was subdean of York from 1520 until his death, and in 1523 was Wolsey's vicar-general in the province of York (see Emden BRUO I 143). One might with equal plausibility identify the boy's tutor with one Gamaliel Clifton or Clyfton (d 1541) who was Bachelor of Canon Law at Cambridge by 1500 and was studying canon law at Turin in 1508 (cf G.B. Parks *The English Traveller in Italy* (Rome 1954) I 640); later he took a doctorate, possibly at Turin. In 1513 he obtained a papal dispensation on account of a charge of homicide incurred at Cambridge; see Emden BRUC 141. The charge of homicide suggests a violent temper like that of the brawling Clyfton who so annoyed Erasmus. There is no direct evidence, however, for either identification.

196 / To Roger Wentford

Paris, 12 June [1506]

Roger Wentford was the headmaster of St Antony's School in Threadneedle Street, one of the leading schools in London. Erasmus resumed his intimate friendship with him on his return to England (cf Epp 241 and 277). In 1518 he indicated his intention of dedicating the first edition of the *Colloquia* to Wentford (cf Allen Ep 772:9), but did not do so, possibly because Wentford showed some disapproval, urging the suppression of one of the principal colloquies (cf Allen Ep 833).

ERASMUS TO HIS FRIEND ROGER

Among the many highly congenial friends England has made for me you, my dear Roger, are one of the very first I think of; for your love to me was so unwavering, your company so delightful, your kind services so helpful that, wherever upon earth my fate shall carry me, I am destined to take with 5 me there a most pleasant memory of my friend Roger. If only your fortune should free you to follow me to Italy! You would then take entire possession of your friend Erasmus, whom you have already in many ways, if I may so put it, made superlatively your own.

The journey turned out well enough, except that the sea voyage was 10 horrible to me; four nights we were at the mercy of wind and wave, and as a result I picked up a headache, from which I hope soon to be relieved. France presents a wonderfully pleasant aspect to me, all the more delightful because I have not seen it for some time. I miss England, particularly because I have left behind there so many learned, virtuous, affectionate, obliging, 15 and pleasant friends – friends who have done so much for me, in short; and you are to be reckoned chief among these. So be sure to maintain the affection you have for your Erasmus; I, in turn, shall daily surpass myself in love for my Roger. Farewell.

Paris, on the morrow of Corpus Christi [1507] 20

197 / To Jean Desmarez

[Paris? July? 1506]

Allen suggests that this preface to Lucian's *De mercede conductis* was actually written while the *Luciani opuscula* (cf Ep 187 introduction) was being printed since it was placed at the end of the volume. Desmarez (Paludanus) had been Erasmus' host at Louvain (cf Ep 180 introduction).

* * * * *

9 superlatively your own] *tuissimum*

ERASMUS OF ROTTERDAM TO MASTER JEAN DESMAREZ, PUBLIC ORATOR OF LOUVAIN UNIVERSITY

In order to let you know, my dear Paludanus, that your friend Erasmus, even as he flits about over land and sea everywhere, still carries always with him a memory of you, I am sending you as a token, so to speak, Lucian's 5 dialogue *De mercede conductis*, which I turned into Latin as I was setting out for Italy, and indeed virtually booted and spurred. You will see here reflected, as in a looking-glass, not unenjoyably, the drawbacks of life at court; the same that you often used to tell me of, naturally from personal experience, to be sure, and like a shipwrecked castaway who had just 10 managed to struggle back to the independent literary life you now pursue. I have done this quite deliberately on purpose to challenge you, by my example, to attempt some daring enterprise on your own, after your long acquaintance with Greek. Why should I not use the word dare, when there is, as I believe, no more daring feat than to try to make good Latin out of 15 good Greek? Farewell; and since I love you most dearly, pray love me in return.

198 / To the Reader [Paris, about July 1506]

This preface to the translation of Euripides' *Iphigenia* was evidently added hastily while the Bade edition was in the press (cf Ep 188 introduction). In the second edition (Venice: Aldus December 1507) it was replaced with a new and fuller preface addressed to Archbishop Warham (Ep 208).

ERASMUS TO THE READER, GREETINGS

I am well aware that different things please different people; in order, therefore, to satisfy everyone as far as might be, and also to leave nothing untried for myself, in translating this play I have given up some of the old attention to exactitude and paid somewhat more regard to attractiveness 5 and clarity. In addition, I have restricted the excessive variety of metres in the choruses; not out of concern for my own convenience, but partly because I saw that such a mixture of kinds yielded a result not very far removed from prose, and partly because I was conscious that even Seneca in his tragedies refrained from imitating such metrical variety. Farewell, dear 10 reader.

199 / To René d'Illiers Paris, [beginning of August 1506]

Like the preceding one, this preface to the translation of *Alexander seu Pseudomantis* was probably composed while the *Luciani opuscula* (cf Ep 187 introduction) was in the press, the translation itself having been brought to Paris and printed before Erasmus decided to whom to dedicate it.

René d'Illiers (d 1507) had been bishop of Chartres since 1492. He belonged to a noble family which had something like a monopoly of ecclesiastical offices in the diocese of Chartres.

TO THE RIGHT HONOURABLE FATHER IN CHRIST, HIS LORDSHIP RENÉ, BISHOP OF CHARTRES, FROM ERASMUS OF ROTTERDAM, A CANON OF THE ORDER OF ST AUGUSTINE, GREETINGS

Having in divers ways become aware that you have friendly feelings towards my poor talent and the trifles I write – and this too though you are usually a fastidious critic – I am sending you the *Pseudomantis*, or 'False Prophet,' by Lucian, as I am about to leave for Italy, so that it may serve as a memento of your Lordship's humble servant in his absence. Now this false prophet is a rascal indeed; but of all men he is the most serviceable for the detection and refutation of the impostures of certain persons who even today cheat the populace, either by conjuring up miracles, or with a pretence of holiness, or by feigned indulgences and other tricks of the kind. So you will, I hope, read him with a certain amount of profit – but also with a vast degree of pleasure; for whereas in addition to noble birth and high estate and responsible office your Excellency is perfectly instructed in those studies which are grave and austere by nature, nevertheless with your gay wit and extremely affable manners you do not altogether shun even the more elegant arts such as this, and are in the habit of admitting some frivolous interludes of this useful sort among exacting public duties. You will, besides, be able to find in Lucian, in fullest measure combined, both that 'black wit' with which Momus is credited, and the 'fair wit' which is associated with Mercury's name.

I am inexpressibly grieved to hear that the splendid and famous cathedral in the town of Chartres has been struck by lightning and set on fire. Farewell.

* * * * *

6 fastidious critic] *Adagia* II viii 59

11 cheat] Cf *Adagia* I v 52.

24 cathedral] The wooden spire of the northern tower in the west facade of the cathedral of Chartres was struck by lightning on 26 July 1506 and burned. It was rebuilt in 1507.

200 / To Servatius Rogerus [Florence, 4 November 1506]

This rather curt note is the first surviving letter written by Erasmus from Italy. He had left Paris in August (cf Ep 194 introduction) and travelled by way of Orléans, where he stopped for a few days as guest of Nicolas Bérault (cf Allen Ep 535:39ff), to Lyon (cf Allen Ep 2473:9f and Thompson *Colloquies* 147f), and thence over Mont Cenis to Turin. While crossing the Alps he wrote one of his most important poems, the *Carmen de senectute* addressed to Wilhelm Cop (cf Reedijk 280ff). At Turin he was granted the degree of doctor of theology on 4 September. His original intention to take the degree at Bologna (cf Ep 75:15) may have been abandoned because of the greater expense or more numerous formal requirements at the more famous university. Erasmus was not proud of his Turin degree and nowhere in the correspondence does he explain where he got his Italian doctorate, leaving the way open to the assumption that he got it at Bologna. He was careful, however, to preserve his diploma, which is now in the university library in Basel. When he arrived in Bologna he found the city threatened by siege and so moved on with his party to Florence.

ERASMUS OF ROTTERDAM TO HIS FRIEND SERVATIUS

I have come to Italy for many reasons, though I found her disturbed by the great tumult of the wars, so much so that, since the pope with the help of the French army was preparing to besiege Bologna, I was forced to leave and take refuge in Florence. But now that it is reliably reported that Bentivoglio has been caught by the French as he fled with three of his sons, I hope that the situation will settle down and allow me to return to Bologna, where the pope and his cardinals are to winter. 5

I have received my doctorate in theology; really I took this in disregard of my own inclinations and in response to my friends' insistence. I hope to come and see you next summer. Farewell. 10

* * * * *

3 pope] In the fall of 1506 Julius II launched a campaign to restore papal authority in Bologna. Having secured the aid of French troops through the influence of the cardinal of Rouen with Louis XII, he threatened the city with siege. The Bolognese, fearing a sack by the French troops, were forced to surrender and Julius entered the city (cf Creighton IV 86ff).

5 Bentivoglio] Giovanni Bentivoglio, though nominally ruling Bologna as papal vicar, was in reality an independent *signore*. When the Bolognese were forced to surrender to Julius, Bentivoglio took refuge in the French camp. Cf C.M. Ady *The Bentivoglio of Bologna* (Oxford 1937) 130ff.

6 three of his sons] Annibale, Ermes, and Antongaleazzo

201 / To Jan Obrecht [Florence, 4 November 1506]

Nothing is known of Jan Obrecht from the correspondence, except that he was apparently a kinsman of Willem Obrecht (cf line 3n) and lived near Gouda (cf Ep 202 introduction).

ERASMUS OF ROTTERDAM TO THE WORSHIPFUL JAN OBRECHT

I am pleased at the friendly feelings you entertain for me, and the friendly remarks you make about me as reported to me by Master Willem, tutor to the lord high treasurer's sons. He is very fond of you. At present he is staying at Bologna, where he lives on intimate terms with me. I have 5 recently been awarded a doctorate in theology, against my own inclinations, which were overborne by my friends' insistence. They were of the opinion that this label might bring me some degree of authority. I hope to come and see you again next summer, when we shall exchange all our news in person. Please give my warmest greetings to the friends we have in 10 common; I wish them every happiness. If my own trifles give you pleasure, many of my compositions have recently been printed at Bade's press in Paris.

Farewell.

202 / To Jacob Mauritszoon Florence, 4 November [1506]

This letter was obviously sent by the same messenger as Ep 200 since Mauritszoon, like Servatius, lived in Gouda (cf Ep 176 introduction). The enclosure of Ep 201 and the request that it be delivered to Jan Obrecht argues that Obrecht lived not far from Gouda.

ERASMUS OF ROTTERDAM TO MASTER JACOB MAURITSZOON, A MOST LEARNED LICENTIATE IN CIVIL AND CANON LAW

Heaven be thanked, your Erasmus is alive and well, and continually remembers you. He asks you to be so kind as to deliver the enclosed note as soon as possible to Master Jan Obrecht. I beseech you not to take amiss the 5

* * * * *

201:3 Willem] Master Willem Obrecht of Delft was at this time in Bologna. The university records show him to have been tutor to the three sons of Hieronymus Lauwerijns, heer van Watervliet, chamberlain and treasurer to the archduke Philip. The second son Marcus remained an intimate friend and correspondent of Erasmus for many years.

request for this small favour on my behalf. There is much news from Italy that would be worth writing about; but the messenger is hurrying off at this moment. Give my greetings to the learned Master Reyner the physician; also to Hendrik and all my other friends. My best wishes for your prosperity and that of all your household. 10

Florence, 4 November

203 / To Servatius Rogerus Bologna, 16 November [1506]

ERASMUS OF ROTTERDAM TO HIS FRIEND SERVATIUS

Though I recently wrote from Florence, still, since letters often miscarry over so long a distance, I will write again on the same topics. I came to Italy mainly in order to learn Greek; but studies are dormant here at present, whereas war is hotly pursued, so I shall look for ways of hastening my 5 return. I have taken a degree in theology, not by any means because I wished for it, but because others insisted I should.

Bentivoglio has left Bologna; the French, who have been laying siege to the town, were driven back by the citizens with the loss of a few soldiers. On St Martin's Day Julius, the supreme pontiff, entered Bologna; the 10 following Sunday he celebrated mass in the cathedral. The emperor's arrival is awaited. Preparations are afoot for a war against the Venetians also, if they do not withdraw from those territories that belong by right to the pope. Meanwhile all studies are in abeyance. Farewell.

Bologna, 16 November 15

* * * * *

8 Reyner] Snoy (cf Ep 190:14n)

9 Hendrik] Cf Ep 190:15n.

203:8 Bentivoglio] Cf Ep 200:5n.

10 Julius] The triumphant entry of Julius II into Bologna on 11 November 1506 was a magnificent spectacle. Erasmus, who was back in Bologna in time to witness it, was scandalized by the appearance of the vicar of Christ in the role of an armed conqueror and compared Julius' entry to a Roman triumph (see sources cited in *Opuscula* 85 line 358n).

11 emperor] Maximilian I. That his arrival was expected was evidently an unfounded rumour.

12 Venetians] Julius was determined from the beginning of his reign to recover the towns in the Romagna that had been annexed by Venice, but actual preparations for the war did not begin until the formation of the League of Cambrai in December 1508, which Julius joined in the following March (cf Creighton IV 98ff).

204 / To Prince Henry [Bologna, about 17 November 1506]

This fragment of a letter addressed to Prince Henry (later Henry VIII) was quoted from memory in a letter to Johannes Cochlaeus, 1 April 1529 (Allen Ep 2143:75–8) as an introduction to Erasmus' statement that Henry's answer (Ep 206), a copy of which was appended, was actually written by the prince.

... We have received here a report that is too sad for anyone willingly to believe it, but too persistent to appear altogether unfounded, to the effect that Prince Philip has departed this life ...

205 / To Jérôme de Busleyden Bologna, 17 November 1506

The translations of some of Lucian's dialogues which accompanied this letter were intended to supplement the *Luciani opuscula* which had already been published by Bade, 13 November 1506 (cf Ep 187 introduction). They were, however, printed and added to some copies of the *Opuscula*. They were also printed separately by Martens at Louvain in 1512 (NK 3434; cf Ep 264:25n).

Jérôme de Busleyden (1470–1517) was the brother of François de Busleyden, archbishop of Besançon (cf Ep 157:67n). He was studying law at Orléans in 1500 when Erasmus met him. Later Erasmus regretted having been unable at that time to secure Busleyden's patronage (cf Ep 157:69ff). After studying at Bologna and Padua and receiving an LL D, Busleyden returned to the Netherlands, where he held a number of ecclesiastical benefices and was sent by the prince on several diplomatic missions. He was a generous patron of scholars, one from whom Erasmus had great expectations (cf Ep 178:15ff). On his death he left a large bequest to found the *Collegium Trilingue* at Louvain, with the inception of which Erasmus was closely associated (cf Allen Epp 691, 699, 804, 805). See also H. de Vocht *J. de Busleyden, his Life and Writings* Humanistica Lovanensia 9 (Louvain 1950).

TO JÉRÔME DE BUSLEYDEN, PROVOST OF AIRE AND MEMBER OF THE ROYAL COUNCIL, FROM ERASMUS OF ROTTERDAM, GREETINGS

For some time a report has been circulating here too grievous for anyone to wish to believe it, but yet too persistent to appear unfounded, to the effect that our own Prince Philip has departed this life. My dear Busleyden, what 5

* * * * *

204:3 Philip] Archduke Philip, who since the death of Queen Isabella in 1504 had claimed the crown of Castile by virtue of his marriage to her daughter and heiress Joanna, died in Spain on 25 September 1506.

complaint, what cries of woe am I to utter, and 'whom shall I accuse – man or god'? What tears, what lamentation would be tragic enough to do justice to this terrible blow? Too great, too great the price we paid for you, ye kingdoms of Spain; first you took from us François de Busleyden, archbishop of Besançon; yet, not content with destroying so great a man, you 10 have even swallowed up the prince himself, than whom, had he but lived, the whole earth should have seen nothing greater, nothing finer. Yet what, I ask you, remained for him to do, young as he was, save to surpass himself by his own efforts?

But how cruel is Fortune's sport here; how unprecedented the malice 15 of Fate! O Death, as envious as you are unjust, how you always carry off the best things first, and scarcely show them to us before you sweep them away! For whom shall I now most deeply mourn? For the father, Maximilian, since he has lost a son so splendid, a son he loved more than all his many domains? Or rather for the children, inasmuch as their tender years 20 are now bereft of so loving a father? Or for his country, that has known joy so belated, and mourning so premature, for its dearest prince? Or lastly for the whole world, deprived of so bright a glory so long before his time? This, then, was the doom portended by that fateful storm which drove him in mid-voyage to England's shore, the very fates clearly turning him back from 25 Spain. I myself wrote a panegyric, of no great merit, in praise of the young prince. Ye gods, how many panegyrics I then promised myself, and full of matter too! And now, behold, by this sudden change of fortune I sadly write his epitaph instead. Let us go now, poor frail humanity that we are, and put our trust in what we call our fortunes, when Death snatches away at 30 his whim even those in whom length of days benefits all mankind.

But why, my dear Jérôme, do I refresh your pain by indulging my own? For the rest, I beg that Heaven may generously grant the children the gift of their father's good fortune, but add to it the long life of his late imperial majesty Frederick. May you be accorded your brother's success in 35 managing them, but a longer life than your brother's. I have appended to this letter some dialogues by Lucian, so that it should not approach so dear

* * * * *

6–7 'whom … god'] An echo of Virgil *Aeneid* 2.745

17 show them to us] Cf Virgil *Aeneid* 6.869.

26 panegyric] Cf Ep 179 introduction.

35 Frederick] Frederick III, Philip's grandfather, was seventy-seven when he died in 1493.

35 brother's success] François de Busleyden had been tutor to Philip (cf Ep 157:67n). Jérôme, however, did not become tutor to Philip's sons.

and so learned a friend as you without a literary gift in hand. I have turned these dialogues into Latin these last few days while I was escaping to Florence for fear of the siege; I did this, of course, rather than do nothing, 40 for at this moment studies are remarkably dormant in Italy, whereas wars are hotly pursued. Pope Julius is waging war, conquering, leading triumphal processions; in fact, playing Julius to the life. Farewell; pray convey my cordial greetings to the right reverend Father Nicolas Ruistre, bishop of Arras. 45

Bologna, 17 November 1506

206 / From Prince Henry Richmond, 17 January [1507]

Henry's answer to Ep 204 was added as an appendix to Allen Ep 2143 (cf Ep 204 introduction). Here Erasmus was attempting to allay the doubts of Cochlaeus and others concerning the authenticity of Henry's *Assertio septem sacramentorum adversus Martin. Lutherum* (London: Pynson 12 July 1521; STC 13078). The prince's letter was added as proof of his mastery of Latin at an early age. Erasmus had used the same argument in writing to Duke George of Saxony (cf Allen Ep 1313:71ff). There he added that it was no wonder that the prince had a pleasing style since he had been encouraged by his tutor, Lord Mountjoy, to read Erasmus' writings, which he himself had used when he was Erasmus' pupil. In the letter to Cochlaeus Erasmus admitted that he had at first refused to believe that Henry's letter was his own work written at the age of fifteen, but was convinced when Mountjoy showed him a number of letters in Henry's hand with additions, deletions, and corrections showing the stages of composition. Henry's letter had in fact the earmarks of a schoolroom exercise, and may well have been polished by his tutor. Erasmus probably owed to Mountjoy the privilege of receiving a letter from the prince (cf Ep 296:117ff).

PRINCE HENRY SENDS GREETINGS TO DESIDERIUS ERASMUS, A CONSUMMATE SCHOLAR

Jesus is my hope

I was greatly touched by your letter, most eloquent Erasmus, for it was too charming to seem as though it were composed hastily, and yet too clear and 5 direct to be considered as the premeditated work of so subtle a mind as yours. For in some way it happens that the elaborate productions of men of

* * * * *

43 Julius to the life] Erasmus frequently compared Julius II to Julius Caesar (cf *Julius exclusus*, *Opuscula* 68 n89, and Ep 229:21n.

44 Ruistre] Cf Ep 177 introduction.

talent which are the object of too much devoted care bring with them an additional element of deliberate obscurity, since when we try to express ourselves more elegantly we imperceptibly lose the open straightforward manner of speaking. But the clarity of that letter of yours is as limpid as its charm is effective, so that you seem indeed to have won every vote. Still, why do I go about to praise the eloquence of a man like you whose learning is world-famous? I cannot invent anything in your praise which could be truly worthy of your consummate scholarship. Accordingly I omit your praises; I think it better to be silent than to speak inadequately. 10 15

I had, long before I received your letter, heard with great unhappiness the report about the death of the king of Castile, my deeply, deeply regretted brother; but I would that the report had been brought to us either much later or with less truth. For no less welcome news has ever come here since the death of my very dear mother. And, if I may confess the truth, I was less enchanted with this part of your letter than its marvellous elegance deserved; for it seemed to re-open a wound which time had healed. But it is right for mortals to submit to whatever pleases Heaven. Pray continue to tell me by letter if there is any news where you are, so it be more pleasant. May God prosper whatever has occurred that is worthy of mention. Farewell. 20 25

Richmond, 17 January

207 / To Aldo Manuzio Bologna, 28 October [1507]

Having completed his year's contract with the Boerio boys, Erasmus was preparing to return to the north. Before leaving, however, he wanted to have his translations of Euripides reprinted by the famous Aldine press, the Bade edition of 1506 being full of errors (cf Ep 188 introduction). This letter casts some light upon business arrangements between author and printer at that time. Erasmus' suggestion that he would have been willing to have the printing done at his own expense and risk had he had time, and his offer to take one or two hundred copies off the printer's hands, suggest that these arrangements were not unusual, especially perhaps in the case of an author whose reputation was not yet well established. He may have made similar arrangements with Bade for the printing of the *Adagia* of 1500 since he was concerned with selling copies (cf Epp 128:2n, 139:192n, 181:69ff).

Aldo Manuzio (1449–1515), commonly known simply as Aldus, was the most

* * * * *

12 won every vote] *Adagia* I v 60

18 king of Castile] Cf Ep 204:3n.

21 mother] Elizabeth of York (d 11 February 1503)

Aldo Manutio Romano Erasmus Roterodamus S.P.D.

Illud apud me saepe numero optavi, doctissime Manuti, ut quantum lucis [struck]
attulisses utriusque litteraturae, non solum arte tua formulisque longe nitidissimis,
verum etiam ingenio doctrinaque non trivali, tantundem emolumenti
illa tibi vicissim retulissent. Nam quantum ad famam attinet, dubium non
est, quin in omnem usque posteritatem Aldus Manutius volitaturus sit
[struck] omnium ora quicunque litterarum sacris sunt initiati. Erit autem
memoria tua, quemadmodum nunc est fama, non illustris modo, sed favora-
bilis quoque et amanda, propterea quod (ut audio) [illegible] propagandisque
bonis authoribus das operam, summa quidem cura, at non pari lucro,
planeque Herculis exemplo, laboribus exerceris pulcherrimis quidem illis,
et immortalem gloriam allaturis aliquando, verum aliis interim fru-
[margin: magis] ctuosis quam tibi. Audio Platonem graecanicis [struck] abs te [struck] formulis ex-
cudi, quem docti plerique iam vehementer expectant. Quos authores medi-
cinae impresseris cupio cognoscere. Atque utinam Paulum Aeginetam nobis
dones. Demiror quid obstiterit, quo minus novum testamentum iampridem
emulgaveris, opus (ni me fallit coniectura) etiam vulgo placiturum, maxime
nostro, id est, theologorum ordini. Mitto ad te duas tragoedias a me ver-
sas, [struck] [illegible] sane foeliciter. Ipse iudicabis.
Thomas Linacre, Gulielmus Grocinus, Gulielmus Latimerus, Cutbertus
Tunstallus, tui quoque amici, non tantum mei, magnopere probarunt, quos ipse
[margin: nosti] doctiores esse, quam ut iudicio fallantur, syncoriores quam ut amico velint adula-
ri. Nisi si quid amore nostri caecutiunt. Neque damnant conatum meum Itali
quibus adhuc ostendi. Badius impressit, sibi sat foeliciter, ut scribit,
Nam ex animi sententia divendidit exemplaria iam omnia. Verum
non satis consultum est famae meae. Usque adeo mendis scatent omnia.
Atque offert quidem ille operam suam, ut superiorem editionem posteriore
resarciat. Sed vereor ne iuxta Sophocleum adagium, malum malo sarciat.
Existimarim lucubrationes meas immortalitate donatas, si tuis excusae
formulis in lucem exierint, maxime minutioribus illis, omnium nitidissimis. Ita fiet, ut volumen sit pusillum, et exiguo sumptu res conficiatur.
[struck] Id si tibi videbitur negotium suscipere, ego
[struck line]
exemplar emendatum quod mitto per hunc iuvenem gratis suppeditabo, nisi si
paucula volumina mittere volueris, amicis donanda. Neque ego vererer rem
meo sumptu meoque periculo moliri, nisi mihi esset intra paucos menses Ita-
lia relinquenda. Quare perlim rem quamprimum absolvi, est autem vix decem dierum
negotium. Id si modis omnibus postulas, ut [illegible] volumina ad
me [illegible], tametsi non solet mihi admodum gratus esse [illegible]
κερδῷος: et incommodissimum sit [illegible] transportare, tamen ne id quidem
gravabor, modo tu equum precium praestes. Vale doctissime Alde et
Erasmum in eorum numero ponito, qui tibi ex animo bene cupiunt.
Si quid est in officina tua non vulgarium authorum, gratum facies si indicabis.
Nam docti illi Britanni hoc mihi negocii dederunt, uti pervestigarem.
Si de imprimendis Tragoediis nos animo tuo non sedet omnino, Reddes exem-
plar huic ipsi qui attulit ad me referendum. Bononiae [illegible] Novembr.

Autograph letter, Erasmus to Aldo Manuzio, 1507 (recto page)
Biblioteca Apostolica Vaticana, Reg. lat. 2023, f 163

celebrated scholar-printer in Italy. His press, founded in 1494, was noted for its scholarly editions of the Greek classics and for the small octavo editions of the Latin classics in fine italic type.

This letter and Epp 209, 212, 213 in Erasmus' handwriting were discovered in the Vatican library by Pierre de Nolhac and are published with a facsimile in his *Erasme en Italie* 2nd ed (Paris 1898).

TO ALDO MANUZIO OF ROME FROM ERASMUS OF ROTTERDAM

I have often privately wished, most learned Manuzio, that literature in both Latin and Greek had brought as much profit to you as you for your part have conferred lustre upon it, not only by your skill, and by your type, which is unmatched for elegance, but also by your intellectual gifts and uncommon 5 scholarship; since so far as fame is concerned, it is quite certain that for all ages to come the name of Aldo Manuzio will be on the lips of every person who is initiated into the rites of letters. Your memory in after-time, like your reputation at present, will inspire not merely honour but also affection and love, because, as I hear, you devote yourself to reviving and dis- 10 seminating good writers, taking infinite pains indeed but failing to receive an adequate reward; and you strive at enormous tasks in the manner of Hercules, splendid tasks it is true – tasks that will one day bring you undying renown – but which for the time being profit others rather than yourself. I am told that you are printing a Plato in Greek type; most scholars 15 are already eagerly awaiting it. I am desirous to know what medical writers you have printed; I wish you would present us with Paul of Aegina; I very much wonder what has prevented the publication, long before now, of your New Testament, a work which, unless my guess is mistaken, will please even the general public and especially those of my own sort, that is, the 20 theologians.

I am sending you my translations of two tragedies. It was audacious to attempt them, of course, but it is for you to decide for yourself whether I

* * * * *

12–13 in the manner of Hercules] In *Adagia* III i 1 Erasmus compared the work of restoring ancient literature to the labours of Hercules.

15 Plato] The Aldine Plato was published in September 1513.

17 Paul of Aegina] A medical writer of great renown (seventh century AD). The first edition of the Greek text was published by Aldus in 1528.

19 New Testament] Probably a reference to Aldus' plan to publish the Bible in Hebrew, Greek, and Latin. It was begun in 1501 but not carried through. The Aldine Bible in Greek was finally published in 1518 and embodied in it Erasmus' text of the New Testament (cf Allen I 64 n280).

have translated them properly. Thomas Linacre, William Grocyn, William Latimer, and Cuthbert Tunstall, who are your friends as well as mine, had a very high opinion of them. You are aware that these men are too scholarly to be at sea in their judgment, and too honest to be ready to flatter a friend, unless they are sometimes blinded by personal affection for me; and those Italians to whom I have thus far shown my attempt have not been censorious. Bade has printed them with happy enough results for himself, as he tells me in a letter; for he has already sold his entire stock to his own satisfaction. But he did not take proper precautions to protect my reputation, for the whole thing is chock-full of errors. It is true he is now offering his assistance in repairing the defects of the first edition by a second printing; but I fear he may seek 'the ill to remedy with further ill,' in Sophocles' words. I should consider that my efforts were given immortality if they were to be published in your type, especially that small fount which is the most elegant of all. In this way the book will be very small, and the publication will cost but little. If you find it convenient to undertake the commission, I shall furnish you with the corrected copy, which I send by the bearer's hand, free of all obligation, unless you should be willing to send me just a few copies for presentation to my friends.

And I should have no hesitation in arranging for the printing at my own expense and risk had I not to leave Italy in a few months' time; so that I should like the business to be finished as soon as possible. It would hardly take ten days. Now if you absolutely insist on my taking charge of a hundred or two hundred copies, though Mercury, the god of profit, is not as a rule particularly favourable towards me and it will be highly inconvenient

* * * * *

24 Linacre] Cf Ep 118:27n.

24 Grocyn] Cf Ep 118:26n.

25 Latimer] William Latimer (1460?–1545) was an English scholar highly respected for his knowledge of Greek. He had studied for years in Padua where he became acquainted with Aldus. He was back in England by December 1503 (cf Emden BRUO II 1106). He and Erasmus remained friends for many years.

25 Tunstall] Cuthbert Tunstall (1474–1559), like Latimer, had studied in Padua where he took an LLD and was back in England by 1506. He soon won the favour of Archbishop Warham whose chancellor he became in 1509 and through whom he received numerous preferments. He was dean of Salisbury 1521, bishop of London 1522, bishop of Durham 1530, and president of the Council of the North 1530–8. He was also sent on a number of royal embassies. He proved a generous patron, frequently contributing to Erasmus' support.

36 Sophocles] *Ajax* 362; cf *Adagia* I ii 6.

to have this parcel conveyed, still I will not boggle even at this so long as you fix a fair price in advance. Farewell, my scholarly friend, and reckon Erasmus among those who sincerely wish you well. 50

If you have any rare authors in your printing-house, I shall be obliged if you will give me a note of them; for those English scholars have asked me to look out for such things. If the business of printing the tragedies does not suit your plans at all, then please return the copy to the bearer, so that he may bring it back to me. 55

Bologna, 28 October

To the consummate scholar Aldo Manuzio of Rome, in Venice

208 / To William Warham [Bologna, November 1507]

In the Bade edition of his translations of Euripides Erasmus had dedicated the *Hecuba* to Warham (Ep 188), but, perhaps because he was pressed for time, had inserted only a brief preface to the *Iphigenia* addressed merely to the reader (Ep 198). This was replaced in the edition published by Aldus in December 1507 by the present expanded preface addressed, as Erasmus had apparently originally intended (cf Allen I 5), to Warham.

TO WILLIAM, ARCHBISHOP OF CANTERBURY,
FROM ERASMUS, GREETINGS

My lord Archbishop, after I had begun to labour at this tragedy it seemed to me that I detected a different flavour in the language, and another style of poetry; for, if I am not mistaken, it has somewhat more naturalness and its 5 style is more flowing. For which reason it might seem to be by Sophocles: but again it rather suggests Euripidean paternity by its close-packed themes and a sort of rhetorical ability in marshalling arguments on one side or the other of a question. However it is not my province to determine to which of the two it should be ascribed, nor do I think it matters much. All 10 the same, I have decided to relax my former strictness somewhat in order to avoid failure to do justice to the theme in this respect as well. Accordingly I have translated the *Iphigenia* a little more freely and also a little more expansively, but again in such a way as in no degree to fall short of a translator's duty to convey the meaning. In one respect I have dared in both 15 plays to depart from my author's practice: I have to some extent reduced the metrical diversity and licence of the choric parts, hoping that scholars would take my difficulties into account and pardon me for this; after all, Horace did not strive to reproduce the great freedom in prosody and variety in metres shown by the lyric poets, nor Seneca those of the tragedians, 20 although each of them was merely imitating the Greeks, not translating

Aldo Manuzio
Portrait medal, with anchor and dolphin device,
the trademark of the Aldine press, on the reverse
By an unknown Venetian medallist
Museo Civico Correr, Venice (Foto Toso)

them as well. But even if I had time among my more important studies to translate a number of other tragedies, not only should I not repent of this boldness, but I should not be reluctant to alter the style and topics of the choruses; and I should prefer either to treat of some commonplace or to 25 deviate into some agreeable digression, rather than to waste effort upon what Horace calls 'melodious trifles.' For it seems to me that nowhere did the ancients write more foolishly than in choruses of this sort, where, through excessive striving for novelty of utterance, they destroyed clarity of expression, and in the hunt for marvellous verbal effects their sense of 30 reality suffered. Farewell, my honoured patron.

209 / To Aldo Manuzio [Bologna, November 1507]

TO ALDO MANUZIO OF ROME, FROM ERASMUS

The spectacle of so famous a city, and the business itself, and especially that kind and friendly disposition of yours pressed me to fly to you if it had been spring, or the autumn were springlike; but as things stand I am deterred by the climate, to which I am not yet accustomed, and which at the moment is 5 very inclement, especially since a few days ago the weather here at Bologna gave some trouble to my health, which is delicate in itself, even at the best of times.

Perhaps there will be some points on which you will not agree with me, and for this reason I was particularly anxious to visit you in person. 10 There are certain passages, too, where I have some underlying doubts of my own; in a few I suspect that the printer's copy was faulty. For example, in the *Hecuba* B4, on the right-hand page *οὐ μήν γε πείθῃ* I read *οὐκ ἦν γε*. At the end the words *οὗτος σὺ μαίνῃ* should, I think, more properly be given to Agamemnon than to Hecuba. In the *Iphigenia in Aulis* z6, left page *ταχ-* 15

* * * * *

27 Horace] *Ars poetica* 322

31 honoured patron] *meum decus*: a quotation, meant to be detected by Warham, from the dedicatory ode of Horace addressed to Maecenas

209:13 *Hecuba*] Erasmus' reading of this phrase from *Hecuba* B4 (line 399) is now known to be that of the better MSS. MSS vary in giving the words at the end of the play (*Hecuba* line 1280) to Agamemnon or Hecuba, but modern editors agree with Erasmus.

15 *Iphigenia in Aulis*] Erasmus' suggested reading of *Iphigenia* z6 (line 1170) is accepted in Gilbert Murray's Oxford text, but is attributed to the French scholar Jean Brodeau, who was seven years old when this letter was written. Erasmus' references were all to the signatures of the Aldine edition of Euripides of 1503 edited by Marcus Musurus, which he evidently used as the basis for his translation (cf Ep 158:10n).

θεῖσα τοῖσι φιλτάτοις I read τἄχθιστα. Also in certain other places, which I cannot remember at present, I have dared to diverge from the text before me. I should very much like to discuss these matters with you face to face, inasmuch as I value your judgment very highly, were I not obliged to look after my health. But if you find an obvious mistake anywhere, for I am 20 human, you have my permission to alter it at your discretion; by doing so you will act the part of a friend, which is what your letter says that you now are. But if anything seems doubtful, yet defensible – a case where I may seem not so much to have made a slip through error as to have differed from you in opinion – please either leave it or, if you so desire, even change it: for 25 there is no responsibility that I would not now venture to entrust to my dear Aldus.

About the poetry: it does not seem to me to matter much. First, I have not in the choruses used the same metres as Euripides, except in one or two cases. For in the majority of the choruses there are almost as many kinds of 30 metre as there are verses, and there is also the Greek licence in varying the prosody; and when I saw that neither Horace in his lyric verse nor Seneca in tragedy imitated their great confusion or freedom (whichever it is), I thought it foolish for me to try to do so amidst all the difficulties I had to face. Accordingly I was content with somewhat fewer metrical patterns. 35 Second, if I should wish to add the names of the metres I have used in the choruses, of which there are a good many in each, and the combinations, and the rules of prosody, and the permitted substitutions, I shall have to do the same in the rest of the play; for those sections are not always in uniform iambic trimeters, but now and again change their metre. And it seemed out 40 of place for so small a volume to be swollen by so large an appendix. It will look more elegant, I believe, to publish a clean text; and at this moment I do not have by me the authorities I need for the purpose; so it would be better to leave the task unattempted than to do it incompetently.

Nor do I indeed have the time; for I wish the business to be finished as 45 soon as possible on many grounds, in order to present my learned friends with it as a New Year's Day gift. And I have a link of friendship with all those who are versed in, or profess, good literature here. Next, I am going to Rome immediately after Christmas, with the express intention of renewing old friendships there and making new ones by a little gift of this sort. I am 50 sending you my letter with a very few changes; I entrust to your judgment

* * * * *

47 gift] For the custom of giving gifts on New Year's Day, see Ep 187:3ff.

51 letter] Erasmus probably sent a complimentary letter to the printer which might be included in the book, a not unusual gesture.

everything to do with your dedication, and I shall be delighted to have a testimonial from Aldus. But if there is anyone else you think you should oblige in this way, do as you think best. As soon as it is ready, I should very much like twenty or thirty copies to be sent, with the price marked. 55 Payment will be made to the person who delivers the books or to anyone else whom you may appoint; but if you would rather have payment sent to you there in advance, this too can be arranged. Farewell, most learned and genial Aldus; include your friend Erasmus among those who both admire you and wish you well. 60

If there is anything you wish to alter in my letter to you I authorize you to do what you think best. Please leave out the short poem added at the end of the tragedies, for it is the work of a young Frenchman who was in my service at the time, and whom I had persuaded by way of a joke that his poem would be published. When I left I gave it to Bade in the young man's 65 presence, in order to keep his expectation alive; but I wonder what on earth got into his head afterwards to make him print it, considering that I told him of my intention to pull the youth's leg by making him hope for publication.

I have changed my short preface to the *Iphigenia*, so please remove the 70 old preface and put the new one in its place. In case my letter seems too long in any respect, I have underlined the passages that could quite conveniently be left out. I have no doubt that you will still find a host of compositor's errors; but please keep a sharp look-out for such things.

Write as soon as you can to let me know whether you have received my 75 letter (for the bankers occasionally delude me), and when the work should be finished. Farewell; you may command your friend Erasmus as you please.

To the consummate scholar, Aldo Manuzio of Rome, in Venice

* * * * *

62 poem] At the end of the Bade edition there was a short poem, 'Gervasi Omenii Drocensis ad lectorem epigramma.' It does not appear in the Aldine edition.

63 Frenchman] Gervase Amoenus of Dreux was a servant pupil of Erasmus for a time, probably during his stay in Paris in 1506. That he was also a protegé of Mountjoy is evident from a MS collection of his compositions presented to the English king in which he so describes himself. (British Museum MS Royal 16 E. XIV) He had, in fact, a modest career as editor and poet.

71 old preface] Ep 198, replaced by Ep 208

76 delude me] Cf *Adagia* I v 49.

ERASMI ROTERODAMI ADAGIORVM CHILIADES TRES, AC CENTVRIAE FERE TOTIDEM.

ALD. STVDIOSIS. S.

Quia nihil aliud cupio, q̄ prodesse uobis Studiosi. Cum uenisset in manus meas Erasmi Roterodami, hominis undecunq; doctiss. hoc adagiorũ opus eruditum. uarium. plenũ bonæ frugis, & quod possit uel cum ipsa antiquitate certare, intermissis antiquis autorib. quos parauëram excudendos, illud curauimus imprimendum, rati profuturum uobis & multitudine ipsa adagiorũ, quæ ex plurimis autorib. tam latinis, quàm græcis studiose collegit summis certe laborib. summis uigiliis, & multis locis apud utriusq; linguæ autores obiter uel correctis acute, uel expositis erudite. Docet præterea quot modis ex hisce adagiis capere utilitatem liceat, puta quẽadmodum ad uarios usus accõmodari possint. Adde, qd' circiter decẽ millia uersuum ex Homero. Euripide, & cæteris Græcis eodẽ metro in hoc opere fideliter, & docte tralata habẽtur, præter plurima ex Platone, Demosthene, & id genus aliis. An autem uerus sim, ἰδοὺ ῥόδος, ἰδοὺ καὶ τὸ πήδημα. Nam, quod dicitur, αὐτὸς αὑτὸν αὐλεῖ.

Præponitur hisce adagiis duplex index. Alter secundum literas alphabeti nostri. nam quæ græca sunt, latina quoq; habentur. Alter per capita rerum.

Erasmus *Adagiorum chiliades* title page
Venice: Aldus 1508
Houghton Library, Harvard University

210 / From Paolo Bombace [Bologna], 6 April 1508

The letters from Bombace to Erasmus (Epp 210, 217, 223, 251, 257) survive only in the form of summaries of their contents in Italian, with some direct quotations in Latin, in G. Fantuzzi *Notizie degli scrittori bolognesi* (Bologna 1782) I 279–80.

Paolo Bombace (d 1527) was an aristocratic Bolognese who lectured in Greek and in Latin rhetoric and poetry at the university. Erasmus formed a firm and lasting friendship with him during his stay in Bologna. In the *Adagia* I vi 1 he paid warm tribute to Bombace as 'the first to teach Greek and Latin there with equal ability' and also as a man whose 'manifold learning and the extreme pleasantness of his ways' attracted Erasmus to him.

A LETTER OF PAOLO TO ERASMUS DATED 6 APRIL 1508

He recommends to him a certain Merlin, just as he recommends him to Aldo Manuzio, and says 'Your friend Paolo is buffeted by storms of unpopularity, just because he dared to intrude among the doctors.' He then adds. 'Your tragedies began to be put on sale a little while ago,' and congratulates 5 himself that the verdict he had already pronounced has been endorsed by scholars. Next he enquires about Aldus' plans with regard to Plutarch.

211 / To William Blount, Lord Mountjoy [Venice, September 1508]

The publication of the Aldine edition of the *Adagiorum chiliades* in September 1508, dedicated to Mountjoy, was a landmark in the career of Erasmus as well as in the dissemination of the classics. Erasmus had never been satisfied with the slim *Adagiorum collectanea* of 1500, which Gaguin had criticized as jejune (cf Allen Ep 531:405ff), or the only slightly enlarged edition of 1506 (cf Ep 126 introduction). He had been collecting further adages for some time before going to Italy and he added still more at Bologna. Aldus having agreed, in a letter since lost, to print the adages, Erasmus gave up his plan of going to Rome (cf Ep 209:48ff) and arrived in Venice early in January 1508 to see the new book through the press. For the next nine or ten months he lived in the household of Aldus and his father-in-law Andrea Torresani d'Asola (cf Ep

* * * * *

2 Merlin] Perhaps Jacques Merlin 'Victurniensis' who edited Origen (Paris: Bade 15 October 1512)

5 tragedies] The *Hecuba* and *Iphigenia* printed by Aldus, December 1507 (cf Ep 208 introduction)

7 Plutarch] Aldus published the Greek *editio princeps* of Plutarch in March 1509.

212:6n), adding many more adages and writing feverishly while the printing was going on. Here he was in daily contact with the learned Greek scholars who formed the Aldine Academy and who generously supplied him with Greek MSS. Erasmus paid warm tribute to Aldus and to the helpful Greeks in the adage 'Festina lente' and described the difficulties of carrying out so vast a task in such a short time in the adage 'Herculai labores' (trans in Phillips 171ff and 190ff). Many years later, in 1531 when he had been irritated by scandalous stories about his life in Venice, he published a satirical description of the meagre fare provided by Andrea Torresani in the colloquy 'Opulentia sordida' (Thompson *Colloquies* 488ff). The new edition was immensely enlarged, the 819 adages of the first edition having grown to 3,260, and the title was changed accordingly from *Adagiorum collectanea* to *Adagiorum chiliades*. It was also very different in character. It drew much more heavily on Greek authors, many of them still unprinted, and the commentaries were greatly enriched, tracing the permutations of the adage from author to author and in many cases developing the theme suggested by the adage into a short essay. For full discussion see Phillips 62–95; see also Renaudet *Erasme et l'Italie* 83ff, and D.J. Geanakoplos *Greek Scholars in Venice* (Cambridge, Mass. 1962) 256ff.

ERASMUS OF ROTTERDAM TO THE NOBLE LORD, WILLIAM MOUNTJOY, GREETINGS

Some time ago in Paris I collected a sort of nosegay of proverbs. I did so in a few days at most, without much care, and also with hardly any Greek books to refer to; my object was to provide you, my most honoured William Mountjoy, with a personal handbook, since I had noticed that you took especial pleasure in this kind of thing. Certain persons went so far as to have it printed and published, industriously, it is true, though with untoward and excessive devotion to my interests, but so filled with errors that otherwise it might seem to have been spoilt on purpose. Yet, thrown together and put out as it was, it was better received than I had expected, whether this was due to your patronage, or the book's merits. It seemed to have lent such assistance to beginners in humane letters that they acknowledged a great debt to your Lordship, and something also to my own diligence. Accordingly, in order at one and the same time to repair the damage done by other persons to the previous edition, and to lay every student under a still deeper obligation to both of us, and especially to promote the interest in the humanities which is increasing in England day by day in this way, I waited until I had got together an adequate supply of Greek books, and then put my original version back on the anvil. Thus I

* * * * *

20 put ... anvil] *Adagia* I v 92

included in my handbook adages drawn from a great many authors, to the number of more than three thousand two hundred; for why should we not count them up, like treasure?

To this I planned to add, as it were using the same lamp-oil, as the saying goes, a number of remarkable metaphors, witty sayings, noteworthy 25 epigrams, unusually delightful allusions, and poetic allegories, since all these resources were, I thought, close in their nature to adages and, like them, contributed to a rich and attractive style. I had previously decided also to append with some care those scriptural allegories which are found in the famous theologians of early ages; first, because there, it seemed to me, I 30 should be on familiar ground and performing the functions of my proper profession; and second, because that section of my work would have to do not merely with the cultivation of the intellect but also with the good life. But when I saw this part of my enterprise assuming such vast proportions, I was put off by the labour involved, which was well-nigh limitless, and 35 cancelled my move; and, limiting myself to the course I have run, I now hand the torch to anyone else who may be willing to take over the race from me. As for myself, I am not yet really sorry I undertook this drudgery, inasmuch as it has to some extent revived for me the memory of my youthful studies, which was already beginning to fade. But, while it seemed proper 40 to have left my own field up to the present, still I did not think it was right for me, or would fail to result in some accusations against me, if I were to spend a great part of my life, up to old age, in working at an occupation which was not mine. Accordingly I shall discuss theological allegories, since it belongs to my profession to do so, as soon as I have an adequate 45 supply of Greek books on the subject – and will do so the more willingly because I observe that for some centuries now theologians have neglected this department, which is really of the utmost importance, and bestowed all their efforts on subtle questions – a practice which would be less reprehensible if it were not their one and only concern. As for the remaining parts of 50 the subject, I shall omit these the more willingly because I have come to realise that there is a person who volunteered to undertake them some time ago, namely Richard Pace, a young man so well versed in knowledge of

* * * * *

24 using the same lamp-oil] Cicero *Epistulae ad Atticum* 13.38.1; cf *Adagia* I iv 62.

36 cancelled my move] A metaphor from such games as chess; cf *Adagia* I v 55.

37 torch] *Adagia* I ii 38

53 Pace] Richard Pace (1482?–1536) had been studying at Padua since about 1498, having been sent and supported by Thomas Langton, bishop of Winchester, whose secretary he had been. Before the end of 1508 he went to Ferrara, to study under Leoniceno (cf Ep 216A:21n), where Erasmus visited

Greek and Latin letters that his intellect would enable him unaided to bring fame to the whole of England; and who is of such high character, and so modest withal, that he wholly deserves the favour of yourself and those who resemble you. And so, now that I have a successor as satisfactory as he, the result will be, first, that I have not only occasioned no loss to scholars by avoiding the remaining part of this task, but have even done them a good turn; and second, that this entire work will now be indebted to your country, England, for its author. 55 60

These then are the reasons why I undertook this part, and only this part, of the enterprise. I shall now give you a brief account of the principles on which I proceeded. Instead of consecutive order (if indeed there can be any kind of order in these matters), I substituted an index, in which I arranged by families those proverbs that seemed to be of the same general stamp and to be related. In making this collection I have neither been so pedantic as to be reluctant to include anything under the heading of adages unless it is accompanied by the phrase 'as they say' or some other obvious indication of the kind, nor on the other hand so hasty as to sweep into my net immediately anything that remotely resembled an adage, for fear of justifiable complaints that anything I chanced to touch promptly turned into an adage, just as all that Midas touched became gold. I have translated into Latin virtually all the Greek I quote, though I am quite well aware that this is at variance with the practice of the ancients, and contributes nothing to the attractiveness of the style. Still I have made allowance for the times in which we live. If only a knowledge of Greek literature might be so widely diffused that my tedious task in translating could deservedly be censured as superfluous! But for some reason we are inclined to be a little slothful in our approach to an activity as beneficial as this, and we are quicker to welcome any faint shadow of learning than that without which scholarship cannot exist at all, and upon which alone the integrity of all its branches depends. 65 70 75 80

As to verse, which is to be met with here in vast amounts, I have translated it into its corresponding kind of metre, except for a very few verses in Pindaric or choric metres, because I could see that it would be 85

* * * * *

him on his way to Rome and left a number of papers with him, including the *Antibarbari* (cf Ep 30:17n), the *De ratione studii* (cf Ep 66:introduction), and the *De copia* (cf Epp 260 introduction and 244:7n). Later Pace moved to Bologna to study with Bombace, leaving Erasmus' papers with William Thale. From there he went to Rome where he was in the service of Cardinal Bainbridge until 1514. Returning to England he had a long and brilliant career as royal secretary and diplomat and received a number of benefices. Cf J. Wegg *Richard Pace* (London 1932).

absurdly pedantic to render them syllable for syllable, and in the second place it seemed pointless, had I wished to attach a different sort of metre, taken from the context. But in other verses where metrical rules are concerned I have on a few, though rare, occasions made use of a licence employed by the authors from whom I borrowed the quotations, as for 90 example an anapaest in the even-numbered feet of an Aristophanic trimeter, a tapering effect in the Homeric hexameter, a lengthening of a final syllable in the first arsis of any foot, and anything else of the kind. I thought I ought to give notice of this in case anyone should take me to task, in the belief that I did it out of ignorance. 95

For my part, as far as was possible in the boundless profusion of the material, especially the ancient material, and considering the great scarcity and corruption of manuscripts, and moreover my acute lack of time, which had to be measured rather by my available leisure than by the demands of the enterprise, I have made every effort to see that the fair-minded reader 100 should not find anything wanting. Even so there are still a few things with which I am myself dissatisfied. In this regard, if a better version is supplied later, either by second thoughts, which proverbially are best as a rule, or by a more ample supply of books, I shall by no means be ashamed to recant – and herein too I shall be following the example of the ancients. If in this 105 matter any other person anticipates me and corrects my work, then far from taking offence I shall be extremely obliged to him. Personally I both approve of the conscientiousness of those authors who try to ensure that nothing remains in their writings for even the most captious critic to disapprove of, and marvel at the good fortune of those who actually succeed in this. 110 Certainly my own modest accomplishments would not venture to promise it, especially where the subject is of this sort. But if I have managed to unearth anything that is not generally known – and unless I am mistaken you will find not a few such things in this book – I communicate it freely, without vain display; if, on the other hand, anything has escaped me, I shall 115 no less stand corrected for it, being ready both gladly to teach what I know and with no less frankness to learn what I do not know. I have never liked the example set by those who become excited and boastful and vainglorious over any little word or phrase they have discovered, as though they had

* * * * *

92 tapering] *meiouros*: a rare form of the Homeric line, in which one of the long syllables in the last two feet is replaced by a short syllable

103 second thoughts] *Adagia* I iii 38

104 recant] *Adagia* I ix 59

109 most captious critic] Literally 'Momus'; cf Ep 182:81n.

captured Babylon, and as it were brandish their contribution in scholars' faces as a reproach, yet, should anyone disagree with a single word of it, fight as if for hearth and home to defend it. 120

But I have good reason to hope that these products of my nightly toil will entirely satisfy the generous-minded reader, provided you accept them with your customary good will, inasmuch as you are my studies' one supreme Maecenas (for what other name could more succinctly describe both the unparalleled affection you show me and the extent of your accomplishments?) Indeed you are uniquely deserving of that splendid tribute, once paid by Apuleius: 'most noble of scholars, most scholarly of noblemen, and in both classes the best' – to which one should add, 'of all men the most modest.' As you have adorned your family's ancient renown with scholarship, and adorned your scholarship with splendid integrity, so too you have added to all the virtues the fairest crown and coping-stone, as the saying goes: a wonderfully modest nature. And it should be regarded as the very perfection of your fame, equal to the longest speech that could be made in your praise, that you have won the favour of the most intelligent king whom not only our own age but even the annals of antiquity ever saw, and who is also (a very great virtue in a prince) most chary in choosing whom he would cherish. Admittedly it is the way of authors to fill a great part of their prefaces with compliments to those to whom they dedicate their writings, and it seems but the proper tribute to true goodness that the recollection thereof should be handed down to posterity, which is better done by books than by any other memorials; but I had a greater field of opportunity for praising my patron truthfully and without pretence than any other author ever had. Yet since my frank character, of which you are not unaware, is utterly alien not merely to flattery but to compliment of every sort, while your unique modesty can endure nothing so little as eulogies, even of the most modest kind, I shall omit the latter and proceed to my discussion of adages; which I have decided to open with a definition, as philosophers prescribe. Do but read, and farewell; or rather, while I am thus engaged, give me all the support you can. 125 130 135 140 145 150

212 / To Aldo Manuzio Padua, 9 December [1508]

Soon after the completion of the *Adagia* Erasmus left Venice for Padua. Despite the charm of the university town he did not remain long, for the League of

* * * * *

129 Apuleius] Cf *Florida* 16, quoted from memory.

133 coping-stone] *Adagia* II iii 45

Cambrai, signed 10 December 1508, threatened the Veneto with invasion. He therefore moved on to Ferrara and from there, when it too was threatened, by way of Bologna, Florence, and Siena, to Rome, taking with him the eighteen-year-old archbishop of St Andrews, Alexander Stewart, natural son of James IV of Scotland, whom Erasmus had agreed to tutor (cf Allen I 61f and Allen Ep 604:2n; Renaudet *Erasme et l'Italie* 87ff).

ERASMUS TO HIS FRIEND ALDUS

Germain has delayed me here with his magical spells, though I was already booted and spurred. Please urge Francesco to hurry his copying of my modest treatise, for I shall meanwhile see if I can oblige someone by offering it to him, and thus obtain some reward, so that my activity of these last months does not go for naught. Andrea has shown considerable foresight in paying me everything in écus; but I am sure he will do his duty in this business. 5

Farewell, dear Aldus, most learned and kindly of men.

At Padua, the morrow of the feast of the Conception 10

To the most learned Aldo Manuzio, defender of good literature

* * * * *

2 Germain] Germain de Brie [Latin 'Brixius'] of Auxerre (d 1538) was a young French student whom Erasmus had met in Venice, where he was a servant-pupil of Johannes Lascaris, and again in Padua, where he was a pupil of Marcus Musurus. Years later he became involved in literary controversies with both More and Erasmus.

3 Francesco] Francesco Torresani d'Asola (c 1481–1546) was Aldus' brother-in-law, eldest son of Andrea Torresani.

4 treatise] Probably the *De copia* (cf Ep 260 introduction)

6 Andrea] Andrea Torresani d'Asola (Asulanus) (1451–1529) was Aldus' father-in-law and partner. He had been printing in Venice since 1479. After the marriage of his daughter to Aldus he was closely associated with him, and in 1508 the two presses were united. After the death of Aldus Andrea and his sons carried on the Aldine press (cf Allen Ep 311 introduction).

7 in écus] Most likely the French écus d'or au soleil (1475–1515), then officially valued at 36s 3d tournois = 6s 2d gros Flemish = 4s 3d sterling, slightly less than a Florentine florin; but possibly écus d'or à la couronne, then valued at 35s 0d tournois. Cf CWE I 315–16, 321, and 336–7; and table A below, 327–33, 340. For a confirmation of this and all subsequent references to French coinage values see Denis Richet 'Le cours officiel des monnaies étrangères circulant en France au XVIe siècle *Revue historique* 225 (1961) 377–96.

213 / To Aldo Manuzio [Padua, December 1508?]

ERASMUS TO HIS FRIEND ALDUS

Confound those fine fellow-countrymen of yours, who do not allow me to enjoy the region of Italy I like more and more as time goes on! Tell Francesco to send back my treatise, for we are all leaving here in two days. Farewell, my dear Aldus. I shall explain to Bombace personally what you want him to be told in writing, and also how highly you esteem him. 5

Farewell.

214 / From William Warham [May 1509]

On the death of Henry VII, 21 April 1509, Erasmus' friends in England urged him to return and enjoy the patronage of the new king, whom he had long regarded as a potential patron. This letter is a fragment preserved in the MS *Collectanea* of Gerard Geldenhauer of Nijmegen in the Bibliothèque Royale, Brussels, and is apparently part of a letter from the archbishop offering additional inducements to Erasmus to return. Writing to Servatius Rogerus five years later, Erasmus referred to a gift from Warham of the precise amount mentioned here (cf Ep 296:135).

[BY WILLIAM, ARCHBISHOP OF CANTERBURY: EXTRACT FROM A LETTER ADDRESSED TO ERASMUS OF ROTTERDAM]

... I should like you to rest assured that on your first arrival in England you will receive from me a hundred and fifty nobles, on condition only that you agree to spend the rest of your life in England; but with the understanding 5

* * * * *

2 fine fellow-countrymen] Erasmus is probably referring to the threat of war against Venice about to begin as a result of the League of Cambrai.

214:4 a hundred and fifty nobles] As a monetary term 'noble' then had three possible meanings: (1) the gold ryal coin, worth officially 10s 0d sterling (1465–1526), which was popularly called the rose-noble because its design was similar to that of the previous, traditional gold nobles, except for the inclusion of the Yorkist, then Tudor, roses on both the obverse and reverse; (2) the gold angel coin, sometimes called the angel-noble, because it had the same official value of 6s 8d sterling (1465–1526) as previously placed on the traditional nobles from 1344 to 1464; (3) simply that same money-of-account value of the traditional noble = one-third of a pound sterling = one-half a mark. If the archbishop meant either of the latter two, as seems likely, he was thus offering Erasmus £50 0s 0d sterling = £72 10s 0d gros Flemish = £426 13s 4d tournois; but if he meant the first, then a sum of £75 0s 0d sterling = £108 2s 6d gros Flemish = £637 10s 0d tournois. Cf CWE I 312, 319, 325, 329, and 336–7; and tables A–F below, 327–45.

that you may nevertheless revisit your native land, your family, and others of your friends, on suitable occasions ...

[Copied from the original]

215 / From William Blount, Lord Mountjoy Greenwich, 27 May [1509]

This letter with its glowing and, as the event proved, exaggerated account of the patronage Erasmus might expect from the young king Henry VIII was probably the decisive factor in Erasmus' decision to return immediately to England. Coming from Mountjoy, who had been Henry's tutor and had already aroused in him an admiration for Erasmus, it carried conviction (cf Ep 206 introduction). There is reason to believe, however, that the letter was actually written by Andrea Ammonio, who was Mountjoy's secretary at the time (cf Ep 218 introduction). A manuscript copy of the letter in the Deventer Letter-book has the heading 'Andreas Ammonius' crossed out and 'Guilhelmus Montioius' substituted in Erasmus' handwriting. See facsimile in Allen I following 450. Later Erasmus wrote to Ammonio that he had recognized his style in the letter (cf Ep 283:85f).

WILLIAM MOUNTJOY TO ERASMUS OF ROTTERDAM

I am quite sure, my dear Erasmus, that, the moment you heard that our sovereign lord, Henry the Eighth (not *octavus* so much as *Octavius*) had succeeded to the throne on his father's death, every particle of gloom left your heart. For you are bound to repose the highest of hopes in a prince 5 whose exceptional and almost more than human talents you know so well, particularly since you are not merely his acquaintance but his friend, by virtue of the fact that he has written to you under his own hand, as he has not done to many others. And if you knew how courageously and wisely he is now acting, and what a passion he has for justice and honesty, and how 10 warmly he is attached to men of letters, then I should go so far as to swear upon my own head that with or without wings you would fly to us here to look at the new and lucky star. Oh, Erasmus, if you could only see how happily excited everyone is here, and how all are congratulating themselves on their prince's greatness, and how they pray above all for his long life, 15 you would be bound to weep for joy! Heaven smiles, earth rejoices; all is

* * * * *

215:3 *Octavius*] As a youth the future emperor Augustus was known by his family name of Octavius; under it he was adopted as son and heir by Julius Caesar.

8 his own hand] Ep 206

12 without wings] Cf *Adagia* III v 84.

milk and honey and nectar. Tight-fistedness is well and truly banished. Generosity scatters wealth with unstinting hand. Our king's heart is set not upon gold or jewels or mines of ore, but upon virtue, reputation, and eternal renown. Here is a mere sample: a few days ago, when he said that he longed to be a more accomplished scholar, I remarked, 'We do not expect this of you; what we do expect is that you should foster and encourage those who are scholars.' 'Of course,' he replied, 'for without them we could scarcely exist.' What better remark could be made by any king? But it is foolish of me to set out on the high seas in my frail bark; this responsibility is reserved for you. However the reason why I have decided to place these few scraps of compliment to his divine highness at the very beginning of my letter is just so that I may lose no time in abolishing any vestiges of depression left in your mind; or, if they have in fact all vanished, that I should reinforce, and steadily enlarge, your present hopes. 20 25 30

Now I come to your two letters to me, dated from Rome on 29 and 30 April. The first of these brought me at once pleasure and pain, because you quite properly confessed to your Mountjoy, in a friendly and comradely spirit, all your plans, thoughts, misfortunes, and worries. This was agreeable, but on the other hand I was distressed to find that you, who are so good a friend, and one to whom I wish particularly well, are the target of divers blows aimed by Fortune. I would offer you words of consolation, and urge you to be of good cheer, did not I believe that of your own accord, if you have any expectations at all, you must have no small hopes. You may well believe that your chapter of misery is drawing to a close; for you are about to approach a prince who can say 35 40

Take then these riches, and be first of bards.

So much for the first letter. But one thing I shall not omit, nor will I allow you to deceive yourself: whereas you say you owe much to me, I am on the contrary so much in your debt for giving me immortality through your writings that I believe I must declare myself insolvent. 45

Now for your second letter. You lament the loss, in one single mishap, of both my letter and your friend to whom it was entrusted. If only the losses were on an equal footing! But one of them can never be made up. My letter contained little, save that I had received your *Opus adagiorum*: your *opus*, I repeat, which is by all scholars agreed to be as brilliantly learned as it is 50

* * * * *

31 letters] Evidently the fact that we have so few letters from Italy does not mean that Erasmus did not write to his friends.

42 Take ... bards] Martial 8.55.11

50 *Opus adagiorum*] The edition of the *Adagia* published in Venice in September 1508 (cf Ep 211 introduction).

expressive in style, and, unless my affection for you deceives me, completely finished, and worthy indeed of the mighty labour and effort you bestowed on it; such labour as would have entitled you to the patronage, not of myself (whom you know to be of no great importance, and anyway a friend already) but of anyone you chose, no matter how eminent. But since in fact you have elected to regard me as a more suitable choice for the dedication of this distinguished work, I am immensely grateful; though how I can show my gratitude for making me, as I have said, immortal, I do not know. All the same I wish you had shown more restraint: for you laud, or rather load, me with such weighty compliments that I cannot acknowledge more than a fraction of them as my due. Who indeed, at least if he knew me, would endure being told that I was the most lettered of men, when I ought not even to be regarded as a student of letters? I should be greatly annoyed with you over this did I not wish at least to seem modest (another quality you credit me with), so that you shall not be convicted of misrepresentation on every count.

I also said in my letter that it was because of my many distractions and for certain other reasons which I did not venture to set down on paper that I had not previously replied to some of your letters; that this did not mean that my friendly attitude and feelings towards you had ever been altered or diminished, but rather had unexpectedly increased because of your absence. This, then, is what I put in the letters the loss of which you regret.

I now return to your great work which everyone is praising to the skies – especially my lord of Canterbury, who is so full of approval and admiration for it that I am quite unable to wrest it from his possession. You will of course ask me whether there is nothing but praise so far: well, the same archbishop promises you a benefice if you should return to England, and has just given me five pounds to send you for your travelling expenses, to which I have added another five. This is not to be regarded as a gift, for the word gift must be kept for other purposes, but to speed your journey to us and to keep you from prolonging our anguish at being without you. It remains for me to assure you when we meet that nothing is ever more delightful to me than to receive your letters, and that you must not think that you could ever offend me in any way.

I am distressed to hear that you have fallen sick in Italy. You know that

* * * * *

78 benefice] Warham did not make good the promise, thus conveyed through Mountjoy, until three years later, March 1512 (cf Ep 255 introduction).

79 five pounds] £5 0s 0d sterling = [15 angel-nobles = 10 rose-nobles] = £7 4s 2d gros Flemish = £42 10s 0d tournois, by gold-exchange values. Cf CWE I 328, 347; and tables A–F below, 327–45.

TOP

Ring (at left) containing an antique gem carved with the
head of a figure identified as Terminus,
gift of Alexander Stewart, archbishop of St Andrews,
to Erasmus in 1509,
with impression in wax (at right)

BOTTOM

Seal (at left) with Terminus figure,
plus the inscription 'Cedo nulli' (I yield to no one),
engraved for Erasmus at his own request,
with impression in wax (at right)

Erasmus adopted the Terminus figure as his personal emblem
and used both ring and seal to confirm his most important documents.

Historisches Museum, Basel

I never pressed you to go to Italy, but now that I observe the literary experience and personal reputation you have acquired there I am very sorry not to have accompanied you; for my belief is that such a high degree of scholarship and fame is worth the price of hunger, poverty, and illness, 90 even death itself. Enclosed with this letter you will find a bill of exchange for the money. So look after your health, and come back to us as soon as you can.

Yours with all his being, William Mountjoy
Greenwich palace, 27 May 95

216 / From Jacob Piso Rome, 30 June 1509

The circumstances under which this letter was written and Erasmus' movements at the time present some difficulties. He was certainly in Rome on Good Friday, 6 April (cf *Ciceronianus* ASD I 2 637) and on 30 April (cf Ep 215:31–2). It was probably between these two dates or possibly in May that Erasmus took his pupil Alexander Stewart on a trip to Naples (cf Allen Ep 604:2n; Allen I 62 lines 110ff; and Allen Ep 756:17ff). After this they returned to Rome and Alexander went on to Siena where he had been studying. Erasmus must have either accompanied or followed him, since he recalled in 1528 that it was at Siena that Alexander gave him the ring with the Terminus figure when he parted from him to return to Rome. Allen's suggestion in his introduction to this letter, that it was written while Erasmus was absent on the trip to Naples, seems unlikely, as he himself noted in Ep 604:2n, since Erasmus would scarcely have had time after the end of June to return from Naples and go to Siena and back to Rome before leaving for England. He was certainly in Rome after receiving the offer from England (cf Allen Ep 2465:47ff), probably around mid-June. The suggestion of some biographers that the letter was written after Erasmus left for England seems to be contradicted by the implication in lines 34ff that Erasmus had not yet decided to accept the English offer and had asked Piso's advice. There is in fact every reason to believe that Piso expected to see him again and that this was not a final farewell. A possible solution of the problem is that Erasmus had gone to Siena before the end of June to say goodby to Alexander who had been recalled to Scotland and that this accounted for his absence when Piso wrote. In 1522 Piso recalled having received a letter sent by Erasmus from Siena, possibly the one answered here (cf Allen Ep 1297:66; see also Allen Ep 1206:24ff).

Erasmus left Rome probably in mid-July. Travelling north by way of Bologna, he crossed the Alps by the Splügen pass to Constance, and from there travelled by way of Strasbourg down the Rhine to the Netherlands. There he visited friends at Antwerp and Louvain before crossing to England (cf Allen I 62 lines 216ff and Ep 266:15).

Jacob Piso (d 1527) was at this time Hungarian ambassador to Rome. He returned to Hungary in 1516 as tutor to King Louis II and later served on various embassies for the Hungarian court. He continued to exchange letters with Erasmus at intervals until shortly before his death (see Allen Epp 1662 and 1754).

PISO TO HIS FRIEND ERASMUS OF ROTTERDAM

My late reply – perhaps later than is reasonable – to the letters I received from you some time ago, most learned Erasmus, may seem to indicate that my friendship for you has grown utterly cold. So far is this from the truth, however, that I say with vehemence that not a moment passes when I do not think of you; for you have won a place in my heart from which neither lapse of time nor the wiles of an enemy could ever eject you. I repudiate and deny the assertion that I have ever enjoyed more the company of anyone whomsoever. I say nothing of the good it does me; though indeed I profited greatly by it, and shall be for ever in your debt, inasmuch as it was your civilized and truly educated conversation that began to recall me to literature, from which I had been, as it were, exiled, after a long spell of idleness. If only I might spend my life continually in your company! If I did so, I should perhaps live longer, as well as more happily. But since this cannot possibly come about, let us at least secure what little pleasure we can by exchanging letters. I would not urge you too seriously, in case you might perhaps think me in doubt of your good will towards me. In the same way I am unwilling to be challenged by you on this point, for of my own accord I am already eager before all else to fulfil my duty towards you.

I hope you will be prepared to pardon this delay; for indeed I was, as it happens, so beset with distracting business during that period that for several days on end I was simply not my own master, as Mouscron and Thomas (?Tommaso) will testify, since I am in the habit of living on the closest terms of intimacy with both of them whenever I am free to do so.

* * * * *

22 Mouscron] Jean de Mouscron (d 1535) studied at Padua about 1502. He was later archdeacon of Cambrai.

23 Thomas] Possibly Thomas Halsey (cf Ep 254 introduction) or Tommaso 'Fedra' Inghirami (1470–1516), the librarian of the Vatican, with whom Erasmus was intimate in Rome. For Inghirami cf Allen Epp 1347:264 and n, and 3032:220. In the latter passage the name is given as Petrus Phaedra, erroneously according to Allen. He is mentioned as an orator in the *Ciceronianus* (ASD I 2 637) under the name of Petrus Phaedrus. See also a letter of Beatus Rhenanus to Charles V, dated 1540 (Allen I 62 line 203).

Since you left, I have had only casual dealings with your friend Christopher. You know how outspoken I am; I think frankness is incomparably the first quality in friendship. And you know better than I what his attitude to you is, but it seems to me honest and straightforward. As for myself, I want you to be sure that I take second place to none in affection for you; would that I could prove this in act and deed, as I long to do. Certainly Fortune will never deprive me of heart, nor alter my feeling, which is ever with you and wholly devoted to you. Therefore use my services freely whenever you please. I shall not disappoint what you expect of me. 25 30

My best congratulations on your offer from England. I have not wit enough to advise you on the point (for I would not be a sow teaching Minerva). Look into your heart, but do not lose your head. It is certainly pleasant to be rich, but still more pleasant to be free. If Fortune now offers you both of these at once, grab with both hands. That genius of yours deserves every advantage, distinguished as it is by every excellent quality and by your enviable accomplishments in Greek and Latin literature, which are themselves deeply in your debt and will not for long allow their champion to languish in obscurity. Others may say what they wish, but I frankly confess that it was your works that shook me out of my torpid condition. Farewell, learned and delightful Erasmus. I am well. 35 40

Rome, 30 June 1509 45

I am waiting for you to send me the epitaph on that drunken little buffoon; do not disappoint me, I beg of you. Please extract something else about him from your other learned friends, and send it to me.

216A / From Daniele Scevola — Ferrara, 22 December 1509

The original manuscript of this letter was discovered in 1938 by Paul Oskar Kristeller in a miscellaneous collection of correspondence in the Biblioteca Nazionale in Florence and was published by him in *Renaissance News* 14

* * * * *

25–6 Christopher] Probably Christopher Fisher who was in Rome at this time (cf Ep 182 introduction).

35–6 sow teaching Minerva] Cf *Adagia* I i 40.

46 epitaph] This must be the 'Epitaphium scurrulae temulenti' (Reedijk 291), published in the first edition of the *Concio de puero Jesu*, 1511 (cf Ep 174 introduction). The drunkard referred to is evidently the Portuguese humanist and poet Hermicus (Enrique Cayado, d 1508), who died while Erasmus was in Rome and whose death is described in the adage 'Vinaria angina' (*Adagia* IV viii 2). There Erasmus tells how his death was caused by Christopher Fisher, who urged him to drink wine to cure his fever. Erasmus mentioned Hermicus in a more favourable context in the *Ciceronianus* ASD I 2.

(1961) 6–14. Little seems to be known about the writer, Kristeller having been able to find only one other reference to him, a letter in which Scevola identifies himself as a physician. Erasmus undoubtedly met him in Ferrara when he stopped there for a short time after leaving Padua in December 1508 (cf Epp 212 introduction and 211:53n). When Erasmus left Ferrara he was bound for Siena where his pupil Alexander Stewart was to study (cf Ep 216 introduction). He spent the next six months partly in Siena, partly in Rome, and by July 1509 had left Italy for England. As his letter indicates, Scevola had had no recent news of Erasmus and could only assume that he was still in Siena. The letter addressed to him there probably never reached him and this may account for its being found in a collection of letters in Florence.

TO THE SUBTLEST OF INTERPRETERS OF GREEK AND LATIN AND MOST DISTINGUISHED OF TEACHERS MASTER ERASMUS OF ROTTERDAM, MY INCOMPARABLE FRIEND. AT SIENA, IN THE COLLEGE OR UNIVERSITY

If all is well with you, so it is with me, except that in one point things are not as I could wish. Most anxious as I am for news of your welfare, I am most ignorant as regards both you and your affairs, and this disturbs me no less than would a similar uncertainty about affairs of my own. Had you sent me just one line in reply to my previous letter, I should know that you had not forgotten me. You must do what you will: even against your will I shall always be devoted to you, nor shall I cease to write to you even though I might know that you would never answer. About a year has now gone by during which I have heard no definite news of you, and so I beg you will either put an end to my uncertainty or find me some post in your part of the world where I may be in your neighbourhood and all may go well with you as my guide. Here it is all the war; the whole place is abandoned to Mars rather than the muses. If you put off writing, you will find yourself one day entertaining me as an unexpected guest; for desire for you and for the subjects that you study, in which I take my chief delight, spurs me on and draws me towards you. The rest I leave to Fortune. Mind you love me as a friend. Niccolò Leoniceno, for whom I have an undying veneration, also

5 10 15 20

* * * * *

21 Leoniceno] Niccolò Leoniceno of Vicenza (1428–1524) was a distinguished Latin and Greek scholar and physician who taught at Ferrara for some sixty years (cf Allen Ep 541:55n). Erasmus met him in Ferrara during his stop there, probably through Pace who had come to Ferrara to study under him (cf Ep 211:53n). Erasmus later spoke of Leoniceno with great respect as the foremost medical writer in Italy (cf Allen Ep 862:16), and in 1525 in a letter to Celio Calcagnini recalled meeting him in Ferrara and asked for news of him (Allen Ep 1576:33). Calcagnini's reply of 1 July 1525 informed him of Leoniceno's recent death (cf Allen Ep 1587:274).

sends you his respects. He has published a Latin version of Hippocrates' *Aphorisms* with Galen's commentary and his *Ars parva*, besides a number of notes on Pliny, already printed, which I expect you have seen. Aldus has arrived here and seems likely to take root. But we can now make our own what the pastoral poet sings: 25

Yet, Lycidas, our songs
Amongst the arms of Mars have no more force
Than have Chaonian doves when eagles stoop.

Have a care for your health, and do not forget me. 30

Your sincere friend Daniele Scevola
Ferrara, 22 December 1509

217 / From Paolo Bombace [Bologna, March 1511?]

This is an extract (cf Ep 210 introduction).

A LETTER FROM PAOLO TO ERASMUS

[He explains] that he was on the point of going to Siena; and he informs him that Aldus was at Ferrara, and on the point of moving to Bologna, and was in his own house; and that Carteromachus had gone to Pavia.

218 / To Andrea Ammonio Dover, 10 April [1511]

This letter, the first that survives of those written by Erasmus since December 1508 (Ep 213), ends the longest hiatus in the correspondence of Erasmus since his early days. Moreover no definite evidence has been found of his actual

* * * * *

22 Hippocrates] Leoniceno's Latin translation of *Galeni ars medicinalis et in Aphorismos Hippocratis cum ipsis aphorismis* and Galen's *Ars parva* were both published at Ferrara in 1509.

24 Pliny] Three of the four books of Leoniceno's edition of *Errores Plinii et aliorum qui de simplicibus medicaminibus scripserunt* were also published at Ferrara in 1509, the first book having already been published in 1492.

24 Aldus] The war following the League of Cambrai forced Aldus to flee from Venice to Ferrara (cf Ep 217).

27–9 Yet, Lycidas ... stoop] Virgil *Eclogues* 9.11–13

217:2 Siena] Bombace was going to the baths at Siena for his health (cf Ep 251).

4 Carteromachus] Scipione Fortiguerra, called Carteromachus, of Pistoia (1466–1515) was a close friend of Aldus and one of the founders of the Aldine Neacademia. Erasmus met him first in Bologna (cf Allen Ep 1347:226), then in Venice and Padua (cf Allen I 55 and 61), and later was on familiar terms with him in Rome (cf Allen Epp 1347:229, 3032:214ff). He was highly respected as a Greek scholar.

movements from his return to England in the summer of 1509 until this letter written on the way to Paris. Allen assumes that in the period before this journey he had been living with Ammonio (cf Ep 221:31) in More's house in Bucklersbury (cf line 20 and Ep 232:4). J.K. Sowards attempts to explain the gap in the correspondence partly by the fact that the friends with whom Erasmus was most closely related at this time were in London and so did not need letters, while he seems to have lost touch with his old friends on the continent (cf Ep 256:7–8n); but partly also by an unsupported surmise that Erasmus' letters during this period were so filled with derogatory comments on Julius II that he felt it advisable to suppress them ('The Two Lost Years of Erasmus: Summary, Review and Speculation' *Studies in the Renaissance* 9 (1962) 161–86).

Andrea Ammonio (de Harena; Italian 'della Rena') of Lucca (c 1478–1512), an Italian humanist who had come to England probably in 1504, had met Erasmus before his journey to Italy (cf Ep 283:85) and became one of his most intimate friends. In 1509 he was in the service of Mountjoy (cf Ep 215 introduction) and by July 1511 had become Latin secretary to Henry VIII. In February 1512 he was rewarded with a canonry in St Stephen's, Westminster. See C. Pizzi *Un amico d'Erasmo: l'umanista Andrea Ammonio* (Florence 1956), and E&C 215f.

ERASMUS TO ANDREA AMMONIO

At Dover I seized the opportunity to show your poems to our Maecenas, and he expressed general satisfaction with your talents and your learning. However he did not seem altogether pleased with your preface, for the very reasons that I guessed when I was with you, since I know his disposition 5 well enough. He is most averse to any suspicion of vanity, and accordingly advised me to omit the preface if I published the work, for the poem itself would serve as preface. Again, when you say in the poem 'What is done by the mass of men of your rank' and presently mention dicing and drinking, he is afraid that this passage may bring opprobrium both on you and on 10

* * * * *

2 poems] A book of verse dedicated to Mountjoy which Erasmus was taking to Paris to be printed. Mountjoy apparently found the preface too fulsome in his own praise and at Erasmus' suggestion Ammonio substituted another (Ep 220) with a more generalized praise of English generosity. For the contents of the volume see Allen's introduction to this letter. The poems are reprinted in C. Pizzi, ed *Andreae Ammonii carmina omnia* (Florence 1958).

2 our Maecenas] Mountjoy, with whom Erasmus was travelling

7 poem] The opening verses are addressed to Mountjoy.

him, as if he were glad to have men of his rank censured. If you are changing the preface, I wish you would add just a brief mention of the eclogue dedicated to him; I have come to perceive that he would like this, for the sake of its praises of England and of the king, in which he takes especial pleasure. I shall await a letter from you on this subject, which you can send to Josse Bade; for I will not change a single point in your compositions without first ascertaining your wishes. Farewell, dear friend. 15

Please give my warm regards to More. Also please congratulate Linacre on my behalf, for at the archbishop's I heard something which I was not sorry to hear. Kindly ask More to see that the books that I left in my room are sent back to Colet. 20

Dover, 10 April [1515]

219 / To Andrea Ammonio Paris, 27 April [1511]

Erasmus had evidently not received a reply to Ep 218 which, indeed, seems never to have reached its destination. Even this letter was not delivered until 16 May (cf Ep 221:26). Erasmus stayed in Paris directing the printing of the *Moria* (cf Ep 222 introduction) until June and living in the house of an Englishman named Eden in the Rue Saint Jean de Beauvais on the left bank. There he was waited on by young Stephen Gardiner, later bishop of Winchester and a prominent royal official, as Gardiner reminded him in 1526, recalling at the same time how impressed he was by the number of Greek and Latin books Erasmus bought (cf Allen Ep 1669 and E&C 101).

ERASMUS TO ANDREA AMMONIO

Please reply to me as soon as possible, dear Andrea, saying what you wish done about the preface to your poems; for Mountjoy did not like it at all. Write a note on the proverb you showed me in England, as my work will be reprinted here in Paris. The Aldine editions are being offered for sale, and 5

* * * * *

12 eclogue] The principal poem in the book is a bucolic filled with praise of England.

16 Bade] See Ep 183 introduction.

19 Linacre] Thomas Linacre (cf Ep 118:27). He had just been given the living of Hawkhurst in Kent by Archbishop Warham.

219:4 my work] The revised and enlarged edition of the *Adagiorum chiliades* intended to be printed by Bade (cf Ep 263:22n) are fairly expensive too, at one and a half écus; they were dearer in Rome. Any who wish to have them should apply to that Italian who has a monopoly on the sale of Aldus' books.

Please be sure to give my greetings to the bishop of Durham. I shall write to him when I have time and a more reliable messenger. 10

Paris, 27 April [1510]

220 / From Andrea Ammonio to William Blount, Lord Mountjoy

[London, c 18 May 1511]

This is evidently the substitute preface to the edition of Ammonio's poems (cf Epp 218:2n and 221:3).

ANDREA AMMONIO OF LUCCA TO THE ILLUSTRIOUS WILLIAM MOUNTJOY, GREETINGS

Where I could not return a favour, illustrious Mountjoy, I have always desired at the least to be, and to be thought, grateful at heart. Accordingly, since I have enjoyed every sort of kindness both from you who are a 5 latter-day Maecenas and from many other liberal patrons of literature in your country, a country which has nurtured me for so many years that it would seem not improper if I called it my own, and since poverty, which, as has been said, makes many men ungrateful, barred me from other means of repaying my debt of gratitude, I entered upon the one way that lay open to 10 me: I undertook to eulogize those to whom I thought I owed the most – a service which, says Pliny the younger, was once so highly valued that those who had written encomiums on men or cities were habitually decorated with rewards of honour or money. Look at Choerilus, who at Alexander's hands 15

For verse unkempt, and misbegotten too,
Received gold philips from the royal mint.

Nor did Publius Cornelius Scipio Africanus disdain to make a close friend

* * * * *

6 at one and a half écus] Possibly priced in terms of the old écus d'or à la couronne (1475) as a common money-of-account value; or of the current écus d'or au soleil (1475–1516). If the former, the price would be £2 12s 6d tournois; if the latter, £2 14s 4½d tournois [= 9s 3d gros Flemish = 6s 4½d sterling]. Cf CWE I 315–16, 321, 336–7; and table A below, 327–33, 340.

7 Italian] Perhaps Francesco of Padua (cf Epp 221:19, 240:57n)

9 Durham] Thomas Ruthall (cf Epp 192 introduction, 236:39, 243:46)

220:12 Pliny the younger] *Epistles* 3.21.3

14 Choerilus] Cf Horace *Epistles* 2.1.233–4.

of Ennius, however much in art uncouth his poetry was: he allowed him to take part, crowned with the laurel, in his own supreme triumph, and at the end to be interred in the tomb of the Cornelii. But, to say no more of mortal men, what reward does God require for his measureless benefits towards man? Why, only praise. With what sacrifice does he bid us sacrifice to him? With none other than praise; because, to be sure, this alone is our own gift, while all others come from him.

Such, then, is the gratitude I have tried to show to England my foster-mother, to you, and to my other patrons. What I have extolled – not adequately, but as I might – are your blessings and your virtues. But if I have bestowed little grace of style on my splendid theme, you are aware of the saying 'in great endeavours, 'tis enough to will.' I venture to dedicate these trifles to you, such as they are, because I know you for one who is above disdain, and because I have seen that you, with your great and amazing friendliness, think of my nonsense as being not wholly worthless. So pray accept it, such as it is, with that good humour with which you are wont to accept poor and simple gifts; and, as is your habit, please have regard to the intention of the giver, not to the gift he offers. Farewell.

221 / From Andrea Ammonio London, 19 May [1511]

ANDREA AMMONIO TO ERASMUS THE THEOLOGIAN

I can see, most kind Erasmus, that, as you with your penetrating acumen had divined, the preface to my trifles is not at all acceptable to Mountjoy. For that reason I am sending you a second: newborn as it is, it does seem to me less bad than the former one, and if you should deem it worthy of your judicious corrector's file, I should venture to hope that it might become good. But if your revising hand declines to undertake this kind of task, I have resolved to strive no more to please you with it, whereas I would risk any danger, even life itself, where your interest was concerned. However this may be, I earnestly commend to you the small name and fame that I have. If you judge these trifles likely to bring pity on me, cut them down in any way you like and, in fine, take thought for your dear friend's reputation. I know your wisdom in my cause exceeds my own, and have no doubt

* * * * *

19 however much in art uncouth] Ovid *Tristia* 2.424

21 tomb] Cf Cicero *Pro Archia* 9.22.

30 'in great ... will'] Propertius 2.10.6; cf *Adagia* II viii 55.

33 my nonsense ... worthless] Catullus 1.3–4, 8

that you will do as much: for I know what a good friend you are, and hence will 'no word further add.' 15

I am delighted that your *Adagia* is to be reprinted there, although I should prefer copies from Aldus' press because of the elegance of both his Latin and his Greek type. But I do not understand who is the Italian to whom you refer me, for I do not know any Italian bookseller here. However I shall make careful enquiries, for I am exceedingly anxious to buy a copy. I 20 have commended you most conscientiously to the bishop of Durham. He was pleased with the message, sends you his thanks, and asked me when you planned to return: I replied 'soon, as far as I could guess.' But I am annoyed with the messenger to whom you gave your letter, addressed to me: for I believe it was his fault that, though you sent it on 27 April, it was 25 not delivered to me until 16 May; so that I am very much afraid my reply may already be too late.

As for English news, there is hardly anything worth the hearing except about the king, who every day shows himself in a more godlike guise; but this is old news to you. You yourself are really dreadfully missed; 30 since people know I was a close companion of yours I am being besieged with 'What of Erasmus? When will he come back? He is quite the sun of our age. If only he might come back!' – and many other such remarks, which I am unwilling to set down in case you should afterwards tax me with one or other of them. Our very sweet friend More, and his most agreeable wife, 35 who never mentions you without blessing your name, and his children and entire household are extremely well. Master Linacre has a benefice, for which I suppose all the muses have offered thanks to Fortune. Your Leucophaeus sends greetings. Look after your health and come back safe to us; and also give my greetings to our very dear Polygraphus, and tell him by 40 no means to observe the contract.

London, 19 May [1515]

* * * * *

15 'no word further add'] Horace *Satires* 1.1.121

35 wife] More's first wife. She died shortly after this (see Chambers 94ff, 118ff).

37 Linacre] Cf Ep 218:19n.

39 Leucophaeus] Thomas Grey (cf Ep 66 introduction)

40 Polygraphus] Allen notes Nichols' suggestion (II, 15) that Richard Croke (Ep 227:31n) is meant here. He was in Paris and correcting the *Moria* for the press. But Allen also suggests that Bade might possibly be intended.

222 / To Thomas More [Paris?], 9 June [1511]

Immediately after his return to England from Italy in 1509 Erasmus wrote the *Moriae encomium* in More's house while awaiting the arrival of his books and while being, as he said, prevented by an attack of the kidney-stone from doing any more serious work (cf Allen Ep 337:126ff). He did not publish it, however, until his trip to Paris in 1511 to see it through the press. His assertion that he did not think it worth editing and that it was actually edited by Richard Croke (cf Ep 227:31n) is probably no more than a conventional modest fiction (cf Allen I 19 lines 6ff). This preface dedicating the work to Thomas More was printed in the first edition (Paris: Gilles de Gourmont for Jean Petit n.d.) and in all the numerous editions which appeared in rapid succession from various presses.

ERASMUS OF ROTTERDAM TO HIS FRIEND THOMAS MORE

As I was returning lately from Italy to England, in order to avoid squandering upon vulgar and uneducated talk the whole time I had to spend on horseback, I sometimes preferred inwardly to savour some memory, either of the studies you and I shared once, or of the learned and congenial friends 5 whom I had left behind in this country. Of these you were always one of the very first to come to mind. Indeed my delight in the thought of you when you were absent was like the pleasure I used to take in your company; my life upon it if I have ever in my life enjoyed a sweeter experience than that. Well then, since I thought I must at all costs occupy myself somehow, and 10 since that particular time seemed hardly suitable for serious scholarly writing, I decided to compose a trifling thing, *Moriae encomium*. You will ask how some Pallas Athene came to put that idea into my head. First, I was inspired by your surname of More, which is as close in form to *Moria* (Folly) as you are in fact remote from folly itself – to which, as all agree, you are a 15 complete stranger. Second, I guessed that this flight of fancy might find especial favour in your eyes since you take immense pleasure in frolics of this kind, by which I mean those that are neither crude, which I hope to be the case, nor altogether devoid of wit, and as a rule you play the part of a kind of Democritus in human life at large. Yet, though as a rule you disagree 20 widely with vulgar opinions because of that singularly penetrating wit of yours, nevertheless your affability and kindness are so extraordinary that

* * * * *

20 Democritus] The ancient philosopher who laughed at human follies, while his counterpart Heraclitus wept.

Thomas More
Hans Holbein the Younger

you are both able and pleased to play with everyone the part of a man for all seasons. So I beg you to accept this short essay as a souvenir of your comrade, but also to acknowledge and cherish it, inasmuch as it has been 25 dedicated to you and is no longer mine, but yours.

For there will perhaps be some wrangling critics who will falsely assert either that these trifles are too airy to be quite suitable to a theologian's pen, or that they are more sarcastic than suits the modesty of a Christian. They will loudly accuse me of imitating the Old Comedy or some kind of Lucianic 30 satire, and of attacking the whole world with my teeth. Now as for those who find the triviality and humour of the theme offensive, I should like them to reflect that this is no vein of my own invention, but reflects the habitual practice of great writers of the past; inasmuch as Homer, all those centuries ago, wrote in jesting vein his Battle of the Frogs and Mice, Virgil 35 of the Gnat and the *Moretum*, Ovid of the Walnut; in addition encomiums on Busiris were written by Polycrates and his critic Isocrates, on injustice by Glaucon, on Thersites and the quartan ague by Favorinus, on Baldness by Synesius, on the Fly and the Art of Being a Parasite by Lucian; and finally Seneca wrote a playful apotheosis of Claudius the emperor, Plutarch a 40 jesting dialogue of Gryllus with Ulysses, Lucian and Apuleius an 'Ass' apiece, and someone or other the 'Testament of Grunnius Corocotta the piglet,' mentioned also by St Jerome.

So let them make up stories about me if they wish, alleging that I have sometimes played draughts for recreation, or ridden a hobby-horse if they 45 would rather; for, considering that every way of living is permitted its appropriate recreation, it would be monstrously unfair to allow no diversion whatever to those who pursue literary studies, especially if nonsense leads to serious matters and absurd themes are treated in such a way that the reader whose senses are not wholly dulled gains somewhat more profit 50 from these than from some men's severe and showy demonstrations, as when someone delivers a laborious patchwork speech in praise of rhetoric or philosophy, another expatiates on the virtues of some ruler, another

* * * * *

23–4 man for all seasons] *Adagia* I iii 86

24–5 souvenir of your comrade] Catullus 12.13

36 *Moretum*] Untranslatable as a title. It is defined in Lewis and Short as 'a country dish composed of garlic, red vinegar, oil, etc.'

43 Jerome] *Commentaries on Isaiah* 12, init

45 a hobby-horse] Horace *Satires* 2.3.248

48 nonsense] Horace *Ars poetica* 451

49 absurd themes] Literally 'goat's wool'; *Adagia* I iii 53; cf Ep 103:37.

50 senses ... dulled] Cf Horace *Epodes* 12.3.

recommends opening a crusade against the Turks, another utters predictions about the future, and another coins quibbling questions on some 55 point of goat's wool. For, as there is nothing more frivolous than to handle serious topics in a trifling manner, so also there is nothing more agreeable than to handle trifling matters in such a way that what you have done seems anything but trifling. Others will judge me; but unless my vanity altogether deceives me, I have written a Praise of Folly without being altogether 60 foolish.

Now to reply to the peevish complaint that I am sarcastic. Men's intellects have always been granted freedom to exercise the play of wit upon human life at large, with impunity so long as this freedom does not turn into furious rage. I am therefore the more surprised at those delicate ears 65 which nowadays can scarcely tolerate anything any more except the usual honorific addresses. You can also find some whose notions of religion are so perverse that they could sooner endure the most dreadful abuse of Christ than the very slightest jest which might cast an aspersion on pope or prince, especially if it touches their bread and butter, that is, their income. And yet 70 if someone censures the lives men live in such a way that he does not denounce a single person by name, tell me if he appears to bite and worry mankind, or rather to teach and admonish them? In any case, look at all the points on which I censure myself. Besides, one who leaves no class of human beings unscathed appears angry not with any person in particular 75 but with every kind of vice. So, if anyone arises to cry out that he is hurt, he shows either that his conscience is pricking him or at least that he is afraid. St Jerome let himself go in this way with much greater freedom and incisiveness, sometimes not even sparing names. For myself, apart from the fact that I name no names at all, I have also exercised such restraint of my 80 pen that the intelligent reader will easily realize that my aim was to amuse and not to criticize. Never have I dabbled, after the fashion of Juvenal, in the hidden cesspool of iniquities; and I have taken care to examine practices which are to be laughed at rather than detested. If, again, there are some who cannot be appeased even by these arguments, they should at least 85 remember that it is creditable to be lashed by Folly's tongue; for when I brought her on stage I had to make her speak in character. But why do I say this to you, a lawyer of such eminence at the bar that you can present brilliantly even a case whose brilliance leaves much to be desired? Farewell, eloquent More; and put up a stout defence of *Moria* your kinswoman. 90

From the country, 9 June [1508]

* * * * *

59 vanity] Erasmus uses the Greek word for self-love; cf *Adagia* I iii 92.

70 bread and butter] *Adagia* III vi 31

223 / From Paolo Bombace [Siena? June 1511?]

An abstract of the original letter. Erasmus' letter of August 1511 (cf Ep 226:2) may have been a reply. Bombace was evidently making the visit to Siena announced in Ep 217 and commented on in Ep 251:3. The insertion of 'Desiderio' by the editor, Fantuzzi (cf Ep 210 introduction), is an obvious error.

A letter from Paolo Bombace to Erasmus to the effect that he [Desiderio] was at Siena, and Aldus with him – who had previously been at Bologna in his own house; and that there was talk there about the Academy which the said Aldus wished to found, which seemed to resemble Plato's Republic. He reports to him that his enemy Musurus spoke ill of his *Adagia*, and said that 5
the passages of the Greek authors contained in them were ill-translated.

224 / From Jakob Wimpfeling Strasbourg, 10 August 1511

This letter was appended to Schürer's edition of the *Moria* (Strasbourg August 1511). Jakob Wimpfeling (1450–1528) of Schlettstadt was a devoted but conservative humanist. Born in 1450, he belonged to the older generation of German humanists. He taught at Heidelberg 1469–83 and spent his later years in Strasbourg and Schlettstadt. His *Opera selecta* are being edited by Otto Herding (Munich 1965–). See L.W. Spitz *The Religious Renaissance of the German Humanists* (Cambridge, Mass. 1963) 41–60, and K.P. Hasse *Die deutsche Renaissance* (Meerane 1920) 122–30.

TO DESIDERIUS ERASMUS OF ROTTERDAM GREETINGS FROM JAKOB WIMPFELING OF SCHLETTSTADT; FROM GERMAN TO GERMAN, FROM THEOLOGIAN TO THEOLOGIAN, FROM PUPIL TO MASTER

Do not believe anyone who tells you, my dear Rotterdam, that when I wrote 5

* * * * *

223:3 Academy] The Neacademia, a rather informal group of Greek scholars, had been founded by Aldus at Venice in 1500 or 1501, but he continued to seek support and a permanent home for it from various princes (cf D.J. Geanakoplos *Greek Scholars in Venice* Cambridge, Mass. 1962, 128ff).

5 Musurus] Marcus Musurus (c 1470–1517), a Greek from Crete, was a member of the Aldine Academy and helped edit a number of Greek texts for Aldus. He was appointed professor of Greek at Padua in 1503 and at Venice in 1512. Erasmus named him among the Greeks who had helped him in preparing the *Adagia*. See the adage 'Festina lente,' II i 1 (Phillips 186); cf Epp 269:56; Allen Ep 512:8; and LB IX 1137C (cf Geanakoplos 111–66). It is not clear why Bombace should have regarded Musurus as Erasmus' enemy, since Erasmus' references to him are always cordial.

my defence of the theology of the moderns against Philomusus I meant to have a dig at your *Moria*. I think that for younger men whose minds are still lively Aristotle's famous philosophy and subtle logic, and also his metaphysics, together with the modern theologians, are not entirely without their value both for sharpening the mind and for destroying heresies. 10 All the same, I cannot approve of devoting an entire lifetime to them exclusively, neglecting the teaching of Christ and Paul and the four lights of the church, since such a blind love of the moderns, especially a particular modern of one's own order, has forced some people to suffer fire, and to such an extent estranged others from Augustine, Gregory, Leo, William of 15 Paris, and Jean Gerson, that they seem unfitted not only for history and canon law and preaching, but even for speaking and arguing a case, either in writing or by word of mouth. And, however great the need in the civil or ecclesiastical courts, for the business of contracts, prebends, and the cure of

* * * * *

6 defence] Wimpfeling's *Contra turpem libellum Philomusi defensio theologiae scholasticae et neotericorum* (s.l.n.d.) with preface dated 1510. He had been moved to defend modern theology against the claims of poetry by the immoderate attack upon the aged Ingolstadt theologian Georg Zingel, launched by Philomusus (see following note) who posed as the champion of humanism. In this letter Wimpfeling makes it clear that he does not include the *Moria* among the humanist works he deplored but, on the contrary, was in full agreement with its satire upon the pretentions of those theologians who devote themselves exclusively to medieval metaphysics and logic-chopping while neglecting the Scriptures and the patristic writings.

6 Philomusus] Jakob Locher (1471–1528) was known as Philomusus, the friend of the Muses, a title he is said to have acquired while studying in Italy. He had been a student of Conrad Celtis, whom he succeeded as professor of poetry at Ingolstadt in 1498. He had previously been in Freiburg, where Maximilian made him poet laureate in 1497. He published editions of the classics and numerous other works.

12 four lights] The four Fathers of the Latin church: Ambrose, Augustine, Jerome, and Gregory the Great. 'Ecclesiae sanctae lumen' occurs in the *commune doctorum* of the *Breviarum Romanum*.

14 fire] If burning at the stake is actually meant, the rest of the sentence is anticlimactic. It seems more likely to refer to having one's books burnt.

15–16 William of Paris] Guillaume d'Auvergne, called William of Paris, was a thirteenth-century Realist at the University of Paris and bishop of Paris in 1228.

16 Gerson] Jean Charlier de Gerson (1363–1429) was one of the most distinguished Parisian theologians of the late middle ages and a leader of the movement for ecclesiastical reform which culminated in the Council of Constance.

souls, and the conduct of causes in general councils, there is no one who can employ their help successfully. 20

Let it be granted that it is proper and expedient for them to lecture on quaestiones, read and debate them, and ponder subtleties; let it be granted that it is proper for them to set a learned man of their own religious order and his opinion above a writer of another persuasion, whether from pride or fanaticism. But it is also expedient and proper that the ancient, leading lights of our faith should by no means be suppressed. If I mistake not, my view is shared to some extent by Aulus Gellius in the twenty-second chapter of his ninth book, where he quotes a long and well-expressed opinion from Plato's *Gorgias*. In the same way my friend Oecolampadius, who agrees with me, revolts against those divines who reduce theology to a mere froth of words and, as Gerson says, to a wintry mathematics and who, while they very frequently cite the accepted opinions of Aristotle, Averroes, and Avicenna, adduce no evidence from the law and the prophets, or from the Gospel or the apostolic writings, and, while they brandish a frail shaft in defence of their own position, leave in the sheath that invincible sword, sent from Heaven, on which they could rely. Even though Oecolampadius himself approves of scholastic theology at all points, still it has seemed to him that a goodly number of its devotees become blear-eyed like Rachel, and barren like Leah; as regards their affections, swallowing the food of virtue which they cannot digest, so that as regards their intellect too bad sight must follow; wherein they forget that God shall destroy their knowledge, that knowledge puffeth up but charity edifieth – so much is evident from the causes of offence that arise daily. 25 30 35 40

Accordingly, dear Erasmus, if your attitude and mine are examined aright, neither will your *Moria* seem to conflict with my *Defensio*, nor my *Defensio* with your *Moria*. I have read the *Moria* with great enthusiasm, my desirable Desiderius, and persuaded my fellow-townsman (and kinsman 45

* * * * *

28 Aulus Gellius] *Noctes Atticae* 10.22.3–23; not the ninth book

30 Oecolampadius] Johann Hussgen of Weinsberg (1482–1531) hellenized his name as Oecolampadius, the name by which he is generally known. He was a student of Wimpfeling's at Heidelberg. He later studied Greek and Hebrew and helped Erasmus with his edition of the New Testament. He eventually became one of the leaders of the Reformation at Basel. See E. Staehelin *Das theologische Lebenswerk Johannes Oecolampads* (Leipzig 1939).

37 sword] 'the sword of the spirit which is the word of God': Ephesians 6:17

40 Rachel] Wimpfeling seems to be confused here. It was Rachel who was barren and Leah who had weak eyes (Genesis 29:17, 31).

43 knowledge puffeth up but charity edifieth] 1 Corinthians 8:1

too), Matthias Schürer, to print it afresh so that a great host of my countrymen might become zealous readers of your works, and acquire pleasure and profit from that source. Farewell in the Lord. 50

From Strasbourg, 19 August in this year of grace 1511

225 / To John Colet Queens' College, Cambridge, 24 August 1511

Erasmus left Paris by the middle of June (cf Ep 256:23n) and returned to London, where he fell seriously ill with the sweating sickness (cf Ep 226:5n). He had barely recovered by mid-August when he had to go to Cambridge to take a position especially created for him as lecturer in Greek which John Fisher had persuaded him to accept (cf E&C 102).

ERASMUS TO HIS FRIEND COLET

If my bad luck can make you laugh, my dear Colet, there is plenty of material at hand for your amusement. Apart from the earlier happenings in London, my servant's horse was fearfully lame, since the carrier changed the horse Bullock had sent. Then there was nothing to eat the whole journey 5 through. The following day unending rain, right up to dinner-time; after dinner thunder and lightning and showers; three times my horse fell headlong to the ground. Bullock has studied the stars and says Jupiter is rather annoyed with us. Already I think he is right. I see traces of Christian poverty; and I entertain so very little hope of any gain that I am sure I shall 10 have to spend, here and now, every penny I can squeeze from my patrons.

There is a physician here, a fellow-countryman of mine, who relies on the fifth essence to promise amazing feats: he makes old men young and

* * * * *

49 Schürer] Matthias Schürer (1470–1519) of Schlettstadt began printing in 1508 and published a number of works by Erasmus and other humanists. He printed the *Moria* in August 1511, October 1512, and November 1514.

225:5 Bullock] Henry Bullock, a young fellow of Queens' College, was Erasmus' only friend in Cambridge before his arrival. They may have met in 1506 and certainly after Erasmus' return from Italy in London where Bullock was well known in the Colet-More-Grocyn circle (see E&C 218; Emden BRUC 105).

8 Jupiter] Presumably Pluvius the rain god

12 physician] Probably a Dr Bont whose death Erasmus mentions in Ep 275. He was apparently an alchemist who was seeking the fifth element, *quinta essentia*, supposed to be the substance of which the heavenly bodies were composed.

brings the dead to life. This gives me hope that I may grow young again, if only I can get a taste of this fifth essence. If this comes my way, I shall not be altogether sorry I came. As for earning something, I see no prospect. What can I filch from people who haven't a rag to their backs? – I who am far from brazen, and yet have had Mercury against me from birth. 15

Farewell, my kind counsellor and teacher. When I begin to lecture, I shall report how it goes, to give you even more occasion for laughter. 20

Cambridge, Queen's College, St Bartholomew's Day 1511

I may even begin to tackle your own St Paul: you see how brave your Erasmus is becoming! Farewell once more.

226 / To Andrea Ammonio Queens' College, Cambridge, 25 August 1511

ERASMUS OF ROTTERDAM TO HIS FRIEND ANDREA AMMONIO

I am sending you a letter I have addressed to Bombace. So far there is nothing new to tell you about my own affairs, except that the journey was very uncomfortable, and that my health is still a little shaky as a result of that sweating sickness I told you of. I expect I shall stay at this college for several days anyway. Being anxious to devote my chief attention to getting well, I have not yet given an audience the chance to hear me. The beer in this place suits me not at all and the wines are not quite satisfactory either. If you are in a position to arrange for a small cask of Greek wine, the best obtainable, to be sent to me here, you will have done what will make your friend perfectly happy. But quite dry wine please. You need not worry at all about the payment; I will even have this sent in advance, if you wish. I am already beginning to enjoy the first of the advantages we derive from those most holy bulls – by dying of thirst! You can guess the rest. And I have not even made the crossing yet. Farewell dearest Ammonio. 5 10 15

From Queens' College, the morrow of Bartlemas 1511

* * * * *

22 your own St Paul] Cf Ep 108:76n.

226:2 Bombace] The letter referred to is probably an answer to Ep 223.

5 sweating sickness] Erasmus had been so ill with this disease in London just before coming to Cambridge that rumours of his death had spread as far afield as Mechlin (cf Ep 244A:5f) and Bologna (cf Ep 251:1f).

14 bulls] For possible explanations of this enigmatic reference see Allen's note. The final line of this letter is even more enigmatic, and no explanation has been found.

227 / To John Colet

Cambridge, 13 September [1511]

ERASMUS TO HIS FRIEND COLET

I am enclosing at your request the office of Chrysostom, and also a letter in which, unless I am mistaken, there will be things you will not approve of, because you despise systems and books of rules, whereas I allow them some importance, especially in a teacher. Do not be in a hurry to believe anyone about Linacre. I have solid grounds for my conviction that he holds you in the highest regard, and is not greatly upset by your rejection of his grammar – though it is human nature to be passionately attached to one's own writings, just as parents are to their children. But if in fact this is rather a sore point with him, then you will have to play a skilful part so as to conceal your feelings and avoid reopening that particular wound; and win him back by your looks and your obliging behaviour rather than by making excuses, especially excuses made through other people. In this way any injury that rankles in him will gradually pass away with time. But how excessively impertinent I am to say these things to you, like the proverbial sow teaching Minerva.

So far I have not come across anyone I consider suitable to be second master in your school, but I shall continue to make enquiries, and as soon as I find one I shall let you know. Farewell, best of teachers.

Sometimes I have to do battle here on your behalf against the Thomists and Scotists; but more about them when we meet. I am beginning a translation of Basil's commentary on Isaiah, a work which delights me. I

* * * * *

2 office of Chrysostom] Erasmus's translation from the Greek of the Mass of St John Chrysostom. It was published much later in Paris, first in the Chevallon Chrysostom of 1536, and then separately by Wechel in 1537, and in Froben's edition of Chrysostom's *Opera* of 1539.

2 a letter] The *De ratione studii*, which is cast in the form of a letter (cf Epp 66 introduction 230:3)

4 you despise] Possibly a reference to the sentiments expressed in Colet's *Accidence*, written about 1509 (cf E&C 108, n7).

6 Linacre] Thomas Linacre (cf Ep 118:27n) had written a Latin grammar for St Paul's School, which Colet rejected. A more elaborate work, *De emendata structura Latini sermonis* (London: Pynson 1524; STC 15634), later established his reputation. Both books were widely used especially on the continent for many years.

16 sow teaching Minerva] See Ep 216:35–6n.

17–18 second master] There was a high master, as the headmaster of St Paul's is still called, and a second master (cf Ep 230:19).

22 Isaiah] Cf Ep 229 introduction.

shall give a sample of it to the bishop of Rochester and find out whether he is willing to give me a little something by way of emolument for the toil it causes me. I know very well you are smiling at that and saying, what a beggar! Yes, and I hate myself too. I have quite made up my mind that I must either acquire some position or other to relieve me of this beggarly role or else imitate Diogenes in a thoroughgoing fashion. Farewell again. 25

Cambridge, 13 September

If you have at your disposal any fund entrusted to you for making grants, I beg you to send a few nobles to Richard Croke, a former servant-pupil of Grocyn's, who is at present a student of the humanities at Paris. Unless I am quite mistaken, he is a young man of good promise, one on whom you would be justified in bestowing assistance. Farewell once more, my one best teacher. 30 35

Cambridge, [1513]

228 / To Andrea Ammonio Queens' College, Cambridge [16 September] 1511

ERASMUS TO HIS FRIEND AMMONIO

My dear Andrea, you have raised my spirits twice over not only by sending the very welcome consignment of wine but by adding to it something far more welcome – a letter, which absolutely tastes of your mind and character; and there never was, and never will be, anything more delicious in my opinion than that. So I have a double reason for thanking you. You are indignant at the mention of payment; now I was certainly not unaware that you had a heart generous enough to grace a royal fortune; but I calculated that you would probably send me a rather large cask, one that would last several months, and even the one you did send was larger than any decent man could accept as a free gift. 5 10

* * * * *

23 Rochester] John Fisher (cf Ep 229 introduction)

31 nobles] Erasmus probably meant the Tudor gold angel-nobles, as he did subsequently in Epp 240A:11, 248:40, and 270:30, or their equivalent value in money-of-account (6s 8d sterling); but possibly gold ryals or rose-nobles worth 10s 0d. Cf Epp 214:4n, 248:40n, and tables A and B below, 327–37.

31 Croke] Richard Croke (c 1489–1558), after studying at Cambridge and with Grocyn probably in London, went to Paris in 1511 where he was a pupil of both Erasmus and Girolamo Aleandro. He may have aided Erasmus in the printing of the *Moria* (cf Ep 222 introduction). On his return to England in 1512 Aleandro urged Erasmus to continue to act as his instructor and patron (cf Ep 256:30ff). He became Greek lecturer at Cambridge in 1518.

I had a hearty laugh over the Greek note. It would be hard-hearted indeed of me not to forgive More, plunged as he is in such important business.

I am most surprised that you sit on your nest so unendingly, and that you never fly away. If you should ever be disposed to pay another visit to this university, you will be warmly welcomed here by many people, especially by me. As for your invitation to me to come back to your neighbourhood if my illness continues, I cannot see anything to attract me in London, except the company of two or three of my friends. But let us speak about this another time. I hear the mighty Julius is dead. 15 20

Farewell, dear Ammonio, and please write to me often; you cannot do anything that would please me more.

Cambridge, from Queens' College, [17 August] 1511

229 / To John Fisher Cambridge, [September 1511]

John Fisher, bishop of Rochester, had been friendly to Erasmus who had hopes of still more patronage from him. Specifically Erasmus hoped for some money in return for the presentation to Fisher of a translation of St Basil's commentary on Isaiah (cf Ep 227:21ff). This letter first appeared as the preface to *Basilii in Esaiam Commentariolus* printed in the Froben edition of the *Enchiridion militis christiani* (Basel 1518).

John Fisher (1469–1535) was vice-chancellor of Cambridge University in 1501 and chancellor in 1504–35. Through his influence the Lady Margaret Beaufort, mother of Henry VII, whose confessor he was, founded professorships of divinity at Oxford and Cambridge and two colleges, Christ's and St John's, at Cambridge. He was made bishop of Rochester in 1504 (cf Emden BRUC 229). He remained a friend and patron of Erasmus for many years.

* * * * *

16 another visit] It is not known when Ammonio visited Cambridge. It may have been with Erasmus in 1506 (cf Allen I app VI).

21 Julius] Julius II was taken ill 17 August 1511 and for several days was believed to be dying. The city was in a turmoil; the cardinals began to lay plans for a conclave; and couriers were sent out in all directions to carry news of the pope's death (E. Rodocanachi *Le pontificat de Jules II* (Paris 1928); Creighton IV 134f). Erasmus' ironical reference to the pope as 'Julius Maximus' and again (Ep 233:6) as 'invictissimus Julius' was echoed in a mordant epigram on Julius written at about this time and sent to More (*Opuscula* 36f; Reedijk 391–3; cf Epp 205:43n, 233:6, 245:25, 262:3).

TO THE REVEREND FATHER IN CHRIST, JOHN,
LORD BISHOP OF ROCHESTER, FROM ERASMUS OF ROTTERDAM

Best and most learned of prelates, your acts of great kindness and generosity to me have been a challenge to me to show that I am not blatantly ungrateful; and so I am beginning to consider whether at least I might offer 5 you some literary gift that should be worthy of your Eminence – should be, that is to say, both scholarly and edifying. Now, as luck would have it, I had brought with me from Grocyn's library St Basil's commentary on Isaiah: that is, a commentary on the most eloquent of prophets by the most eloquent of theologians. I began to translate it into Latin, but the deeper I 10 penetrate into the work the less flavour it seems to have of that divine style of Basil's, though at the very outset the title had itself made me somewhat suspicious, revealing that the work was planned indeed by Basil, but published by some other priest after Basil's death. My suspicions were increased by the fact that even those authors who list Basil's publications 15 make no mention of this volume. Accordingly I have come more or less to the conclusion that these books either are the work of some other Basil – there are many of the name – not the bishop of Caesarea, brother to Gregory of Nazianzus; or that the title was added deliberately, on purpose to win the reader's approval. And this, if you do not entirely disagree, seems un- 20 worthy of dedication to your name; unworthy, too, of my bestowing a great deal of care upon it. I give you a tentative sample and, for the rest, will adhere to your decision as if it were that of an oracle. Farewell.

From your own Cambridge, [1510]

230 / From John Colet [London, end of September 1511]

An answer to Ep 227, this letter had not reached Erasmus by 5 October when Ep 231 was written. It is to be found in the Deventer Letter-book.

JOHN COLET TO ERASMUS OF ROTTERDAM

What shall I not approve of? – for these are your words. Is there anything about Erasmus I could fail to approve of? I have read your letter on how to study hurriedly, since I still have no time to go through it carefully because of my distractions; and not only do I agree with all of it as I read, but I am full 5 of admiration for your gifts, as well as your masterly technique, erudition,

* * * * *

230:2 for these are your words] Cf Ep 227:3.

3–4 letter on how to study] *De ratione studii* (cf Ep 227:1n) fluency, and power of expression. I have often wished the boys at my school could be trained by your method, as you have prescribed should be done; also I have often wished that they could be taught by just such men as you in your great wisdom have depicted. When I came to the passage at the end of your epistle where you claim the ability to bring youths to a reasonable command of expression, in both Latin and Greek, in fewer years than the conventional pedagogue requires to teach them to mangle the language, then how I longed to have you, Erasmus, as a teacher in my school! But I am hopeful that you may lend me some assistance, if only in training my teachers when you have taken leave of your Cambridge men. I shall keep your master copies intact as you request. About our friend Linacre, I shall do as you so kindly and so shrewdly advise. Please do not give up your efforts to find a second master for me, if there should be anyone in your neighbourhood who is devoid of arrogance and who is not too proud to be subordinate to the high master. 10 15 20

About that remark in your letter concerning your occasional skirmishes on my behalf with the Scotist ranks, I rejoice to have such a stout fighter and loyal champion to defend me! But from your point of view this is a thoroughly unequal contest, and one that brings no credit; for what lustre do you gain when you have repulsed a swarm of flies and stabbed them to death? And what credit will you earn in my eyes by felling reeds? It is an unavoidable rather than glorious or doughty fray, but at least it shows the concern and loving care you have for me. 25

Pray go on, Erasmus, to give us Basil, for in doing so you will be giving us Isaiah. I think you will do well, and best look after your own interest, if you imitate Diogenes and, rejoicing in your poverty, reckon yourself as king of kings; maybe by despising money you will achieve money, and success. In the lives of Christian heroes the world follows those who flee from it. From whence came so many resources and such wealth in the church but from her shunning of these things? But I know such paradoxes as this are not to your taste. 30 35

I am surprised by what you write about Richard Croke: for what have I to do with others' money, which might make you believe or suspect that I have control of moneys entrusted to me in any way whatsoever? I do not stand by the bedsides of the dying or wheedle rich widows or meddle in the wills and testaments of the wealthy; I do not seek to become the confidant of 40

* * * * *

11 epistle] The passage mentioned refers to the *De ratione instituendi discipulos* which follows the *De ratione studii* (LB I 530AB) in the first edition of the *De copia* (cf Ep 260 introduction).

17 Linacre] See Ep 227:5–14.

rich men, or praise their vices and infirmities, or bid them compound their crimes by putting money at my disposal. I tell you in this country anyone not in that class will find it hard to come by money to give away. I have the handling of my own money and no other; and you yourself know the ends for which I disburse that. Still, I was somewhat amused and at the same time charmed, Erasmus, to see the innate uprightness of character that caused you, in the role of a beggar, which you find so distasteful, to prefer to plead others' causes rather than your own. Briefly then, though I have no one else's money to offer other men, yet if you beg humbly I have some of my own private money for yourself; and if you ask for it without shame, then poverty will, albeit poorly, come to poverty's aid. Farewell, and I beg you be sure to write often to me. 45 50

Your John Colet 55

231 / To John Colet Cambridge, 5 October 1511

ERASMUS OF ROTTERDAM TO HIS FRIEND COLET

I think I am at this moment on the scent of the kind of man you mentioned: more of this when we meet. When I was in London lately I did not call on you, to avoid being a nuisance, for I had to ride off straight away after dinner. One-eyed Pieter, whom chance set in my way, told me you had sent a reply to my last letter, but this I have not yet received. I should be planning to come back to see you about the beginning of December, did not the plague frighten me off, especially should Mountjoy return, so that I can use his house, which at present is impossible because of the Cerberus there. Farewell, best of teachers. 5 10

Cambridge, 5 October 1511

* * * * *

46 my own money] Colet's annual income from the deanery and other preferments was about two hundred pounds. His legacy from his father was used to endow St Paul's school (Lupton *Colet* 122; E&C 111).

231:3 London] Erasmus had evidently made a brief visit to London towards the end of September or the beginning of October.

5 Pieter] Pieter Meghen of 's Hertogenbosch, a one-eyed man, was for some years a copyist and messenger for Colet and his circle.

6 last letter] Ep 227

8 Mountjoy] Lord Mountjoy was still at Hammes. He did not return to London till about 5 November (cf Ep 239:36ff).

9 Cerberus] Cf Epp 240:54 and 247:12. This 'watchdog' has not been identified, although he was evidently well known to Erasmus' friends.

232 / To Andrea Ammonio Cambridge, 5 October 1511

ERASMUS TO HIS FRIEND AMMONIO

A kind of attendant imp of misfortune prevented me from seeing you although I was in your parts lately. For at my first arrival in London nothing seemed less likely than that you should still be staying at More's house, especially as Josse the bookseller had informed me you were now at St Thomas's College. Early next morning I knocked at the door of your room, but you were not at home. After I came back from church, I heard a noise of horsemen. I requested Linacre to look outside, since I was busy writing something or other; he said it was you, taking your departure. But after you had already gone I was full of longing to have a talk with you; however there will be a chance to do this at some other time. 5 10

Please tell me what news you have where you are about Lord Mountjoy's arrival, and, in the second place, whether the plague is as bad as the common report has it; and lastly, give me any news about Italian and French affairs that may safely be entrusted to a letter. Farewell. 15

Cambridge, 5 October 1511

233 / To Andrea Ammonio Cambridge, 16 October 1511

ERASMUS TO HIS FRIEND AMMONIO

I have no pretext for writing, since there is no news, except that I have made up my mind to send away no reliable messenger who comes to hand

* * * * *

2 imp of misfortune] *Adagia* I i 72

4 More's house] Both Erasmus and Ammonio found More's house less comfortable after his marriage to his second wife, Dame Alice, in the summer of 1511 (cf Epp 236:54f and Allen 451:19f).

5 Josse] Allen suggests that this is probably Josse Bade, the Parisian printer who frequently published for Erasmus, but gives no explanation of why he should have been in London at this time.

5–6 St Thomas's] St Thomas's College, more properly called the Hospital of St Thomas of Acon, in Broad Street near More's house. It belonged to the military order of St Thomas the Martyr. The hospital was known to have been heavily in debt in 1510, and no doubt it was taking in boarders to make both ends meet (cf *Victoria County History, London* (1909) I 491–5). Ammonio did not actually move there till late in October (cf Ep 236:52ff).

14–15 Italian and French affairs] Erasmus' repeated demands in letters to Ammonio for news of events in Italy and France show that he had a lively interest in international affairs. It also suggests the source from which he may have obtained much of the political narrative in the *Dialogus, Julius exclusus e coelis, Opuscula* 65ff.

without a letter to you. I wrote just a few days ago; I long to hear how you are, and whether my friend Mountjoy is back yet; and next, how things are in Italy and what the most invincible Julius is up to. Towards midwinter I shall return to you all if the gods allow, provided the winter cold can put a stop to the plague which I hear is spreading in your part of the world. For that matter it is not very far from Cambridge either.

Up to this moment I have been lecturing on Chrysoloras' grammar, but the audience is small; perhaps more people will attend when I start Theodore's grammar. Perhaps also I will undertake lecturing in theology, for that is under discussion at present. The pay is too small to tempt me, but in the meantime I am also doing some service to learning, to the best of my ability; and, to use Ovid's expression, have been 'beguiling' a few months. Look after yourself, my dear Andrea, dearest to me of all mortals, and be sure to write to me often.

Cambridge, 16 October 1511

234 / To Andrea Ammonio — Cambridge, [about 20 October 1511]

ERASMUS TO HIS FRIEND ANDREA

I am sending back your wine cask. I kept it by me for too long empty, just so as to enjoy the very smell of its Greek wine! And now, as a reward for wine of the finest quality, you are to receive verses of the worst – precisely, in Homer's famous phrase, 'bronze in return for gold.' Yes, and I am original too in teaching iambic verses on this occasion to sing songs of praise! My ode shall be appended here:

Whoe'er reflects, Ammonio, on thy dower –
The great and total beauty of thy face

* * * * *

6 Julius] Cf Ep 228:21n.

10 Chrysoloras] Manuel Chrysoloras, the Byzantine scholar and teacher whose lectures in Florence from 1397 to 1400 introduced the serious study of Greek into Italy. His Greek grammar was printed in Venice in 1475. It was the first Greek grammar for the use of students trained in Latin and was widely used in Italy throughout the fifteenth century (cf Rossi 22).

12 Theodore's grammar] Theodore Gaza of Salonika taught Greek in Italy for some forty years before his death in 1475. His Greek grammar was printed by Aldus in Venice in 1495. Erasmus published a Latin translation of the first two books in 1516 and 1518 (LB I 117ff).

15 Ovid] *Tristia* 4.10.114

234:5 Homer] *Iliad* 6.236; cf Ep 145:151n.

6 iambic] The iambic line in Greek was originally a vehicle of biting satire.

7 ode] See critical edition in Reedijk 300f.

(Reward of close beholders); thy tall stature, 10
Fit for the kings of old; grace mixed o'er all
With majesty in countenance and in frame;
Eyes that shine forth in gentle manhood's fire,
A tongue that sounds alluring melodies;
Character, too, that's never out of season, 15
Being friendly, kind, sweeter than honeycombs;
Love, laughter, wit, enjoyment, fun; the three
Graces, in short: a mild, forgiving nature;
Fresh innocence of heart and, strange to tell,
A wise astuteness lacking policy: 20
Also a temper free from love of gain,
Prone to be generous far beyond the scale
Of thy possessions; and a mind how full
(Ready to pour forth too!) and burnished bright
(Can one small head contain so many books?) – 25
All these no less of eloquence adorns,
And kindness, precious as rare, doth season all;
The glare and glittering eye of cruel spite
By that agreeable and modest mien
Thou dost repel; spite of so lordly gifts 30
Nothing of lordliness that nature mars;
Whoe'er, then, weighs such riches, in one man
Composed, will he not justly swear, to thee
Alone was nature truly mother-kind,
Others but stepsons? even though thyself 35
These goods to thine own self dost chiefly owe.
– Fortune, thou'st still thy duty, such great gifts
To match with thine assistance; otherwise
Surely shalt thou seem envious, or quite blind.

I request you to convey to the bishops to whom they are addressed the 40 letters I have added to yours, either when you visit court yourself or when you can find a reliable carrier. Look after yourself. Bullock sends you his greetings; he is an honest friend, and not unlike you. I am looking out for a letter from you, since I have had only one so far. If an opportunity occurs with your friends the bishops, conduct yourself as you have always done 45

* * * * *

40 bishops] Cf Ep 236:39.

42 Bullock] Cf Ep 225:5n.

44 one] The letter referred to in Ep 228:4.

towards your friend Erasmus. If your poems are on sale in London, please send a single copy to me here.

1511

235 / From Johannes Sixtinus London, 20 October [1511]

Sixtinus had met Erasmus at Oxford in 1499 (cf Ep 112 introduction). At this time he had some reason to fear that he had fallen out of favour with Erasmus (cf Ep 244:6n). Erasmus replied in an amiable tone in a letter now lost (cf Ep 244:42). Both this letter and Ep 244, in which Sixtinus offered excuses for his conduct and explained the circumstances, were copied into the Deventer Letter-book.

JOHANNES SIXTINUS TO HIS FRIEND, MASTER ERASMUS

You could not believe how sad I am at your forgetfulness of me. Letters from you are frequently brought here, addressed to your friends, but none addressed to me. What can be the cause of this but your forgetting me? Believe me, I am mindful of your acts of generosity and kindness; and, 5 although I have not yet returned them, still I shall do so as soon as I can; yet such is the distinction and nobility of your mind, you do not greatly look to receiving them. Be sure to tell me, therefore, whether you have deleted me from your list of friends, or not. I shall judge of this by your letters or your silence, understanding, if there be silence, that I am indeed deleted; or if 10 you reply, that I am not. Farewell; and pardon me if I am short and simple.

London, 20 October

236 / From Andrea Ammonio London, 27 October 1511

This letter did not reach Erasmus till 24 November (cf Ep 245:2f).

ANDREA AMMONIO TO HIS DESIRABLE DESIDERIUS ERASMUS

Your letter, dear Erasmus, went far beyond anything I hoped, though it fell short of what I longed for. To tell the truth, you have written to me more often than I thought you would, yet much less often than I wished; and this most affectionate act of kindness means so much to me that, could the 5 bonds that link me to you be firmer than they are, it would have bound me still more closely to you. Nothing I receive gives me more pleasure than a

* * * * *

46 poems] The volume of verse dedicated to Mountjoy which had been published in Paris in the spring (cf Ep 218 introduction).

letter from you; and I think I have had solid evidence for discerning that you have no common affection for me; indeed I thought so before, but now I believe it is possible to be sure of it. But I have had no opportunity to be equally serviceable to you, partly because of his majesty's business (see what a pompous excuse I am making!) and the highly intricate affairs of certain friends, and partly through the fault of those to whom I entrusted my second letter to you, for I understand this was not delivered to you in spite of the substantial fee I gave for its conveyance. 10 15

I have had three letters from you; two of them were full of sugar; but the third was full of honey. And, although at first from the address and the mention of Greek wine I did not doubt it was written to me, yet presently when I came to the poetry I suddenly began to suspect that you were writing to somebody else, since I failed to recognize as mine the qualities you praise there. However, as soon as I realized that you were in fact speaking of me, I said to myself: 'Why do you hesitate to believe what Erasmus says about you? After all, you would trust him even with your life.' In short, I should have deluded myself had I not come to the opinion that your affection for me had deceived your judgment, otherwise worthy of Lynceus. In any case, to keep nothing from you, I have a rather higher opinion of myself as a result of reading your verses, simply for the reason that I have had Erasmus to sing my praises. In this I consider myself luckier than Alexander the Great, and not one scrap do I envy Achilles. But it is I rather than you who can say with truth 'bronze for gold,' since in exchange for the bronze of wine I have gained verses of gold, nay emerald, or, rather, more costly than gold or jewels or any kind of precious ore. But I am vastly greedy, and not content even with this enormous profit: for if I can recover the cask you are sending back empty, I shall command it to make a return voyage to you, recharged with its vital fluid, so as to see if I can coax you to the production of further verses; since, even if your lines are full of fibs, still they sing a most charming tune. 20 25 30 35

I hope in a few days to be able to deliver your letters personally to my lords of Winchester and Durham; and if my words can do anything to

* * * * *

11 business] Ammonio had recently been appointed Latin secretary to Henry VIII.

16 three letters] Epp 232–4

25 Lynceus] *Adagia* II i 54

30 'bronze for gold'] Cf Ep 234:5 and n.

39 Winchester and Durham] Richard Foxe, bishop of Winchester, and Thomas Ruthall, bishop of Durham. Foxe was one of Erasmus' most influential patrons to whom he had dedicated Lucian's *Toxaris* in 1506 (cf Ep 187 introduction). Erasmus had also sought Ruthall's patronage in 1506 with

recommend you further to them, I will outdo Cicero himself. For is there anyone, however inarticulate, whom the possession of such an excellent case would fail to render not merely fluent, but a master of oratory? 40

This is the report of events in Italy: the Spanish king is now on the verge of open war with France and the English will not, it is guessed, stay idly looking on. Julius the supreme has gone to the shrine of the Mother of God at Loreto to congratulate Our Lady on his recovery. The Venetians have, it is said, ambushed and destroyed more than five hundred French horse. The emperor feels the chill so badly that he dares not quit his German stoves. The men of Florence and Pisa have been pursued with dreadful curses because they are lending a council site to those schismatic cardinals. The cardinal archbishop of Reggio has passed away. 45 50

* * * * *

the dedication of his translation of Lucian's *Timon* (Ep 192 introduction). Ruthall responded to Erasmus' appeal rather belatedly by a gift of ten gold pieces (cf Epp 280:36n and 281:8n) in the fall of 1513. Ammonio evidently delivered the letters to Foxe and Ruthall by mid-November (cf Ep 243:46ff) and continued thereafter to press Erasmus' cause (cf Ep 249:20).

43 Spanish king] Ferdinand, king of Aragon and regent of Castile, was in fact already drawn into war with France, together with the papacy and Venice, as a member of the Holy League organized by Julius II and proclaimed in Rome 5 October 1511 (Creighton IV 137).

44 the English] Henry VIII joined the Holy League 13 November 1511 and four days later made a treaty with Ferdinand to attack France before the end of April 1512 (cf Mackie 273).

46 Loreto] Probably an error due to the fact that Julius had gone to Santa Maria del Popolo on 5 October to return thanks for his recovery. The pope had visited Loreto in June 1511 before his illness but apparently did not leave Rome for some months after it (E. Rodocanachi *Le Pontificat de Jules II* (Paris 1928) 134).

46 to congratulate ... recovery] Cf similar use of 'gratulor' in Ep 240:59 where 'Gratulor domino Montioio felicem reditum' can only be translated 'I congratulate Mountjoy on his safe return.'

48 emperor] Maximilian I

50 schismatic cardinals] The schismatic Council of Pisa, summoned by a small group of pro-French cardinals to meet in September 1511 with a view to deposing Julius II. The first actual session was on 4 November. Florence, still allied to France, reluctantly supported the council and was laid under an interdict (Creighton IV 131–51). For a full account of the sessions of the council see L. Sandret 'Le Concile de Pise' *Revue des questions historiques* 34 (1883) 425–56.

51 Reggio] Pietro Isvales (d September 1511) was born in Messina of a family of Spanish origin. He was made archbishop of Reggio in Calabria in 1497 and cardinal in 1500. He was one of the cardinals who remained loyal to Julius at

Here in London we have not yet come to terms with the plague. I myself have at last moved into St Thomas's College, where I am no more at my ease than at More's house. It is true that I no longer see 'the harpy's crooked beak,' but there are plenty of other things to annoy me; so much so that I swear I do not know how I can contrive to live in England any longer. In the first place, they tell me it would be unsuitable to my condition to reside with our Italian merchants, which would be congenial to me; second, I am quite out of sympathy with this nation's dirty habits, habits with which I am already well enough acquainted, and yet my poverty will not permit me to take a lease of a house and live as I should like to live. But to drive away these distasteful reflections I too will turn poet. 55 60

Thy potency in verse, Erasmus mine,
Myself hath urged to move this stock-dull wit
And, Museless, match thee in th' iambick line. 65
But, straight, Apollo scolds me: Art thou fit,
Poor frog, to Master Bull's girth to aspire?
Can swans be rivalled when a crow's beak opes?
Down fell incontinent my leaden lyre,
From a fool's grasp, to break a fool's fond hopes. 70
My seething brain, short-vexed, grew cold again;
Scarce could I send thee one short painful page.
Yet this I'll add (Apollo frowns in vain),
Farewell, Erasmus, glory of our age.

Tomorrow I shall proceed to court and will carry out your business there with zeal and attention; and I shall arrange with someone that, when the Cambridge carriers in due course have returned here, a second cask of wine shall be delivered to you along with this letter. Please return Bullock's greeting a thousandfold for me. Once again, look after your health and continue in your present affection for me. 75 80

London, 27 October 1511

* * * * *

the time of the schismatic Council of Pisa and was highly regarded by the pope who entrusted him with important diplomatic and legatine missions. Domenico Spanò-Bolani *Storia di Reggio di Calabria da' tempi primitivi all'anno di Christo 1797* (Reggio 1797; repr Reggio 1957) II 228

54–5 'the harpy's crooked beak'] A Greek phrase referring unkindly to More's second wife, who seems to have been responsible for Ammonio's move from More's house to St Thomas's (cf Ep 232:4n and 5–6n)

237 / To John Colet Cambridge, 29 October [1511]

A reply to Ep 230.

ERASMUS TO HIS FRIEND COLET

At the moment I am completely absorbed in finishing off my *Copia* (on abundance); so much so that I might seem to make a riddle of it – at once in the midst of abundance and also in utter penury. And how I wish I could put an end to both alike! – for presently I will be writing finis to the *Copia*, 5 provided only that the Muses give better fortune to my studies than Fortune has hitherto given to my purse.

This was the reason why I have answered your letters somewhat briefly and carelessly.

As for the Scotists, the most unbeatable and most successfully compla- 10 cent class of men there is, I am not seriously campaigning against them for fear of wasting lamp-oil and labour and only stirring up a hornets' nest. I have virtually lost interest in translating Basil, not only because certain conjectures suggest that the work is not genuine, but also because the bishop of Rochester seemed rather unenthusiastic after I sent him a sample 15 of my projected translation, explaining in a letter that I intended that Basil should be presented to readers of Latin under the bishop's auspices and from his own university: also, as I have learnt from a friend, he suspects that I am polishing up a previous version and not translating from the Greek. What won't men think of? 20

As for your joke about Diogenes, I am glad I can give you pleasure,

* * * * *

2 *Copia*] The *De copia* had originally been written before Erasmus left Italy in 1509, and he left behind a copy which fell into the hands of Sixtinus (cf Ep 244:7n). He was evidently now revising and enlarging the work for presentation to Colet, to whom he dedicated it on 29 April 1512 (cf Ep 260 introduction).

3 abundance] Literally *copia*, a play on the title of his book

10 Scotists] Cf Epp 227:21f and 230:23ff.

12 lamp-oil and labour] *Adagia* I iv 62

12 hornets' nest] *Adagia* I i

13 Basil] The commentaries on Isaiah, part of which were presented to Fisher in September (cf Epp 227:22ff; 229)

18–20 as I have learnt ... think of] This passage was inserted in the Froben edition of the *Opus epistolarum* (Basel 1529) which was supervised by Erasmus. Allen suggests it may indicate that his feeling for his old patron cooled in later life.

21 Diogenes] Cf Ep 230:32.

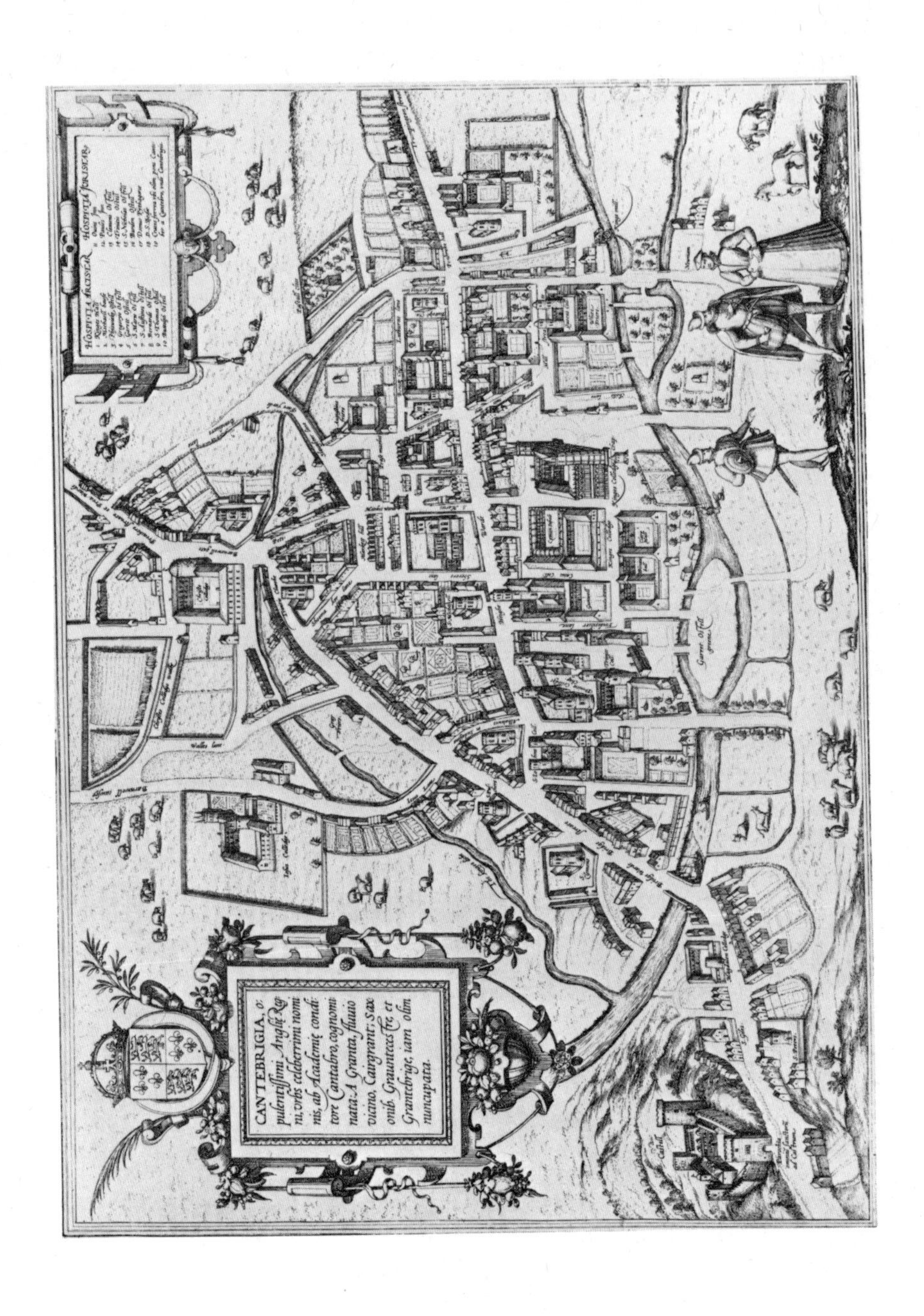

Plan of Cambridge in 1575
George Braun *Civitates orbis terrarum* (Cologne 1575)
Reproduced by permission of the
Syndics of the Cambridge University Library

however I do it. But if my present luck continues, I am like to be playing Diogenes in earnest – not to make myself feel like some great king of kings, but that I may learn quite to despise life itself. How otherwise could one act Diogenes, at my age and in my state of health? For surely a man who neglects his life will spurn all else thereafter. But this he can do anywhere, even among the Garamantes; yet this too would, I believe, have a better outcome than my present ambition which, even if it were not discreditable, is still the most unfortunate by far.

I wrote to you about Croke not because I thought you held other men's money, for I know you have cast from you even money that was given to you unasked, but because I thought you would be more willing to bestow on a fellow-Englishman anything you might chance to have; and, in addition, a favour is better bestowed on a young man, provided he is promising, and this young man is being let down by some people who had promised to help him.

As for your offer of your own money, there I recognize your old kindly attitude towards me and am full of the deepest gratitude. But my feelings were a little piqued by that remark, however much it was made in fun, 'if you beg humbly.' Perhaps you mean – and you are right – that my impatience with my lot comes entirely from human pride; since a truly gentle and Christian spirit takes everything in good part. I am all the more surprised to see how you have linked humility and lack of shame, since you write at once 'if you beg humbly' and 'if you ask without shame.' For if you follow ordinary usage in defining humility as the very opposite of arrogance, what traffic can shamelessness have with modesty? But if by 'humbly' you mean 'in a servile and abject manner,' then, my dear Colet, you are quite at odds with Seneca, who thinks nothing so dear as what is bought by begging – for he who waits for that humble word 'please' from a friend is no friend at all. Once when Socrates was conversing with his friends he said 'I should have bought a cloak today, if I had not run short of cash'; Seneca says that a man who gives only after hearing a remark like this gives too late. Someone else placed money under the pillow of a sleeping friend who was needy and sick but who concealed both these conditions because of a certain sense of honour; when I read this story as a young man, I was as

* * * * *

27 Garamantes] An African tribe noted for their fierceness; they are mentioned by Pliny, Livy, Virgil, and others.

30 Croke] Cf Ep 227:31ff.

44 'if you beg humbly' and 'if you ask without shame'] Cf Ep 230:51–2.

48 Seneca] *De beneficiis* 2.1.4

51 Seneca] *De beneficiis* 7.24

deeply impressed by the modesty of the one as touched by the other's openheartedness.

But I ask you, what could be more shameless or abject than I, who have long been a-begging publicly in England? I have received so much from the archbishop that it would be unspeakably selfish to take anything more from 60 him, even if he were to offer it. From X I have begged boldly enough but he felt less embarrassment in refusing than I had in asking. Now I am appearing too immodest even to our friend Linacre; though he knew I was leaving London furnished with barely six nobles, and he well knows my health, and also that winter is coming on, yet he solicitously advises me to spare the 65 archbishop and Lord Mountjoy and rather to accustom myself to bear poverty bravely. What friendly advice! Yet it is for this reason most of all that I hate my luck, in that it will not allow me to be modest. When my strength was adequate, it was a pleasure to conceal how poor I was. Now it is impossible, unless I were to take pleasure in neglecting my life itself. 70 However I have not put on a brazen mask to such an extent that I ask everyone for everything. As for other people, I fear I may ask them in vain. But how am I to beg from you, pray? – especially when you yourself are not particularly well situated for giving this kind of help. However, if you approve of immodesty, I will end this letter with as shameless a conclusion 75 as is possible for me. I cannot be so brazen as to beg from you with no justification; yet I am not so proud as to reject a gift, if any friend as good as yourself should freely offer it, especially in the prevailing circumstances. Farewell. I have forgotten the brevity I had intended.

Something occurs to me that I know you will laugh at. When I put forth 80 a suggestion about a second master for your school in the presence of several university people, a person of some reputation smiled and said: who would bear to spend his life in that school, among children, if he could make some sort of a living anywhere else? I replied with a good deal of modesty that this function of bringing up youth in good character and good 85 literature seemed to me one of the most honourable; that Christ did not

* * * * *

60 archbishop] Warham (cf Ep 188 introduction)

61 X] Probably Mountjoy

64 six nobles] As in Ep 227:31, Erasmus again probably means the gold angel-nobles, or their equivalent value in money-of-account (6s 8d sterling apiece); but possibly the gold ryals or rose-nobles. By relative gold values six angels (= £2 0s 0d ster.) were then worth about £2 18s 0d gros Flemish or £17 1s 3d tournois. Cf Epp 214:4n; 240A:11n; 248:40n; 270:30n; and tables A–F below, 327–45.

68 will not allow me] Cf Catullus 10.34.

71 brazen mask] *Adagia* I viii 47

72 everyone for everything] *Adagia* II iv 16

despise the very young, and that no age of man was a better investment for generous help and nowhere could a richer harvest be anticipated, since the young are the growing crop and material of the commonwealth. I added that all who are truly religious hold the view that no service is more likely to gain merit in God's eyes than the leading of children to Christ. He grimaced and sneered: if anyone wished to serve Christ properly he should enter a monastery and live as a religious. I replied that St Paul defines true religion in terms of works of love; and love consists in helping our neighbours as best we may. He spurned this as a foolish remark. 'Lo,' said he, 'we have left all; there lies perfection.' That man has not left all, said I, who, when he could help very many by his labours, refuses to undertake a duty because it is regarded as humble. And with this I took my leave of the fellow, to avoid starting a quarrel. Here you see a sample of the Scotists' wisdom and the way in which they talk. Farewell again. 90 95 100

Cambridge, the morrow of Sts Simon and Jude [1513]

238 / To Andrea Ammonio — Cambridge, 2 November 1511

ERASMUS TO HIS FRIEND ANDREA AMMONIO

At long last I have sent back your wine cask, together with some misbegotten verses. The carrier says he delivered this to More since you were absent at the time. I will return to you about the first of January – so at least we shall feel the cold less by keeping each other warm. For I would rather summer than winter here. One last point: it is not good to be, for too long, at such a distance from my personal Jupiter. All the same this place really suits me fairly well. Also I see some prospect of earning, if one could act as a man of all work. I should dearly like to know what effect my letters had on the bishops of Winchester and Durham, and also anything else that is new. If you will have the letter I have attached to yours forwarded to Italy, I shall be much obliged. At present we have just what Homer called 'unquenchable rain.' I suppose Jupiter has heard the prayers of the author whose little book I gave you, where he calls on springs, rivers, lakes, and pools to lend their tears in lamenting Italy's tragedy. 'A wolf saw me first,' so I have to speak by nods and gestures, I have such a sore throat. Farewell. Write to me often. 5 10 15

Cambridge, 2 November 1511

* * * * *

95–6 'We have left all'] Matthew 19:27

238:3 verses] Cf Ep 234. Ammonio's reply acknowledging receipt of the verses and the wine cask (Ep 236) had not yet reached Erasmus.

7 Jupiter] Mountjoy

12 Homer] *Iliad* 13.139

15 'A wolf saw me first'] Cf Ep 144:16n.

239 / From Andrea Ammonio London, 8 November 1511

ANDREA AMMONIO TO HIS DESIRABLE DESIDERIUS ERASMUS

Either my servant is exceptionally unlucky, so that all he does for me turns out badly, or else the Cambridge rabble surpasses even the rest of the disobliging British nation in incivility, so unaware is it of all obligations and so devoid of absolutely every kind of civilized behaviour. I long to see a few of this sort measure their length on a gallows! Why, they have practically no idea what it means to take responsibility for a letter, and fail to deliver it afterwards; to put it in the mildest way possible, they do not know how many people they are cheating of the pleasure that should be theirs, or how many men's good name for conscientiousness they may be ruining; and moreover they are unaware that more than one person's well-being often depends on a single letter. As soon as I got your letter I tried to answer it as quickly as I could, in order to please you, if not by my literary style, at least by conscientiousness in dispatch. I gave the trifle they demanded for the carriage of the letter. Finally I sent back, along with the letter, a second cask of Greek wine; however I see that only a single letter reached you and, along with the good turn I tried to do, the care I devoted to writing has been lost. Oh, these savages! I swear I'd gladly see them torn to pieces any day! However I am consoled by one thing – the reflection that you have so fully grasped my feeling for you that, even though I never wrote, you would still regard me as an admirer and friend. My servant Thomas says that on the last occasion he entrusted the letter and, as I said, a second cask of Greek wine to the man who carried your books down to you; but I do not know to whom he gave other letters. If the wine has been drunk up, try to get back at least the cask. But enough of this bad temper; I am simply seething with it at the moment.

* * * * *

6 measure their length on a gallows] Literally 'make the long letter': the long s, a euphemism for hanging

12 your letter] Ep 234, which Ammonio answered with Ep 236 and a second cask of wine

16 only a single letter] Probably the letter mentioned in Ep 228 as having accompanied the first cask of Greek wine. A second letter, mentioned in Ep 236:14, was apparently not delivered, while Ep 236 itself did not reach Erasmus until 24 November (cf Ep 245:2) although the cask sent with it arrived 10 September (cf Ep 240:4).

21 Thomas] Erasmus later described him as a sensible and wide-awake servant (cf Ep 283:66–7).

I gave your letters personally to my lords of Winchester and Durham; both received them with looks of utmost delight and praised to the skies your rare talents. Winchester seems to blame you for treating him as a stranger and never coming to see him; I replied, as it occurred to me to put it on the spur of the moment, that it was a rather awkward shyness that made you do this, but that so far as I knew you were quite devoted to his lordship; together with some other remarks appropriate to the occasion. But all this was before they had a chance to read your letters. Afterwards they were so busied with public affairs that I decided not to interrupt them with your concerns; but I shall not fail to do so at the proper season. Your patron, as I have heard (for I have not yet seen him), has been in town for three days. Jupiter is very angry with us here; it rains by day and by night and seldom stops. The plague has almost ceased to rage; but, unless the magistrates take some effective measures of relief, a famine is going to follow, and this will be every bit as terrible as the plague. I am not surprised that the price of firewood has gone up: every day there are a great number of heretics to make bonfires for us, and still their number continues to grow. Why, even my servant Thomas's own brother, who is more like a lump of wood than a human being, has instituted a sect on his own, if you please, and has followers too.

But to pass to Italian affairs. At Rome a league has been agreed upon between the pope, the Spanish king, and the Venetians. Its terms, which have been announced, are as follows: the Spanish king shall provide for the aid of the pope 1,200 heavy-armed horse, known as lances, also 1,000 light horse, and 10,000 foot-soldiers; while the pope is to keep up 500 heavy horse and 8,000 infantry, and in addition he is to give a monthly allowance of 40,000 gold pieces to pay the auxiliaries; and the Venetians are to muster such forces as they can. The council at Pisa is falling apart. The cardinal of

* * * * *

31 on the spur of the moment] Cf *Adagia* I v 72.

36 patron] Mountjoy, just returned from Hammes

47 Italian affairs] An amplified version of the news sent in Ep 236:43–51

50 lances] A lance did not represent a single heavily armed horseman, but a unit composed of a man-at-arms or knight in full armour and four or five more lightly armed followers.

53 40,000 gold pieces] Undoubtedly either Florentine florins or Venetian ducats. Both coins were then worth about 4s 7d sterling, so that this papal grant would have amounted to about £9,167 sterling = £13,167 gros Flemish = £77,520 tournois. Cf CWE I 314, 316, 321, 338–9; and tables A–F below, 327–45.

Santa Croce, who began the schism, is said to have won a pardon from the pope by the help of the king of Aragon and fled for refuge to the Kingdom of Naples. I had forgotten to say that it is permissible for any Christian prince to enter the said league within forty days, after which time the pope's sanction shall be required for admission. What my fellow-citizens are going to do they have so far failed to discuss – with, it is guessed, a great saving in oarsmen! The emperor will be merely an onlooker at this business. It is rumoured that the Florentines are preparing to desert the French. 55 60

Now you know all that has been reported on Italian affairs to this date. About your hoarseness: had you been here I should have dealt with it at once by administering one little draught. I am grieved that the hope of your return to us is put off as far as the first of January. At the same time I am happy that your present territory has suited you fairly well; we shall console our yearning for you with the thought of the great advantages you have there. Your other letters shall be diligently forwarded to Italy tomorrow, for they have arrived just in time, almost at the moment when the courier was leaving. Look after yourself, my dear Erasmus, and give many greetings for me to our friend Bullock. Farewell once more. 65 70

London, 8 November 1511

240 / To Andrea Ammonio — Cambridge, 11 November [1511]

ERASMUS TO HIS FRIEND AMMONIO

On the eve of Martinmas your letter was delivered to me – to be specific, your angry one – together with a cask of Greek wine, half full. The fellow who brought it demanded two *drachmae*. I gave him sixpence. Then, after a

* * * * *

55 Santa Croce] Cardinal Bernardino de Carvajal, a Spaniard, was one of the most influential cardinals and had been a rival of Julius II in the papal election. He did not win pardon from Julius, as was rumoured, but was finally pardoned by Leo X in 1513 (cf Creighton IV 188f).

59 my fellow-citizens] Ammonio came from Lucca.

240:2 eve of Martinmas] 10 November

3 cask] The cask sent on 27 October with Ep 236 and mentioned in Ep 239:16, to which this letter replies

4 two *drachmae*] Erasmus was not, of course, referring to the ancient Greek silver coin, but to a current English one, almost certainly the silver 'groat,' worth 4d sterling, as is given (without explanation) in most previous translations. Erasmus undoubtedly thought the Greek coin name appropriate since he was talking of Greek wine. Although 'drachma' does not appear ever to have been used as a synonym for the English groat, it was indeed commonly used to mean the 'gros tournois' in France, where Erasmus had just recently

close look at your letter, I noticed that the cask had not been sent with your last letter, which you wrote on the eighth of November, but with a previous letter; this was evident even from the colour of the wine. Indeed when you sent it the first time, I was surprised that you consigned it unsealed to the hands of men to whom nothing is sealed. Obviously, my dear Andrea, we have here to deal with men who combine extreme boorishness with the extremity of evil cunning; and there is absolutely no reason why you should congratulate me on account of my retreat down here; shame alone curbs my complaints. Let us, however, speak of this privately when we meet.

I was not looking for a second cask, except that you, astonishingly courteous as you are, took my praise of the wine for a fresh order. As far as I am concerned, I am more anxious about recovering your letter than about either the wine or the cask; for, if you have sent only the first and second casks, neither of them is lost. I sent back the first and, unless I am mistaken, received it back again with your last letter. Talk of my carrier! What if you had seen my book-chests, battered on all sides? What would you have said if you had heard his trumped-up story about the horse? And that bald-headed rascal never hove in sight here. I declare it is folly to expect a single act of human decency from these monsters. But I could not restrain my laughter on seeing even Andrea (born to the graces, to friendship, and to gentleness) capable of passionate rage, while I am now practising the role of Micio, after I have almost

learnt at mine own fortune's hand
To mourn for my defeat,

and am beginning to approve of Virgil's words 'Our sole hope in defeat lies in despair.'

In a word it seems to me that I deserve every kind of misfortune whenever I reflect what Italy was, which I have left behind, and how Rome was smiling on me when I left her: alas for the exchange, but one's duty is to make the best of what we have.

* * * * *

resided (cf Ep 219 introd.). Moreover the current 'gros de roi,' at 36d tournois, had approximately the same value as the current English groat (in fact 4.22d ster. by the relative silver contents). Thus one may reasonably assume that Erasmus meant the latter by analogy and that he gave the messenger three-quarters of the sum demanded. Cf CWE 1 320–2, 326 (obolum), 340–1; E&C 126n; F. Schrötter *Wörterbuch der Münzkunde* (Berlin 1930) 160; and tables A, B, and E below, 327–37; 342–3.

26 Micio] Cf Ep 3:11n.

27–8 learnt … my defeat] Virgil *Aeneid* 4.434

29 Virgil] *Aeneid* 2.354

34 make … have] *Adagia* II ix 33

What you tell me of Italian affairs is anything but happy news to me, not because I love the French king but because I hate war. For when every day we see the most trivial of raids taking several years to end (and not easily, at that), what will be the prospect if such an extensive war once breaks out? Yet I have nobody to vent my annoyance upon, except that circumcised physician of the pontiff's; surely either he is a poor workman, or else the sources of hellebore are quite exhausted. But 'the fates themselves must find a way.' I have less sympathy with those heretics you mention, if only because they have chosen the moment when winter is upon us to send up the price of fuel. I am not so troubled as you are about famine, so long as it is possible to exist. Thank you for delivering my letters to the bishops of Winchester and Durham, and also for your most kind support, and for the wine you sent me even though I was not looking for it, and for so diligently forwarding my letters to Italy. But why do I draw up a short list of your various services to me, when you play the part of Ammonio, that is, of a most generous friend in everything? 35 40 45 50

Before I betake myself to your part of the world, I must get ready some warm hive in which to hide myself through midwinter – I should like to be not too far away from St Paul's: for I have made up my mind to avoid Mountjoy's house as long as that Cerberus sits in wait: although I cannot see a place there that would really do for the winter unless I was prepared to 55

* * * * *

40 circumcised physician] Erasmus referred again to the pope's Jewish doctor who cured him from a serious illness in the *Julius exclusus* (*Opuscula* 26 line 220 and n). According to E. Rodocanachi (*Le Pontificat de Jules II* (Paris 1928) 9), Rabbi Samuel Sarfati was the physician in whom Julius had the most confidence. He attended the pope on his death bed (ibid 178). In the addenda to Ep 240:36n Allen (IV xxii) identifies the pope's physician as a Provençal Jew, Jacob ben Emmanuel, known as Bonet de Lates, on the authority of Renaudet (*Préréforme* 392 and 499).

41 hellebore] A drug reputed by the ancients to be a specific for mental diseases; the suggestion is that the pope is incurably insane (cf *Adagia* I viii 51–2).

41–2 'the fates ... a way'] Virgil *Aeneid* 3.395

54 Cerberus] The role and status of this otherwise unidentified Cerberus is puzzling. In October Erasmus wrote to Colet that he hoped to return to London in December if Mountjoy were back so that he could use his house which that Cerberus barred at present (cf Ep 231:9n). But when this letter was written, Mountjoy had returned; yet Cerberus still prevented Erasmus from using his house (see also Ep 247:12).

evict the owner himself. Perhaps there is something with the Augustinians – Francesco of Padua writes to invite me to stay with him and promises me an Italian sort of life; please give me any advice you have to give on this subject. I congratulate Lord Mountjoy on his safe and happy return, and ask you to see that he receives my letter. I wrote also to the bishop of Rochester by the same carrier who brought you my last; if a suitable opportunity offers, please find out whether it reached him. As for the other two bishops, please go on with them as you have begun; I shall await your reply before I leave here. Bullock returns your greetings, and is enormously pleased at having them. If you ever meet More, ask whether he has delivered my letter to the archbishop and whether he himself has sent me any communication, either from himself or from others. Farewell, best of friends.

Cambridge, 11 November [1512]

240A / From William Warham Lambeth, 11 November [1511]

A reply to two letters from Erasmus, neither of which has survived. The first is probably the one entrusted to More (cf Ep 240:65–6), which Ammonio felt sure he must have delivered to Warham since he saw the archbishop almost every day (cf Ep 243:75–6). Both Warham and More would frequent Westminster Hall, which housed the law courts, the one as chancellor, the other as a practising lawyer, and it was there in fact that the letter was delivered. The

* * * * *

56 Augustinians] It is not clear which Augustinian house is meant here. There was a house of Augustinian canons (Erasmus' own order), Holy Trinity in Aldgate, which was prominent but at this time in debt. There was also a priory of Augustinian friars in Old Broad Street. Both were near St Paul's. Cf *Victoria County History, London* (1909) I 465–75, 510f. It seems likely that he would seek lodging in a house of his own order as he had done at Oxford in 1499 (cf Ep 106:10n) unless he feared some unpleasantness on account of his having abandoned the garb of his order (cf Ep 296:181ff).

57 Francesco of Padua] The identity of this person is uncertain. Allen suggests it may be the Italian bookseller mentioned in Ep 219:7; but he was unknown to Ammonio in May 1511 (cf Ep 221:19).

60 Rochester] Erasmus' letter to Fisher, bishop of Rochester, must have been written about 2 November. It has not survived. Fisher's reply is apparently Ep 242, the tenor of which shows that either this letter or an earlier one contained a request for money, probably as a return for his presentation of Basil's commentaries on Isaiah (cf Ep 229). Fisher did send a small gift some time before writing (cf Ep 242:5ff), and Erasmus' letter of 2 November may have acknowledged receipt of the gift.

65–6 letter to the archbishop] Cf Ep 240A introduction.

second letter was contemporary with Ep 238 because it mentions Erasmus' cold and his intention to come to London on 1 January. Like the letter to Fisher mentioned in Ep 240:60 it probably contained a request for financial help. Warham's letter is to be found in the Deventer Letter-book as well as in LB App 205, where Leclerc wrongly dated it 1517. On discovering this to be an error, Allen re-dated it and published it in the corrigenda of volume III (xxxi).

WILLIAM, ARCHBISHOP OF CANTERBURY,
TO HIS FRIEND ERASMUS

[After greetings] I have received two letters from you. The first, which was lengthy, reached me at the court in Westminster, where one is well furnished with leisure, and I should gladly have replied to it, had the mes- 5 senger who brought it re-appeared. The second was brought to me yesterday by a bald-headed fellow, whose head had scarce a single hair to cover it, and it gave me the information that you had caught a troublesome cold. I am sorry to hear this. To enable you to recover more speedily from this ailment I am sending you with this letter, and by the aforesaid courier, twenty gold 10 angels; and among the angels you will find Raphael, the physician of salvation, who can cure you and restore you to your former good health. I am glad to learn that you will come to London on the first of January next, as your letter informs me. Look after yourself.

Your sincere William Cantuar 15
From Lambeth, 11 November

241 / To Roger Wentford [Cambridge? November 1511?]

Wentford was a schoolmaster in London whom Erasmus had met in 1506 (cf Ep 196 introduction).

ERASMUS TO ROGER WENTFORD

In your wish that I should not publish the *Copia*, unless it was consideration

* * * * *

3 After greetings] This was probably inserted by the scribe who copied the letter into the Deventer MS in order to save the space taken up by a formal salutation.

10–11 twenty gold angels] Tudor angel-nobles, officially valued at 6s 8d sterling apiece (1465–1526), so that this sum was then worth £6 13s 4d sterling = £9 13s 4d gros Flemish = £56 17s 8d tournois. Cf Ep 214:4n; CWE I 312, 325, 336–7; and tables A and B below, 327–37.

241:2 *Copia*] Wentford had evidently seen part of, or an early draft of, the *De copia* which Erasmus was still intending to polish (cf line 34). Perhaps it had been sent to Colet who showed it to Wentford, as Allen suggests, or Erasmus may have consulted Wentford in his capacity as a schoolmaster (cf Ep 237:2).

for my fame that influenced you, I for my part recognize your good will by two arguments: first that, being somewhat blinded by extreme affection for me, you esteem your friend Erasmus' trifling work so highly that you treat it 5 as a rare treasure, not, in your opinion to be shared with the vulgar crowd; second, that you are so devoted to keeping up my reputation that in friendship you make the better always the enemy of the good, using one nail, as it were, to drive out another. Still, I myself think it will do my reputation more good if those writings are not published, or even copied, 10 by anyone without most careful revision; and care like this is what I dislike more than dog or serpent, especially as I see no profit come of it but impairment of the eyes, premature old age, and starvation, and a mere scrap of fame accompanied by a great deal of unpopularity. To answer your question about my situation, I am, so far as promises of gold are concerned, 15 unmistakably wealthy, apart from which I live in stark hunger! You express a great deal of sorrow at the emptiness of my purse; you would express still more of it if you knew that I brought it to London well stuffed with more than seventy-two nobles, of which not a farthing remains. From this you will be able to guess how money slips away here, where I have to spend out 20 of my own pocket for every single purpose, and must deal with two devouring Charybdises.

When you so generously and, as I feel sure, so sincerely offer me money of your own, I cherish and warmly salute that same Rogerian spirit which I long since tested and proved true. If only Fortune had given you 25 means that equalled your kindness! And so she will some day, unless she is an open foe to kind-natured men. Where you are I cannot see how I could live, except with Grocyn; and certainly there is nobody in the world I would

* * * * *

8–9 one nail ... another] *Adagia* I ii 4

11–12 dislike more than dog or serpent] *Adagia* II ix 63

18 London] Literally 'istuc.' Allen notes: probably on his return from Paris in June (cf Ep 225 introduction).

19 seventy-two nobles] If Erasmus meant gold angel-nobles, as he did in Epp 240A:11, 248:40, and 270:30, or their equivalent value in money-of-account (6s 8d ster. apiece), then this sum would have amounted to £24 0s 0d ster. = £34 16s 0d gros Flemish = £204 16s 0d tournois; if he meant gold ryals (rose-nobles), then a sum of £36 0s 0d sterling. Cf Epp 214:4n, 227:31n; and 248:40n; and tables A–F below, 327–45.

28 Grocyn] This passage suggests that Erasmus had been staying with Grocyn in London after his return from Paris and before leaving for Cambridge (cf Ep 225 introduction). On leaving London he took with him to Cambridge a book from Grocyn's library (cf Ep 229:8). It is possible that he may also have stayed with Grocyn for part of the two years during which we have no definite word of his movements (cf Ep 218 introduction).

sooner live with, but I am ashamed to cause him the expense, particularly when I have no means of returning the favour, and he will not allow me to 30 contribute anything, so kind is he. I was not particularly anxious to leave you, but it was this consideration of price above all that moved me to do it. Meanwhile to avoid being idle I am finishing my *De conscribendis epistolis*, and I also intend to polish up my *Copia*, while at the same time I often curse these miserable literary pursuits of mine, that produce so little. Farewell, 35 dear Roger, dearest of mortals. Please give my warmest greetings to Master Grocyn, who was patron and teacher to us both. About the boy, I have spoken to Master William X, though Linacre had already discussed the same thing with him.

[1514] 40

242 / From John Fisher London, [c 18 November 1511?]

This letter from the Deventer Letter-book is probably a reply to the letter mentioned in Ep 240:60.

FROM JOHN, BISHOP OF ROCHESTER, TO ERASMUS

Greetings, Erasmus, and I beg you to take no offence at my failure to write a letter when last I sent to you: the bearer was in haste to be out of town, and I myself was on the point of leaving my house when I met him. So, though I had no opportunity to write, still I sent you the small present you had asked 5 for. To be sure I did not give it out of that fund over and above my modest means you suppose to be in my hands. Believe me, Erasmus, whatever

* * * * *

33 *De conscribendis epistolis*] Erasmus had been working on this at intervals for years (cf Ep 71 introduction).

37 boy] This probably refers to John Smith, who became Erasmus' servant-pupil and remained in his service until 1 November 1513. He had been a pupil at Wentford's school. His father was a friend of the Cambridge schoolmaster William Gonell who later used his influence with him on Erasmus' behalf (cf Epp 276, 277, 279). It therefore seems likely that the Mr William (D. Gulielmo N) mentioned here was Gonell rather than Mountjoy as Allen suggests (cf E&C 130, n61).

242:5 the small present] Erasmus had sent a portion of his translation of St Basil's commentary on Isaiah to Fisher with a preface addressed to him (Ep 229) and accompanied it by a letter asking for something in return (cf Epp 227:21ff and 237:15). In it he apparently suggested to Fisher, as he had to Colet (cf Ep 230:38ff), that he might have money in trust for such purposes. While denying that he had any such funds, Fisher did send Erasmus a present which he probably acknowledged in the letter mentioned in Ep 240:60.

people may say, there is no money lodged with me which could be dispensed as I solely chose. The bestowal of the money you refer to is prescribed for me so strictly that I cannot alter it, however much I may wish to do so. 10

For my part, I will not see you in want so long as there is anything left over from my slender resources; for I can see how indispensable you are to our university. At the same time I will also take pains, as often as the chance comes my way, to beg for others' help when my own shall fail. Your friend – our friend – Mountjoy will, I am sure, remember you if ever he has pledged his help; and I shall be glad to urge him to do it, for he is now at court. Best wishes, dear Erasmus. 15

From London

243 / From Andrea Ammonio London, 18 November [1511]

ANDREA AMMONIO TO ERASMUS, HIS DESIRED DESIDERIUS

Your carriers had already left when John More brought me your letter without any letter to Mountjoy; and so I must wait for those scoundrels' return, or else for some chance that may bring me a bearer to whom to give this letter. I understand you have at long last received the cask with the seal broken, and half-empty, and not by any means free; for I think you bought dear at sixpence that flat stuff, all that those ruffians had left you, and moreover I know how that bald-headed fellow has got into the habit of playing tricks. But you are right to give me a warning that no act of human decency is to be expected of these monsters; I must say, if Socrates himself had had a brush with that kind of brute, even he would never have been able to keep unvarying patience or good countenance. In any case I did not send a further consignment of the wine because you had praised it, but because I had in fact done a good stroke of business. For I had received gold where I had given bronze, and so I was trying to see if you had other verses you would be willing to exchange in the same way, not because I take delight in the falsehoods they contain, but because of their elegance and ease and that friendly myopia which makes you think me other than I am. 5 10 15

I have heard from Linacre that your friend the archbishop has decided

* * * * *

243:2 John More] A younger brother of Thomas More to whom he acted as secretary (cf Ep 246:4)

3 letter to Mountjoy] Cf Ep 240:59.

7 sixpence] For the current value of 6d sterling cf CWE 1 340–1; and tables A and B below, 327–37.

14–15 gold ... bronze] Cf Ep 145:151n.

to give you financial help and is looking for a place to serve as a reliable base 20
for your support. If this is so, it will cut down your complaints. But if you
have any left, pour them into your friend's lap, and you will get them back
from me with interest; for I think you are lucky compared with me. You see
you have gained what you were after, consummate learning, a name supremely famous wherever eloquence in the Roman tongue extends, and 25
finally immortality, while I have chased after Fortune even to 'Britain's
farthest shore' and never been able to overtake her; for she continually
recedes further away from me, nay, frightens me still more. I had two
friends who were devoted to me, yet were men for whom the predictions
and speculations of all their fellows foretold lifelong poverty and humility; 30
Fortune, quite marvellously and as if on special purpose to spite me, has
promoted them both to the highest dignity: one she has made vice-chancellor of the Holy See, the other, just recently, supreme penitentiary.
Each of them now reproaches me with folly for preferring Britain to their
company and to the city of Rome, the home of Fortune; and looks down on 35
me and not altogether undeservedly. I may add that you send your reputation before you wherever you turn, and cannot fail to find powerful patrons
everywhere; but I, unless I can scrape together some means to support my
declining years among those whom I have given much hard work, many
years, and no little expense to oblige, know not where I can take refuge, 40
seeing that I have quite grown old in this Cimmerian darkness: premature
grey hairs, which they call the standard-bearers of death, are rushing out in
serried ranks all over my head. But this is a long and sad story; and this is
the interest I keep for you!

I have not yet paid my respects to Lord Mountjoy; it is my misfortune 45
to keep postponing my duty from day to day. The bishop of Durham
promises you his aid and keen support, while the bishop of Winchester has

* * * * *

20 place] Warham conferred the living of Aldington on Erasmus 22 March 1512 (cf Ep 255 introduction).

26–7 'Britain's farthest shore'] Catullus 11–12

32–3 vice-chancellor] Cardinal Sisto Della Rovere of Lucca (d 1517), nephew of Julius II, was made vice-chancellor of the Holy See in 1508.

33 penitentiary] Cardinal Leonardo Grosso Della Rovere (d 1520) was a nephew of Sixtus IV and was given the office of supreme penitentiary by Julius II.

41 Cimmerian darkness] *Adagia* II vi 34

46 Durham] His promise of aid and the friendly comments of the bishop of Winchester were evidently called forth by their receipt of Erasmus' letters mentioned in Ep 236:38.

said less in public but in a more friendly vein. He was under the impression that you already held a benefice; I replied that you had been given the expectation of a benefice but that none had yet been forthcoming. He 50 smiled and asked whether that particular hope was something you could use to buy food. I smiled in turn, and said: 'Rather Erasmus has purchased these expectations by spending money and time.' Thereupon he told me to speak to him about this on another and more suitable occasion. I have not yet seen the right moment, but I was extremely glad that the bishop of 55 Winchester spoke so affectionately about you. As to the future, I shall see to it that you do not lack any kindness at my hands.

About the hive for you to withdraw to, I have no definite news for you. The Augustinians have nobody with whom you could share a dwelling. I do not know whether you would like me to ask the blind poet. I hear there are 60 certain empty rooms there, which could be rented, but they would have to be furnished. As to the community where I myself am living, they say every corner is filled; besides, the table they keep is worse than mediocre. There is, as you know, a college near St Paul's belonging to certain doctors, who, they say, live rather well; but in my opinion it would be living in a sewer. 65 Perhaps it might do no harm to try Francesco, but he seems to me a more pitiable object than the old beggar Irus himself. In a word, I have nothing yet to report about this business; if anything comes into my mind, you shall hear about it. Why should I ask you about Griffo's friendliness, especially at

* * * * *

60 blind poet] Bernard André of Toulouse (c 1450–1522) came to England in 1485. He was by that time blind. He became court poet under the patronage of Henry VII and was tutor to Prince Arthur from 1496 to 1500 when he resigned to become royal historiographer. He wrote a biography of Henry VII and a history of his reign. He also wrote a number of educational treatises. Erasmus was somewhat unwilling to appeal to him for lodgings as he owed him money and wished to avoid him (cf Ep 248:39ff).

62 community] St Thomas's Hospital (cf 232:5–6n)

64 college] A community or college of doctors of law, called Doctors' Commons. In 1511 it was recently founded and lodged in Paternoster Row. It was abolished in 1857 (cf E&C 133, n68).

66 Francesco] Cf Ep 240:57n.

67 Irus] Cf Martial 5.39.9 and 6.77.1. He was the aged beggar in the eighteenth book of the *Odyssey*.

69 Griffo] Pietro Griffo, deputy collector of papal revenue in England from 1509 to 1512. See Denys Hay 'Pietro Griffo, an Italian in England' *Italian Studies* 2 (1939) 118–28. Ammonio was apparently suggesting that Erasmus might find lodging with him (cf 249:24, 250:27).

this particular time when Messer Giambattista Boncanti is away? Write back and tell me your wishes; meanwhile if you should return to London you shall not want for a room. 70

Up to the present I have not seen More; I thought, too, that it would not do to make a special point of asking him whether he has delivered that letter. He can hardly have helped delivering it, for never a day passes but he either sees the archbishop or addresses him. I have no news from Italy; but then I have not received so much as a line myself. I should like you to give Bullock once more my warmest greetings, since he so much appreciates them. About the best turn you can do me is to take every possible care to stay in excellent health. 75 80

London, 18 November

244 / From Johannes Sixtinus London, 19 November [1511]

JOHANNES SIXTINUS TO HIS VERY DEAR FRIEND ERASMUS

I was enormously delighted by the pointed, nay sharp, wit of your letter, except at the place where you found a want of straightforwardness in me: but so well and so skilfully do you heal this tiny wound, though it does hurt me a little, that I cannot complain; especially since you adduce certain arguments which would lead even a responsible man to suspect me of deceit and fraud if I were not as well known to him as I am to you. Thale's persistent assertions that he did not give me the manuscript of your *Copia* as a gift but as a loan, to be returned to you, together with my continued silence amid frequent references to the *Copia*, a silence that would have been broken by accident if not on purpose, had I been consistently straightforward – considerations such as these would assuredly, at first sight, have an effect on a person of sober judgment, to say nothing of an irresponsible one. Yet when I die, Erasmus, I shall die in the full consciousness that to the best of my belief the book was given to me. When Thale left and could not sell his books, he shared them out among his friends: some to 5 10 15

* * * * *

70 Boncanti] This person has not been identified.

244:2 letter] Erasmus's answer to Ep 235, now lost.

7 Thale] William Thale was the man to whom Pace gave the papers Erasmus left with him at Ferrara in December 1508 (cf Epp 30:17n, 211:53n). Among them was a draft of the *De copia* which Thale apparently gave to Sixtinus. As Erasmus was once more working on the *De copia*, he was anxious to recover the earlier copy and was also afraid that it might be published in an unauthorized edition (cf Ep 260:69ff).

Allen, some to me, and also I think some to Shurley – but I will not make any rash statement. Your brain-child was given to me since he knew that anything of yours was very acceptable to me; I am not quite sure whether or not I read the title and list of contents for as far as I know I never read a single page. I kept a full perusal for my leisure, leisure which I could not obtain at Bologna on account of my study of law; and so it was quite possible for a straightforward person to say nothing, despite frequent mention of the *Copia*, since as far as I know that title never occurred to me. To your penetrating mind this will perhaps seem farfetched; but indeed, so far as I am aware, I have never lied to you or dealt craftily with you in any way; and I am very sorry that this has happened. So I beg you to banish, as I think you will, any suspicion of fraud and guile you have entertained concerning me. It appears, however, that you have already done so, since you say that that little cloud, so to call it, has easily been wiped away by the force of affection and that you have been thinking about securing a place for my relative, as Bullock promises to do. And as for your statement that you know of no services on your part towards me, apart from affection for me, that is just like your noble and generous nature, for it is your custom to do good to all men, and you think it your duty to perform kind acts to all men of good will. But indeed I am well aware of them and shall remember them as long as I live, and this I shall always maintain.

The hope of a visit from you soon has given great pleasure to our dean, who has forty shillings in readiness for this visit, unless he sends them to Cambridge for you before you arrive. I wish that you were here, and you

* * * * *

17 Allen] John Allen (1476–1534) was a churchman and diplomat who had spent some nine years in Italy partly as Warham's agent (cf Ep 249:26–30). He was Erasmus' predecessor in the living of Aldington (cf Ep 255 introduction). Later he was one of Wolsey's agents in the suppression of the monasteries and in 1528 was made archbishop of Dublin and chancellor of Ireland.

17 Shurley] Richard Shurley was granted the living of Pembridge in Herefordshire in October 1509. He was apparently in Ferrara after Erasmus left, but must have returned to England shortly thereafter.

38 dean] Colet

39 forty shillings] A sum worth £2 0s 0d sterling = £2 18s 3d gros Flemish = £16 18s 0d tournois, by the relative silver values. Although Erasmus may have been thinking simply of the money-of-account evaluation, he may indeed have meant the actual silver coin, popularly called the teston (testoon, tester), which Henry VII had issued only seven years earlier as the first shilling in English history. The teston-shilling was struck from 1504 to 1526 at the traditional fineness of 11 oz 2 dwt silver (= 92.5 per cent pure) and a weight of 144 grains Troy (= 9.331 grams = 8.631 grams pure silver). Cf tables A–F below, 327–45.

and I were fortunate enough to be always together, and could talk instead of writing to each other. Yet I did at length cajole a letter from you, when I thought (but not quite seriously, for this I never could have done) that I had virtually been blotted out of your list of friends, seeing that among all the frequent bundles of letters from you there was none addressed to me. If you 45 had not sent letters to anyone at all, I should have put this down to the honourable labours that have taken up your time; just as you ought to attribute to my own labours the fact that I have written to nobody; but when I saw that you had time enough to write packages of letters, indeed bags full of them, not just now and again but very frequently, I thought that I too 50 might receive just one of them if I were still upon your register of friends; yet you are clever too in the way you meet my protest by adding greetings to me in correspondence addressed to others.

But need I go on? You have made amends to me; while if I have cleared myself adequately in your eyes, I shall be more delighted than you can 55 easily suppose. Farewell, my very sweet friend.

The reason for my somewhat late reply is that your letter dated on the feast of Sts Simon and Jude was not delivered to me until 17 November, later than you might imagine. Once again, my very best wishes.

London, 19 November 60

244A / From Jérôme de Busleyden [Mechlin? November 1511?]

This letter was found in a manuscript volume of Busleyden's poems, letters, and speeches in the Bibliothèque Royale in Brussels. The manuscript bears no date and that assigned to it by Allen is conjectural, though supported by cogent arguments which make it more plausible than the date June 1516 suggested by Nichols (II 277) on the assumption that it refers to the time when Erasmus was hoping for a benefice from Jean Le Sauvage, chancellor of Burgundy. A rumour of Erasmus' death following a serious attack of sweating sickness in the summer of 1511 was widely circulated at the time when this letter was written (cf Ep 251:2n), while there is no evidence of any such rumour in 1516. The benefice referred to seems more likely to be the living of Aldington, the gift of which was forecast by Ammonio in November 1511 (cf Ep 243:20) though it was not actually conferred until March of the following year. The suggestion that it had been long promised would apply to Warham's gift (cf Ep 215:78), but not to anything from Le Sauvage, nor could he be described as a patron whom Erasmus had long served. Allen notes a resemblance between the advice given by Busleyden and that passed on by Erasmus to Ammonio in Ep 250. It may also be worth noting that Busleyden would

* * * * *

58 feast of Sts Simon and Jude] 28 October

scarcely have urged Erasmus to moderate his strictures on kings when revising his comments for publication if he had already read the *Moria*, which he almost certainly would have done by 1516, though not necessarily by November 1511 when it had been in print for only a few months.

TO ERASMUS OF ROTTERDAM, THE GLORY OF GERMANY

Your elegant letter gave me the utmost pleasure, both because it came from you and I had to wait a long time for it, and also because it brought the news that you are still alive, whereas a rumour of unknown source had been circulating for months to the effect that you are dead. I was as appalled by 5 that gloomy report at the time as I am now completely restored to happiness, knowing it to be false, for a little while ago, having lost you in this way, I had almost died myself; overcome by mourning for you, of all people, I had almost left others to mourn for me. So thanks be to God, who, gauging the deliverance of us both by that of one of us, saved me in you and 10 you for my sake; to the end that by this act of saving grace he may in the end vouchsafe to us a closer and more intimate friendship; for we have long been joined by our common love of virtue, by common studies and a common bond of heart and mind, in unbroken affection.

To go back to your letter: I have given much thought to what you wrote 15 in it at some length, and rather freely, about kings; and, since your sentiments are such as could more safely be confided in person to trusty ears than set down in a letter, I hope you will be discreet enough to moderate them in revising them for publication and treat of them (the kings) with caution, lest some day you give the ill-disposed crowd of blackmailers and informers the 20 opportunity to say a word against you in the ear of princes. Such men always swarm in princes' courts, as you are well aware and as I have eventually, to my peril, discovered for myself.

What you say besides about the plan to get you a benefice gives me some satisfaction, granted that the matter is not yet quite on the last page, as 25 they say. But I have great hopes that the undertaking so solemnly given to you and so often renewed will bear fruit for you in the end. Only, if any delay should occur, please do not lose patience but endure the drudgery. Continue cheerfully in your plans, and press your Maecenas daily, for he is far more in your debt, inasmuch as your intellect has already been hard at 30 work on his behalf for so many years and your ready obedience has always been open and obvious. So, to sum up in brief, you simply must forget your usual modesty, and be brazen; forget that you are a wise philosopher, and

* * * * *

25 granted] Literally *esto*

25 on the last page] *ad umbelicum*: *Adagia* I ii 32

33 be brazen] *Adagia* I viii 47

play the role of some shameless petty dependent, knocking on his patron's door in the early morning and wearing away his threshold, urgently demanding until at last he obtains what he asks for. Farewell. 35

245 / To Andrea Ammonio Cambridge, 26 November 1511

This letter answers Ep 237. It is exceptionally full of phrases in Greek.

ERASMUS TO HIS FRIEND AMMONIO

At long last on 24 November I received your letter written on 27 October – a letter, my dear Andrea, to give it the briefest possible praise, entirely worthy of you, which means that it was as learned as it was open-hearted. If I reply to it rather briefly, you must put this down to St Jerome, whom I have 5 undertaken to expound – a much harder assignment, by the muses I swear it, than one would think. And yet it is not the effort that torments me so much as the worry involved. In praising my verses as much as you do I see you are merely playing the rhetorician and, to show your skill with words, deliberately making an elephant out of a fly. I personally think them both 10 very clumsy and entirely truthful; in this, if in nothing else, I sing the whole gamut away from you. And I borrowed the idea of those verses from nowhere but yourself. Indeed I painted my Ammonio in the most lively colours, it is true (for they were your own), but the artist was not lively and there was no life in his brush. But tell me, what is this great discovery of 15 yours of which you write, namely that Erasmus is fond of Ammonio? For if I were capable of refusing to love a man of your character, one too to whom I am so much indebted, then indeed I should be Erasmus not from Eros but just the opposite, the most unlovable, one who deserves to be called brute by wild brutes and savage by the very tribes of Tartary. 20

What is this you tell me? The pope gone to Loreto? What piety! As to the war that has been set on foot, I am afraid that the Greek proverb about

* * * * *

245:5 St Jerome] This may be Erasmus' tenure of the Lady Margaret Professorship in Divinity. The appointment required only a month of lecturing (cf Ep 248:47).

10 elephant out of a fly] *Adagia* I ix 69

11–12 the whole gamut] *Adagia* I ii 63

18 Erasmus] He plays on two Greek words: *erasmios* 'lovely' and *era* 'earth' or *eris* 'strife.'

21 Loreto] Cf Ep 236:46n.

the moth in the candle-flame will soon be appropriate. For if anything happens to the Roman church, then who, I ask you, could more properly be blamed for it than the all-too-mighty Julius? But pray suppose the French 25 are driven out of Italy, and then reflect, please, whether you prefer to have the Spaniards as your masters, or the Venetians, whose rule is intolerable even to their own countrymen. Priests are something that princes will never put up with; and yet they will never be able to agree among themselves because of the more than deadly feuds between their factions. I fear Italy is 30 to have a change of masters and, because she cannot endure the French, may have to endure French rule multiplied by two. But this is fate's business; we fight these battles from an armchair.

I am sorry your change of country has not suited you, but even so I am rather happy that a kindred spirit has come my way. For although your 35 neighbours are Cyprian oxen and eaters of ordure, they still believe that they alone eat heavenly fare and feast on the brain of Zeus. I am quite delighted that you are Lucianizing, and when I get back to London, that is, before the middle of December if Heaven so wills, we will pursue Greek studies together. Meanwhile I shall await your letter, in which please tell 40 me any news of my friend Mountjoy, for, although I have written to him twice, I know his ways – he never utters a syllable in reply; next, what hope your bishops hold out; third, whether the plague has subsided yet, and what nest you think I had best withdraw to.

I have now received three letters from you. I wrote to Colet and to 45 one-eyed Pieter, but suspect these letters have been stopped. I gave More a letter to deliver to the bishop of Rochester; I do not know whether he has delivered it. Illness was the cause of my failure to reply to your poem; when my vigour returns, I shall not be completely silent. Farewell, Andrea; you are a better friend to me than any Pylades. 50

Cambridge, 26 November 1511

* * * * *

23 the moth in the candle flame] *Adagia* I ix 51

25 Julius] Cf Ep 228:21n.

33 armchair] *Adagia* I iii 93

36 Cyprian oxen] The oxen in Cyprus were said to eat human excrement (*Adagia* I x 95).

37 eat heavenly fare] *Adagia* III i 91; I vi 60

42 never ... a syllable] *Adagia* I viii 3

46 Pieter] Cf Ep 231:5n.

246 / To Andrea Ammonio Cambridge, 27 November [1511]

ERASMUS OF ROTTERDAM TO HIS FRIEND ANDREA

Pray observe how shameless I am! I am sending you the *Icaromenippus* for you to copy out, if you can do this without boredom or inconvenience, or else arrange with More to give it to his brother for copying. You see I am preparing something by way of bait in readiness for New Year's Day, 5 though, unless I am mistaken, it will be futile. And here – what a university! No one can be found who will write even moderately well at any price. But, my dear Andrea, I would rather anything than that you should assume any tedious task for my sake. Please see that my letters are delivered to the people to whom they are addressed. Make sure that I find you in the best of 10 health.

Cambridge, 27 November [1512]

247 / From Andrea Ammonio London, 28 November [1511]

ANDREA AMMONIO TO ERASMUS

For one reason or another I have twice now failed to write to you by those rascals of yours. Still, three or four days ago I handed to a priest a letter addressed to you, finishing it in haste because he said he was hurrying off in your direction; in it I made it clear that my lord of Winchester is very well 5 disposed towards you, but he is so much engrossed in these present disturbances that he can hardly find leisure for anything else. Nevertheless, if you wish me to insist, I will not be idle. Consider all the same whether you ought not to be here in person, for I think you would have great influence. If you come, you need not worry about your health; everything is 10 perfectly healthy in these parts, and the plague is not so much as mentioned. Moreover, if you are absolutely terrified of Mountjoy's Cerberus, you and I together could easily find a room somewhere else which would suit you well enough; for if I were looking for it by myself on your behalf, I should be hard indeed to satisfy. 15

I have had a letter from Italy, from which I learn that the French side is

* * * * *

2 *Icaromenippus*] Erasmus' translation of one of Lucian's dialogues, to be printed with others in the edition dedicated to Warham 29 April 1512 (see Ep 261 introduction).

4 brother] John More (see Ep 243:2n)

5 bait] Cf Ep 187:4n.

247:12 Cerberus] Cf Ep 231:9n.

in the ascendant so far, while only a few Spaniards are showing up, and those half-starved and barefoot too. The Council of Pisa is going ahead; the cardinals of Santa Croce, Cosenza, Bayeux, and Narbonne have been stripped of their rank in a general conclave and deprived of all their benefices; 20 and finally the lord of Bologna is paying in hunger, pestilence, murder, and pillage the penalty he deserves for his treachery. No more Italian news. Look after your health, my dear Erasmus, and give my greetings to our friend Bullock.

London,28 November [1512] 25

248 / To Andrea Ammonio Cambridge, 2 December [1511]

ERASMUS OF ROTTERDAM TO HIS FRIEND AMMONIO

Your letters, my dear Andrea, make me want to fly to you for an opportunity to enjoy closer communion with so pleasant a friend. On the other hand, the same letters make it possible for me to endure staying here, just because they refresh me so often with your conversational nectar that it seems to me 5 that I am not away from London at all.

But what is this, pray? Are you really comparing my fortune with yours – the anemone with the rose? I ask you, is there a single respect in which you are not miles ahead of Erasmus? Take my reputation, such as it is: I cannot say I owe it anything, except that it holds a candle to my distress 10 and refuses to let my misery remain a secret, so that the embarrassment of my situation is now heavier to bear than its discomforts. But this is a wound I would rather not reopen. Say that my fortune is worthy of me; I should like

* * * * *

18 Council of Pisa] Cf Ep 236:50n.

19 Santa Croce] Carvajal. (See Ep 239:55n). His deprivation and that of the other cardinals here mentioned, Cosenza (Francesco Borgia), Bayeux (René de Brie), and Narbonne (Guillaume Briçonnet) took place in public consistory on 24 October 1511 (E. Rodocanachi *Le pontificat de Jules II* (Paris 1928) 144).

21 lord of Bologna] This probably refers to Annibale II Bentivoglio, one of the sons of Giovanni Bentivoglio (cf Ep 200:5n), who was the *de facto* ruler of Bologna from May 1511 to June 1512 (cf Ep 251:13–14n). During this time the papal troops besieged Bologna and laid waste the surrounding countryside. Allen's suggestion that it refers to Achille de' Grassi, bishop of Bologna, cannot be accepted since he was not in the city during this period and was, moreover, a staunch supporter of Julius II.

248:8 the anemone with the rose] *Adagia* II vi 41

9 miles ahead] *Adagia* II iii 82

12 wound] *Adagia* I vi 80

to put this construction on it. As for your fortune, you are quite right to complain about it if anyone were to assess your gifts: anyone who could measure these would surely assign you the supreme pontiff's place. But, my dear Andrea, you are familiar with the celebrated blind sport of Fortune, and the sight of men whom her unpredictable behaviour has swept to the heights ought not to give you such acute pain. If, however, you are quite determined to better yourself, you must abandon some part of that which more than anything makes you attractive to all good men – I mean your modesty. I myself think that, as things are, even if nothing is added, you are the luckiest of men, considering your nationality, appearance, age, talents, character, and the approval you have from the best sort of people. And unless my predictions are hopelessly out, the day is not far distant when your splendid gifts will be matched with the fairest rewards that fortune has to offer.

You lament leaving Rome; but what good does it do to count the waves in one's wake? 'We must make the best of what we have.' Furthermore I think I can pretty well guess why the thought of grey hairs vexes you so much: you are afraid the girls will tease you! Oh, what a bitter blow, yes, a thing 'to gnaw the heart'! I am grateful both to you and to the bishop of Winchester, and with good reason, to you because you have furthered my interest in such a friendly way, while he gives me such warm support. But be sure to avoid insisting in any way.

About a room: all I am after is an apartment well protected from draughts, with a good fire – I will organize my supplies in my usual fashion. I would rather you did not breathe a word about the following matter for a while; but if you can get wind of anything, I should like to know whether my Maecenas has paid those twenty nobles to Bernard; this is what makes me tend to avoid London, as I hate nothing so much as being dunned. Still, you are free to negotiate with him about a house if you happen to meet him.

Two days ago I sent off the cask with a very short letter. I have received

* * * * *

28–9 count the waves in one's wake] *Adagia* I iv 45

29 make the best ... have] Cf Ep 240:34n

32 'to gnaw the heart'] Euripides *Hecuba* 235; *Adagia* I i 2

40 twenty nobles] As Ep 254:3 would indicate, these nobles were evidently the Tudor gold angels, officially worth 6s 8d ster. (1465–1526), and not ryals or rose-nobles. This debt would thus have amounted to £6 13s 4d sterling = £9 13s 4d gros Flemish = £56 17s 8d tournois. Cf Ep 214:4n; CWE I 312, 321, 325, 329, 336–7; and tables A–F below, 327–45.

40 Bernard] André (cf Epp 243:60n and 254:2)

two letters from you and am answering them with this one. If, however, Jerome were not torturing me so acutely, I should take up the contest with you, not only in verses but in whole volumes. Still, within ten days my month will be up. Bullock has written to you. If you happen to see Colet and any mention of me arises, offer your help if he wishes to write to me. If Sixtinus comes your way, please tell him that his letter gave me the utmost pleasure. I still have to work at this treadmill for seven or eight days; after that we will enjoy ourselves together at our ease and pleasure. Farewell, best of friends. 45 50

Cambridge, 2 December

I have written also a second letter to you; it was delivered, I think, by a bookseller named Gerard. 55

[1512]

249 / From Andrea Ammonio — London, 5 December 1511

ANDREA AMMONIO TO ERASMUS OF ROTTERDAM

Is this your way, Erasmus, of teasing your friend and making fun of him? You ask me if there is any respect in which I am not miles ahead of you, whereas I am fully conscious of being a hundred leagues at least behind. But if it were possible to make a complete exchange, I should soon make you eat your words, for I should immediately invite you to exchange with me. Now do you really think I am worth a bishopric, and the most exalted at that? Either you are as fond of me as I could wish, or at any rate your joke is Erasmian. In your judgment of me as 'the luckiest of men, even if nothing is added,' I see a touch of rhetorical embellishment; but your fine predictions are very welcome, even if they have their source in your good will rather than in any genuine foresight. Ah, you prophet – so you have at last guessed the reason why I grieved over my grey hairs! As if the girls you mention looked at a man's hair and not rather at his purse! I swear I have only to let a gold coin glitter at my fingertips to become more handsome 5 10 15

* * * * *

45 Jerome] Cf Ep 245:5n.

49 Sixtinus] The letter referred to is Ep 244.

55 Gerard] May be identified with Gerard or Garrett Godfrey (d 1539), a Dutch stationer and bookseller who had been living in Cambridge since 1503. Erasmus apparently lived with him for part of his stay in Cambridge and sent him greetings over the years. Erasmus himself refers to him simply as Gerardus. For his identification with Garrett Godfrey see Allen's notes here and Allen Epp 456:281 and 777:29–30nn.

than Nireus himself. No, I am not depressed for this reason, but because I can see that I have wasted my life and am growing old. Once again your advice is sound – we must make the best of what we have. But I should like you to advise me where to go, without altogether playing the philosopher.

I reminded the bishop of Winchester about you once more, but the moment was ill-chosen. Still, when you come yourself we can find some perfectly suitable time. I understand, more or less, your wishes about the room, but you do not reply to my question whether you would like to take a lodging with Griffo. I shall meet Sixtinus and tell him what you say about the letter. Also I shall speak to Mountjoy and worm out of him, as discreetly as I can, whether those gold nobles have been paid. I do not know whether you have heard that Allen is here in person; I have often intended to tell you this, but always forgot. He was recalled on some honourable pretext, but in fact because, I hear, he conducted my lord of Canterbury's business in Rome unwisely.

I wish that the eight days you tell me you must spend where you are may be shorter than winter days, and the nights likewise, so as to hasten the time when you and I may be frivolous together in spite of Fortune and I may enjoy the gaiety of Erasmus.

I have received from the bookseller your two letters with the *Icaromenippus*, and have also answered them. Bullock's letter, and the cask, and those two short letters of yours have not yet reached me. Look after yourself.

London, 5 December 1511

250 / To Andrea Ammonio Cambridge, 9 December [1511]

ERASMUS OF ROTTERDAM TO HIS FRIEND AMMONIO

May all the muses hate me, my dear Andrea, if I am pretending at all about your luck; no it is all from the heart.

On the feast of the Conception I was brought painfully to bed, where-

* * * * *

16 Nireus] The handsomest man among the Greeks at Troy (Homer *Iliad* 2.673)

24 Griffo] Cf Ep 243:69.

27 Allen] Cf Ep 244:17n.

33 Fortune] Literally (the goddess) Nortia (Juvenal *Satires* 10.74)

36 *Icaromenippus*] Cf Ep 246:2n.

250:4 the feast of the Conception] 8 December, commonly called the feast of the Immaculate Conception

upon I was delivered of several large rocks. Please include this kind of stone among the pebbles you use for working out the calculus of my happiness! Take care to avoid saying anything inappropriate in your conversations with the bishop of Winchester. 5

You want my advice about making the best of what we have. Very well then; I will act the sow teaching Minerva without playing philosopher too much, which you will not allow. To begin with, put a bold face on everything to avoid ever feeling shame. Next, intrude in all the affairs of everyone; elbow people out of the way whenever possible. Do not love or hate anyone sincerely, but measure everything by your own advantage; let your whole course of behaviour be directed to this one goal. Give nothing unless you look for a return, and agree with everyone about everything. 10 15

But, you say, there is nothing special about all this. Come then, here is a piece of advice just made to order for you, since you wish it; but, mind you, I whisper it confidentially. You are familiar with British jealousy; use it for your own profit. Always sit on two stools at once; bribe different suitors to cultivate you. Threaten to go away, and actually get ready to go. Flourish letters in which you are tempted away by generous promises. Sometimes remove your presence deliberately in order that, when your society is denied them, they may feel the need of you all the more keenly. 20

I have no business to do with X. If he had done a single thing wisely, it would have seemed a marvel in my eyes, for he is 'more foolish than folly itself'; but his successor is not much wiser. Griffo is a man I like tremendously in every way, but still I like my freedom better. The carrier claims he delivered the letter and the cask. Farewell, my dear Ammonio. 25

Cambridge, morrow of the Conception [1512] 30

251 / From Paolo Bombace [Bologna], 21 December 1511

This letter may be an answer to the one mentioned in Ep 226:2. It is an abstract of the original (cf Ep 210, introduction).

* * * * *

5 stone] Cf Ep 296:65n.

6 pebbles] *Adagia* I v 55

10 the sow teaching Minerva] Cf Ep 216:35–6n.

19 British jealousy] The phrase is in Greek in the text, evidently a measure of prudence.

20 sit on two stools] *Adagia* I vii 2

25 X] Probably Allen, whom Erasmus was to succeed in the living of Aldington (cf Ep 244:17n), and whose presence in London Ammonio had mentioned in the preceding letter

[Letter from Bombace to Erasmus, 21 December 1511]
He expresses his pleasure that the rumour which had been circulating about Erasmus' death was false. He tells him about the ill-health, especially the headaches, from which he is suffering; hence he had gone to the baths of Siena, but without any benefit. He says that on his return from this journey he found that his Greek lectureship in Bologna had been awarded 5 'to a Greek, who was a wooden log rather than a human being,' but the salary had not been withdrawn, and that the loss of the lectureship was engineered by his rivals. All the same, he says, he still kept the lectureship in rhetoric and poetry, which he held until Christmas, after which date he gave it up, following also the advice of Carteromachus who resided in his 10 house at the time, and with whom also he betook himself to Venice in the springtime, and there fell ill.

After returning to his own country, he adds, he found that the Bentivoglio had again come back to their city and were ruling it, which pleases him; that he thereupon received his salary for the preceding years, although 15 he had not been lecturing at the university. He goes on to say that at the present time, while the pope was making every effort to recapture Bologna by force of arms and the Bentivoglio throwing up fortifications in order to defend it, with every citizen labouring at the defensive works, he himself was obliged to take part in the labour of construction and take his pick and 20 shovel, in company with the others, and work on the defences. Following which, he thanks Erasmus for inviting him to come to England; he adds that he has read his *Adagia* and has made notes upon certain things about which he would write to him later.

252 / To Antoon van Bergen London, 6 February [1512]

Erasmus returned to London in December 1511 or January 1512. At this time he was invited by Fisher, bishop of Rochester, to accompany him to the Lateran

* * * * *

1 rumour] Cf Ep 226:5n.

6 Greek] A certain Peter of Aegina, according to the editor of Bombace's letters: G. Fantuzzi *Notizie degli scrittori bolognesi* (Bologna 1782) II 276.

10 Carteromachus] Scipione Fortiguerra (cf Ep 217:4n)

13–14 Bentivoglio] The sons of Giovanni Bentivoglio, who had died in exile, returned to Bologna with the aid of French troops in May 1511. Julius II was determined to reconquer the city and, after the proclamation of the Holy League in October, Bologna was besieged by papal and Spanish troops. The collapse of the French army after Ravenna forced the Bolognese to surrender and the Bentivoglio left the city for good 10 June 1512. Cf C.M. Ady *The Bentivoglio of Bologna* (Oxford 1937) 202ff.

Council which had been summoned by Julius II for 19 April 1512 (cf Creighton IV 148ff). Erasmus received the invitation too late to make arrangements. This and the following two letters were to have been delivered by someone in Fisher's party, but in fact Fisher did not go (cf Ep 255:4n). Antoon van Bergen had been a patron of Erasmus since about 1500 (cf Ep 143, introduction).

ERASMUS OF ROTTERDAM TO THE EMINENT FATHER ANTOON VAN BERGEN, LORD ABBOT OF ST BERTIN

Best greetings, reverend Father. I very nearly came to revisit you in the company of the present English mission; for the bishop of Rochester – who is endowed not only with wonderful holiness of life but with profound and 5 abstruse learning, and moreover has an amazingly pleasant disposition that recommends him to the highest and the humblest – has always vouchsafed me out of his kindness the greatest possible favour, though I am of no account whatever; and it was he who wished me to join the mission. However I heard of it too late to have time to set my affairs in order. For this 10 reason I thought it incumbent upon me to give my greetings by letter at least to so rare a patron, especially as I took my leave without greeting you when last I returned from Paris. Yet this itself happened by chance. I thought I was to stay for several months at the castle of Hammes, but in this I was completely mistaken. Your physician, Master Ghisbert, knows all about it. 15

If you have any desire to hear how I am, your Erasmus is now almost entirely transformed into an Englishman, so extremely kind have many persons been to me, including especially the archbishop of Canterbury, my incomparable Maecenas – or rather, not mine, but that of all scholars, among whom I occupy the last place, if any. Great heavens, how well- 20 endowed and fertile and quick his mind is! What skill he shows in the conduct of highly important business, and how distinguished his scholarship! At the same time his demeanour towards everyone is uniquely affable; he has the pleasantest manner in the world towards those he meets, so that he never leaves anyone depressed in spirit on parting, which is a truly 25 royal trait. Besides, his generosity is lavish and prompt; and lastly, for all the eminence of his station and his rank, he has not a trace of arrogance, so that he gives the impression of being the only person who is unaware of his

* * * * *

14 Hammes] When Erasmus left Paris in June 1511 (cf Ep 256:23n) he intended to stop on the way to London at Hammes for a visit with Mountjoy. He did not do so, possibly because Mountjoy was expecting to return to England in the near future (cf Ep 231:8n). Hammes is very near Saint-Omer, the abbot's home.

15 Ghisbert] The town physician of Saint-Omer (cf Ep 95:13n)

greatness. No one stands up for his friends more loyally or more stoutly. In a word he is the primate indeed, not only in rank but in all praiseworthy qualities. When I have him on my side, ought I not to consider myself exceptionally lucky even if that were all? 30

How exceedingly fortunate is our illustrious Prince Charles in the prospect of gaining such a bride! Nature could make nothing that was lovelier, or more perfect, than she is; and she surpasses all women as much in goodness and wisdom as in beauty. I bid your Reverence farewell. 35

London, the sixth of February [1515]

253 / To Robert Guibé London, 8 February [1512]

Robert Guibé (c 1456–1513) was a Breton who had long been resident in Rome. He had been made a cardinal in 1505 and bishop of Nantes in 1507. He sided with Julius II in his quarrel with Louis XII and was compelled by the king to resign his bishopric in 1511. Erasmus, however, still styled him cardinal of Nantes here and in Ep 296:110, where he mentioned the cardinal among those who had shown him kindness in Rome.

TO HIS EMINENCE THE CARDINAL OF NANTES FROM ERASMUS, GREETINGS

Most reverend Father, the purpose of my present letter is but to assure you that I have never been, and am not, and never shall be forgetful of the kindness which your most reverend Lordship showed to me, both upon the journey and while I was staying in Rome, though I had done nothing to deserve it. I should have to look for a new river of Lethe if I wished to forget that city and to be no more racked with longing for it; for I cannot without anguish recall the climate, the green places, the libraries, the colonnades, and the honeyed talks with scholars – the lights of the world, the position, the prospects, that I put from me so readily. Nevertheless this longing is mitigated by the extraordinary courtesy shown to me by the most reverend the archbishop of Canterbury, and not merely courtesy but good will, so warm that his affection could not be exceeded though he were my father or my brother. I am also receiving a kindly welcome from many other prelates of this realm, first among whom is the eminent bishop of Rochester, a man who to great uprightness of life adds varied and abstruse learning and has a 5 10 15

* * * * *

33 Prince Charles] Later the emperor Charles V. His marriage to Mary Tudor, daughter of Henry VII, was arranged by treaty signed at Calais 21 December 1507 (Mackie 187). The engagement was broken off in 1514 (Mackie 283f).

mind above all meanness, and because of these qualities is much esteemed. I should have gone to Rome in his company had I been informed of it a little sooner. 20

Should there be any matter in which your most reverend Lordship deigns to employ the assistance of the humblest of your servants, pray command and instruct me. The archbishop of Canterbury, whom I have just mentioned, the primate of England, endowed with primacy not merely in his rank and title but in learning, morals, honour, graciousness, and 25 modesty, treats me with exceptional favour, for all that I do not deserve it. He has a quite unequalled regard for the glories of the Roman see, though indeed this whole realm of England is extremely well disposed thereto. I pray God to give concord and union throughout the world by his holy peace; and so I bid your Eminence farewell. 30

London, 8 February [1515]

254 / To Thomas Halsey London, 8 February [1512]

Thomas Halsey was penitentiary of the English nation in Rome.

ERASMUS OF ROTTERDAM TO HIS FRIEND THOMAS HALSEY

At long last Bernard and I, using every stratagem, have won the day! Lord Mountjoy has paid the thirty ducats.

If my lord the bishop of Rochester had known of my desires in time, and I of his, I might perhaps have been with you already. If I am not utterly 5 mistaken, he is unchallengeably supreme among our contemporaries for holiness of life, for learning, and for generosity of mind – only excepting, as an Achilles, my lord of Canterbury, who alone keeps me here, though not entirely in accordance with my own wishes.

Give my greetings to our friend Master Pace and recommend my 10 writings to him so that they not be lost. I have already written six letters, but received none, save one from Pace, and that had been opened and arrived

* * * * *

254:2 Bernard] Bernard André, to whom Mountjoy had finally paid the money Erasmus owed him (cf Ep 243:60n).

3 thirty ducats] These Venetian ducats, then worth about 4s 7d sterling apiece, were apparently the equivalent of the 20-nobles debt in Ep 248:40. Thus 30 ducats = £6 17s 6d sterling = 20.6 angel-nobles = £9 17s 6d gros Flemish = £58 2s 10d tournois. Cf CWE 1 312, 314, 338–9; and tables A–F below, 327–45.

10 Pace] Erasmus is here referring to the papers left with Pace at Ferrara in 1508 (cf Ep 211:53n).

late. Greet also that most courteous ambassador of the Hungarians (for I guess he is with you), and your colleague Master John, the Pole, and our other friends. Farewell. 15

London, 8 February [1510]

255 / To Andrea Ammonio Cambridge, 19 February [1512]

Erasmus made a short visit to Cambridge at this time. He was anxious to conclude the arrangements for the parish of Aldington in Kent, of which Warham was about to appoint him rector. Hence his demand for speedy news. The rectory was conferred on him 22 March and by the twenty-sixth he was back in London to nominate proctors to represent him at his induction. He gave up the rectorship 31 July 1512, being succeeded by John Thornton, titular bishop of Syra in Crete and suffragan to the archbishop, but was allowed to draw a pension from the living. For details of the arrangement, with varying estimates of the value of the living and the amount of the pension, see Allen's introduction to this letter; Nichols II 64ff; E&C 145ff; for Erasmus' own account see his *Ecclesiastes* LB V 811f, and Ep 296:130n.

ERASMUS OF ROTTERDAM TO HIS FRIEND AMMONIO

I beg you earnestly to pass on to me as soon as possible any news there is where you are; for when I left London I heard that the ambassador had been recalled from his journey by a letter from the king, because the pope had proclaimed that there would be no general council until November. 5

I have a new story: your cask is still at Cambridge, together with its wine, I hear – but the wine is sour already. Oh, the blockheads!

Do not hesitate to send me a messenger on horseback with any important news you think may urgently concern me, but tell Colet about it first. Farewell. My good wishes to Master John. 10

Cambridge, 19 February [1511]

* * * * *

13 ambassador of the Hungarians] Jacob Piso, who had been friendly with Erasmus in Rome in 1509 (cf Ep 216 introduction)

14 John, the Pole] Not identified, except as a colleague of Halsey and therefore presumably a Penitentiary at the papal court

255:5 council] After the second session of the Lateran Council on 17 May the council was prorogued until 3 November (Creighton IV 150). The English delegation was therefore recalled. A new delegation appointed 1 April did not include Fisher (SP Henry VIII I 3 109).

10 John] Allen suggests that this may refer to Jean of Lorraine, a servant-copyist of Ammonio's who is mentioned in several letters and whom Erasmus liked (cf Epp 281:4n and 282:44–8).

256 / From Girolamo Aleandro

Paris, [end of February] 1512

Girolamo Aleandro (1480–1542) was a brilliant classical scholar and teacher with whom Erasmus had formed an intimate friendship in Venice in 1508 when both were working in the Aldine press and for a time shared a room in the house of Andrea d'Asola (cf Ep 211 introduction). When Aleandro left for Paris Erasmus gave him letters of introduction to his scholarly friends there (cf Allen Ep 1195:51). From 1508 to 1513 Aleandro taught Greek with great success at the University of Paris, except for a brief period from December 1510 to June 1511 when he was at Orléans, thus missing Erasmus' visit to Paris (cf Renaudet *Erasme et l'Italie* 87 and 146). This letter, as from one Greek scholar to another, is liberally sprinkled with Greek phrases. It was discovered in a MS in the Vatican by M. Paquier in 1895.

GIROLAMO ALEANDRO TO ERASMUS OF ROTTERDAM

I am not quite sure whether it is you or I or both of us whom I ought to regard as open to the charge of negligence, inasmuch as neither of us has written a line to the other since your departure from Italy, despite the fact 5 that we have been as good friends as professors of the same subject ever were. And although we have both offended in this respect, surely your lapse is much the less excusable; for whereas I myself sent you three letters while you were still in Italy, I have received nothing from you either before or after, save three short words. Even if it happened that my letters were not 10 delivered to you (as might easily have happened, because war interrupts all communications and also because you never, as I hear, stayed very long in one spot), still you could and should have written to me a little more often, considering that you knew exactly where I was and that hundreds of people come daily from Italy into France. 15

How are you going to explain the fact that even when you were in Paris and had plenty of news, you did not write to me as you did to Pyrrhus? Whereas I myself, hearing you were in France, postponed business that was quite important to me and left Orléans with all speed to go to Paris, solely that I might call upon you, embrace you, laugh gaily with you, and enjoy 20 your learned and amusing company, and that you and I might take turns in recalling the life we once shared. Nothing in the world could have happened to please or delight me more than this; but my fates were not so kind, for friends told me you were gone already – four days before I arrived.

* * * * *

16 Pyrrhus] Jean Pyrrhus d'Angleberme (cf Ep 140:38n)

21 once shared] From about December 1507 to April 1508

23 gone already] According to his *Journal*, Aleandro was in Paris 19 June 1511, so Erasmus must have left no later than the fifteenth.

Still, all will be forgiven if you continue to cherish the feelings you used to have for me. As to my own deep affection for you, Richard Croke, 25 your pupil and mine, will inform you in person. He is removing to your part of the world, rather because he himself fears armed conflict than because of any imminent danger, since the talk in ruling circles here is of naught but peace between the French and English, apart from one foolish piece of common gossip which is said to have its source at your end. And I ask you, 30 dear Erasmus, to continue to encourage our good Croke, as you have begun to do, not only by writing but by your personal support, which will make it easy for him to obtain advancement from the rulers in your parts. He is a youth of excellent character and agreeable disposition, extremely devoted to us, and so well advanced in his Greek studies that he is not unworthy of 35 both his instructors. But I need say no more than this concerning one of whom, on a closer look, you are sure to think well.

Here is some news for you: I have to tell you that I was elected, with the applause of gods and men, to deliver the address on behalf of our university at the second Council of Pisa. But I am not so enthusiastic as to 40 prefer business, which may be somewhat perilous to soul and body, to my life of learned leisure – though even here there are responsibilities to distract me from my studies. Every day the fathers of this university assign me offices, more properly described as onerous than honourable, which do not really suit my convenience, but which in their view bring me honour 45 and which I certainly could not honourably decline. To take only one example: three days ago they elected me to represent the faculty of philosophy, in company with those of theology and law, in the examination of a certain tract that had been sent to our university by the council at Pisa and had been commended in a letter from the king. Its theme is the relative 50 authority of the pope and of the church, and its title indicates its contents. So we meet frequently; and Heaven knows what intrigues and quarrels I

* * * * *

25 Croke] Cf Ep 227:31n.

40 Council of Pisa] This was the pro-French second council which opened in November 1511 (cf Ep 236:50n). The first Council of Pisa was that held in 1409. Aleandro was elected to be orator at the council on 4 February, but resigned three days later.

49 tract] The *De auctoritate papae et concilii ultraque invicem comparata* (Rome: M. Silber 1511) of Tommaso de Vio of Gaeta (called Cajetanus) who was a strong defender of papal authority as against that of a council (cf Allen Ep 891:25n and Creighton v 78ff). It was sent by the Council of Pisa with the approval of Louis XII to the University of Paris for examination in the hope that it would be condemned. The faculty, however, refused to condemn it.

witness at those meetings! So much talking for the sake of effect, such monstrous expressions I hear! A great deal of quite pointless noise made by certain persons who share with me the authority to consider this book. 55 There are some things I close my eyes to and swallow like a draught of physic; they do me no good, yet I cannot extricate myself, for now I am the mouse, as they say, Erasmus, that has had a taste of pitch, to quote Theocritus. Yet even in our community there are some very eminent men whose scholarship and character alike deserve great respect, theologians, lawyers 60 and physicians, including a number of those entrusted with the examination of the said book; although they mingle the useful with the agreeable, yet I always hear things that give me considerable satisfaction, though my taste, as you know, is normally hard to please.

At the same time I trust I have in prospect some kind of end to 65 business of this sort; for other hydra-heads are sprouting, which I shall be hard put to cut off, even if Iolaus himself should be my torch-bearer. I am the daily target of candidates from everywhere for the offices of rector and procurator, and as it happens I have now become the broker of merchandise of this kind, or more precisely an accountant and treasurer; and if I cannot 70 disengage myself with ease – for it is risky to let a dog taste the tripes – then all I have left is the method adopted by Alexander for undoing the Gordian knot; which would of course mean that I must decamp, even without warning, since I can neither stand aside, being such as you know me, Erasmus, nor yet tolerate the deep disquiet and seething storms of elec- 75 tions.

So much for my foolish nonsense. As for my hopes of an income, I am not in a position to tell you anything; for I have no such hopes, nor need I fear that, when I get back to my own country and decide to divide up my private property, my heirs will be after me to reclaim for the common fund 80 what I have earned for myself. All the same I am living – but living from day to day: I do not want for clothing or books (though, as you know, I brought most of these from home) or plate, but if you look in my treasury you will find there only spiders' webs. You are, it will be said, a philosopher, and it

* * * * *

58–9 Theocritus] Theocritus 14.51; cf *Adagia* II iii 68.

62 useful with the agreeable] Horace *Ars poetica* 343

66 hydra-heads] Hercules in his fight with the Lernaea hydra, which grew fresh heads as soon as the old heads were struck off, was assisted by his nephew Iolaus (*Adagia* I x 9 and I v 39).

71 it is risky … tripes] *Adagia* II iv 22

72–3 Gordian knot] *Adagia* I ix 48

is not really becoming for you to bother about such things. Indeed I admit to being a philosopher and a Christian, and hence a mortal man, subject to anxieties and illness, to age and death; and if you lack money for such contingencies as these, literature will bring you no succour save a vain and arrogant faith, like that of the Stoics; to whom I myself, in agreement with the judgment of the ages, greatly prefer Aristotle, who held that riches should be sought before philosophy, though that rascal, your friend Lucian, has most maliciously dubbed this great man 'the most cunning of flatterers' – out of spite, I suppose, because he failed to achieve success like Aristotle's, while he himself was both flatterer and prattler. 85 90

But you have had more than enough of my nonsense. For my part, Erasmus, I do not regret, and never will, the advice you gave me about going to France, although all Italy protested as you know. For just as Mercury spirited Horace away from the battlefield, so you removed me, as if guided by some divine power, out of the path of the coming wars into peace; even though from time to time during those early months, when I was not yet habituated to the climate, or French customs, or the French language, I used to lie sick on my bed and curse my own luck as much as your advice, while I recalled the familiar customs of my own country. However, as was clearly revealed to me later, my luck was better than I could foresee at the time; I am Davus, not Oedipus. But as for hoping that I or anyone else could become rich in this city merely by following my profession, what nonsense! Do not so much as entertain the thought. Perhaps what I am about to say is untrue, but I may be permitted to repeat what I am told by almost everyone, that never before in Paris (and I speak only of those who practise our profession) has anyone been more admired by all kinds of people or more frequently pointed out with cries of 'There he is!' or more greatly missed whenever I have absented myself from the city than myself. And yet now and then I am hard put to produce ten gold pieces saved up in my purse, partly because of the huge expenses without which nobody could possibly live like a gentleman in Paris, partly because my income is not so much small as uncertain. Every day I scrape together a 95 100 105 110 115

* * * * *

91–2 Lucian] *Dialogi mortuorum* 13.5

98 Horace] *Odes* 2.7.13–14

105 Davus] *Adagia* I iii 36

111 pointed out] *Adagia* I x 43

113 ten gold pieces] Probably écus d'or au soleil (1475–1515), the current French gold coin, then officially valued at 36s 3d tournois = 6s 2d gros Flemish = 4s 3d sterling apiece; or possibly écus d'or à la couronne (1474), valued at 35s od tournois. Cf Ep 212:7n; CWE I 315–16, 321, 336–7; and tables A–F below, 327–45.

sufficient amount, and I can recall earning sometimes seventy francs and more in a single month; but Fortune is so changeable, or my employers so unreliable, that for the next two months I may scarcely gain a crust of dry bread; and so what I had earned by protracted labours is quickly swallowed up in books, clothing, and victuals. Yet if I had some kind of fixed salary from the king (though this is more than I can hope for in difficult times such as these), I have no doubt that, besides being able to endure the hard work better, I could store up something that would pass down to posterity and win me some fame. 120 125

In all this I think you are a happy man, my dear Erasmus; you have already achieved that which I most desire, while I, tired out by the daily uproar of lectures until I am not only hoarse but on the edge of physical collapse, can neither satisfy that desire for the present nor even provide a home for my old age; for, since there appeared on the scene the things they call glosses, regular dunghills if I may so describe them, tainting the air with their noisome vapours, a myriad humbugs have exploited the enveloping darkness of these works to cover their own indiscriminate thefts and perversions; the chairs of the professors are shattered by endless shouts and catcalls, while all those lecturers cause the 'marbles to rupture, the columns to break.' And not only in the provincial towns, which are the refuge of all such as soon as they have got their discharge from university teaching, but even in this city there is no one who does not presumptuously flaunt his follies and hazard his ignorance. This they do either free of charge (which is very common indeed, for how else could they find an audience?) 130 135 140

* * * * *

117 seventy francs] The word 'franc' is used here as the popular synonym for livre tournois, as a money-of-account, and does not refer to the actual gold coin, last struck in 1423. By relative silver values £70 0s 0d tournois = £12 0s 4d gros Flemish = £8 4s 6d sterling. Cf CWE I 318, 331–2, 336–7; and tables A–F below, 327–45.

127 that which I most desire] This might suggest that Aleandro had heard that Erasmus had been given, or at least promised, a benefice in England. Erasmus was not actually appointed as rector of Aldington until about a month after this letter was written (cf Ep 255 introduction), but the rumour that he was about to be given a living by the archbishop of Canterbury had been in the air for at least three months (cf Ep 243:19) and, indeed, seems to have spread to the continent by November 1511 (cf Ep 244A:24ff).

131 glosses] The commentaries that surrounded and frequently obscured the texts prescribed in medieval universities were particularly resented by the zealots for the new learning whose aim was to go directly to the original texts.

135–6 'marbles ... break'] Juvenal 1.12–13; cf *Adagia* IV iii 77.

137 discharge] *Adagia* I ix 24

or sometimes for a very small fee; so greatly do men value the privilege of making fools of themselves! Yet the vast majority of the uneducated, whose number is legion, understand such people better and generally esteem them more highly, than they do scholars – and rightly, for (to go a little too far in proverbializing at a connoisseur of proverbs) one stammerer best 145 understands another and mule scratches mule. What never ceases to amaze me is that, when I give a free lecture on any subject, they all pour in to hear me in flocks, starling- and jackdaw-fashion (if I may use foolish expressions like the pupils of Beroaldo and of Battista Pio), while other men's lecture-rooms are deserted; and no one else is talked about, and my audiences, 150 especially on Latin topics, are larger than any that have ever been seen in Paris within living memory. This is greatly resented by some, inasmuch as they can scarcely swallow the fact that not only students but doctors and men of gentle birth and most of those grown-up lecturers too come to my lectures. Yet, when I ask for the customary fee, you can see them all run off 155 'as do Chaonian doves when eagles stoop.' Thus my lecture-hall, so full of students, thins out suddenly and, though it is ever graced by the presence of many distinguished men, is not so crowded that I do not consider myself to deserve a better attendance. Consequently the idea has frequently occurred to me, and still does, that in spite of what I have written above those 160 men's offence lies in greed or poverty rather than in shallowness of mind or contempt and dislike of sound learning. If I say of my own self that I deserve a better attendance, please take this in good part; put it down to a failing I share with others of my kind, since Quintilian describes it as a weakness with which all lecturers are afflicted. 165

But I have already gone beyond the proper length for a letter. However my reason for writing so much was first my wish to repay with interest the debt I owed you through my long silence, and second the fact that as I write to you I feel myself to be conversing with you in person. Will you, in turn,

* * * * *

145–6 one stammerer ... another] *Adagia* I ix 77

146 mule scratches mule] *Adagia* I vii 96

149 Beroaldo] Filippo Beroaldo the elder (1453–1504) was a popular and highly respected professor of rhetoric at the university of Bologna for some thirty-seven years. He also edited a number of Latin classics. Aleandro belonged to a younger generation and was somewhat contemptuous of him.

149 Pio] Battista Pio (c 1460–1540) was a pupil of Beroaldo. He taught at Bologna and elsewhere and edited a number of classical works.

156 Chaonian] Virgil *Eclogues* 9.13; cf Ep 216A:27–9n.

164 Quintilian] 1.2.9

write and tell me all about yourself – a long, solid letter with some good news in it? You can easily do this, for I hear that nothing bad ever comes out of England. 170

Farewell; and my very best greetings to Grocyn, Linacre, More, Latimer, and the rest of our fellow-scholars. I strongly recommend you to make a friend of Doctor Joachim; I have found him to be particularly distinguished for uprightness of character and literary attainments. Farewell again. 175

Paris, 1512

257 / From Paolo Bombace [Milan? spring 1512]

This is an abstract of the original letter (cf Ep 210, introduction). Bombace had given up his post at the university (cf Ep 251) and was eager to leave Bologna because of the continued threat of war. In the spring of 1512 Bologna was still occupied by the French, but was recovered by Julius II in June 1512 (cf Creighton IV 152). G. Fantuzzi gives an abstract of a letter from Bombace to Aldus, written from Milan probably at about this time, asking him to find some way of saving him from having to return to Bologna (*Notizie degli scrittori bolognesi* Bologna 1782).

An undated letter from Paolo to Erasmus, in which he says that Aldus has been trying to obtain a lectureship for him at Padua, now that in Bologna 'the entire aspect of affairs is that of disorder and death.'

258 / From John Colet [London, March 1512]

Erasmus was evidently still in Cambridge and had written to Colet as well as to Ammonio for news about his expected benefice (cf Ep 255). This letter is from the Deventer Letter-book.

The fact is, my dearest Erasmus, that I have heard no news that concerns you since you left here. If I find out anything in future, I shall certainly inform you, as you ask me to do. I have been in the country for the last few days, staying with my mother in order to comfort her grief at the death of my servant, who died in her house. She loved him as a son and mourned his death even more than that of her own son. Your letter reached me on the night when I was about to return to the city. 5

* * * * *

175 Joachim] Joachim Egellius of Ravensburg, a kinsman of Michael Hummelberger (Ep 263:26n)

I have just one funny story to tell you. A certain bishop, or so I heard, and one who passes for a man of some wisdom, spoke ill of my school in a large gathering of people, saying that I had founded a useless institution, or rather an evil one, or even, to use his very words, 'a home of idolatry.' This he said, I believe, because the poets are taught there. Such remarks do not anger me, Erasmus, but they make me laugh heartily. 10

Franz has come back, and demanded the book; but Master Johannes decided that I should keep it. I am sending you the little book which contains my oration; the printers have said they will send a few copies to Cambridge. Farewell, and do not forget the poems you are writing for my boys; I should like you to finish them with all your ease and charm. Be sure to let me have the second part of your *Copia*. 15

259 / From John Babham — Oxford, 12 April [1512?]

Little is known of John Babham except that he was at this time a student at Oxford, where he took his BA degree in February 1514. Erasmus had evidently met him earlier and had sent him a letter of encouragement and a request that he render him some service there. The date is probably between 1512 and 1515. The letter is from the Deventer Letter-book.

JOHN BABHAM TO ERASMUS

You could more easily guess, most learned Erasmus, than I myself could properly express, how much pleasure your letter brought me; not so much because I now have found a chance to do your bidding, as because I am the owner of a letter from Erasmus, which I can read over and over again. As 5

* * * * *

14 Franz] Franz Birckmann of Cologne was a bookseller in Antwerp who was in London at this time (cf Ep 263:54). He evidently served at times as an agent and messenger for Bade and other printers (cf Epp 263:22n; 264:11). He seems to have been an untrustworthy character and Erasmus was suspicious of him, with good reason as the event proved (cf Epp 265:5f; 283:184n). The book Birckmann demanded, probably with the hope of taking it to Bade, was the *De copia*, the first part of which had already been sent to Colet (cf Ep 241:2n, and line 19 below).

14 Johannes] Allen suggests that this probably referred to Johannes Sixtinus who is spoken of in this way (*dominus Johannes*) in Ep 291:3.

16 oration] The oration urging the necessity of reformation in the church, delivered to convocation 6 February 1512. It was immediately printed by R. Pynson. The text is in Lupton *Colet* 293–304.

17 poems] The five poems grouped under the title 'Carmina scholaria,' written for St Paul's School, had actually been published already, probably in September 1511, in Robert de Keyzere's edition of the *Concio de puero Jesu* (NK

Heaven is my witness, I would rather have a rich store of these than anything else in the world. Had I words to match my feelings, I should endeavour to praise your letter and its eloquence, your refined, nay lovely, style; but I am afraid of being forced 'by want of gifts thy great renown to harm,' as Horace says. I have repeatedly reflected that the task I have laid upon myself in undertaking to write this letter is far above my ability; and yet, though I was aware that it would bring no pleasure to a scholar of your distinction, still I thought I ought to acknowledge your letter at least by a reply, since I had no other means of doing so. You have always been so kind that I believe you will take in good part anything that comes from me. Farewell, protector of the muses.

Oxford, 12 April

260 / To John Colet London, 29 April 1512

Erasmus had been working off and on since 1499, if not earlier, on a textbook designed to supply beginners in Latin composition with an abundance and variety of words and phrases. It was finally published as *De duplici copia verborum ac rerum commentarii duo* (Paris: J. Bade 15 July 1512) with this letter as preface (cf LB I 3ff). A short preliminary sketch for his students in Paris, entitled *Brevis de copia praeceptio*, had been retained along with his copy of the *Familiarium colloquiorum formulae* by Augustin Vincent and was eventually published in the unauthorized edition of the latter (cf Ep 130:108–9n). Erasmus mentions work on it in 1499–1501 (cf Epp 95:39, 136:57, 138:187, 145:178ff). When it was first mentioned in May 1499, he included it among several school books on which he was working and which he told Batt he intended to dedicate jointly to him and his young pupil, Adolph of Veere (Ep 95:35–7); but it was still unfinished when he went to Italy. He did more work on it there, but it was among the papers left with Pace at Ferrara and was never recovered (cf Epp 30:17 and 244:8n). The edition of 1512, Erasmus says in the *Catalogus lucubrationum*, was composed hastily at Colet's request for St Paul's School (Allen I 9 1–4; cf Ep 258:19). By that time Batt, to whom the dedication had been half-promised, was long since dead. The book became immensely popular. At least 85 editions were published during Erasmus' lifetime and more than 150 before the end of the century.

* * * * *

2887; cf Ep 175 introduction and Reedijk 291f). They were reprinted in the Bade edition of *De copia* dedicated to Colet (cf Ep 260 introduction). See text in Reedijk 297–300; cf J.H. Rieger 'Erasmus, Colet and the Schoolboy Jesus' *Studies in the Renaissance* 9 (1962) 187–94.

259:10 Horace] *Odes* 1.6.11–12

FROM DESIDERIUS ERASMUS OF ROTTERDAM TO JOHN COLET, DEAN OF ST PAUL'S IN LONDON, GREETINGS

I for one am bound to pay warm tribute, dear Colet, to the remarkable and truly Christian goodness that leads you continually to devote all your efforts and all your life's endeavours, not to serving your own advantage, but to benefitting your country and your fellow-citizens as far as you possibly can. Equally do I admire the wisdom you show in having chosen two particular fields for the greatest possible achievement of this aim. First, you observed that the richest rewards of charity lie in bringing Christ into the hearts of one's countrymen by means of continual preaching and by holy instruction. Now you have already been engaged in this for a great many years, I will not say with great glory, for glory is a commodity you so little regard as even to refuse it, but at least with great fruitfulness; and it is on this account that your own Paul, for all his pronounced modesty in other respects, occasionally turns boastful and vaunts himself with a kind of sanctified insolence. Second, and it was next in importance in your opinion, you founded a school that far excels the rest in beauty and splendour, so that the youth of England, under carefully chosen and highly reputed teachers, might there absorb Christian principles together with an excellent literary education from their earliest years. For you are profoundly aware both that the hope of the country lies in its youth – the crop in the blade, as it were – and also how important it is for one's whole life that one should be initiated into excellence from the very cradle onwards.

Besides, no one could help loving your generous high-mindedness and, so to call it, your holy arrogance in insisting that both of these services to your country must be unpaid, and your motives above reproach; so much so that the laborious preaching you undertook for so many years has not enriched you by a single penny. For though you sowed unto them spiritual things, you have never reaped any man's carnal things, and you have resolved to take upon yourself the entire expenses of the school, which were clearly vast enough to appal an oriental potentate. And whereas most people welcome a partner in this, almost more than in any other kind of enterprise, you elected to lavish your patrimony, your entire fortune, even your household possessions, upon it rather than admit anyone on earth to

* * * * *

14 your own Paul] Cf Ep 181:17n.

23 from the cradle] *Adagia* I vii 53

28 single penny] *Adagia* I viii 9

28–9 though you sowed ... carnal things] Cf 1 Corinthians 9:11.

share the honour with you. This means, surely, that you assume the role of a father, indeed more than a father, towards all your fellow-citizens' children and indeed all your fellow-citizens. You rob yourself to enrich them, strip yourself in order to equip them, wear yourself out with hard work in order that your offspring may prosper in the Lord. In short, you devote your entire energies to winning them for Christ. 35 40

One would have to be brimfull of ill will not to give enthusiastic support to efforts such as yours, wicked indeed to cry out against them, and an enemy of England not to do what one could to lend assistance. For my part, since I am well aware how much I am indebted both to the English nation at large and also to you personally, I thought that it would be appropriate for me to make a small literary contribution to the equipment of your school. So I have chosen to dedicate to the new school these two new commentaries *De copia*, inasmuch as the work in question is suitable for boys to read and also, unless I am mistaken, not unlikely to prove helpful to them, though I leave it to others to judge how well-informed this work of mine is, or how serviceable it will be. What I can really claim is that I have been the first to envisage the subject and give an account of it. For anyone may see how different from my purpose was that of the ancient Greek writer, Julius Pollux, when he classified under topics the names of different things and made up neat piles, so to speak, of a number of synonyms and related terms. Nor am I disposed to mention authors like Isidore or Marius or Philiscus, who are at so many removes from *copia* that they are unable to express their thoughts in good Latin even once. As for the little book ascribed to Cicero (but I am rather of the opinion that it is a patchwork collected from the works of Cicero by some devoted follower), it surely contains nothing more than a hurried compilation, covering but few expressions. 45 50 55 60

My own endeavour has been to point to certain fixed types of *copia* as the primary sources, the method being to progress by stages from the general to the particular. Yet I confess with regret that the present work has 65

* * * * *

54 Julius Pollux] A grammarian of the second century AD whose *Onomasticon*, a classified collection of the Greek names for things, had been published by Aldus in 1502.

56 Isidore] Bishop of Seville, AD 600, compiled, beside his great encyclopaedia the *Etymologiae*, a short work called *Synonyma*.

56 Marius] Marius Victorinus was a fourth-century grammarian.

57 Philiscus] Stefano Fieschi of Soncino (fl 1453) was a grammarian whose *Synonyma* was often published in the fifteenth century.

58 little book] The *Synonyma* attributed to Cicero

William Warham
Copy by Hans Holbein the Younger
of his original portrait of 1527, now lost
Musée du Louvre, Paris (Cliché des Musées Nationaux)

not received the careful revision it should have had. It is some time since I unsystematically amassed the raw material for my future work, seeing that I should require a great deal of time to polish it and must read through a great many authors. Accordingly I was not particularly anxious to publish it; but when I discovered that certain persons were laying traps to catch these commentaries and had all but managed to publish them in a thoroughly bad text, I was obliged to give them such revision as I could, and get them out, as the lesser evil of the two. Farewell, my dear Colet. 70

London, 29 April 1512

261 / To William Warham London, 29 April 1512

Since his presentation of Erasmus to the living of Aldington in March (cf Ep 255 introduction), Warham had become one of his principal patrons. As a gesture of thanks Erasmus promptly dedicated to him a group of translations from Lucian, some already published, some new. They were printed as *Luciani Erasmo interprete Dialogi ... quorum quaedam recentius, quaedam annos abhinc octo sunt versa, sed nuper recognita* (Paris: Bade 1 June 1514). A copy was sent to Bade at this time (cf Ep 263:2n), but publication was delayed. The first edition of Lucian (Paris: Bade 13 November 1506) had been dedicated to Foxe (Ep 187).

FROM ERASMUS OF ROTTERDAM TO THE MOST REVEREND FATHER IN CHRIST, HIS GRACE WILLIAM, ARCHBISHOP OF CANTERBURY, PRIMATE OF ALL ENGLAND, GREETINGS

I am sending you a few dialogues by Lucian, some of which I have lately translated and some revised. You will say that the things I send are trifles. 5 Why yes, they are; but scholarly trifles, such indeed as may make you laugh, if indeed one who is distracted by a multitude of cares and overwhelmed by floods of business, as you are, can ever find time to laugh. But no matter whether this creation of my muses be frivolous or serious, there is surely nobody to whom I could more appropriately offer it than to you, who 10 are my one unrivalled Maecenas: to you who alone encourage me, nourish my talent, vouchsafe me leisure, and dignify my studies. Farewell.

London, 29 April 1512

262 / To Andrea Ammonio Cambridge, 9 May [1512]

TO ANDREA AMMONIO FROM ERASMUS DESIDERIUS

Please pass on to me any reliable rumours circulating at your end; for I am very anxious to hear whether it is true that Julius is really playing Julius and also whether Christ keeps his ancient way of testing most severely in misfortune's storms those whose discipleship he most desires to reveal. For 5 my part, dear Andrea, I have taken a solemn vow for the happy outcome of the church's affairs. I see you approve my piety already! I am to pay a visit to Our Lady of Walsingham, and I will there hang up a votive offering of a Greek poem. Look for it if ever you visit the place.

Bullock is applying himself busily to Greek. You are second to none in 10 his affections. Be sure to give my greetings to Master Jean, who is the high priest of kindness in every respect. Will you pass on my thanks to Master Carmiliano for writing such eminently friendly falsehoods about me in that superbly accomplished letter he wrote to Bryan in which he calls me most learned of learned men. Of course I cannot accept words of praise like these; 15 but this fact itself makes me all the more indebted to his extraordinary good will and devotion towards me. For me it was undoubtedly both an honour and a pleasure to be praised by a man himself so greatly praised. Farewell, my learned and courteous Ammonio.

Cambridge, 9 May [1509] 20

263 / From Josse Bade Paris, 19 May 1512

This letter is taken from an autograph in the Basel university library (on Bade see Ep 183 introduction).

* * * * *

3 Julius] The comparison of Julius II to Julius Caesar was a common theme with Erasmus. Cf Ep 228:22n and the *Julius exclusus, Opuscula* 68 line 89 and n).

8 Walsingham] The shrine of Our Lady built at Walsingham about sixty miles from Cambridge in 1061 was one of the most popular pilgrimage attractions in Europe. It was served by Augustinian canons of the Walsingham Priory. See J.C. Dickinson *The Shrine of Our Lady of Walsingham* (Cambridge 1956). Erasmus described this journey in 1526 in the colloquy 'Peregrinatio religionis ergo' (Thompson *Colloquies* 287–312).

9 Greek poem] Text in Reedijk 303

11 Jean] Cf Ep 281:4n.

13 Carmiliano] Pietro Carmiliano of Brescia (d 1527) had been Latin secretary to Henry VII and at this time was, like Ammonio, a canon of St Stephen's, Westminster. As a poet laureate he wrote verses on official occasions. See Emden BRUO I 358. At a later time Erasmus thought less highly of his accomplishments as a Latin stylist (cf Epp 282:5 and 30–6; and 283:61–4).

14 Bryan] John Bryan, a student at King's College, Cambridge

18 to be praised ... praised] Cf Cicero *Tusculanae disputationes* 4.31.67.

ASCENSIUS TO HIS FRIEND DESIDERIUS ERASMUS

Your servant Maurice has conscientiously delivered to me several elegant and polished products of your celebrated pen, together with a letter from you, very pleasant except for one slightly distressing fact – it contained no indication what I must pay for them, on this score leaving me quite up in 5 the air. For while I have no wish to let the pursuit of profit brand me with the stigma of ingratitude, a detestable quality, my business rivals will not permit me to pay a suitably high price for them; they are even now getting their presses ready to re-issue whatever I print. Besides, their rivalry would have some justification; for if I print the *Enchiridion* I shall offend Dirk and 10 cause him loss; if I do the *Folly* I shall similarly offend Gourmont; if I print those published at Keyzere's press I shall offend Keyzere; so they might be capable of printing the rest as well. Besides, the *Tragedies* of Seneca, which I should have been extremely eager to do if they had been brought to me in time, have lately been printed by Jean Petit; and a certain 15 bookseller who is a countryman of mine has also arranged for an edition to be printed in my shop from that Florentine text; I wish it could have been equally well revised. Still, I am delighted to have your work. If I have a

* * * * *

2 Maurice] One of Erasmus' servants, probably from Saint-Omer, since Erasmus later asked Ammonio to inquire there what had become of him (cf Ep 273:38–9).

3 products] Bade furnished a list of these in a letter to Hummelberger, 7 July 1512. They include the *De copia*, tragedies of Euripides and Seneca, some dialogues of Lucian, the *Moria*, and some others. Bade published the *De copia* 15 July 1512; the *Moria* 27 July 1512; Lucian 1 June 1514; Seneca 5 December 1514.

10 Dirk] Dirk or Thierry Martens (c 1450–1534) of Alost had a long and distinguished career as a printer, mostly in Antwerp and Louvain. He was a devoted friend and admirer of Erasmus for whom he printed nearly sixty volumes. He first published the *Enchiridion* in the *Lucubratiunculae* of 1503. Cf Ep 164 introduction.

11 Gourmont] Gilles de Gourmont, a printer in Paris, 1506–33. He published the first edition of the *Moria* (1511) (see Ep 222 introduction).

12 Keyzere] Robert de Keyzere of Ghent (cf Epp 175 introduction, 258:17n)

15 Petit] Jean Petit (active 1492–1530) was one of the most celebrated Paris booksellers who published a number of books by various printers. The edition of Seneca's *Tragedies* is probably that printed for him by Jean Marchand in 1511.

17 Florentine text] Filippo Giunta brought out an edition of Seneca's *Tragedies* in Florence, 3 April 1506. Bade had published them (jointly with Keyzere of Ghent) in March 1512.

chance to view the prospects in a somewhat rosier light I will shortly print it on my own account, together with your *Tragedies*, accompanied by our brief explanations, at least on Seneca's plays. 20

Now about your *Adagia* I entertain far more sanguine hope, and there would be less jealousy involved, for everyone is aware that I have undertaken it. All the same, when people hear that it is not ready even yet, I fear it will soon be printed from Aldus' text; for it is now in the press in Germany, 25 if the letter Michael Hummelberger wrote to me is correct, and it will, as I have said I feared, be printed here too, and I shall not be able to prevent its publication any longer. If it had been printed last year, the edition would have practically sold out already; and if it is printed now, even in an incorrect text, this will still serve to rob later and better editions of their 30 profits. Of Jerome's letters, too, all that have already been printed are sold. For this reason, because I have put about a rumour that I am waiting for you to furnish me with a better text, I am afraid that when it is found that I have received nothing as yet I shall be unable to postpone sending them to the press. As a matter of fact, I know of no work that suits me better or, if I judge 35 aright, does more credit to your profession than those letters. I should like, therefore, to have at least some of them, if possible, before the Nativity of St John the Baptist, in order to make a beginning, since at that time I shall have three presses free, one of which I shall assign first to your *Copia* and the other two to those letters – if they should come to hand. 40

As to the rest, let me briefly tell you the price I have personally settled

* * * * *

21 Seneca] Bade published a revised edition with Erasmus' notes 5 December 1514.

22 *Adagia*] This was a revised and much enlarged edition of the *Adagiorum chiliades* which Erasmus had planned to have printed by Bade in Paris (cf Ep 219:4n). Bade still hoped to publish it despite the rumour that the Aldine edition of 1508 (cf Ep 211 introduction) was about to be printed in Germany. Froben in fact printed it at Basel in August 1513 (cf Ep 283:182n). Erasmus entrusted a copy of the revised edition to Birckmann (cf Ep 258:14n), who, instead of giving it to Bade, took it to Froben (cf Ep 283:184ff) who published it in 1515 (cf Ep 269 introduction).

26 Hummelberger] Michael Hummelberger (1487–1537) of Ravensburg in Swabia was a German scholar who studied in Paris for some years and who helped Bade with several editions. He was an enthusiastic Greek scholar and studied under Aleandro. In 1511 he left Paris to return to Ravensburg.

31 Jerome's letters] The revised edition of the correspondence of St Jerome, which Bade hoped to print, was eventually sent to Froben, Erasmus having heard that the firm of Amerbach-Froben had already begun an edition of Jerome's works.

upon. We agreed on fifteen florins for the *Adagia*, if I remember correctly. You have received ten, and I am to pay you five more, and three for the original text. I shall gladly agree to pay another fifteen florins for the revision of the letters of St Jerome, and as much again for what you have just 45 sent me. You will protest loudly at the smallness of the price. I admit that I could offer no recompense to match your ability, application, scholarship, and toil; but the most glorious rewards will be accorded in the first place by Heaven, and then by your own virtuous character. As you have eminently well served secular literature, both Greek and Latin, so you will in this way 50 serve sacred literature also, and help your humble friend Bade, who has a large family and no income save the fruits of his daily toil. Come then, Erasmus, my cherished refuge; send me your agreement by the hand either of Franz of Cologne or of Johann of Coblenz the booksellers; both of them are in your part of the world at present, and are coming here presently. 55 There is no need to send a special messenger for this purpose.

In the matter of purchasing books, nothing has so far come from Lyon for Jean Pierre. If he has anything that you asked for or that I think worth your reading, it can be sent to Antwerp quite safely in the present circumstances. I have given two francs as journey-money to your servant Maurice. 60 Farewell.

One thing: if you accept the terms I propose, payment can be made whenever you wish, and I shall carefully keep the books you sent (except the *Copia*, which I shall print on St John the Baptist's day, according to the agreement we made about it) until I am informed of your intentions. 65 Farewell.

* * * * *

42 fifteen florins] In all likelihood Florentine florins (fiorini d'oro), then worth about 38s 9d tournois apiece = 6s 7d gros Flemish = 4s 7d sterling. A payment of 33 florins for both the *Adagia* and the St Jerome letters would thus have been worth about £63 19s 1d tournois = £10 17s 3d gros Flemish = £7 11s 3d sterling. Cf CWE 1 316, 321, 338–9; and tables A–F below, 327–45.

54 Franz] Birckmann (cf Ep 258:14n)

54 Johann of Coblenz] A bookseller and stationer in Paris

58 Jean Pierre] Jean Pierre de Verade or Varade, son of a Milanese gentleman who was a refugee from the Italian wars. In Paris he became a bookseller. Cf P. Renouard *Répertoire des imprimeurs parisiens* (Paris 1965) 419.

60 two francs] As in Ep 256:117, this reference is undoubtedly to the money-of-account evaluation, two livres tournois, rather than to the actual gold coin. The sum of £2 0s 0d tournois would then have been worth 6s 10½d gros Flemish = 4s 8½d sterling (by relative silver values). Cf CWE 1 318, 340–1; and tables A–E below, 327–43.

64 John the Baptist's day] 24 June. The *De copia* was actually published 15 July 1512 (cf Ep 260 introduction).

The eve of Our Lord's ascension, Paris, 1512

God willing, I shall print everything in the format and type you told me to use, even if I make enemies of the whole world.

To the most learned and eminent orator and theologian, Erasmus of Rotterdam 70

264 / To Pieter Gillis [London, autumn] 1512

This letter is in part an indirect answer to Ep 263. Since England was now at war with France, Erasmus seems to have feared that his letters might not reach Bade in Paris and was therefore using Gillis in Antwerp as an intermediary.

ERASMUS TO PIETER GILLIS

Your letter, my dear Pieter, was the most delightful thing that has ever happened to me. If my reply to it is brief, you would not find it hard to excuse this if you knew the quantity of studies under which I am all but crushed. As soon as I have time to spare, I shall load my friend Gillis not 5 merely with letters but with proper books. Please see that this is delivered to Josse Bade as soon as possible. I have got ready my work on proverbs, expanding it so much that I have quite changed its character – and improved it a great deal, unless I am mistaken, though it was not so bad before; so he has no need to fear editions by others. There had been an 10 understanding with Franz, the bookseller, that I was to give him the manuscript; but he went off without coming to greet me. I gladly accept the price proposed by him in his letter; money, for what it is worth, does not greatly move me. He should take all measures to ensure that the work may emerge from his press in a style that will make it difficult for anyone else to 15 compete. I intend to finish the revision of the New Testament and the letters of St Jerome; if I have time, I will also emend the text of Seneca. Possibly I may come back to see you after Easter; but, if this proves impossible, the first thing I shall do is to send you my proverbs, as soon as I find a reliable

* * * * *

264:7 proverbs] The revised *Adagiorum chiliades* (cf Ep 263:22n)

10 editions] That is, competition from reprints by other publishers of earlier and unrevised texts of the works, now superseded

11 Franz] Birckmann (Ep 258:14n). He was later given a copy to take to Bade (cf Ep 263:22n).

13 price] Cf Ep 263:41ff.

messenger. I am somewhat concerned in case Bade cannot muster enough Greek type for this work; it is half Greek. So he should make his preparations as carefully as possible, and practise himself somewhat in Greek, which will be useful to him for producing other books as well. He is not to send either money or books here until I write to him explaining what I wish. I have not yet seen any sign of the publication of Lucian's dialogues which I sent him, while I do notice that some of them have been printed at Louvain; I am anxious for information about this. I have translated several works by Plutarch, which I shall revise and send in addition. An Englishman has delivered to me Bade's latest letter, in which he remarks that he has printed the *Moria*, but I have not seen it here. Farewell.

[Louvain], 1512

265 / To Pieter Gillis [London, autumn 1512]

ERASMUS TO HIS FRIEND PIETER GILLIS

Your letters usually take the initiative in urging me to write, but nowadays you do not even reply when I need you! I wrote to you previously about the commentaries which formed the subject of my agreement with Bade. I have been a little suspicious about Franz, feeling that he had not been quite above-board in his conduct in the affair; this is why I wished to hear about it in a letter from you.

I cannot tell you how grieved I am to see our fellow-countrymen gradually slipping into the present conflict, when they have already been harassed by so many wars or, to put it more correctly, robberies. Ah, those tongueless theologians, those mute bishops, who look on at such dire human disasters and say nothing! Do write to me, my dear Pieter; and farewell.

* * * * *

25 Lucian] The *Dialogues* were not published by Bade until 1 June 1514 (cf Ep 261 introduction). They were, however, in Bade's possession as early as July 1512 (cf Ep 263:3n). The Lucianic dialogues printed at Louvain by Martens, 24 August 1512, were the group dedicated to Busleyden in 1506 (cf Ep 205 introduction).

28 Plutarch] See Epp 268 and 284.

30 *Moria*] Bade published a revised edition of the *Moria* 27 July 1512.

265:4 commentaries] The *Adagia*

5 Franz] Birckmann (cf Epp 258:14n, 263:22n, 283:184n)

Adolph of Burgundy, heer van Veere
Drawing by Jacques le Boucq (fl 1559) in Recueil d'Arras,
Bibliothèque de la Ville d'Arras, MS 266, f 256
Bibliothèque Municipale d'Arras

266 / To Adolph of Burgundy, heer van Veere London, [autumn] 1512

With the second marriage of Anna van Borssele in 1502 and the death of Batt at about the same time (cf Ep 172:4ff), when young Adolph was only about twelve, Erasmus seems to have lost contact with the family of his old patroness. By 1512, however, Adolph was grown up and in high favour at court (cf Ep 93 introduction) and Erasmus was hopeful of regaining his patronage.

ERASMUS TO ADOLPH, THE NOBLE PRINCE OF VEERE

My warm greetings to your Highness. I have for some time now been planning to migrate hence to your part of the world, but have thus far been restrained from this course by the great kindness shown to me by certain people, particularly the archbishop of Canterbury. Lord Mountjoy, who is 5 lieutenant of Hammes and is most affectionately disposed towards you, always favours your people in the upheavals of the present war and helps them as much as he can. I cannot express the deep grief I feel at the occurrence of such calamities for the human race and the fact that no one tries to prevent them. Even more do I grieve that our own country is 10 gradually becoming involved in these troubles, especially as she has been not merely sorely tried but very nearly crushed by those protracted wars; and I wish it were safe for me to put my feelings on this subject into a letter.

How often I have been sorry that I did not eagerly accept the position you offered me at Louvain three years ago! But at that time I had been 15 emboldened by my extravagant hopes and the mountains of English gold I saw in my fancy. Fortune, however, has since lowered my crest, and at present I long like Ulysses to see the smoke ascending from my native place, if only a moderate competency awaited me in your part of the world. I beg you to assist me, long ago your devoted Erasmus; for this you are able, and 20 no less willing, to do, if you can but keep it in mind. Farewell.

London, 1512

* * * * *

5 Mountjoy] As commander of the castle of Hammes (cf Ep 231:8n) Mountjoy was in a position to grant military support to Adolph's nearby castle of Tournehem.

15 three years ago] Presumably on his way back from Italy in 1509

16 mountains of gold] *Adagia* I ix 15

18 Ulysses] Homer *Odyssey* 1.58

267 / To Giovanni Battista Boerio London, 11 November 1512

Giovanni Battista Boerio was a Genoese who settled in England where he became physician to both Henry VII and Henry VIII. Erasmus had accompanied his two sons to Italy in 1506 and supervised their studies there for a year. Though he seems to have fallen out with Boerio for a time (cf Epp 289:5ff, 292:22ff), he remained on cordial terms with the family for many years after they returned to Italy (cf Ep 194:33n). Lucian's *Astrologia* was printed at the end of Bade's edition of Lucian's *Dialogues*, 1 June 1514 (cf Ep 261 introduction), but without this preface, possibly because of Erasmus' quarrel with Boerio at about that time.

FROM ERASMUS OF ROTTERDAM TO GIOVANNI BATTISTA, PRINCIPAL PHYSICIAN-IN-ORDINARY TO HIS MAJESTY THE KING OF ENGLAND, GREETINGS

Lately, as I was hunting for a little present to give to such a great friend, I happened to come upon a treatise on astrology by Lucian. The very title 5 delighted me, and I began eagerly to hope that it might be something which would seem worthy, in the first place, of your kind services to me and my affection for you; second, of a person who by his exceptional scholarship, loyalty, and wisdom has for many years already earned the position of principal physician-in-ordinary, and that too at the courts of the two 10 greatest English kings in history, namely Henry the Seventh, a prince of unrivalled wisdom, and his son, who so recalls his sire, not in looks alone or in name, but in all the endowments of a king, that the father seems not to have died but to have entered into a second youth in the son; worthy, last of all, of a man who has so distinguished himself in this most excellent science 15 of astrology that others, compared with you, appear to 'flit about like wan shades,' as Homer puts it. But in the first place, the donor's good will should make the modest gift acceptable to you, such as it is; second, your kindness – your habitual kindness, indeed – will see to it that it becomes a great present instead of a small one, distinguished and choice instead of 20 mediocre; this will come about if the little book sees the light of day not only with the added recommendation of your good esteem but also with the polish added by your revision. What particularly appealed to me in the book was the fact that it was an ancient work; but your keener perceptions will enable you to discover more aspects that merit your approval; for in 25 general all Lucian's productions are far from uninteresting. The service I

* * * * *

17 Homer] *Odyssey* 10.495; cf *Adagia* II iii 53.

have discharged was that of a not unfaithful translator; it will be for you to pronounce judgment as much upon the translator as upon the author. Farewell.

London, Martinmas 1512 30

268 / To John Yonge

London, 1 January 1513

John Yonge (c 1456–1516) was a churchman, lawyer, and diplomat who held numerous ecclesiastical preferments and royal offices, including that of Master of the Rolls. He was, therefore, a potential patron whose favour Erasmus hoped to gain by the present of a translation of Plutarch's *De tuenda bona valetudine precepta* on which he had been working in the autumn of 1512 (cf Ep 264:27–8). The present must have been in MS, since the first printed edition was that of Pynson in London in July 1513 (STC 20060). Erasmus sent a copy of this edition to Ammonio, who was in camp with the royal army in France, with instructions to deliver it to Yonge, which he did (cf Epp 273:9, 280:16–19). It was reprinted by Th. Martens in Louvain 10 November 1513, with this letter as preface, but in the Froben Plutarch of 1514 the leaf which would have contained the preface is cut out in all the copies we have seen, a fact which still awaits explanation.

TO THE RIGHT HONOURABLE JOHN YONGE, MASTER OF THE ROLLS, FROM ERASMUS OF ROTTERDAM, GREETINGS

You should not wonder at my sending so small a New Year's gift to so great a friend; for you are aware that it is the nature of presents to be made acceptable by the good will of which they are tokens and not by their value. 5 In the second place, what literary present could be short enough when it is offered to one who is eternally busied in such a multitude of embassies and so much public business of the realm? Not to add that in these times of great confusion – this veritable age of iron – it is well that anything that has to do with the Graces or the Muses should be extremely short. But if I may, even 10 so, add a few verbal flourishes to my small present – first, it comes from the treasures of Plutarch, and you know that all the productions of this particular author are excellent; second, it is quite fresh – with the ink still wet upon it; and besides, you would hardly credit the exertions this tiny book has cost me, not so much because Plutarch is a trifle difficult, partly through his 15 style, partly since he endlessly accumulates a great deal that he does not clarify, but much more because, though he is the most learned of writers, his text is equally the most corrupt. Thus while he, of all authors, deserves to be read, he more than any other is impossible to read, so much does the reader have to struggle with monstrous faults at well-nigh every line. If, 20

John Yonge, Master of the Rolls
Effigy by Pietro Torrigiano, c 1516
Public Record Office, London

finally, you should ask what the subject is, the work explains how to preserve one's good health even without the aid of medicines; and even though everyone places a high value on his health, still I can think of few men who more deserve to keep their health as long as possible than you; for you place all your exertions at the disposal of the public, so that you seem to have come into the world to serve your country rather than yourself. And if Plutarch's instruction on this subject is less medical than that of Galen or Paul of Aegina, still it is more philosophical. 25

It only remains for my little book, such as it is, to pass into use, not only commended by the blessing of your name, but also emended by the touch of your revising hand; indeed the more you emend it, the more you will commend it. Farewell. 30

London, 1 January 1513

269 / To the Reader London, 5 January 1513

This is the preface to a revised and enlarged edition of the *Adagiorum chiliades* (cf Ep 211), which had been planned by Bade in Paris as long ago as April 1511 (cf Epp 219:5 and 263:22–31) and was expected to appear in 1513. Erasmus gave the corrected copy to Franz Birckmann for transmission to Paris (cf Ep 283:181ff), and he passed it not to Bade but to Froben in Basel. Froben had just published in August 1513 an unauthorized page-for-page reprint of the first edition of the *Chiliades* (Venice: Aldus September 1508) and therefore waited to produce the new edition until his reprint was sold out. When Erasmus reached Basel in August 1514 it had not yet appeared. He was thus able to add some retouching to this preface (eg, 34ff), but did not trouble to alter the date 1513 at the end. The revised edition with this preface appeared, undated, some time in 1515. On the importance of this edition, in which many essays were expanded and several long essays added, all tending to introduce a new note of criticism of contemporary society, see Phillips 96ff.

ERASMUS OF ROTTERDAM TO THE GENEROUS-MINDED READER, CONCERNING THE SECOND EDITION OF HIS *Chiliades*

I suppose, generous reader, that as soon as some person of keen critical instincts observes that this work on adages is now appearing in a third edition, he is likely to raise the objection that, according to the poets, 5

* * * * *

269:4–5 third edition] The first being the *Adagiorum collectanea* of 1500 (cf Ep 126); the second and third the Aldine *Adagiorum chiliades* of 1508 and the present revision.

Bacchus was born but twice, whereas the present book is being reborn over and over again. But when snakes and some insects slough away their old age and are, as it were, reborn several times a year, surely it is no scandalous matter for a book to reappear in fresh guise from time to time, so long as it is purified, revised, and enriched? For if, in the animal kingdom, mothers 10 that produce a litter of four or five at a time, because of their numbers, usually give birth to them still rough and unformed, intending to lick them into shape later, why should I hesitate to follow nature's example when I am confronted with all those thousands of proverbs? This is especially justified since it was the course followed by those great men and true aristocrats of 15 literature, Aristotle in his *Rhetoric* and *Ethics*, Cicero and Quintilian in their advice to the orator, Origen in his commentary on the mystic marriage-song, and St Jerome in his commentary on the holy prophet Obadiah, not to mention Seneca, Tertullian, Boethius, and a host of other authors of the highest reputation, who have not shrunk from correcting or superseding a 20 previous edition by means of a new one. As for me, who am nothing at all compared to them, surely I am entitled to suppose that I should do likewise, first because my subject is less momentous than theirs, and second because it is one that by its very nature is bound to be expanded or improved by my daily reading, especially at a time when new relics of ancient literature are 25 continually being brought to light. Suppose that by some lucky chance we were to discover the writings of Clearchus and Aristotle and Chrysippus and Didymus on the subject of proverbs; ought I then to be deterred by shame from using their treatises to re-issue the present *Chiliades* once again in an ampler or a more correct form? If only other authors too could show 30 this kind of disposition to surpass themselves from time to time! Plato indeed says that this is the most splendid victory anyone could win. Such as it was, my first edition – or more properly that hasty effusion – was well

* * * * *

6 Bacchus] When his mother Semele died, the unborn Bacchus was rescued by his father Jupiter, who sewed him up inside his thigh until he was of age to be born, as it were, a second time.

27 Clearchus] Clearchus of Soli in Cyprus (c 340–c 250 BC) was a disciple of Aristotle who wrote paradoxes, erotica, an encomium on Plato, and various theological and zoological works. He is also said to have made a collection of proverbs.

27 Chrysippus] A Greek philosopher of the third century BC

28 Didymus] Didymus Chalcenterus (c 63 BC–10 AD) was a Greek scholar who taught in Alexandria and wrote commentaries on Greek authors of which only fragments remain.

31 Plato] *Laws* 1.626E

received and proved useful; while the second had a still warmer reception, as is sufficiently shown by the fact that so many reprints have appeared 35 within three years, both in Italy and in Germany – which cost me some discomfort, inasmuch as they anticipated the laborious efforts I was already making to get this third edition ready. But since in preparing it I have once again outdone myself, I am confident that it too will be still better received than the former ones. Certainly it ought not to look like a new creation, 40 since I have said at the very opening of my preface that it was not.

On this point, however, the reader must be the sole judge. I shall state the facts plainly: it becomes a German both to act openly and speak frankly. Well then, in the first (or Paris) edition, which was exceedingly hurried, the subject entirely deceived my youthful judgment. I had supposed myself to 45 be faced with a fairly easy task, but I learned by experience that it involved harder work than any other kind of literature; also I was not equipped with Greek books, and to elect to write about proverbs without them is simply to fly without wings, as Plautus puts it. Again when I was preparing a second edition in Venice, and was by that time well aware how hard and onerous 50 my chosen subject was, still I got through the whole business within about eight months, and a single frail mortal had to undertake a mass of work that would be too much for Hercules himself unaided. There are still men alive who could refute me if I spoke falsely: Aldo Manuzio, in whose house I finished this edition while he printed it; Joannes Lascaris, at that time 55 ambassador of the king of France; Marcus Musurus; Battista Egnazio; and

* * * * *

36 within three years] This is evidently an addition to the 1513 preface, inserted when the book was actually published in 1515, and refers to the reprints of the Aldine *Chiliades* by Froben in 1513 and by Mazocco at Ferrara and Anshelm at Tübingen in 1514.

49 Plautus] *Poenulus* 871; *Adagia* III v 84

55 Lascaris] Joannes Lascaris was born in Constantinople and was brought to Italy as a child. He was patronized by the Medici, and after 1494 by Charles VIII and Louis XII. He was French ambassador to Venice, 1504–9, where he was closely related to the scholars of Aldus' circle. He is mentioned along with Egnazio and others in the adage 'Festina lente,' II i 1, as among the scholars who had aided Erasmus in preparing the Aldine *Adagia* (cf Phillips 186).

56 Musurus] See Ep 223:5n. These names were added to *Adagia* II i 1 in the Froben edition of January 1526.

56 Egnazio] Giovanni Battista Cipelli, a Venetian who adopted the name Egnazio, edited many of the editions of the classics published by Aldus, and was for many years professor of rhetoric at Venice. He and Erasmus exchanged occasional letters until 1534 (see Allen Ep 2964).

Girolamo Aleandro; together with many others who witnessed with what drudgery I ground out this task. The reasons for the haste in which I produced that edition I have also fully explained in the first proverb of the third chiliad. Even if I do not seem to have acquitted myself very creditably, 60 I shall surely be excused even by biased critics for the somewhat unfinished condition of the *Adagia* at its first creation, inasmuch as I was the first of Latin writers to tackle this subject; and, as the proverb itself says, 'one must be indulgent towards a first attempt.'

In the second edition again, so far as I am concerned, each may judge 65 for himself what credit I ought to receive for scholarship or literary skill. But in the matter of care and fulness I believe the result shows that I am far in advance not only of the Latins but even of the Greeks. I refer to such authors as have left treatises of this kind. There is, in fact, nothing extant save a scanty compilation by Zenobius, a scantier one by Diogenianus, and one, 70 still more brief, by Plutarch, unless it is falsely attributed to him. In addition there is a collection by Apostolius of Byzantium which is somewhat fuller or, to speak more truthfully, bigger, but worse than all of them for ignorance and errors. As for Hesychius of Alexandria and the promise he makes in his preface that he will give a fuller account of the adages which 75 Diogenianus had merely catalogued without comment, it is obvious from his performance that the preamble is by another hand than that of the author, since the former promises expanded treatment, whereas in the book one can find nothing but the bare bones. At a later period I acquired a better-stocked library and also a little more leisure, all this due to the 80 extraordinary, the almost incredible, kindness of a man, or rather a great man, who deserves to be remembered to the end of time, William Warham, archbishop of Canterbury and primate of all England, or rather of the whole world, if such a person could be valued according to his true qualities. If one were to attempt to sing his praises in the manner he deserves, one would 85 require more chiliads than I have allotted to the *Adagia* and the list of his

* * * * *

57 Aleandro] Cf 256 introduction.

62–3 first of Latin writers] Cf Ep 126:112–13n.

63–4 'one must ... first attempt'] *Adagia* I ix 61

70 Zenobius ...] These compilers of Greek proverbs, dating from the second century AD and later, are printed by E.L. von Leutsch and F.G. Schneidewin *Corpus paroemiographorum Graecorum* 2 vols (Göttingen 1830–51). It was from them that Erasmus borrowed not only much material but the idea of arranging his material by thousands and hundreds.

79 bare bones] *Adagia* II x 100

distinctions would exceed the proverbs in number. But that would be inappropriate here, as well as unacceptable to his modesty, the only side of his nature that is exaggerated, indeed, so to say, immodest. Great as he is in all respects, he seems to me particularly great for one reason: he, and he alone, declines to recognize his own greatness. Thus his supreme distinction lies in the very fact that, though his merits transcend any possible praise, he will not, even to a limited extent, accept praise at all. But, and this I may say as being properly relevant to my present purpose, among the tumultuous storms of affairs that beat upon him from every quarter, and at the present time – a veritable age of iron, when the world is so fiercely ablaze with the conflagrations of war, and so profoundly disturbed that even in Italy, the mother of good letters, there is no room or respect for them – still in heroic isolation he not only pays attention to the muses in their grievous condition, but even encourages them with rewards, obliges them by generosity, attracts them by graciousness, and binds them to him through good will, fosters them by kindness, protects them with his authority, and by his distinction endows them with dignity and lustre. To sum up: in every way he plays the part of an unrivalled Maecenas towards all men in whom he has discerned the combination of distinguished learning and sterling character. Among these, he gave so warm a welcome to me, though I was the lowliest among them all and rather an aspirant to such praise than entitled to it, that I felt I had found, in one single person, all the qualities I had left behind in Rome, in that mighty throng of the world's great men.

It was accordingly with the help and encouragement which his kindness afforded me that I proceeded to remodel my commentaries on proverbs. I went over the entire work from head to foot, as the saying goes; and first of all I corrected the printers' errors, of which there were a good many. Besides this I added, in quite a few places, the translations of the Greek words, which I had left out in haste as I went on to deal with other matters, for many readers had felt the want of them. Also I somewhat amplified those passages which seemed thin, using for this purpose authors not generally encountered. Next I have written in everywhere the names of authors which at that time did not come to mind, or which I lacked the leisure to insert. Finally I have here and there come to disagree with myself (why should I pretend otherwise?) and am frankly obeying the maxim praised by much-praised men: second thoughts are best. I have expelled, as

* * * * *

111 remodel] *Adagia* I v 92
112 head to foot] *Adagia* I ii 37
122 second thoughts are best] *Adagia* I iii 38

it were, from the class of adages a few that seemed to have been undeservedly included by compilers who nodded, or were merely showing off. But on the other hand I have added to the centuries a moderate quantity of fresh adages, with the result that, by these and other increments, more than one-quarter has been added to the bulk of the former volume. 125

Such, my dear reader, is the present *Adagia*; the same work as before, or, if you prefer, a different one, but in any case more correct, more comprehensive, and, unless I am mistaken, generally better. May all the muses be angry with me if this refurbishing of the *Chiliades* has not cost me almost as much nightly effort as the former edition. How much that cost me perhaps no one would believe who has not tried it for himself. Yet, as the country proverb says, I have flavoured this stew and I must eat it up. If I was rash to plunge into this laborious undertaking, I have paid the penalty for my rashness; while if I was destined for it by fate, it was useless to struggle against the gods. And if among the lovers of good letters there shall be any who gain either profit or pleasure from my exertions, then I shall not be sorry I undertook them. To have accomplished the one thing I set out to do will be reward enough. If my agreeable and benevolent reader should further deem some portion of thanks or of praise to be due, then I would request him to apportion all of it in equal measure between my two patrons: William Mountjoy, a noble baron of the English realm, and the archbishop of Canterbury. Of these the former should receive credit for the principal, the latter for the interest and additions, where the *Chiliades* are concerned. 130 135 140 145

Farewell; and whoever you may be who show interest in my works, may you benefit therefrom.

London, 5 January 1513

270 / To John Colet Cambridge, 11 July [1513]

This is evidently a reply to a letter from Colet in response to a request for money. The *De copia*, for the dedication of which Erasmus says he had been

* * * * *

134 country proverb] *Adagia* I i 85

136–7 struggle against the gods] *Adagia* II v 44

142 two patrons] Erasmus owed a debt both to Mountjoy, to whom he had dedicated the first two editions of the *Adagia*, and to Archbishop Warham, whose patronage had been his principal support for the past year (cf Ep 255 introduction). This preface, however, consists largely of material more suitably addressed to the reader than to a patron, a fact which enabled Erasmus to avoid the embarrassment of dedicating the work to either of his patrons, while leaving him the opportunity to express his thanks gracefully to both in the concluding paragraph.

promised fifteen angels, had been published a year before, 15 July 1512 (cf Ep 260 introduction). Allen suggests that the gap of six months in Erasmus' correspondence at this time may have been due to illness. Rumours of his death were current on the continent by late summer.

ERASMUS OF ROTTERDAM TO HIS UNRIVALLED PATRON, JOHN COLET

You reply in earnest to a letter I wrote in fun. Perhaps it was a breach of decorum to jest with such a powerful patron. All the same, I had a fancy at the time to be witty and frivolous in company with a friend as peerless as 5 you; I was not thinking of your rank so much as of your kindness. Your good nature will enable you take my foolish sally in good part.

You write that I am in your debt even against my will. Generally speaking, my dear Colet, it is unpleasant, as Seneca says, to be in debt to a man to whom one does not wish to owe anything. Still, I know nobody on 10 earth whose debtor I would rather be than yours. And your attitude towards me has always been such that, if no services had been thrown into the scale, I was bound all the same to pile up an enormous load of obligation to you. In fact, however, such a quantity of kindnesses and material benefits too has been added that I should be the most thankless of men if I 15 failed to acknowledge the debt. You say you are far from well off. I fully believe this and fully sympathize. However unusual pressure from my own poverty made me trouble you in yours. How reluctantly I did so you may guess from just one fact – my extreme delay in asking for the fulfilment of an old promise of yours. I am not surprised that your promise has slipped your 20 memory, immersed as you are in a great variety of affairs. Once in your garden, when there happened to be some talk about my *Copia* and I had expressed my intention of inscribing it as a boy's book to our boy prince, you requested that I should dedicate my new book to your new school. I replied with a smile that your school was rather modestly endowed: that 25 what I needed was somebody in a position to furnish a little ready money; and you began to smile in agreement. Next, when I had mentioned my many categories of expenses, you said after some hesitation that, while you were unable to provide what my circumstances demanded, still you would

* * * * *

23 our boy prince] Probably Prince Charles, later Charles V, who was Erasmus' prince and whom he calls 'our prince' even when writing to Englishmen (cf Ep 287:14). The alternative suggestion (cf E&C 153 n128) that it refers to Henry VIII seems unlikely, since the conversation alluded to could not have been earlier than Erasmus' return to England in 1509, by which time Henry was already king and could scarcely be called 'princeps noster puer.'

be happy to give me fifteen angels. And when you cheerfully repeated this offer, I asked if it seemed sufficient. You replied, even more cheerfully, that you would certainly be glad to pay it. Upon this I said, 'I, too, shall be glad to accept it.' 30

Perhaps you will recall the episode now that I have mentioned it. I could add further proofs if you did not freely believe me already. There are of course a few people, friends too (for I have nothing to do with any enemies of yours, nor do I care a straw for their remarks), who are apt to describe you as a somewhat hard man and as being over-careful in disbursing money; and they said (so I interpreted it, with their approval) that this was not through any fault of meanness, but that, because your natural shyness prevented you from saying 'no' to people who were shamelessly importunate and pressing, you were less generous to your friends who did not trouble you, since you could not satisfy both. None of this, however, applies to me, for though I am not very shameless and troublesome in my demands I have always found you most generous. I did not, then, hear this from your detractors but from men who sincerely wish you well. However I neither agree with their opinion nor dispute it except by acknowledging your unsurpassed kindness to me. If you find it not displeasing to grant the balance of what you have promised, I shall accept it, my circumstances being what they are, not as a debt but as a favour, which I shall return in any way I can, and at least shall hold in grateful remembrance. 35 40 45 50

I was distressed to read what you wrote at the end of your letter: that the burden of business was oppressing you more vexatiously than usual. I should like to see you withdrawn to as great a distance as possible from the world's affairs: not because I fear this world, with all its barbs, may claim you as its own and seize possession of you, but because I would rather see your distinguished talents, eloquence, and learning wholly devoted to Christ. But if you cannot completely get clear, still beware of sinking daily 55

* * * * *

30 fifteen angels] Tudor gold angel-nobles, officially worth 6s 8d sterling apiece (1465–1526), so that the sum offered amounted to £5 0s 0d ster. = £7 5s 0d gros Flemish = £42 13s 4d tournois. Cf CWE 1 312, 325, 336–7; and tables A–F below, 327–45.

37 care a straw] *Adagia* I viii 4

53 business] At about this time Richard Fitzjames, bishop of London, charged Colet with expressing certain erroneous or heretical ideas. Warham acquitted Colet but allowed him to be suspended from preaching for a time: P.S. Allen 'Dean Colet and Archbishop Warham' EHR 17 (1902) 306. Erasmus' story of the incident is in his biographical sketch of Colet (Allen Ep 1211:528ff).

deeper in that bog. Perhaps defeat would be better than victory at such a cost; for the greatest of all blessings is peace of mind. These are the thorns which always accompany riches. Meanwhile confront the malicious gossip of ill-disposed people with an upright and pure conscience. Immerse yourself in the one and simple Christ and the complexities of the world will disturb you less. But why do I as the sow teach Minerva, or, being sick myself, attempt to cure the physician? Farewell, best of teachers. 60 65

Cambridge, 11 July [1511]

I have finished the collation of the New Testament and am now starting on St Jerome. After this is done, back I fly to you. Your protégé – yes, yours indeed – Thomas Lupset is helping me and delighting me greatly with his company every day and with the assistance he is giving me in the revision of these texts. And I return aid for aid: which is something I would do more liberally if his studies allowed the time, for I should not like to take a young man away from them. Believe me, no one on earth outdoes him in affection for you. Again, farewell. [1511] 70

271 / To Thomas More — Cambridge, [July 1513]

ERASMUS OF ROTTERDAM TO HIS FRIEND MORE

Lupset thinks that with my help he has been reborn and has fully returned from the underworld. But the masters are trying every trick to drag the youth back to their treadmill, for at once on the same day he had sold his books of sophistry and bought Greek ones instead. Please see you play your part well when the right time comes along. Nothing is more attractive or affectionate than this youth's disposition. Farewell. 5

I am translating a book by Plutarch on how to tell a flatterer from a friend – rather long, but I like it the best of them all. I shall finish it, God willing, within a week. This seems to me almost more to the point than an 10

* * * * *

64 the sow teach Minerva] Cf Epp 216:35–6n and 227:15–16.

69 Lupset] Thomas Lupset (1498?–1530) was the son of a London goldsmith and one of the first pupils at St Paul's School. Colet then sent him to Cambridge, where he came under the influence of Erasmus (cf Ep 271:2ff). He remained on friendly terms with Erasmus and corresponded with him until at least 1525 (cf Allen Ep 1624).

271:5 books of sophistry] A favourite term with Erasmus for medieval scholastic writings

8 Plutarch] See Ep 292 introduction.

unsparing combat with Vigilantius under the banner of Jerome. Farewell again.

If you see our friend Lazarus, a man plainly born for the muses and the graces, please be sure to greet him and encourage him to finish making a fair copy of those things of mine he has in hand, for I have a few brand-new things I am sure he will like very much. A thousand good wishes. 15

Cambridge, [1510]

272 / To Henry VIII [Cambridge, July 1513]

The translation of Plutarch's *De discrimine adulatoris et amici* with this preface was sent to Henry VIII in MS. It is now to be found, not autograph but in the original binding, in Cambridge University Library, MS Add. 6858. In a dedication of the third edition of the same work to Henry in 1517 Erasmus recalled that when he had first presented the work the king had been too busy with war to pay attention to literature. Erasmus was therefore sending it to him again although it had since been published (cf Allen Ep 657:32ff). Henry was in fact with the army in France when this preface was written. It was printed for the first time in *Plutarchi opuscula* (Basel: Froben August 1514), the first book printed for Erasmus after his arrival in Basel. It may have been among the MSS entrusted to Birckmann (cf Epp 263:22n, 269 introduction, and 283:189ff).

TO THE INVINCIBLE KING OF ENGLAND, HENRY THE EIGHTH, FROM ERASMUS OF ROTTERDAM: GREETINGS

Although this world contains no more agreeable society than that of a true and genuinely candid friend and there is nothing a man needs more in the conduct of his affairs, at the same time nothing is harder to find than such a friend, just as whatever is most estimable generally proves excessively rare. But, as Hiero ably maintains in the pages of Xenophon, none stand more sorely in need of this important constituent of happiness than princes, happy as they may be in other respects; for a prince more than any other requires both many friends and right loyal ones too. Indeed he needs to be clear-sighted who all by himself must see to the well-being of thousands. It 5 10

* * * * *

11 Jerome] This refers to Jerome's *Contra Vigilantium* a violent attack (AD 406) on a Gaulish priest for opposing, among other things, excessive veneration paid to the tombs of the martyrs.

13 Lazarus] Apparently a copyist, but otherwise unidentified

272:7 Xenophon] *Hieron* 3.6, of which Erasmus later published a translation (cf Allen Ep 2273)

is fitting, therefore, that the prince should be endowed with many eyes, or in other words with a multitude of wise and loyal friends. This was sagely understood by Darius, king of the Persians, who, having been offered a pomegranate of extraordinary size, expressed the wish that he had a Zopyrus for every seed in it. This Zopyrus was a man of the finest character and a friend of the king, who rightly therefore regarded him so highly that he maintained he would rather have a single Zopyrus unharmed than capture a hundred Babylons; whereby he publicly declared his belief that a friend is more valuable than any treasure. His son Xerxes, too, when he was on the point of invading Greece, found among a horde so vast that no one on earth has yet ventured to believe in it only one man, Demaratus, to give him frank and friendly counsel; yet he failed to see how devoted he was until the outcome proved it. Croesus, king of the Lydians, had the same experience with Solon; while Alexander the Great is said to have had, among all his many companions, only Callisthenes, a pupil of Aristotle, and even he was frank rather than friendly. For Dionysius of Syracuse the only such person was Dio, together with Plato; for Nero it was Seneca – and if Nero had obeyed his advice he would have reigned longer, and might have earned a place among the good emperors as well.

But though it may be that the character and disposition of the monarchs I have named would not admit of frankness in friends, still even where the nature of the prince is abundantly gracious – the very pattern of your own, the most gracious that could be imagined – yet his exalted station, which attracts a host of friends, is the very circumstance that makes it difficult to distinguish true friends from false. For there is sense in the well-known saying 'prosperity makes friends; adversity tests them.' Moreover, in proportion as a true friend is a valuable possession, so is he the more poisonous who acts the role of a friend in order to insinuate himself into one's favour. Considering, therefore, how carefully we assay the purity of gold by means of touchstones, and how we can tell natural gems from artificial by certain distinguishing marks, would it not be utterly absurd not to exercise the same degree of care in a matter so vastly more important – namely, in distinguishing a flatterer from a friend, in other words, that which is most harmful in life from that which is most beneficial? Now to avoid the necessity for detecting a friend by trial and error at considerable cost to oneself, as one detects poison by tasting, Plutarch, who is indubitably the most learned of Greek authors, has promulgated a remarkable

* * * * *

14 Darius] Plutarch *Moralia* 173A

37 saying] The quotation is from the spurious Seneca *De moribus* 51.

technique, making it a simple task to discriminate between a candid, true friend and the impostor who poses as such. Moreover, since the art of 50 admonishing friends, like the art of medicine, requires not merely devotion but tact as well, in case we undermine friendship itself even while we clumsily try to cure our friend's faults, he has added a final section in which he makes it clear how gently one ought to admonish a friend if there is any good reason for it. Such, then, is this most useful treatise, which I have 55 endowed with a Latin dress for your Majesty's sake, in order that I might now attest to a king, of all kings the most illustrious, the continuance within me of that same loyalty and devotion which I expressed to you long ago when you were a boy full of promise. Farewell.

273 / To Andrea Ammonio [Cambridge], 1 September [1513]

Ammonio was at this time on the continent as part of the royal entourage with the army which had just defeated the French, 16 August, in the Battle of the Spurs at Guinegate near Saint-Omer.

ERASMUS OF ROTTERDAM TO HIS FRIEND AMMONIO

I have already written you a letter, which has probably by now been delivered. But I was highly gratified that you mentioned your Erasmus, and moreover so affectionately, in your letter to Jean. The *De tuenda bona valetudine precepta* which I previously inscribed to the Master of the Rolls 5 has recently been printed, quite nicely too, in London. Your Jean has promised that he will send you one or two copies of it. If the recipient of my little book's dedication is present in camp, and if you happen to have a chance, please give him my greetings and present him with a copy. I have revised it so thoroughly that he will hardly believe it is the same book. 10

The plague is raging as fiercely in London as the war is with you. I am therefore staying at Cambridge, looking every day for a convenient moment to take wing, but no opportunity occurs. Another thing that holds me

* * * * *

58 long ago] Erasmus had congratulated the young prince on his classical scholarship in 1499 (cf Ep 104).

273:4 Jean] Jean of Lorraine (cf Ep 281:4n). He had evidently stayed in England while Ammonio went to France.

4–5 *De tuenda bona valetudine precepta*] Precepts for good health: cf Ep 268 introduction.

back is the thirty nobles I expect to receive at Michaelmas. Sixtinus has already flown off to Brabant. My mind is so excited at the thought of 15 emending Jerome's text, with notes, that I seem to myself inspired by some god. I have already almost finished emending him by collating a large number of ancient manuscripts, and this I am doing at enormous personal expense.

I was heartily amused by the picture of life in camp, so vividly 20 sketched in your letter to Jean: so well did you bring before one's eyes the neighing, shouting, cavalry charges, braying of trumpets, the roar and flash of cannon, vomiting of the sick, and groans of the dying. You will be lucky indeed if (may God of his goodness vouchsafe this issue) you return to us unscathed. And what enthralling tales you will be able to tell for the rest of 25 your life about the hardships you are suffering now! But I beseech you urgently by the muses and graces, my dear Ammonio, to see to it, as I warned you in my last letter, that you fight safely. Be as fierce as you like with your pen and slay a hundred thousand foes in a single day. I rejoice in the success of our cause to a degree that it would not be permissible to 30 express, either orally or in a letter.

If ever you visit Omer, and a suitable occasion arises, please give my greeting to the abbot of St Bertin, my most esteemed patron; also to his steward Antonius of Luxembourg, canon of Saint Omer, and to Master Ghisbert, physician to the abbot and the town, two of my best friends; and, 35 in addition, to the dean of the said church, who is a man of exemplary

* * * * *

14 thirty nobles] The first payment of the pension from Aldington, which was to be paid in half-yearly instalments, at Michaelmas (29 September) and Lady Day (25 March). Cf Epp 255 introduction and 296:130n. If these nobles were gold angels, as in Epp 240A:10–11, 248:40, and 270:30, or their equivalent value in money-of-account (6s 8d ster. apiece), then this payment would have been £10 0s 0d sterling = £14 10s 0d gros Flemish = £85 6s 8d tournois. But if reckoned in ryals (rose-nobles), at 10s 0d apiece, it would have been £15 0s 0d sterling. Cf Ep 214:4n; CWE 1 338–9; and tables A–F below, 327–45, especially table D, 341.

14 Sixtinus] Cf Ep 235 introduction.

33 abbot] Antoon van Bergen (cf Ep 143 introduction)

34 Antonius of Luxembourg] See Ep 137 introduction. He was now canon of Notre Dame at Saint-Omer.

34–5 Ghisbert] Cf Epp 95:13n; ; 252:15.

36 dean] Sidrach de Lalaing (d 1533) became dean of Saint-Omer in March 1513.

character and a great lover of literature. If you should get a chance to speak to him, I beg you to ask him what has become of my former servant Maurice, whom I shall assuredly be glad to help in any way I can. I would not dare to ask you, harassed as you are by numerous hardships and at the 40 same time, as I guess, by many distractions, to write to me sometime too. However, if ever you find it no imposition, it will give me as much pleasure as anything could.

I know it is unnecessary for anyone, much less myself, to ask you to support your own Jean's scheme and help him to advance it as successfully 45 as possible; I am well acquainted with the high esteem in which you hold him. On his side, he is completely devoted to you; and it is not Ammonio's way to be surpassed in affection. It is in you that he has reposed his principal hopes of success in the business.

I beg you most particularly to be sure to give my greetings to Battista. 50 The letter I am looking for from him must be written in Greek, or not at all! I pray that some benevolent deity will send more favourable breezes; for 'this wind allows one neither to stay nor sail.' Farewell.

[London], 1 September [1511]

274 / To William Gonnell Cambridge, 26 September [1513]

William Gonnell (d 1560) was a young man living at Landbeach, a village five miles northeast of Cambridge, and apparently in charge of a school. He did copying for Erasmus and looked after his horse when he was away from Cambridge. Later he became tutor to More's children. Earlier in September Erasmus had left Cambridge to avoid the plague, probably staying with Gonnell at Landbeach.

ERASMUS TO HIS FRIEND GONNELL

My horse, dear Gonnell, always comes back to me fresher and in better condition, thus proving how carefully and wisely he has been fed. Therefore I heartily beseech you to continue to look after our nag as you have begun to do. Why should I not call him ours? After all, friends have 5 everything in common. I will take care that you do not appear to have spent

* * * * *

39 Maurice] Cf Ep 263:2n.

45 scheme] For Jean's scheme for advancement see Ep 282:44ff.

50 Battista] Probably Boerio (cf Ep 267 introduction)

52–3 'this wind ... sail'] *Adagia* II v 21

274:6 everything in common] *Adagia* I i 1

your efforts on a man who forgets, or is lacking in gratitude. Farewell, dearest Gonnell.

Cambridge, 26 September [1512]

275 / To [William Gonnell?] [Cambridge, October 1513]

This letter and the one following were found among the state papers of Henry VIII in the Public Record Office (SP Henry VIII 9 f.100). This letter has no heading but has at the end: 'Honorato viro G. ludi magistro amico singulari.' Allen's argument for assuming the letter to be by Erasmus and addressed to Gonnell is convincing. Plague was still rife in Cambridge, so severe in fact that the university was closed during October. Cf C.H. Cooper *Annals of Cambridge* I (Cambridge 1842) 295. As a result Erasmus was considering returning to Gonnell at Landbeach, whence he wrote to Colet on 31 October (cf Ep 278).

Things here are just as before; so I am thus far undecided whether I ought to return to join you. Once again there has been a death not far from the college, and Bont the physician has died, out in the country, as has his little daughter at home. Therefore please oblige me by not changing the beds for four days. If I come, I shall come with our friend Watson. Farewell. 5

To the esteemed G, schoolmaster and most valued friend

276 / To [William] G[onnell?] and H[umphrey Walkden?]
[Cambridge, October 1513]

From the similarity of subject to Epp 275 and 279 it is clear that the 'G' to whom this letter is addressed was William (Gulielmus) Gonnell; the 'G' may refer to either his first or his last name but in Epp 274, 287, and 289 he is addressed as Gonnell. The Omfredus to whom the letter is also addressed was probably Humphrey Walkden, a fellow of Queens' to whom Erasmus sent affectionate greetings after leaving Cambridge (cf Allen Epp 456:280, 1656:19). The enclosed letter which Erasmus asked Humphrey to put into English for him was addressed to the father of John Smith who had been his servant-pupil since November 1511 (cf Ep 241:37n). Robert Smith, who was apparently a man of some substance in Cambridge, had been staying with the Gonnells when

* * * * *

275:3 Bont] Cf Ep 225:12n.

5 Watson] John Watson (d 1537) had been a fellow of King's College, Cambridge, and was later master of Christ's (cf Emden BRUC 622). Earlier he had travelled in Italy and met many of Erasmus' friends (cf Allen Ep 450).

Erasmus was there and had then asked to have his son sent back to him, which Erasmus agreed to do despite the fact that he had not yet been able to find a new servant (cf Ep 277:3ff).

ERASMUS TO HIS G AND O

I cannot talk to this monster; you must give him to understand that I have been more than a father to the boy, looking after him as I did in mind and body alike; and that he has not wasted his time, but made progress, better progress than he would have made in any school whatsoever. 5

If my horse needs shoeing, see that this is done, for he may possibly have a rather long journey to face. There is a piece of business which looks like keeping me here, little as I wish to stay. On Wednesday I shall arrive with Watson. Goodbye, and for my sake show some courtesy to this donkey of a man. 10

If Humphrey has time, I should like him to put the gist of the following into English and send John with it for my signature:

TO MY ESTEEMED FRIEND ROBERT SMITH, GREETINGS

I have still no definite prospect of a servant, for the one I thought, at the time, that I could rely on has changed his mind and gone overseas. 15 However, because I have resolved to conform entirely to your wishes, I am sending John to you, John to whom I have been just like a father, or better than a father, in caring for his body and mind. Since his talents deserved good treatment like this, I do not regret having given it. He has not completely wasted his time. Although the boy's pro- 20 gress is not at once apparent, he possesses more of good Latin than he would have gained in three years at Roger's school. If he has not been thrashed, it is because while with me he has not deserved it, and a fine-spirited pupil is far better led than dragged. If you have found a more suitable master for him, I myself am glad, both for the boy's sake 25 and yours, since this boy's natural endowments are material worthy of a first-class craftsman. You may find a more learned, but never a more affectionate one though you search the country through. My good wishes to yourself, your excellent wife, and all your house.

To Master G and Master O, his valued friends 30

* * * * *

22 Roger's school] St Antony's School in Threadneedle Street, London, of which Roger Wentford was headmaster (cf Ep 196 introduction)

277 / To Roger Wentford [Landbeach? October 1513]

Since John Smith had been a pupil at Wentford's school (cf Ep 241:37n), Erasmus hoped that Wentford might persuade John's father to let him remain with Erasmus until he could find another servant.

ERASMUS TO ROGER WENTFORD, THE MOST ACCOMPLISHED HEADMASTER OF ST ANTONY'S SCHOOL

When John's father was with us, he told me he wished to entrust his son to another man, and I did not utter a word against the proposal. He gave me notice for All Saints day and I accepted. I added that if he wished to take him 5 away that very moment I should take it in good part. I cannot be angry at him, knowing as I do that whatever he does about the boy is done at the suggestion of another person. A good while ago, when he had taken him away, he subsequently returned him to me on your initiative, though I was not really very eager, having by this time turned my attention elsewhere. 10 Another time when he had withdrawn him for a fortnight he brought him back himself and was willing to allow him to accompany me even on my crossing the sea. In my house the boy has had a liberal education and at my own personal expense; and, though he has not made such good progress as I desired, still I will confidently maintain that he knows more Latin than he 15 would have been likely to get in any school, even Lily's, in the space of three years, and you are aware that the first steps are hardly visible; so it is far from true that he has at all thrown away his time. But since I see the numskull of a father driven hither and thither by the suggestions he receives, the mother foolishly fond, I am not disposed to waste my good 20 services. Now nothing is so completely lost as what is bestowed upon the ungrateful – not that I think they are ungrateful; but even more does one lose what is bestowed on those who do not understand. For an ungrateful person, even if he pretends to owe nothing, will still feel inwardly a sense of obligation, and will at some time repay for mere shame; but he who does 25 not understand a benefit goes so far as to think he himself is the creditor! Thus, just as it is foolish to lay under obligation people who are devoid of understanding, so it is the height of madness to do good turns to unwilling recipients. The man remarked to a close friend of mine that my ignorance of

* * * * *

5 All Saints day] 1 November

8 another person] The boy's mother, who was chiefly responsible for taking him from Erasmus (see line 20 below).

16 Lily's] St Paul's School, of which William Lily was high master

English was a hindrance to the boy's learning, whereas on the contrary this is the very thing that makes him, willy-nilly, learn Latin all the better. 30

'Where do these remarks lead?' you ask. Why, to this: when the father was negotiating with me about this matter, I was almost sure of acquiring a certain person as my servant, but he has changed his mind and gone over to Brabant, though he intends to return before Christmas. If I go over there 35 myself, which will be a little after the first of November, I shall leave John wherever he chooses. But if I do not, will he kindly allow the boy to stay with me until my aforesaid servant returns, to keep me from changing my servant too often within a short time? Perhaps you can persuade him to do this. But if he totally refuses this request, though I am sure he will allow it 40 without much reluctance, he is to do as he pleases. I shall not be unduly distressed at the waste of kindness on my part, inasmuch as I have bestowed my assistance on good talents in this case. Farewell, my dear Roger, and write to me occasionally.

It has just occurred to me why I should seem to him the only one 45 suitable to teach, clothe, and feed his son at my own expense: the boy has had less drudgery to undergo than he would have had at your place. He has been treated as a gentleman and done no writing for me. I have neither fed nor clothed him meanly, nor given him perfunctory teaching. Had he been as eager to learn as I was to teach him, he would have no need by now of 50 anyone to teach him his letters or take him through his grammar, cane in hand. And I do think my reputation for letters ought to be considered at least equal to those of the general run of teachers. I do not say this because I am unduly concerned about money, but that I, of all men, should seem fit to receive such treatment and then to be robbed of my servant without a sign 55 of thanks. However more about this, and at greater length, another time. Again best wishes, my dearest Roger.

[1514]

278 / To John Colet [?Landbeach near] Cambridge, 31 October [1513]

Although this letter is headed Cambridge, lines 26–7 indicate that it was written while Erasmus was in the country, presumably at Landbeach, after he had fled from Cambridge to avoid the plague.

* * * * *

34 servant] Allen suggests that this refers to Stephen Gardiner, who later had a distinguished career as statesman and prelate, appointed bishop of Winchester by Henry VIII in 1531, and lord chancellor by Queen Mary in 1553–5. In a letter of 1526 (Allen Ep 1669) he recalled meeting Erasmus in Paris in 1511 and later being offered a position as his servant-pupil through the Cambridge bookseller Gerard (cf Ep 248:55n), evidently while Erasmus was in Cambridge.

ERASMUS OF ROTTERDAM TO HIS FRIEND COLET

I cannot tell you how much I congratulate you on recovering your quiet. I wonder what the suffragan means, since he knew that this tax had been imposed before he took upon himself the responsibility for paying my annuity, and yet he said not one word at the time about sharing the burden 5 of the tenths.

I feel you are a little vexed that I have once again left London without paying my respects to you; and you twit me for impatience. Well, that is my particular affliction; I do not deny it myself; but nothing of the kind you suspect took place then. First of all, I had no business to see you about; and 10 your William frankly cautioned me that you were very busy writing letters, so that I should not disturb you, though I had not come to do that either, but to receive from your William the letters addressed to me. Also I was in such haste to get away from there for fear of the plague that I decided not to enter even my lodgings. Again when I went back to remove my books, I got 15 together all my books and my gear in complete solitude, and, having done this, by which time also it was quite late, I hurried away and never even slept in my room; the business of bringing the boxes over I entrusted to Josse. Such were my motives for failing to call upon you.

* * * * *

2 quiet] The recovery of his quiet refers to the end of his troubles with Bishop Fitzjames, who had charged him with heresy and suspended him from preaching (cf Ep 270:53n).

3 suffragan] Bishop John Thornton, a suffragan of Canterbury, had been appointed rector of Aldington 31 July 1512, subject to a pension to be paid to Erasmus (see Ep 255 introduction and 273:14n). The question at issue here is whether the royal tax of 10 per cent voted by convocation and due on 7 July 1512 for the following five years was to be paid out of the income from the living or to be shared by Erasmus. Since the tax had been imposed on the living before Thornton agreed to pay Erasmus' pension, Erasmus argued that it did not apply to his pension but was solely the rector's obligation. The pension may also have been subject to payment of papal taxes on annate or first fruits amounting to possibly half its value for the first year (cf E&C 147). On the whole problem of clerical taxation see J. Scarisbrick 'Clerical Taxation in England, 1485–1547' *Journal of Ecclesiastical History* (April 1960) 41–54.

7 again left London] Erasmus had evidently made two flying visits to London some time during September or October. Colet's letter of 7 October (cf line 19) seems to have been concerned chiefly with Erasmus' copy of St Matthew which he had lent to Fisher. It need not have been the one in which Colet expressed his displeasure at Erasmus' failure to greet him, as is assumed in E&C 159. That Erasmus made two trips to London at this time is suggested first by the phrase 'again left London,' and second by the reference to his return for the removal of his books, which were presumably in the lodgings which on the first occasion he had not entered.

On the thirty-first of October I got your letter written on the seventh; 20
and I had written a second letter to you on the same subjects. If my Matthew is not in your possession, it must be in the bishop of Rochester's. This was what I rather guessed anyway. But he failed to add it to the others because I had given them to him separately. If it is lost, I shall blame myself, and shall punish myself by the tedium of work done over again as a penalty for being 25
obliging.

Everyone is running away from Cambridge in all directions; I myself have already withdrawn to the country, but perhaps the want of wine will drive me back to Cambridge.

I congratulated you in my last letter and now congratulate you again 30
for having returned to preaching, the holiest, most beneficent task of all. Yes, I think that brief interruption will even be turned to good account; men will listen more thirstily to one whose voice they have missed awhile. May the supreme Lord Jesus guard and keep you.

Cambridge, 31 October [1507] 35

279 / To William Gonnell [Cambridge, first part of November 1513]

ERASMUS OF ROTTERDAM TO HIS FRIEND,
MASTER WILLIAM GONNELL

There is no reason, my dear Gonnell, for you to be much perturbed at the death of one or two people, unless the scourge begins to spread in all directions; especially when, as things are in England at present, changing 5
one's domicile means simply changing, and not escaping from, one's danger. Avoid the contagion of a crowd as much as you can; live temperately as you are doing; and keep the members of your household from contact with crowds in the same way. Winter is upon us now; and winter commonly cures troubles of this sort. 10

I believe you are far too deeply vexed, almost to the point of despair, over the loss of your purse and the little cash that was in it. In the first place, what has the Muses' nursling to do with money, or Apollo to do with Midas? Next, what concern to a young man are the cares that beset the old? And lastly, why should the loss of such a very tiny sum affect the spirits of a 15
Gonnell? Why, when I was on the point of returning to France fifteen years

* * * * *

21 Matthew] Erasmus' Latin translation from the Gospel, which he had apparently lent to Fisher

ago I lost money to the value of twenty pounds on Dover beach, shipwrecked before I even got aboard. I had lost all I had in the world at once, but I was so undismayed that I went back to my books all the keener and fuller of energy; and presently, a very few days after this, out came my book of proverbs. Make the Muses your delight, Gonnell, and Fortune will somehow give you back that money of yours – and with interest. Meanwhile you are to reckon my bit of money, however paltry it is, as being yours for the sharing. If you miss me, I miss you just as wretchedly; but Fortune will not be cruel to us for ever! 20 25

I was greatly put out at first when my servant John left me. However my mind is quite inured to this now, so much so that I had rather he did not come back; for what is the use of obliging people who do not comprehend? 'Nothing is so utterly lost as what is bestowed on the ungrateful'; yes, but the loss is far worse when the recipients cannot understand what is given. Where the ingrate covers himself by pretences, the uncomprehending man does not even feel obligation. If you should begin anything new, please let me know of it. When there is a chance to talk, I shall tell you about something which, I hope, will give you some pleasure and be of some use to you in your studies. Farewell. 30 35

Will you please give my kind regards to that most gracious lady your mother and to the rest. I am surprised Lupset does not write at all; I long to hear how he is and what he is about. Farewell once more.

[London, 1515]

280 / From Andrea Ammonio — London, 25 November [1513]

Henry VIII had returned to England at the end of October and Ammonio had presumably returned with him.

ANDREA AMMONIO TO DESIDERIUS ERASMUS

Three letters from you have reached me in camp, and I have enjoyed nothing more – not even the time when the Frenchman ran away; I answered the first in the language of the camp; I do not know whether you got

* * * * *

17 twenty pounds] Cf Ep 119:9n.

20–1 book of proverbs] *The Adagiorum collectanea* of 1500 (cf Ep 126 introduction)

37 Lupset] Cf Ep 270:69n.

280:2 three letters] Of these only Ep 273 survives.

4 the first] This letter never reached Erasmus (cf Epp 282:6–7 and 283:50ff).

this letter. As for the last letter, delivered to me, as it was, just before I left France – that is, when we were going home to acknowledge the cheers – I sent no reply, but I did as you told me. I took pains to recommend you to the abbot of St Bertin, and read out to him that long list of yours, enumerating your good friends in his service. It was marvellous how he brightened up at once when your name was mentioned. Really he was like a widowed mother who hears news of her young son abroad. He buttonholed me and took me aside, for there was a large crowd present, and after many affectionate enquiries about you finally asked me how you had fared in England. I answered him with truth that you had in every way fared far worse than you deserved. In short, he was quite clearly most well disposed towards you. Next I met the Master of the Rolls, and showed him personally what you were writing about him, and offered him the little work by Plutarch; he thanked me briefly and, because he was quite obviously very busy, rushed away somewhere else, and I had no further chance to speak to him.

As soon as I touched English soil I began to enquire into your whereabouts, since you had written to say that you were running away from the Cambridge plague. Eventually Sixtinus, and he alone, told me that you had indeed left Cambridge because of the plague and withdrawn somewhere or other; but that, since you were in difficulties, he said, because of a shortage of wine and you thought the want of that worse than the plague, you had gone back to Cambridge and now were there. Ah, what a mighty companion in arms of Bassareus thou art, who hast refused to desert thy captain in direst danger! Wherefore I send thee from thy great commander's hand a gift, a bowl of Cretan wine; that very wine which Jupiter, while nursed as a baby in the island, pissed from his baby penis – a mysterious product of milk and nectar! If you repair swiftly to my house in London you shall be privileged to drink far ampler draughts of it.

For the rest, you congratulate me on the improvement in my circumstances; not a very friendly thing to do, unless you congratulate yourself as well and use my fortune as your own. I in my turn congratulate you for many reasons, including particularly the ten gold pieces which were pre-

* * * * *

8 abbot] Antoon van Bergen (cf Epp 143 introduction, 252, 273:33)

16 Master of the Rolls] John Yonge (see Ep 268 introduction)

22 Sixtinus] See Ep 113 introduction.

27 Bassareus] A rare name for Bacchus, borrowed from Horace's *Odes*

36 ten gold pieces] These were not English gold nobles but, as indicated in Ep 281:8, French gold écus à la couronne, received from the 'Gallic spoils' of the recent campaign in France. Cf CWE 1 315, 336–7; and table A below, 327–33, 340.

sented to you by the bishop of Durham; not so much for the sake of the gift, as because he is not usually generous in this fashion to anyone except those for whom he has an unusual degree of respect and affection. But, as for the fact that he gave you no answer that was to the point when you asked him about me, I am not surprised, though I do not know what the reason was; for shortly before he left our camp he made it clear to me that he was a little aggrieved, though I cannot guess why. He is full of suspicions, and takes ill some things you would never imagine. So long as I personally do whatever my duty dictates and incur no blame, I shall not be much perturbed about the attitude towards me of any person in particular. 40 45

There are many other things I might say in reply to your letter. And I have a full purse of gossip too; I am all agog to pour it into your lap. So as soon as you can get back here, let me know at once. Do not, however, forget this: Pietro Carmiliano has lately published an epitaph on the king of Scots which is full of womanish abuse. It is being printed by Pynson, and you will soon be reading it; and in it Carmiliano is more complacent and self-admiring than the famous Suffenus in Catullus; yet, if I had not pulled him up, he would have put in the word *pullulare* with the first syllable short! Still there is a great deal left for you to laugh at; especially the fact that people can be found to praise this sort of nonsense in all seriousness. Farewell, dearest Erasmus, and love me as you do. 50 55

London, 25 November [1515]

I will get even with you for calling me most courageous.

* * * * *

37 Durham] Thomas Ruthall, bishop of Durham (see Ep 192 introduction). It is uncertain when or where Erasmus met Ruthall and received from him the ten gold pieces and the evasive replies to his questions about Ammonio (cf Epp 281:7 and 282:20ff). Since the tone of this letter makes it clear that Ammonio had not been in touch with Erasmus since his return to England, and since Erasmus mentions in Ep 281:3–4 that he had written to Ammonio frequently when he was in camp but makes no mention of letters written to him in England, it seems fair to assume that the information about Erasmus' meeting with Ruthall was contained in one of the letters sent to the camp. In that case Ruthall must have left the camp to return to England (cf line 42) some time in advance of the royal party. Erasmus could, then, have met Ruthall at any time in September or early October either in London or, possibly, in Cambridge, where Ruthall might stop on his way north to Durham.

40 to the point] *Adagia* I v 45

43–4 He is full of ... imagine] This sentence is omitted in the *Epistolae* of 1521.

48 purse] Cf Catullus 13.8.

50 Carmiliano] See 262:13n. The epitaph he had written was on James IV of Scotland, who had been killed at Flodden, 9 September 1513. Pynson's publication is not recorded in STC.

53 Suffenus] Catullus 22.17

281 / To Andrea Ammonio Cambridge, 26 November [1513]

This letter crossed Ep 280.

ERASMUS OF ROTTERDAM TO HIS FRIEND ANDREA AMMONIO

I am already waiting to hear of those glorious deeds of generalship; next, how much booty was brought away stuffed in your belts. I wrote to you more than once by the hand of Master Jean of Lorraine when you were living in camp. Meanwhile I was carrying on as bitter a struggle with 5 blemishes in Seneca's and Jerome's text as you were with the French. Though I have never been in camp, the bishop of Durham has given me ten French gold couronnes out of the Gallic spoils. But more of this when I see you; meanwhile I am waiting for your campaign letters. Farewell.

Cambridge, 26 November 10

It is unnecessary to ask you to do what you always do on your own initiative; still, I do beg you, if ever you have a chance, to help my interests by saying some words of commendation. I have made up my mind to 'cast my sheet anchor' in a few months' time. If this goes well, I am ready to pretend that this country, which I have chosen in preference to Rome and in 15 which old age is overtaking me, really is my own, but if not, I shall cut myself loose from it and go off, it does not much matter where, at least to die elsewhere. I will call all the gods to witness to the trust thanks to which you-know-who has ruined me. But if I had in three words promised what he has undertaken so often and with such splendid-seeming expressions, 'I 20 know what I am promising; I will fulfil it to the letter,' may I be undone if I would not rather die than desert a man who depended on me. You have my congratulations, Ammonio, because Fortune I hear is smiling kindly on you and not behaving spitefully all the time; she is only so-so to me. Farewell once more. 25

[1509]

* * * * *

4 Jean] Jean of Lorraine was a servant or secretary to Ammonio. He is also mentioned in Epp 273:4; 282:44; 255:10; 262:11.

8 French gold couronnes] Ecus d'or à la couronne, last issued in 1474–5, currently valued at £1 15s od tournois, so that this sum was then worth £17 10s od tournois = £2 19s 2d gros Flemish = £2 1s 8d sterling. Cf Epp 212:7n, 280:36n, 296:138n; CWE I 315, 336–7; and tables A–F below, 327–45.

14 sheet anchor] *Adagia* I i 24. The adage means that it was his final effort.

19 you-know-who] Allen suggests that this refers to Mountjoy who, except for a pension of twenty pounds (cf Ep 288:14–15), had done little to fulfil the hopes aroused by Ep 215.

19 three words] *Adagia* IV iv 84

24 she is only so-so to me] This clause was added in the *Epistolae* of 1521.

282 / To Andrea Ammonio Cambridge, 28 November [1513]

This letter answers Ep 280.

ERASMUS TO HIS FRIEND AMMONIO

If anything that has happened this year gave me more delight than your letter, I wish the Graces, together with charm and wit, in a word, the Muses and literature at large may curse me with the same high displeasure as they do Carmiliano! This is an oath you certainly deem to be as binding as if 5 Jupiter were to swear to you 'by his Stygian brother's streams.' It is the only letter I have had, the earlier one not having been delivered. I should have overwhelmed you too with more frequent letters, except that there was no hope that they would reach you; but as soon as your Master Jean offered the chance, the nicest thing I could do at that moment was to have a talk with 10 you by the only available method. Remembering Erasmus in the enormous welter of your affairs, attending so conscientiously to my trifling business – there is nothing new in your doing all this, but I am moved by your sincere friendship, as though you were really doing something new, and am most grateful for your readiness to help me. I am just as grateful as if I had actually 15 received the wine. However I am surprised that you entrust anything of that kind to rascals like these, after more than one experience of their dishonesty. The carrier who delivered the letter says he was not given any cask.

The bishop of Durham has replied, but irrelevantly and not to the 20 point; and when I pressed him with questions, he said, looking as though he would be glad to abandon that particular topic of conversation, 'I think the bishop of Winchester has it, but I am not certain' – and quickly picked up the thread of talk he had interrupted. He was quite evidently hostile to Battista though I gave him no excuse. But these are dire secrets. 25

The reason why it is unlikely I shall go to London before Christmas is partly the plague and partly highway robberies – there is a crop of them in

* * * * *

5 Carmiliano] Cf lines 30ff below and Ep 280:50ff.

6 Stygian] Virgil *Aeneid* 9.104

20 Durham] Allen suggests that Ammonio seems to have been endeavouring to obtain some appointment which lay in the hands of both Ruthall, bishop of Durham, and Foxe, Bishop of Winchester. What is clear, however, is that Ruthall intended to do nothing about the business, whatever it was, and he may have referred Erasmus to Foxe simply as a way of avoiding a direct refusal. Ammonio had already been told of Ruthall's failure to reply to the point and feared he was out of favour with him (cf Ep 280:37n and 42ff).

25 Battista] Boerio (see Ep 267 introduction)

England at present. The day before your letter was delivered to me I wrote by the hand of Bryan, who has written a history of these French in the space of a volume. I saw Carmiliano's epitaph, and when I read *pullulare* with a false quantity, I said 'Here's a disfigurement' – and when I asked, and they told me it was Carmiliano's, I replied: 'Quite worthy of him too.' Some people understood this to mean 'worthy of the Scottish king'; and those with more judgment amongst them smiled. But come, are you not being just a little too kind-hearted when you seek to defend that monster? I swear I would have given a great deal to induce you to say nothing. I am surprised that you leave such a great blank in your letter on the subject of Battista. Bullock's imminent arrival is being announced. Come, you call me most holy; but here you do some injustice to the pope; though what adjective would fit a campaigning and conquering soldier better than most courageous? Even though your 'trifles' may be measured in waggonloads and not merely in sackfuls, you will not be able to satisfy me once I get a chance to talk to you. 30 35 40

I see that your Master Jean, or rather ours, has been most assiduous in looking after our letters. So I hold him in still higher esteem, though I was fond of him before. He says he is aiming at no small elevation, but a bishopric, no less! I wish him all success, for I think he has a warm and friendly heart. 45

I have been living a snail's life for several months now, Ammonio; enclosed and bottled up at home, I brood over my studies. Everything is very deserted here, most people being away for fear of the plague; though even when all of them are present, it is a lonely place for me. Expenses are impossibly high, and not a penny to be made. Imagine that I have just sworn this to you by all that is holy. I have been here for less than five months so far, but in this period I have spent about sixty nobles. I have 50 55

* * * * *

29 Bryan] Cf Ep 262:14n.

34 more judgment] Cf *Adagia* I vi 81.

38 Bullock] See Ep 225:5n.

38–9 most holy] *sanctissimus*: This may have been in the address of the original MS of Ep 280.

40–1 most courageous] *fortissimus*: cf Ep 280:59.

44 Jean] Cf Ep 281:4n.

55 sixty nobles] If these were gold angel-nobles, as in Epp 240A:11, 248:40, and 270:30, or their equivalent money-of-account value (6s 8d sterling apiece), his expenditures would have amounted to £20 0s 0d sterl. = £29 0s 0d gros Flemish = £170 13s 4d tournois. But if they were ryals (rose-nobles) the amount would have been £30 0s 0d sterling. Cf Epp 214:4n; 241:19n; 273:14n; and tables A–F below, 327–45, especially table D, 341.

received just one from certain hearers of my lectures, and I took that under strong protests and with unwillingness. I have determined in these winter months to leave no stone unturned and in fact to 'cast my sheet anchor' as they say. If this is successful, I shall then find myself some retreat; but if it fails, I have made up my mind to fly away from here, I do not know where. If nothing else, at least I shall die elsewhere. Farewell. 60

Cambridge, 28 November [1511]

283 / To Andrea Ammonio Cambridge, 2 December [1513]

This letter evidently answers a reply to Ep 282 and alludes to Ep 280. The phrase 'epistola familiariter jocosa' in the greeting was added in the *Epistolae* of 1521.

ERASMUS OF ROTTERDAM TO HIS FRIEND ANDREA AMMONIO

A letter written in friendly jest

In your letter you philosophized quite beautifully about the Muses and wealth. And to me our friend Pace seems deliberately to affect to forget his good literary training and to attempt a style that is calculated to please the Midases rather than the Muses. If the way to wealth is, as you tell me it is, for a man to be divorced from the Muses, certainly Erasmus will not be one of the very last, even in Carmiliano's opinion. For it is obvious that you are openly jesting when you place yourself in this category. Further, I interpret those magnificent phrases 'the Muses' darling' and others of the same sort as signs that you are either deluded by fondness for me, or else generously giving me out of your warm-heartedness praise I do not deserve; or, and I think this is nearest the truth, you wish to raise the spirits of an unfortunate friend and console him with little panegyrics like yours. However this may be, I am either indebted to you for taking an interest in me or appreciative of your characteristic generosity or filled with regard for your practical kindness. 5 10 15

When you urge me to try and secure a position, I acknowledge the sincerity and the friendly spirit in which you advise me; and I will try it too, though my judgment protests sharply and prophesies no successful or 20

* * * * *

56 received] Elsewhere he said he taught Greek and Holy Scripture gratis (Ep 296:141f). He probably meant that he got practically nothing from his students, although he was paid a salary by the university. For detailed estimates of his income and expenditure at this time see E&C 69ff.

57–8 leave no stone unturned] *Adagia* I iv 30

283:4 Pace] Richard Pace (see Ep 211:53n).

happy outcome. If I had exposed myself to Fortune's hazards, I should accept the rules of the game and take rebuffs in good part, knowing that it is Fortune's sport to elevate some men and turn others away at her whim. But I thought I had taken steps to see I had nothing to do with so wanton a mistress when Mountjoy summoned me into harbour as though it were an accomplished fact. On my oath, I am not the least bit tortured by the thought of Fortune's indulgence to others, however unworthy they may be; your own success and that of other men like you bring me, on the contrary, a true pleasure of no ordinary sort. And if, finally, I were asked to sum up and assess the merits of the case, I think my present position is more than I deserve. I measure myself, in fact, by the length of my own foot and not by those compliments of yours. There is just one thing that grieves me: being defrauded by the man I so supremely trusted. And again, though poverty may be a very harsh burden, especially on the toilsome threshold of old age, still I am moved more by shame than by want. I must, however, digest this bitter pill too and put a good face on it; but, if I was born to this fate, it is useless to struggle against the gods.

I am very glad, my dear Ammonio, that your interests are progressing, borne by a favourable wind and tide; glad that this is happening not only to a friend but also to one who thoroughly deserves it. Still, what has Fortune so far given you that is good enough for literary talents and a character like yours? I should be somewhat afraid of being thought to flatter in your hour of success if I were not aware that you well know my disposition, a disposition which makes me unwilling to be compliant even to rulers; but either you are destined for very high office or my judgment misleads me.

Just see how vain I am about my *Adagia*, thinking nobody knows it but myself, since I had a notion you had forgotten the proverb 'nothing to the point'! But what encouraged me to make this mistake was your addition of a pronoun and, if I remember correctly, omission of a preposition in the original language of the proverb. Your letter could not have been at hand when I wrote, because ὑπόκρινεν might easily lead me to conjecture that you had intended to write ἀπέκρινεν. I am glad your previous letter and Battista's were not delivered; glad at least to the extent that I have been

* * * * *

31 the length ... foot] *Adagia* I vi 89

34 toilsome] *Adagia* II x 46

37 struggle against the gods] Cf Ep 269:136–7n.

39 borne ... tide] Homer *Odyssey* 3.300

47–8 'nothing to the point'] Cf Ep 280:40n; the adage is in Greek.

53 Battista] Boerio (cf Ep 267 introduction)

spared the anxiety and grief that the announcement of his illness would have brought me, while at the same time I am not cheated of the benefits of happily hearing that he is better, combined with self-congratulation on having stayed at home. I was more afraid of that enemy than I was of the French, however dubious the issue of a war may be. I am grateful that he, good fellow, is offering to share his roof and his table with me. I see he has changed his mind entirely since he sent for his sons. 55 60

As to Carmiliano: not only do you make a successful apology for him, but I admire your patriotism when, defending your country's honour, you overlook his rascality! All the same I wish you could remove all the man's faults – if you did this you would do still better for your country's reputation – I mean remove the accursed creature entirely. I am most surprised that you can be angry with your man Thomas, who is such a sensible and wide-awake servant that he looks after your interests better than you do. Let us give the blame for this not to him, but to my bad luck. 65

Now I come to your *Panegyricus* whose judge and critic you make me, and give me all the power Homer gives to Jove, to nod approval or disapproval at anything I choose and pronounce sentence of doom whenever I feel like it. For my part I do not claim to have enough ability, or learning either, to be able to correct or criticize what you write. I will frankly say that there is nothing which comes from your pen that I do not heartily admire; this may be a result of critical judgment (for even modest craftsmen can sometimes pass judgment on first-rate work), or again it may result from a kind of instinctive feeling. Certainly my opinion is not distorted by friendship, since it was on my admiration for your written works that this very friendship was founded. However, as different eyes are pleased by different beautiful shapes and as different food delights different palates, so I think there is also a certain lack of uniformity in taste – a latent kinship or antipathy, so to speak – between minds. A long time ago our friend Holt showed me some brief pages on trivial subjects you had written quite 70 75 80

* * * * *

66 Thomas] Ammonio's servant, mentioned in Ep 239:21

69 *Panegyricus*] Ammonio's poem *Panegyricus ad Henricum VIII*. It does not seem to have been published.

70 Homer] *Iliad* 16.250

82 Holt] Possibly John Holt, fellow of Magdalen College, Oxford, 1490–5. He was a distinguished schoolmaster of Oxford and Chichester, and a friend of Thomas More. His *Lac puerorum* (published before 1500) was one of the first Latin grammars in English. If he is in fact the man referred to here, the incident must have occurred in 1499–1500 during Erasmus' first visit to England, since Holt's will was proved 14 June 1504 (cf Emden BRUO II 953).

casually. A taste of them awoke in me at once an admiration and indeed a love of your genius, which I took with me to Italy. And again I recognized 85 the same inspiration in Mountjoy's letter, even though I had quite forgotten your handwriting. There you have my opinion of your writings as a whole. I am glad they give pleasure, not only to men of learning who, unless they are utterly soured by envy, cannot help applauding them enthusiastically, but also to those in high places, my lord of York in particular. You have 90 indeed won approval from the votes of the learned, but on that account I cannot call you blessed. Most blessed of men I shall rightly call you, if you gain so much favour from that great man, and you owe our lady of Rhamnus a great debt.

But now you have been insisting for quite some time on a more 95 detailed critique, crying out that I am making flattering speeches, not judging your work. Well then, so that I may not seem disobliging towards a friend, no request from whom I could conceivably refuse, I shall now put on the lion's skin and assume the critic's scourging rod and frown.

Your narrative of events is so good that I could not have gained a fuller 100 knowledge of them from anybody's memoirs. First, how the bandits were cut off; next, how the enemy unsuccessfully tried to surround the king; and again, how on the resumption of the fight they fled in disgraceful rout, their leaders themselves taken. Also the capture of Thérouanne, the Scots meanwhile cut down almost to a man in two engagements; and in addition the 105 capture of Tournai under a sky so cloudless that, as if by celestial encouragement, it clearly invited action. To crown all, the intimate atmosphere of his imperial majesty's arrival in camp. Some would have it that a poem is not a poem unless you summon up all the gods in turn from sky, sea, and land, and cram hundreds of legendary tales into it. I myself have always 110 liked verse that was not far removed from prose, albeit prose of the first order. Just as Philoxenus delivered the opinion that the sweetest-tasting fish were those that were not fish, the most delicious flesh that which was

* * * * *

86 Mountjoy's letter] Ep 215, probably written by Ammonio as Mountjoy's secretary

90 my lord of York] Thomas Wolsey. He was appointed dean of York 19 February 1513. The title Erasmus uses, which would be more fitting for the archbishop, may have been changed after Wolsey's promotion.

93 our lady of Rhamnus] Nemesis; cf Ep 143:61n.

98–9 put on the lion's skin] Cf Ep 145:135n.

100 events] For the events of the French and Scottish campaigns narrated in Ammonio's *Panegyricus* see Mackie 279ff.

112 Philoxenus] *Adagia* I ii 91

not flesh; and reckoned, again, that the most delightful sea-voyages were those close to the shore and the most delightful land walks those by the seaside; so do I take the greatest pleasure in rhetorical poems and in poetical rhetoric, such that one can sense poetry in the prose and the style of a good orator in the poetry. And whereas some other men prefer more exotic elements, my own very special approval goes to your practice of depending for your effects on the bare narrative and your concern for displaying the subject rather than your own cleverness. 115 120

In a few lines only I think you should have adopted a rather less harsh style of composition; but this often happens either when the author has no time to rewrite the same passage again and again, or when we overlook these things in our pursuit of higher qualities. There is one line that seems to me unduly pedestrian: 125

That you may dash out both the Frenchmen's eyes.

If already I appear to make these points too freely, you must blame yourself for forcing me to play the critic. The following passage I liked very much indeed: 130

Whilst thou, far-sundered from the English realm,
Breakest, in distant fields, the Frenchmen's power,
And where thou goest, victorious e'er dost range.

It brought the situation perfectly before my eyes anyway. Already I seemed to see Alexander the Great rampaging in arms even beyond India and, after crossing the ocean, looking for a second world to conquer, wandering far and wide with his all-conquering army through all the tribes on earth; I seemed to see the capture, the conquest, the surrender of everything he met. 135

A few people have found a genuine difficulty about the verse, 140

Prince of our Kings in fact as much as name.

The copyist, Vaughan, a learned man and an honest one, having changed 'our' to 'all,' I suggested 'no Kings,' but this did not find favour. Again I suggested 'foolish Kings,' with a similar result. Then I tried 'not in fact but in name' – it was rejected; and 'neither in fact nor name,' which they turned down. Conclusion: since neither what you wrote nor what I have substituted is acceptable, it is up to you to decide what you would like to have set down. 145

The following verse

He who of late the narrow crown did loose 150

also pleased me, since investigators of the hidden properties of matter

* * * * *

142 Vaughan] John Vaughan, fellow of Queens' College, 1505–18

maintain that gold has the faculty of loosening and dilating things which are tightly bound. Similarly I like the line

Came, by a happy omen, to the camp;

gold is the 'one omen' that is best, particularly to a man in difficulties! There are numerous other things worth marking with an asterisk: if I point them out, adding some explanatory notes on your poem, will there be any reward? I add my prayer that you may be as lucky as you are learned and clever in your work of flattery. There you are: the great critic has finished delivering his critique on your poem, and I now command you in your turn to sit in judgment on the judge. 155 160

From Pace's letter I understand you to have written a historical account of the brush with the Scots; I will read this when I come. I am most glad that Pace is so well disposed to you; there is nothing on earth more affectionate, more upright, than he is. I too wrote a squib some time ago on the flight of the French, but 'no Muses nor Apollo heard.' I am enclosing it, and it cannot annoy you more than once for it is extremely short. The man who burdened you with my letter did not do as I should have wished: he himself had brazenly asked to be given letters to everyone, boasting that he was going everywhere and would be visiting almost the whole of England. If there is a convenient opportunity, send it back; but if there is not, I would rather you would throw it on the fire than be embarrassed by the charge of it. About the letter I said I had not received, I had no doubts; all the same I am glad your suspicion has produced dividends, for the relief your letters bring is quite remarkable, especially when life is so irksome. We are shut in by the plague and beset by highway robberies; instead of wine we drink vinegar and worse than vinegar, and our coffers are emptying; but 'hurrah for victory!' – that is what we sing, being the world-conquerors we are. Even here, on all sides your poem is being snatched up, recopied, and praised by everyone for its learning and cleverness. 165 170 175 180

I have had a bad time at the hands of those booksellers in the business

* * * * *

155 one omen ...] Homer *Iliad* 12.243

159 great critic] Literally Aristarchus; *Adagia* I v 57

162 Pace] Cf Ep 211:53.

165–6 on the flight of the French] This epigram on the flight of the French army in the Battle of the Spurs near Guinegate, 16 August 1513, was published in Erasmus' *Epigrammata* (Basel: J. Froben March 1518); critical edition in Reedijk 304.

166 'no Muses nor Apollo heard'] Martial 2.89.3

of my proverbs. A certain person printed them at Basel, but so much in imitation of the Aldine edition that to a careless eye it might seem identical. I had entrusted an emended and enlarged text to Franz, who is accustomed to import almost every book into this country, intending him to hand it over 185 to Bade or, if he advised it, to another publisher. That worthy immediately carried it off to Basel and put it in the care of the man who had already printed it, so that he will publish this edition only when he has sold all the copies of his own, that is, ten years from now. Also there are several books translated from Plutarch and Lucian which I had entrusted to him to give to 190 Bade, to be added to the previous books he has in his possession; and I suspect he has given these also to the other man, and now he is asking me to send more of them. There is German honesty for you! But there is a way in which I can get my own back: a copy of the *Adagia*, and, in fact, a rather more comprehensive one than the copy he took, has been kept. He will find 195 one Cretan can be a match for another.

Immediately after Christmas I shall rush to join you, unless the weather keeps me at home. Please give my greetings to Master Larke, the

* * * * *

182 Basel] This refers to the Froben edition of the *Adagiorum chiliades* (August 1513). It was merely a reprinting of the Aldine edition of 1508 (see Ep 211).

184 Franz] Birckmann (cf Ep 258:14n). The revised and enlarged third edition of the *Adagia* had been intended for Bade, but was taken by Birckmann to Basel and given to Froben (cf Ep 263:22n). Erasmus' fear that Froben, having just reprinted the Aldine edition, would not publish the new one for another ten years was in fact unfounded; he published it in 1515 (Ep 269 introduction). Erasmus had been suspicious of Birckmann at the time when he entrusted the *Adagia* to him (cf Ep 265:5f), and years later in the colloquy 'Pseudocheus and Philetymus' (1523) he caricatured Birckmann as a dishonest person and a trouble-maker. Cf P. Smith *A Key to the Colloquies of Erasmus* (Cambridge Mass. 1927) 18; see also Allen Epp 1514:41n; 1531:43n; 1560:13f.

190 Plutarch] Among the translations of Plutarch were probably those dedicated to Yonge (Ep 268) and Wolsey (Ep 284), both translated in the summer of 1512 (cf Ep 264:25f), and also the one dedicated to Henry VIII (Ep 272) and published by Froben in August 1514, probably through Birckmann's agency. It was translated in the summer of 1513 (cf Ep 271:8). Apparently none of these reached Bade.

190 Lucian] The dialogues sent to Bade in the spring of 1512 (cf Ep 263:3n). They were dedicated to Warham in April 1512, but Bade did not publish them until June 1514 (Ep 261 introduction).

196 Cretan] The Cretans were proverbially shifty; cf *Adagia* I ii 29.

198 Larke] Thomas Larke (d 1530) was the king's chaplain and, like Ammonio, a canon of St Stephen's, Westminster.

Ornatissimo viro, christianissimi
Regis Anglorum elemosynario magno
epo Lyncolnien. noiato. Erasm9. Rot. S.D.
Cum et antea iam dudum vererer
tantum virum tantulo aggredi mu
nusculo, contantemq hinc tua
inuitaret bonitas, hinc deterre
ret magnitudo, accessit interim
tot ornamentis dignitas etiam e
piscopalis Verum ubi mecum re
putarem, nihil humanitati de
cessisse, si quid accessit honori
bus, ausus sum hoc qualicunq
xeniolo et meum in te animum
testificari, et tuum ambire fauo

manu Dni Erasmi
Roterodami

Autograph letter, Erasmus to Thomas Wolsey, 1514
Preface to the copy of Erasmus' translation of Plutarch's
De utilitate capienda ex inimicis which he presented to Wolsey

The clerkly hand Erasmus used on formal occasions was in marked contrast to the rapid script of his ordinary letters, like that to Aldo Manuzio shown on p 130.

Universitäts-Bibliothek Basel, MS AN VI, f 1

most courteous man and the truest friend of all my English acquaintance. I beg you to be so good as to add a note in your next letter to Pace, asking him 200 to tell you what has happened to the books I left behind at Ferrara. His silence looks rather suspicious to me; not that I have any doubt about his good faith, but because I fear something may have happened to my notebooks, which neither of us would like to see. Best wishes, Ammonio.

Cambridge, St Thomas's Day [1510] 205

284 / To Thomas Wolsey Cambridge, 4 January [1514]

This is the preface to a bound MS copy in Erasmus' own hand of his translation of Plutarch's *De utilitate capienda ex inimicis*, now in the university library at Basel. It was probably one of the works given by Birckmann to Froben (cf Ep 283:189ff and n). Allen conjectures that Erasmus, on finding that the Plutarch was not yet published, made a special copy for presentation to Wolsey as a New Year's present. An attack of the kidney-stone, however, kept him in Cambridge over the New Year (cf Ep 285:2), and even after he reached London fear of the plague kept him from seeing Wolsey (cf Ep 287:3f) until it was too late for the present to be timely. When it was finally published by Froben in July 1514 Erasmus wrote a new and longer dedication (Ep 297). Wolsey had just been nominated bishop of Lincoln in January 1514, the first major step in his meteoric rise to power.

TO THE RIGHT HONOURABLE THE BISHOP-DESIGNATE OF LINCOLN, LORD HIGH ALMONER TO HIS MOST CHRISTIAN MAJESTY THE KING OF ENGLAND, FROM ERASMUS OF ROTTERDAM, GREETINGS

I have for a long time hesitated to approach so great a personage with a gift 5 so small, for although encouraged by your goodness yet I was deterred by your greatness, and in the meantime the dignity of the bishopric has been added to your many other distinctions. Yet when I reflected that no increase in your honours had brought about any decrease in your kindness, I ventured by this little present, such as it is, both to express my regard for 10 you and to plead for your favour. Indeed it is a very tiny book, but, to praise it in few words, it is Plutarch's; and even Greece herself, that fertile mother of great wits, never produced an author to surpass him for learning and charm. I doubt if anyone has ever managed, as he has, to unite distinguished style to the most exact knowledge of affairs; and here his discourse 15

* * * * *

201 books] Cf Epp 30:17n; 244:7n.

is a series of pure gems. If he gives you any cause for displeasure, pray blame me. Farewell, and I beg you to inscribe the name of Erasmus (even if it be at the very foot) upon the list of your humble dependents.

Cambridge, 4 January

285 / To William Warham Cambridge, [January 1514]

This is Erasmus' last letter from Cambridge. He left there permanently early in February.

ERASMUS OF ROTTERDAM TO THE ARCHBISHOP OF CANTERBURY

A dangerous grapple with the stone, the worst he has ever suffered, has befallen your friend Erasmus. He has got into the hands of surgeons and apothecaries, alias scoundrels and harpies.

I am still in the throes of labour: the pest is still lodged inside my ribs, 5 and when or what the issue will be is unknown. I suspect that this sickness of mine is due to the beer which, for the lack of wine, I have been drinking for some time. Of course these must be the first fruits we are to acquire from the glorious war with the French. I have merely dictated this letter, and even so with some discomfort; be sure to look after your own health to the 10 utmost, excellent Maecenas.

Cambridge, [1515]

286 / From William Warham London, 5 February [1514]

WILLIAM, ARCHBISHOP OF CANTERBURY, CHANCELLOR OF THE REALM AND PRIMATE OF ALL ENGLAND, TO ERASMUS OF ROTTERDAM

My dear Erasmus, if we begin our letters by wishing health to those who are well, much more is it appropriate to desire health for you since you are ill; 5 though I suppose that long ere now you have been fortunately purged of those stones, at any rate since we have celebrated the Purification of Mary. What is the point of stones in your frail physique? What could one build upon this rock? You are not, I imagine, building fine houses, or anything like that. Wherefore, since stones are not your line of business, be sure to 10 get rid of your superfluous burden as soon as you can; spend money to have these stones taken away; unlike me, who am spending money every day to

* * * * *

285:2 stone] Cf Ep 296:65ff and n.

286:7 Purification of Mary] 2 February

have stones brought to my buildings. To help you do this as you ought to, I have given ten nobles to the son of a goldsmith of London; I should like to see them turn into ten legions. This gold medicine has a certain potency; 15 use it to recover your health, for which I would gladly pay much more. Yes indeed, you still have many important works to publish, and you cannot tackle them unless you are strong. Look after yourself, and do not by your sickness deprive us of the splendid promise and sweetest harvest of your learning. 20

London, 5 February [1512]

287 / To William Gonnell [near London? c 14 February 1514]

Allen dates this letter from London, but the wording suggests rather that Erasmus had made a brief visit to London, during which he had greeted Warham and Mountjoy and visited the royal palace at Richmond, but had been deterred by the plague from staying long enough to give his present to Wolsey. The supposition that the letter was written from some place outside the city is borne out by his calling London by name three times (lines 2, 5, and 9), which is most unusual. Normally he would simply have said 'here.' He also says that London displeased him because the plague was raging there (*illic*). Finally the fact that he had sent his horse to Gonnell raises the faint possibility that he may even have returned to Cambridge, but for this there is no solid evidence.

ERASMUS TO HIS FRIEND GONNELL

When I was in London I paid my respects to my patrons, the archbishop and Mountjoy. I had intended to approach a few of my friends with a small present, among them my lord the almoner, now bishop of Lincoln, but London displeased me in that it is still unsafe to go about there because of 5 the plague, so I postponed this to a later occasion. The king was ill while I

* * * * *

14 ten nobles] If these were gold angel-nobles as in Ep 240A:10–11, 248:40, and 270:30, or their equivalent money-of-account value (6s 8d ster. apiece), this gift would have amounted to £3 6s 8d sterling = £4 16s 8d gros Flemish = £28 8s 11d tournois. But if they were ryals (rose-nobles), it would have been £5 0s 0d sterling. Cf Epp 214:4n; 227:31n; 241:19n; 248:40n; 273:14n; and tables A–F below, 327–45, especially table D, 341.

14 son] Possibly Lupset, whose father was a London goldsmith (cf Ep 270:69n)

287:4 Lincoln] Wolsey (cf Ep 284 introduction)

was there, at Richmond I mean, last Saturday; but his physician's word was that he was now out of danger.

The papal nuncio, the bishop of Chieti, is in London at present. They say he is a man of consummate learning. His intention is to negotiate for peace between the sovereigns, but he is having no success. Unless I am mistaken, he will serve his own interests rather than ours. The king proposes to cross the channel next May, bringing with him his sister Mary as the bride-to-be of our own prince. Gossip has it that Maximillian's daughter Margaret is to marry that new duke whom the king has recently turned from a stable boy into a nobleman.

I have sent back the horse; do be instant in urging your father to look after him well. I have something by me that I think you will like, but there is an amazing shortage of copyists here. Give my greetings to Dr Green, and farewell, dearest Gonnell.

[1515]

288 / To Antoon van Bergen — London, 14 March 1514

In the spring of 1514 it seemed that Henry VIII was about to renew the war with France. Erasmus addressed his protest against war to Antoon van Bergen because of his influence with the Hapsburg-Burgundian court (cf Ep 143 introduction). The argument in this letter was soon after expanded into the adage 'Dulce bellum inexpertis' (*Adagia* IV i 1) published in the Froben edition of 1515 and printed separately by Froben in April 1517. There were fourteen other separate printings before 1540, though not by Froben (trans in Phillips

* * * * *

9 nuncio] Gianpietro Caraffa, bishop of Chieti and one of the founders of the Order of Theatines. He was made archbishop of Brindisi in 1518, cardinal in 1536, and was elected pope as Paul IV in 1555. His mission to make peace between Henry VIII and Louis XII was successful, largely because of the defection of Henry's allies, Ferdinand of Aragon and the emperor Maximilian, and also because of the efforts of Foxe and Wolsey. The peace treaty was signed in August 1514. Cf J.J. Scarisbrick *Henry VIII* (London 1968) 53ff.

14 our own prince] Charles (cf Ep 252:33n)

15 new duke] Charles Brandon, created duke of Suffolk 1 February 1514. He later married Henry's sister Mary after the death of her first husband Louis XII. There was apparently a rumour at this time that he might marry Margaret. The sentence beginning 'Gossip,' printed in the *Farrago* in October 1519, was cut out in the *Epistolae ad diversos* in August 1521.

16 stable boy] Literally 'Dama' (a slave's name); cf *Adagia* I viii 11.

19 Green] Probably Thomas Green, master of Catharine Hall and at this time one of the commissaries or assessors in the vice-chancellor's court.

308ff). A German translation of this letter itself by Georgius Spalatinus was published c 1520–1. For an analysis of this letter and the adage, and an estimate of their place in the humanist peace propaganda, see R.P. Adams *The Better Part of Valor: More, Erasmus, Colet and Vives on Humanism, War and Peace* (Seattle 1962) 82ff, 93ff.

DESIDERIUS ERASMUS OF ROTTERDAM TO THE ILLUSTRIOUS LORD AND REVEREND FATHER IN CHRIST, ANTOON VAN BERGEN, LORD ABBOT OF ST BERTIN, GREETINGS

Most honoured Father, in conversation with the bishop of Durham and with Andrea Ammonio, the king's secretary, I have heard of your interest in 5 me and your truly paternal affection which makes me long all the more to be restored to my native country if I could but obtain from the prince a competence that might suffice to sustain me in modest leisure. It is not that I am ill-pleased with England, or dissatisfied with my patrons. Here too I have a great many friends, and many bishops have shown me exceptional 10 kindness, among them the archbishop of Canterbury, who treats me with such solicitude and affection that no brother, or father even, could be more loving. By his gift I hold a substantial income from a living, which I have resigned. To this my other Maecenas adds a similar sum from his private resources. A considerable amount of further support is given to me by the 15 generosity of prominent men, and there could be much more if I were in the slightest degree ready to beg. But the war that is being prepared for has brought about a sudden change in the character of this island. Here the price of everything is going up every day, while liberality declines. Why should not people give more sparingly after all those tithings? I myself 20 nearly perished lately of the stone that I got from some horrible flat stuff I had to drink because wine was scarce. Besides, while it is a kind of exile to live on any island, our confinement is closer still at present by reason of the wars, so that one cannot even get a letter out. I can see vast disturbances in

* * * * *

4–5 Durham and ... Ammonio] Both had been with the royal army in the Netherlands in 1513 (cf Ep 280:37ff) and probably met Antoon there. Erasmus had, in fact, asked Ammonio to give his greetings to him should he visit Saint-Omer (Ep 273:34).

13 income] The annuity from Aldington. Cf Ep 255 introduction and Ep 296:132 and 138, where Erasmus says that the annuity from Aldington and his pension from Mountjoy were both the same: one hundred écus d'or à la couronne, then officially worth £175 0s 0d tournois = £20 16s 8d sterling = £29 11s 8d gros Flemish. Cf also Epp 212:7n; 296:130n; CWE 1 315, 336–7; and tables A–F below, 327–45, especially table D, 341.

21 stone] Cf Ep 296:65n.

the making, and what their outcome will be is not clear; may God in his mercy vouchsafe to quiet the storm that now afflicts Christendom. 25

I often wonder what it is that drives the whole human race, not merely Christians, to such a pitch of frenzy that they will undergo such effort, expense, and danger for the sake of mutual destruction. Indeed, what do we do but wage war, all our lives long? Not all dumb animals engage in combat, 30 only wild beasts, and even they do not war among themselves but only with animals of other species. Furthermore they fight with the weapons nature has given them, not as we do with machines invented by a devilish science. Again they do not fight on any kind of pretext, but only for food or in defence of their young, whereas our human wars are generally caused by 35 ambition, anger, lust, or some such disease of the mind. Finally they do not muster serried ranks of troops by the thousand, as we do, for the purpose of mutual slaughter. For us, who boast of naming ourselves 'Christians' after Christ who preached and practised naught save gentleness, who are members of one body, one flesh, quickened by the same spirit, nurtured upon 40 the same sacraments, joined in union to a single head, called to the same eternal life, hoping for that supreme communion whereby, even as Christ is one with the Father, so we too may be one with him – how can anything in this world be so important as to impel us to war, a thing so deadly and so grim that even when it is waged with perfect justification no man who is 45 truly good approves it?

Consider its instruments, I pray you: murderers, profligates devoted to gambling and rape, and the vilest sort of mercenary soldiery to whom pay is dearer than life. These are splendid material in war; for then they earn rewards and glory for doing what they were doing at their own peril before. 50 These are the dregs of mankind whom you must welcome into your countryside and towns alike if you have a mind to make war. In brief, if we seek to take vengeance upon another, to such as these must we enslave ourselves. Think, next, of all the crimes that are committed with war as a pretext, while good laws 'fall silent amid the clash of arms' – all the instances 55 of sack and sacrilege, rape, and other shameful acts, such as one hesitates even to name. And even when the war is over, this moral corruption is bound to linger for many years. Now assess for me the cost – a cost so great that, even if you win the war, you will lose much more than you gain. Indeed what realm, do you suppose, can be weighed against the life, the 60 blood, of so many thousand men? Even so the worst evils fall upon those

* * * * *

39–40 members of one body] Ephesians 4:4

55 'fall silent … arms'] Cicero *Pro Milone* 4.11

who have no stake in the war, while the blessings of peace affect all. In war, for the most part, even the victors mourn. Such a crowd of evils does war bring in its train that poets have with good reason pictured it as sent from Hell by the furies; I need not go on to specify the plundering of the 65 populace, the secret agreements between the leaders, and the profound disturbance of the established order, which can never be transformed without a vast amount of trouble. And if it be a lust for glory that lures us to war, it is not glory that is won, especially by criminal acts. If we would find something to call glorious, it is far more glorious to found states than to 70 destroy them; but, as things now stand, it is the common people who build and keep up the cities, whereas the folly of princes brings about their ruin. Or if our motive be gain, there has never been a war that proved so successful as not to produce more harm than good; nobody injures his enemy in war without first inflicting numerous evils on his own people. 75 Lastly, observing as we do how the fortunes of mankind, in change and confusion, ebb and flow like the tides of Euripus, how does it profit us to devote such laborious efforts to the acquisition of an empire which will presently pass on some pretext, no matter what, into the hands of others? What expenditure of blood it cost to build the Roman empire, and how soon 80 its collapse began!

But, you will say, the rights of princes must be upheld. While it is not for me to speak lightly of princes' conduct, I only know that often the greater the right, the greater the wrong, and that there exist princes who first make up their minds what they want and afterwards search for a specious pretext 85 to cover their action. And in the midst of such revolutionary changes in the affairs of men, so many treaties concluded and abrogated, could anyone, I ask, want for a pretext? If the dispute is mainly about the question who exercises sovereignty, what is the need of so much bloodshed? For it is not the people's safety that is at stake, but merely whether they ought to call one 90 person or another their ruler. There are popes and bishops and men of discretion and honour through whom petty issues of this kind can be resolved without conducting incessant wars and throwing Heaven and earth alike into confusion. It is the proper function of the Roman pontiff, of the cardinals, bishops, and abbots, to settle disputes between Christian 95 princes; this is where they should wield their authority and reveal the power they possess by virtue of men's regard for their holy office. Julius, a pope who was by no means universally approved, succeeded in rousing

* * * * *

77 Euripus] Cf Ep 157:35n.

84 right] *Adagia* I x 25

this hurricane of wars. Cannot Leo, who is scholarly, honourable, and devout, succeed in quieting it? Julius' pretext for going to war was a threat 100 to his own safety; but, even though its cause has been removed, the war still goes on.

We should also remember that human beings, especially Christians, are free; and when they have enjoyed a long period of prosperity under some ruler and have come to acknowledge his rule, there is no need to turn 105 the world upside down with a revolution. Even in pagan societies general consent, long continued, creates a title to rule; much more so among Christians, for whom sovereignty means not ownership but government, so that a ruler who loses some part of his sovereignty becomes a person relieved of a part of his load, rather than wronged. But, you object, suppose 110 one of the two parties refuses to accept the arbitration of honourable men; what would you have me do then? First of all, if you are a true Christian, I should wish you to suffer in silence and forgo your rights, such as they are. If, second, you are merely a man of sense, then reflect how much it will cost you to defend your rights; if the cost is excessive, and this it will surely be if 115 you defend them by force of arms, then refrain from causing so much misery to mankind in pressing your claim, which is perhaps a false one, accompanied by such slaughter, such bereavement, such countless tears among your own people. What do you imagine the Turks think upon hearing that Christian princes rage so wildly against one another for the 120 sake of a mere title to sovereignty? Now Italy has been liberated from the French. What has been achieved by all this bloodshed, except to set a new governor in place of the king of France? And the country is no longer as prosperous as it was before.

But to go too deeply into such questions is not to my purpose. If, 125 however, there are any rights that offer occasion for war, they are crude rights which smack of an already decadent Christianity, overburdened with worldly possessions. Even so, I doubt whether they in any way justify acts of war; only I observe that pious authors have sometimes avoided condemning war in cases where, out of zeal for the preservation of the faith, 130 the peace of Christendom is defended against barbarian invasions. But why should we think of these few passages from purely human sources, rather than of the numerous utterances of Christ, of the apostles, and of orthodox and highly respected Fathers, on peace and on tolerating evils? There is no proposition that could not be defended by some argument or 135 other, especially when those in charge of affairs are men whose very crimes receive flattering praise in many quarters, while none dares to censure their errors. And all the time there is no doubt what it is that honest souls pray for, hope for, and long for. Indeed if you look at the matter closely, the private affairs of princes are generally the cause of war. I ask you, is it 140 consistent with humanity for the whole world to be roused to arms every time this prince or that becomes angry, or pretends to be angry, with another prince for any reason under the sun?

We may hope for the best, but only hope. As for myself, such position as I hold is in England, but I should gladly give it all up on condition that a Christian peace might be made between Christian princes. Considerable weight in securing this can attach to your influence, which counts for much with Prince Charles, and a great deal more with Maximilian, and even has the ear of the English nobility. I have no doubt that you already know from experience how expensive even one's friends can be in wartime. It will thus also be in your own interest to endeavour to bring this war to an end; so you need not think you will undertake this responsibility with no reward. I shall hasten to pay my respects to you, as soon as I can fly from here. Meantime farewell, illustrious Father. My warmest greetings and good wishes to Master Ghisbert the physician and to Master Antonius of Luxembourg.

London, 14 March [1513]

289 / To William Gonnell London, [about April 1514]

ERASMUS TO HIS FRIEND GONNELL

I am much distressed by the prevailing state of affairs, my dear Gonnell. The plague is kindling sparks everywhere here, and looks like becoming a roaring blaze any day now. War, with its sea of troubles of every sort, is looming close. In addition, I am being tormented by certain personal embarrassments, besides which a new kind of devil has raised its head at me, a sort of minute creature which, though it is very tiny, is so filled with poison that a viper or even an asp would appear innocent of venom in comparison with it. Please write to me by Watson and give me word how my Pegasus fares; or, better still, how you yourself are; also your most obliging host, and your mother, who is the pattern of goodness. Be sure to give my salutations to Commissary Green, the friend, or to speak more truly the patron, of both of us. Farewell.

London, [1515]

* * * * *

155 Ghisbert ... Luxembourg] Erasmus had coupled these two with Antoon van Bergen in the greetings he had sent via Ammonio in September 1513 (cf Ep 273:33ff and nn).

289:6 devil] This *malus genius* is clearly identified with Giovanni Battista Boerio (cf Ep 267 introduction) in Ep 292:22ff.

9 Watson] Cf Ep 275:5n.

11 mother] Cf Ep 279:36.

12 Green] Cf Ep 287:19n.

290 / From Johann Reuchlin

Frankfurt, April 1514

This letter from the Deventer Letter-book is the first surviving letter in the correspondence between Erasmus and Johann Reuchlin (1455–1522), the German Hebrew scholar whose defence of Hebrew literature led to his condemnation by the theologians of Cologne and his trial for heresy. The resultant controversy assumed international proportions and rallied humanists everywhere to support him against the conservative theologians who refused to admit the necessity of the three ancient languages for the study of theology. For a full account of the controversy, see L. Geiger *Renaissance und Humanismus in Italien und Deutschland* (Berlin 1882) 205–454; also W. Andreas *Deutschland vor der Reformation* (Berlin 1934) 497ff.

JOHANN REUCHLIN OF PFORTZHEIM TO DR ERASMUS

On the instructions of our emperor, Kaiser Maximilian, I have written an opinion on the question of burning the books of the Jews. It was attacked by some professors of theology at Cologne, not in a manner suited to learned 5 doctors, but with violent tirades and insults directed at myself in the fashion of quite irresponsible buffoons. When, moreover, I defended my reputation, as I must, by publishing an *apologia*, the same men became very angry and got together a contrary opinion containing a great deal of falsehood and some abominable slanders, and, using this contrivance as a 10 pretext to discredit me in the eyes of the common people, they resolved to burn in the city of Mainz, by order of the inquisitor of the Preaching Friars, the said volume of my opinion, which I entitled the *Augenspiegel*. But in spite of the opposition of the Preachers, who swarmed to the spot like summer flies, I prevented this by dexterous use of the law, appealing to the

* * * * *

3 opinion] In response to the mandate issued by the emperor, 6 July 1510, calling for opinions regarding the burning of Jewish books, Reuchlin wrote a 'Ratschlag ob man den Juden alle ihre Bücher ... verbrennen soll,' 6 October 1510, which was sent under seal to the archbishop of Mainz to be forwarded to Maximilian.

7 *apologia*] *Defensio contra calumniatores suos Colonienses* (Tübingen March 1513).

11 inquisitor] Jacob van Hoogstraten (c 1465–1507) was inquisitor of the archbishoprics of Mainz, Cologne, and Trier, and the most active of the Dominicans, i.e., Preaching Friars, of Cologne in the prosecution of Reuchlin.

12 *Augenspiegel*] Reuchlin's original *Ratschlag* was expanded and printed under the title *Augenspiegel* in August 1511. It was condemned by the faculty of theology of Mainz, 13 October 1513, and by that of Cologne, 10 February 1514.

apostolic see, which thereupon entrusted the entire inquiry to the bishop of Speyer and prohibited all judges and other persons whatsoever from any interference or attack upon me in the matter of the *Augenspiegel*, on pain of excommunication. 15

Accordingly the aforesaid papal judge proceeded to the examination. The Preaching Friars sent their representative: he was not appointed in due form of law, however, in order to bring the judge into contempt and derision, and to prejudice my case and so deter me from my undertaking. Meanwhile the Preaching Friars burned the said book privately at Cologne while the case was still pending and after the prohibition had been issued against them. Nevertheless the papal judge continued his proceedings without interruption, and on the advice of theologians and professors of law pronounced the definitive judgment which I am sending to you herewith, for the sake of your most kind good will towards all lovers of sound learning, so that, if over the past year my enemies have blackened my name in the eyes of your English and British friends, now at any rate I, a Swabian born near the Hercynian mountains, may be championed by you, and thus restored to credit, in opposition to the burners of books. My good wishes for your prosperity. 20 25 30

Frankfurt, during the April fair 1514

291 / From Jan Becker van Borssele Middelburg, 19 April 1514

Jan Becker van Borssele, probably a kinsman of Anna van Borssele, Lady of Veere, was an enthusiastic classical scholar who was given a canonry at Middelburg, an important town near Veere, in 1513. Erasmus had probably met him during one of his visits to Tournehem or Veere. As this letter from the Deventer Letter-book shows, he had connections which might make it possible for him to secure patronage for Erasmus, which may account for the three letters Erasmus had recently written him. Erasmus met him again at Louvain in 1517–18 (cf Allen Epp 687:16, 717:21). He was nominated first Latin professor at the new Collegium Trilingue at Louvain, but declined the offer (cf Allen Epp 794:13, 805:4f).

JAN VAN BORSSELE TO DR ERASMUS OF ROTTERDAM

Last summer I received three letters from you; and the last letter I had

* * * * *

15–16 bishop of Speyer] The Reuchlin affair was turned over to Georg Palatinus, bishop of Speyer, by a bull of Leo x dated 13 November 1513.

27 judgment] It was pronounced 29 March 1514.

reached me six months ago by the hand of Master Johannes Sixtinus, who was accompanied by Augustinus Aggeus. In addition to what you wrote they told me a great deal about your studies and your situation in general; 5 for we had supper together, and they would have taken dinner with me next day had they not already departed on their voyage to Friesland. I expected them to pass this way shortly afterwards on their return to you, as they had promised to do, and intended to give them a letter addressed to you. But after several months, during which I waited for them in vain and neglected 10 to look into other chances of getting in touch with you, the winter weather became exceedingly stormy; thus it has come about that I have given you no answer yet. Now, however, that I have at long last found someone who is going to visit the dean of St Paul's in London, I hope the present letter can easily be delivered to you with the dean's care and assistance, even though I 15 do not know exactly where it may find you. I felt that I must not let slip so good an opportunity without sending you at least the few words my limited time allows, and I mean to write at greater length afterwards, as soon as I can come by a more reliable courier to deliver my letter.

I am most obliged to you for your kindness in telling me so readily 20 about your position and prospects in England and the latest results of your daily studies. It is splendid, and very welcome, news to me that you are well and that your affairs are prospering; splendid also to hear of the works that emerge from your study each day and are received with unrivalled applause and admiration throughout the scholarly world, no matter whether you are 25 turning excellent things in Greek into no less excellent things in Latin, editing sacred texts worthy of your theological training and unsurpassed learning, or occupying yourself with profane letters as a temporary solace, in order to bear the wearisome burden of more serious studies with greater ease. There is, indeed, nothing that would give me greater pleasure now 30 than to receive some portion of your own contributions to the critical revision of the New Testament or the annotation of Jerome's letters. I will gladly pay for it – I do not say an adequate price (for what price could possibly be adequate to merchandise as precious as yours?) but such a price as you could obtain elsewhere: and this should be a matter of no difficulty if 35

* * * * *

3 Sixtinus] He had gone to the Netherlands not later than 1 September 1513 (cf Ep 273:14) and returned to London by 25 November (cf Ep 280:22).

4 Augustinus] Augustinus Aggeus, a native of The Hague, studied in Paris, taking his BA in 1506. He was probably a kinsman of Sixtinus and through him became acquainted with Erasmus. In a letter to Erasmus in 1517 he described himself as a physician (cf Allen Ep 511).

those critical notes or annotations of yours have already gone to press. Augustinus Aggeus has presented me with a newly printed copy of Plutarch's *De tuenda bona valetudine*, published at Louvain in the Latin dress you gave it; so enthusiastically received by the learned is everything you write. 40

For the rest, I will tell you a little about my own progress which you will be glad to hear (I only wish it might also be some use to you), to encourage you to tell me, as soon as you have time and opportunity, how everything goes with you. As I wrote to you a year since, I hold a preferment at Middelburg which is styled a canonical prebend. It was conferred upon 45 me by Philip van Spangen, with a kindness unknown in this modern age, though I neither deserved nor sought it nor even dreamt of it, much less hoped for it. He stayed with us for several days lately, and I had long and frequent talks with him on a variety of topics, including literature now and then, for he is not without knowledge of letters; indeed he is devoted to 50 literature and literary men and is a keen student. And, as I always do when the talk turns on letters, I mentioned your name respectfully; and he kept asking me how your life there suited you and what your prospects were. In reply I told him what I had learned, both from your letter and from what Sixtinus and Aggeus told me; and all that in such a way as would tend to 55 further and not diminish your reputation and fame. I showed him a great many of the books you had composed, and made him a present of your most polished and beautifully written book of *Lucubrationes*, including the *Enchiridion militis christiani*. He read this piece through before leaving us and was loud in its praises. Fond of you as he had been before, he there and 60 then conceived a fervent admiration for you, invoked a blessing on you, and expressed a longing to have you with us in these parts. He also hinted that he would help you generously if ever he had the opportunity. I egged him on as far as I could, adding comments of my own which afforded plenty of fuel to this blaze of affection for you. 65

To give you a picture of my generous friend Philip: he is far below our prince Philip, whose encomium you composed long ago, both in birth and

* * * * *

38 Plutarch] A reprint of the London edition (cf Ep 268 introduction) by Th. Martens (Louvain 10 November 1513)

46 Philip] Philip van Spangen (c 1477–1529) was lord of Spangen in Schieland, the district around Rotterdam.

59 *Enchiridion*] In the edition of the *Lucubratiunculae* printed by Martens in 1503 or that reprinted by him in 1509 (cf Ep 164 introduction)

67 encomium] Cf Ep 179 introduction.

in station, but in terms of good will, or rather generosity, he takes second place neither to that great man nor to any man whatsoever. He is a fellow-countryman of your own, virtually a next-door neighbour, in fact, and 70 particularly devoted to you for this reason also. As you know there is a castle not far from Rotterdam, commonly known as Spangen; some of us call it Spanga, others Hispania; it is from this place he derives his name, like his father and family before him. The family has always held a position of regard among the gentry of Holland; it is distinguished as an ancient, even 75 noble, line. From it he is descended, and bears the family name; as the eldest son, moreover, he has title to the greater part of the patrimony. His mother was closely related by blood to the lord of Bergen and his brothers – you know whom I mean; that is to say, she came of the most noble house of Grimbergen in Brabant, from which were descended also these brothers in 80 Bergen. These Bergen brothers and my Philip's mother, if I remember aright, were the children of two brothers. You realize how highly you have been, and, I think, still are, regarded by that same household, which also gave a wife to your own prince of Veere. My Philip has a brother in the community of St Bertin, who by a special grant and privilege, conferred by 85 the supreme pontiff, was appointed coadjutor in both sacred and secular affairs to the abbot of St Bertin, and by the same privilege was appointed to succeed to the abbacy upon the demise of the present abbot. Now the abbot, who is already infirm by reason of age, plans not merely to share with him the general charge and governance of affairs, but to entrust it 90 entirely to his hands, in order to test in his own lifetime the quality of the successor he has himself selected. If this comes about, you can see how enormous will be the powers and authority of this personage, distinguished in this way by his birth, foremost at our prince's court, closely connected with the families of Bergen and several others, and finally most 95 powerful by virtue of his own position. My own patron Philip will be

* * * * *

78 mother] Anna van Glimes, daughter of Philip van Grimbergen, younger brother of Jan van Bergen (d 1494) (cf Ep 42:21n)

78 lord of Bergen] Jan van Bergen (d 1532), brother of Erasmus' patrons, Hendrik van Bergen, bishop of Cambrai, and Antoon van Bergen, abbot of St Bertin (Ep 42:21n)

84 prince of Veere] Adolph of Veere, married Anna, daughter of Jan van Bergen, in 1513 (cf Ep 93 introduction).

84 brother] Philip's brother, Englebert van Spangen, was appointed coadjutor to Antoon van Bergen 2 October 1511, and succeeded him as abbot of St Bertin in 1532.

all-powerful with him, as his brother, through whose sole agency and responsibility for the entire business, even contributing the outlays and expenses, the negotiations in Rome were not long since carried through.

I have told you all this in rather a prolix fashion, not merely to extract congratulations from you on securing such a splendid patron for myself, but to cause you to ponder whether these same facts may not at some time serve your interests also. To put it candidly, Philip has promised that he will be most happy to give you assistance should this ever lie in his power, particularly if there is any matter in which his brother's exalted rank and his own influence over his brother can count. Farewell, and please do not take exception to my verbosity; it is caused, I do assure you, by the great warmth of my affection for you. 100 105

I have attached to this letter another, which I have received from Diest, a town in Brabant. You will easily recognize the writer's name and profession, and also his characteristic learning. He has long been most eager to learn Greek, but has no one to teach him; so he is not, I think, making much progress. He is utterly devoted to you, and a very dear friend to me. I recommend him to you, and beg you to write him a reply, even a brief one; please send this to me at Middelburg, and I shall see that it is forwarded to him. By so doing you will oblige me considerably for my friend's sake, and will beyond doubt earn his deep gratitude. Once again my best wishes. 110 115

Middelburg, in Zeeland, 19 April 1514

292 / To William Gonnell London, 28 April [1514]

ERASMUS OF ROTTERDAM TO HIS FRIEND WILLIAM GONNELL

Your news about the horse delights me, dear Gonnell, and in it I perceive yet another proof of your good nature.

The *Cato*, with the other things I have added to it, has long since been finished, but for want of transcribers I possess only a single copy. I have added to my former collection a great number of *similia* from Pliny; I think they will be most useful to you and yours, but there is no one to make a fair copy of them. Among the Britons the avoidance of hard work is so prevalent 5

* * * * *

110 Diest] Allen suggests a possible identification of the writer with Nicolaas Cleynaerts of Diest (1493–1542), author of a Greek grammar and a great admirer of Erasmus.

292:4 *Cato*] Cf Allen Ep 298 introduction.

6 *similia*] Published as *Parabolae sive similia* (cf Allen Ep 312 introduction)

and the love of ease so great that they cannot be roused even if a bright glimpse of flattering money dawns upon them. If you come here, I will be delighted to put these things and all the others at your disposal. It is for you to decide whether this would be to your advantage; since, while your visit will bring the utmost pleasure to me at least, yet the plague is still 'kindling sparks' (to use our friend Green's expression) in several places here and recently has even had the effrontery to force its way into the royal palace itself, causing two or three deaths. But if you are planning a flying visit, you must hurry: for I am preparing to take wing myself in forty days' time, unless some new piece of fortune should befall me of which I cannot yet see even the slightest hint. I have put the latest news in a letter to Green. Farewell, dearest Gonnell.

London, 28 April

I had almost forgotten the thing you most wished to know, namely the identity of the devil that confronted me lately! It is a kind of creature which, though very tiny, contains more poison and plague than anything reared in the sea or on land, for it is made of the pure essence of poison, capable of infecting friend and foe alike, even at a distance. This scourge was sent us by Liguria, which is a more fertile source of such poisons even than Spain. If you wish to know its name too, it does not agree with the character of John the Baptist. I had, being an unduly open and straightforward sort of man, almost agreed to share lodgings with him, but, when I got a taste of the poison, I recoiled: whereas he, in grief at my slipping away from him, breathes his venom at me from a distance and seeks to wound me with the poison of his tongue. I am comforted by two considerations: one, that I am personally blameless; two, that nobody believes him – a man so universally detested that he is loved neither by his brothers nor his children, and is an enemy to his wife. Best wishes again, dear Gonnell.

London, [1515]

* * * * *

10 money] Cf Persius Prologue 12 (Connington's translation)

23 identity of the devil] The following lines clearly refer to Giovanni Battista Boerio (cf Ep 267 introduction). Erasmus had earlier complained of Boerio's attacks (cf Ep 289:6ff). The otherwise meaningless comparison of Liguria with Spain is probably a reference to the fact that Pope Julius II was a Ligurian (ie Genoese), while his predecessor Alexander VI was a Spaniard (cf Opuscula 80 lines 288 and 293n).

293 / To William Warham [London, June 1514]

Erasmus had sent his translation of Lucian's *Dialogi* to Bade for publication with a dedication addressed to Warham more than two years earlier (cf Ep 261 introduction). When the book was finally published 1 June 1514 he felt it necessary to write another letter to accompany the gift of a copy.

TO HIS GRACE, THE RIGHT REVEREND WILLIAM,
ARCHBISHOP OF CANTERBURY, PRIMATE OF ENGLAND,
FROM ERASMUS OF ROTTERDAM, GREETINGS

Ingratitude fills me with the same repugnance that Homer's Achilles felt towards a lie. Yet, as I reflected upon the immense debt I owe to your 5 generosity, a further thought occurred to me: it is proper to express one's thanks to ordinary friends for ordinary benefits, but with a benefactor of such eminence, a primate in very deed, to attempt to return his favours is so remote from the duty of a grateful recipient that it might sooner appear a kind of ingratitude, or at least presumption. And so I decided that in fact the 10 best thing I could do was to employ a small literary gift, plucked, as it were, like some nosegay from the muses' garden, to display to you as best I might the gratitude and affection of my heart. Accordingly I have furnished Lucian's *Saturnalia* with a Latin dress, and now send it to you with my good wishes; it is a witty enough book if I am not mistaken, nor have I hitherto 15 inscribed it to any other person; and it will serve your purpose very well, if ever you have a mind, I should say a moment, to laugh, surrounded as you are by the press of affairs that, in Horace's words, 'do leap upon your head and dance about you.' And why should it be thought a reproach to persons of the highest importance if now and then they refresh care-wearied minds 20 with laughter, when Hesiod tells us how even Jupiter laughs, 'the father of men and of gods'? This is especially true if their laughter be such as I think is contained here; civilized laughter, not without art – nay, such as I think contains somewhat more of profit than even that serious, but so vexatious, business side of life. 25

Farewell, most reverend Father, and pray continue to protect your Erasmus, as you are now doing, from that monster worse than the Hydra.

[1515]

* * * * *

18 Horace] *Satires* 2.6.33–4

21 Hesiod] Cf *Theogony* 36f.

294 / To Pieter Gillis London, [July] 1514

In July 1514 Erasmus left England for Basel, drawn by the opportunities for publication offered by the Amerbach-Froben press, and also somewhat disappointed by his failure to secure patronage in England befitting his expectations. His heavy baggage was sent by boat to Antwerp while he himself crossed from Dover to Calais.

ERASMUS TO HIS FRIEND PIETER GILLIS

The shipmaster Antonius, the bearer of this, will deliver to you three cases: one square, made of wood and roped; the other two of French type, covered in pigskin. Store them either at your house or in some other place of safety until I arrive. Please pay the shipmaster, unless he happens to have exacted 5 payment from me here, for I have not made any bargain with him yet. Once I have paid my respects to Mountjoy and a few other good friends, then, God willing, I shall soon be with you. Then we can have a good talk together about everything. I am only surprised that Franz, the bookseller, came here without bringing a letter from you. Look after my belongings, and regard 10 them as your own. Farewell, best of friends.

London, 1514

295 / To Andrea Ammonio Hammes castle, 8 July 1514

Since Hammes was near Calais it was natural that Erasmus should stop there to visit his patron Mountjoy, who was commander of the castle.

ERASMUS TO ANDREA AMMONIO,
SECRETARY TO HIS MAJESTY THE KING OF ENGLAND

I called at your house more than once in order to bid a last farewell to the best of all my friends, and at the same time to enjoy your company as long as I could, for I can scarcely think of anything in my life that has given me 5 greater pleasure. The crossing was a very good one, but distressing all the same, at least for me. True the sea was quite calm, the winds favourable, the weather glorious, and the hour of sailing most convenient. We weighed anchor in fact at about one o'clock. But those pirates had transferred the portmanteau, crammed with my writings, to another vessel. They make a 10 habit of doing this deliberately, in order to steal something, if they can; and if not, then to extract a few pieces of money and sell you back your own

* * * * *

294:9 Franz] Birckmann (cf Ep 258:14n)

property. Accordingly, believing that several years' work was lost, I was afflicted by a degree of anguish as keen, I think, as any parent would suffer upon the death of his children. And of course in everything else, too, they treat foreign visitors so badly that it would be better to fall into any Turk's hands than theirs. I often wonder to myself that such dregs of mankind are tolerated by the English government, to the great annoyance of visitors, and the vast discredit of the whole island when each visitor recounts at home what an uncivil reception he got, and other nations judge the whole people by what those robbers do. 15 20

I am not sure whether I have told you that I paid my respects to his majesty in person. He received me with the friendliest expression, after which the bishop of Lincoln encouraged me to be full of confidence and hope. For his part he made no mention of a present, and I did not venture to introduce the subject in case I should seem rather grasping. When I took my leave, the bishop of Durham gave me six nobles of his own accord, and, if I remember correctly, for the fourth time. The archbiship went out of his way to find an opportunity to match this sum, while the bishop of Rochester gave me a ryal. This is the whole of the wealth I am bringing away with me. I wanted you to know this, in case anyone should suppose that I have amassed a large sum of money on the pretext of taking my leave. 25 30

At present I am staying at the castle of Hammes, where I mean to stay for a few days with my friend Mountjoy, and then go to Germany, visiting a few friends on the way. If Fortune answers my hopes and other men's promises, I shall hasten back. If not, I shall do what seems best in the circumstances. May almighty God grant that I may return to England safe and sound, to find my dear Ammonio not only safe but enriched with all that Fortune can offer. If you ever have a chance to promote the interests of your friend Erasmus, I am sure you will treat him as well in his absence as 35 40

* * * * *

24 bishop of Lincoln] Wolsey had recently received the bishopric of Lincoln (cf Ep 284 introduction).

27 six nobles] If these were gold angel-nobles, as in Epp 240A:11; 248:40; and 270:30, or their equivalent money-of-account value (6s 8d ster. apiece), this gift would have been worth £2 0s 0d sterling = £2 18s 0d gros Flemish = £17 1s 4d tournois; but if they were gold ryals (rose-nobles), as in line 30 below, then it would have been worth £3 0s 0d sterling. Cf Epp 214:4n; 227:31n; 241:19n; 248:40n; 273:14n; 286:14n; and tables A–F below, 327–45.

30 a ryal] English gold coin, also known as the 'royal' or 'rose-noble,' direct successor of the traditional noble, worth 10s 0d sterling (1465–1526). Cf Ep 214:4n; and CWE I 319, 325, 329, 336–7.

you have always done hitherto whether he was present or absent. Farewell, best of friends.

Hammes castle, 8 July 1514

296 / To Servatius Rogerus Hammes castle, 8 July 1514

This is the last and by far the longest of a series of letters (Epp 185, 189, 200, 203) which Erasmus addressed to Servatius Rogerus, prior of Steyn since 1504, excusing himself for his failure to return to his home monastery. Erasmus never published it, although copies were in circulation before his death. Two manuscripts survive, one at Deventer, the other, in the hand of Erasmus' friend Martin Lypsius and probably written about 1518, in Brussels. The letter was also printed separately three times. Two of the printed versions without place or date are probably prior to Erasmus' death, the third, dated 1536, immediately after. In 1533 Erasmus complained that passages in the letter had been misquoted and used against him (cf Allen Ep 2892:105ff). It has something of the air of an apologia written for a wider audience than the comrade of his early days at Steyn who certainly knew the whole story of Erasmus' entry into the monastery (cf Ep 4 introduction).

TO THE REVEREND FATHER SERVATIUS, FROM ERASMUS

Most gracious Father, after a stormy passage through many hands, your letter finally reached me, but only after I had left England. It has given me infinite pleasure, redolent as it is of your feelings towards me in the past. My reply shall be brief, for I am already travelling as I write, and I will 5 concentrate upon those points which, as your letter tells me, are most germane to the issue. The opinions of men vary so greatly – each bird has his own song – that it is impossible to satisfy everyone. For my part, as God is my witness, I desire to follow the best course of action. For the youthful passions I felt long ago have been checked by advancing age and experi- 10 ence. Never have I planned to alter my mode of living or my dress, not because I approved of them, but to avoid giving offence to anyone. You know, indeed, that it was my guardians' obduracy and the relentless insistence of other people that drove me, rather than persuaded me, to adopt that kind of life. Afterwards I was kept there by the scolding tongue of 15 Cornelis of Woerden, together with a kind of boyish diffidence, although I

* * * * *

296:16 Cornelis of Woerden] This is probably a reference to the Cornelis mentioned in the *Compendium vitae* as having been a schoolmate of Erasmus at Deventer and as having been active in persuading him to enter the monastery (cf Allen 150 lines 81ff). Woerden is to the north of Gouda.

was clearly conscious how ill-adapted I was to the life; for not everything suits everyone. Through some peculiarity of my constitution I have always found it hard to endure fasting. Once I was awakened I never could go to sleep again for several hours. My mind was attracted solely to literature, 20 which is not practised in your community. In fact I feel certain that, had I entered upon some free kind of life, I could have been accounted good as well as happy.

Thus when I fully grasped that I was totally unsuited to your way of living and had been obliged to embrace it against my will, yet because 25 nowadays it is by popular convention regarded as disgraceful to abandon a profession once one has adopted it, I decided to bear with courage this part of my unhappiness also. For you know that I have been unfortunate in many respects. But I have always regarded as the worst of my misfortunes the fact that I had been forced into the kind of profession which was utterly 30 repugnant to my mind and body alike: to my mind because I disliked ritual and loved freedom, and to my body because, even had I been wholly satisfied to live such a life, my bodily constitution could not tolerate its hardships. Perhaps someone may object that I underwent a year of so-called probation and was of mature years. What nonsense! As if one could require 35 a youth of sixteen, with a largely bookish upbringing, to know himself – a considerable accomplishment even for an old man – or to learn, in a single year, what many greybeards have not yet grasped! Yet I myself never approved of it, much less so when I had given it a trial. However I was ensnared by the methods I have spoken of. All the same, I grant that the 40 truly good man can live the good life, no matter what his occupation may be. And I will not deny that I had a tendency to grievous faults; however my nature was not so corrupt that I could not have been led to yield a harvest of good, given a suitable director, one who was truly Christian, not full of Jewish scruples. 45

Meanwhile, therefore, I have searched for the kind of life in which I should be least bad; and indeed I believe I have found it. During this time I have lived among men of sobriety, and among literary studies which have kept me away from many vices. I have been able to enjoy the society of such as have the true flavour of Christianity and have been improved by their 50 conversation. As for my books, I do not boast of them. Possibly you despise them. But there are many people who will testify that reading them has

* * * * *

36 sixteen] Erasmus was certainly more than sixteen when he entered the monastery in 1487 (cf Allen I 583), even if we place his birth at the latest possible date. He may have been referring to the minimum age prescribed by his order for entrance rather than to his own case.

made them not only better educated, but better men. A craving for money I have never felt, nor am I in the least moved by the glitter of fame. I have never been a slave to pleasures, though I was once inclined to them. 55 Drunkenness and debauchery have always revolted me, and I have avoided them. On the other hand, whenever I thought about rejoining your community I envisaged the envy of many, the contempt of all, the conversations so cold and inept, with no savour of Christ, the banquets so profane in their spirit, in short the whole tenor of life such that, if the ceremonies were 60 removed, I cannot see what would be left that was desirable. Finally I thought of the weakness of my flesh, now increased by age, sickness, and toil, which makes me on the one hand unlikely to please you, on the other hand certain to kill myself. For several years now I have been a prey to the stone, a most troublesome and dangerous ailment. For several years I have 65 drunk nothing but wine, and only choice wine at that, unavoidably, because of my infirmity. I cannot tolerate every kind of food, nor yet any and every climate. This sickness of mine recurs so readily that I have to be extremely temperate in my habits – and I know the Dutch climate; also I know your Dutch theories about diet, to say nothing of your practice. If, 70 therefore, I had returned to you, I should have achieved nothing but to bring trouble on you, and death upon myself.

Perhaps, however, you think it to be an important condition of blessedness to die in the midst of the brethren. But this belief deceives and imposes on you, and not you alone, but almost all other men. We make 75 Christianity and piety consist in place, dress, diet, and a number of petty observances. We regard as a lost soul one who exchanges his white habit for a black one, or replaces his cowl with a cap, or changes his abode from time to time. I should go so far as to say that so-called religious obligations of this kind have done great harm to Christian piety, even though it may be that 80 they were first introduced as a result of pious fervour. Later on they gradually increased, and extended into myriads of distinctions. They were backed up by the authority of the popes, given too readily and indulgently in many cases. What indeed is more corrupt or impious than such easy obligations as these? Again, if you turn towards approved, even highly 85 approved, practices, I do not know what picture of Christ you could find

* * * * *

65 stone] Erasmus suffered periodic attacks of this painful disease. He experienced the first attack while working on the *Adagia* in Venice (cf the adage 'festina lente,' *Adagia* II ii; Phillips 186). He had at least two serious attacks while at Cambridge (cf Epp 250:4 and 285:2). The second attack he thought due to his having to drink beer instead of wine.

there, beyond certain cold and Judaic rites. In the practice of these they find self-satisfaction, and by these they judge and condemn others. How much more consonant with Christ's teaching it would be to regard the entire Christian world as a single household, a single monastery as it were, and to think of all men as one's fellow-canons and brethren, to regard the sacrament of baptism as the supreme religious obligation, and to consider not where one lives, but how one lives. You wish me to settle down permanently somewhere, and old age itself adds its prompting. Yet Solon and Pythagoras and Plato are praised for their travels. The apostles too, Paul especially, used to make journeys. St Jerome, albeit he was a monk, turns up now in Rome, now in Syria, now in the region of Antioch, now in this place or that, engaging in the study of sacred literature even in his old age. 90 95

I confess I am not fit to be compared with him; still, I have never changed my residence except when the plague made me, or for reasons of study or health; and wherever I have lived (perhaps I may speak with some presumption of myself, but I will tell the truth), I have won the approval of those men who were most approved, the praise of those most praised. There is not a single realm, neither Spain, nor Italy, nor Germany, nor France, nor England, nor Scotland, which does not invite me to be its guest. If I do not win everyone's approval, which I do not even seek, at least I am favoured by the highest in the land. In Rome there was not one cardinal who did not welcome me as a brother, though I myself sought no such reception: in particular, the cardinals of St George and of Bologna, cardinal Grimani, the cardinal of Nantes, and even the cardinal who is now the 100 105 110

* * * * *

87 Judaic] That a rigid insistence on ritual regulation was Pharisaical rather than Christian was a frequent theme with Erasmus from the *Enchiridion* onwards (cf Ep 164:30).

109 St George] Raffaele Sansoni, called Riario (1461–1521), had been made cardinal of the titular church of San Giorgio in Velabro in 1477 through the influence of his uncle Girolamo Riario with Sixtus IV. He was at this time one of the richest and most powerful prelates in Rome (cf Allen Ep 333 introduction).

109 Bologna] Cardinal Francesco Alidosi (d 1511) was governor of Bologna from 1507 until the French recaptured the city in May 1511. He was murdered a few days later by Francesco Maria Della Rovere, nephew of Julius II (cf Creighton IV 91 and 121 ff). Erasmus probably met him during his stay in Bologna in 1507.

110 Grimani] Cardinal Domenico Grimani (1461–1523), a Venetian, was created cardinal in 1493. He was a patron of literature and a collector of MSS (cf Allen Ep 334 introduction).

110 Nantes] Robert Guibé, cardinal bishop of Nantes (cf Ep 253 introduction)

supreme pontiff, not to mention bishops, archdeacons, and scholars. Now this was not honour paid to wealth, which I do not possess nor covet even now; nor yet to ambition, to which I have always had a great aversion; but purely and simply to letters, which our countrymen laugh to scorn, whereas the Italians worship them. In England there is not a bishop but rejoices at 115 my greetings, longs to have me as his guest, and would be glad if I joined his household. The king himself sent to me shortly before his father's death, when I was in Italy, a most affectionate letter written in his own hand, and he still speaks often of me, no one indeed with more admiration and affection. Whenever I go to pay my respects to him, he receives me with 120 most courteous attention and the friendliest looks; clearly, therefore, he really feels the high regard for me that he expresses in conversation. Also he has repeatedly commanded his almoner to look out a benefice for me. The queen has tried to gain my services as her tutor. Everyone is aware that I should only have to spend a few months at court to heap upon myself as 125 many benefices as I cared to have; but I put my present free time and the labour of my studies before all else. The archbishop of Canterbury, primate of all England and chancellor of this realm, a learned and worthy man, is so devoted to me that his love equals that of a father or a brother; and I can prove his sincerity to you, for he gave me a benefice of about a hundred 130 nobles in value; and later at my request commuted it for an annuity of a hundred couronnes on my resignation; in addition to which he has made

* * * * *

111 pontiff] Leo X, with whom, as Cardinal Giovani de' Medici, Erasmus had been familiar at Rome (cf Allen Ep 335:11)

118 letter] Ep 206

123 almoner] Wolsey had been appointed royal almoner on the accession of Henry VIII.

130 benefice] The living of Aldington (cf Ep 255 introduction)

130–1 a hundred nobles] In this and the subsequent lines Erasmus probably meant the Tudor gold angel-nobles, as in Epp 240A:11, 248:40, and 270:30, or their equivalent money-of-account value (6s 8d sterling), so that this benefice had a value of £33 6s 8d sterling = £48 6s 8d gros Flemish = £284 8s 10d tournois. But possibly he meant gold ryals (rose-nobles), which, at 10s 0d sterling apiece, would have increased the value to £50 0s 0d sterling. Cf Epp 214:4n; 227:31n; 241:19n; 248:40n; 273:14n; 286:14n; 295:27n; 295:30n; and tables A–F below, 327–45.

131–2 a hundred couronnes] In all likelihood the equivalent value, possibly in sterling, of the French gold écus à la couronne, still officially valued at £1 15s 0d tournois apiece, but shortly afterwards, in November 1516, increased to £1 19s 0d tournois. By the current rates the annuity was thus worth £175 0s 0d tournois = £20 16s 8d sterling = £29 11s 8d gros Flemish. Cf Epp

me gifts amounting to more than four hundred nobles within the last few years, even though I have never asked him for anything. Once he gave me a hundred and fifty nobles in a single day! From other bishops I have received 135 more than a hundred nobles, offered freely out of their generosity. Lord Mountjoy, a baron of this realm, formerly my pupil, yearly gives me a pension of a hundred couronnes. The king and the bishop of Lincoln, who is all-powerful with the king at present, are showering me with splendid promises. There are two universities here, Oxford and Cambridge, and 140 both of them are endeavouring to have me; for I taught Greek and divinity for a considerable number of months at Cambridge – always free, however, and I have made up my mind never to depart from this practice. There are colleges here in which there is so much devotion, such regularity of life, that you would reject any monastic rule in comparison, if you could see them. In 145 London lives Dr John Colet, dean of St Paul's, a man who has married profound scholarship to exceptional devoutness, and exercises much influence in all quarters. As everyone knows, his love for me leads him to prefer nobody's company to my own. I omit countless others, in order to avoid being doubly tiresome through garrulity and boasting. 150

Now to tell you something about my books. I believe you have read the *Enchiridion*; many people testify that it has fired them with religious enthusiasm. I claim no personal credit for this, but I am glad for Christ's sake if of his gift any good thing has come about through me. Whether you have seen the *Adagiorum opus*, printed by Aldus, I do not know. It is a 155 profane work, of course, but most helpful for the whole business of educa-

* * * * *

212:7n; 288:13n; and CWE I 315, 321. For other estimates cf E&C 146f.

133 four hundred nobles] Probably the equivalent of £133 6s 8d sterling = £193 6s 8d gros Flemish = £1137 15s 6d tournois; but possibly amounting to £200 0s 0d sterling. Cf note to lines 130–1 above; and Ep 214:4n.

134–5 a hundred and fifty nobles] Probably the equivalent of £50 0s 0d sterling = £72 10s 0d gros Flemish = £426 13s 4d tournois; but possibly amounting to £75 0s 0d sterling. Cf note to lines 130–1 above; and Ep 214:4n.

138 a hundred couronnes] As suggested above in note to lines 131–2, this was very likely the equivalent value of the French gold écus à la couronne (£1 15s 0d tournois), so that this pension was also about £20 16s 8d sterling. Cf Ep 288:10ff, where Erasmus notes that his pension from Mountjoy was the same as his annuity from Aldington, and table D below, 341.

142 free] Cf Ep 282:55f.

152 *Enchiridion*] Cf Ep 164 introduction.

155 *Adagiorum opus*] Cf Ep 211 introduction.

tion, while to me personally it represents the expenditure of untold effort and laborious nights. I have published a book entitled *De rerum verborumque copia* and dedicated it to my friend Colet; it is a useful handbook for future preachers, but such things are scorned by those who despise all sound learning. In the course of the last two years I have, among many other things, revised St Jerome's epistles; I have slain with daggers the spurious or interpolated passages, while I have elucidated the obscure parts in my notes. I have also revised the whole of the New Testament from a collation of Greek manuscripts and ancient manuscripts and have annotated over a thousand places, with some benefit to theologians. I have begun a series of commentaries on Paul's epistles, which I will finish when I have published this other work. For I have made up my mind to give up my life to sacred literature. These then are the concerns upon which I am bestowing my leisure and my busy hours alike. I have, so eminent men are saying, a talent for them which others do not possess; while I shall never have any talent for living your kind of life. In all my conversations with the many men of learning and authority whom I have met both here and in Italy and France, I have never yet come across one who advised me to return to your community, or thought it the better course. Even your predecessor, Master Nicolaas Werner of blessed memory, always used to dissuade me, urging me rather to attach myself to some bishop, and adding that he was aware of my nature and also of the habits of his little brothers (these were the words he used, in the vulgar tongue). In my present situation in life I can see what I must avoid; but I cannot determine what alternative I should prefer to it.

160

165

170

175

180

It only remains for me to explain to you about the dress I wear. Until now I have always worn the garb of canons, and when I was at Louvain I sought and received permission from the bishop of Utrecht to make free use of the linen scapular instead of a complete linen robe; also a black cassock

* * * * *

158–9 *De rerum verborumque copia*] Cf Ep 260 introduction.

162 St Jerome's epistles] Cf Epp 264:17; 270:68; 273:15–19.

164 New Testament] Cf Epp 264:16; 270:66; 278:20.

167 commentaries] Cf Ep 164:40n.

175–6 Nicolaas Werner] Cf Ep 48 introduction.

181 dress] Erasmus retells the story of his various changes of habit and the trouble it caused in Bologna in the letter to Grunnius in 1516 when he was appealing to Leo x for a full dispensation from canonical restrictions (cf Allen Ep 447). It is also recounted by Beatus Rhenanus in his biographical sketch (cf Allen I 59f).

183 bishop of Utrecht] David of Burgundy (cf Ep 28:22n)

instead of a black cloak, after the fashion of Paris. But when I went to Italy and everywhere on my travels saw canons using the black habit with a scapular, I there began to assume that black habit with scapular in order not to give offence by the strangeness of my attire. Afterwards the plague broke out at Bologna; and in that city those who attend to persons sick of the plague customarily wear a white linen scarf hanging from their shoulders and try to avoid contact with people. So one day when I was visiting a learned friend some ruffians drew their swords and prepared to attack me, and would have, had not a certain lady warned them that I was a cleric. Another day, too, when I was on my way to see the treasurer's sons, men carrying clubs rushed at me from all sides and assailed me with a horrible uproar. This is why I fell in with the warning of decent citizens and concealed my scapular, and obtained permission from Pope Julius II either to wear the habit of my order or not at my own discretion, provided only that I dressed like a priest. And by the same letter a full pardon was granted to me for any faults I had previously committed in this respect. Accordingly I continued to dress like a priest while I was in Italy, in order that no one should be offended by the change. After I returned to England, however, I decided to assume my usual dress. Having invited to my house a friend who is eminently distinguished for his life and learning, I showed him the dress I had decided to adopt, and asked him whether it was acceptable in England. He approved, and I went forth thus attired. At once I was admonished by other friends that that form of dress could not be tolerated in England, and that I ought rather to cover it up. I concealed it; and, since it cannot be hidden in such a way as not to be detected at some time and thus give rise to offence, I have stowed it away in a chest, and have up to the present made use of the supreme pontiff's previous dispensation. Papal ordinances provide for the excommunication of anyone who has thrown off the religious garb in order to mingle more freely with the laity. In my own case, however, I was obliged to put it aside in Italy to save my life, while afterwards I was obliged to put it aside in England because it could not be tolerated, though I myself should have much preferred to use it. As things now stand, however, I should occasion greater offence by assuming it once again than I gave by the original change.

* * * * *

194 the treasurer's sons] Cf Ep 201:3n.

197 Julius II] The dispensation granted by Julius II in January 1506 before Erasmus went to Italy (Ep 187A) does not mention dress, but it does suggest that Erasmus would have had no difficulty in securing an indulgence in that relatively unimportant matter.

I have now told you the whole story of how I live and the principles on which I act. I should very much like to alter even this course of life, should I see a better one. But I cannot see what I might do in Holland. I know that the climate and diet do not agree with me; and I should become the cynosure of all eyes, returning as a grey-haired old man, and in poor health too, to the place I left as a youth. I should be a target for the contempt of the lowest after being used to receiving honour from the very highest; I should exchange my studies for drinking parties. As for your promise of assistance in searching for an established place where I might, as your letter asserts, live on a most ample salary, I cannot guess what this could be, unless perhaps you are going to place me with some nuns, to be a servant to women, I, who have never consented to be a servant, even to archbishops or kings! The amount of my salary has no interest for me, for I do not aim at becoming rich, so long as I possess just enough means to provide for my health and free time for my studies and to ensure that I am a burden to none. If only we could talk of these matters in person! It is impossible to do this satisfactorily, or with complete safety, in letters. Your own letter, for all that it was sent by entirely reliable hands, went so far astray that I should never have set eyes on it if I had not happened to come to this castle; and, by the time I received it, it had already been seen by a great many others. Do not, therefore, put anything confidential into a letter, unless you are quite sure where I am staying and have secured a messenger who is to be trusted absolutely. At present I am making for Germany, Basel in fact. There I intend to publish my writings, and perhaps I shall be in Rome during the coming winter. On the way back I shall try to arrange for us to have an interview somewhere. At the moment, however, the summer is almost over, and I have a long journey to make. I had heard from Sasbout and his wife about the deaths of Willem, Franciscus, and Andrew. Be sure to return my greetings to Master Hendrik and all the others who live with you; my feelings towards them are what they should be, for I put down those early upsets to my errors or, if you prefer, to my destiny. On 7 July I received your letter, which was written two days after Easter. Please do not fail to commend the salvation of my soul to Christ in your prayers. If I were sure that I could serve him better by a return to your community, I should make

* * * * *

245 Sasbout] Cf Ep 16 introduction.

246 Willem] Hermans (d 1510); cf Ep 33 introduction.

246 Franciscus] Theodoricus (d 1513); cf Ep 10 introduction.

247 Hendrik] Cf Ep 83:87n.

ready to depart this very day. Farewell, once my sweetest companion and now my revered Father.

Hammes castle, near Calais, 8 July 1514 255

297 / To Thomas Wolsey [Hammes? July 1514?]

This preface to the translation of Plutarch's *De utilitate capienda ex inimicis* is a revision and expansion of that sent earlier with a MS copy (Ep 284) and is the one actually printed in the *Plutarchi opuscula* (Basel: Froben August 1514).

TO THE RIGHT REVEREND FATHER IN CHRIST, THOMAS, LORD BISHOP OF LINCOLN, LORD HIGH ALMONER TO HIS MAJESTY THE KING OF ENGLAND, FROM ERASMUS OF ROTTERDAM, GREETINGS

Although I desired, most distinguished prelate, by this small literary gift 5 both to bear witness to my regard for you and to seek your favour in return, since your authority and influence with his majesty are such that there is no man in all England but longs for and aspires to them; still I was long discouraged therefrom by the magnificence of your high station, while I deemed it to be exceedingly disrespectful to solicit the attention of so 10 august a personage with a present so minute. Much more however did your affability and kindness encourage me, when I reflected how untainted your character is by success, and how ready you are to help everyone. Well did I know that it was by God's providence that you had been accorded the largest measure of power among mankind, to the end that you might accord 15 to mankind that largest measure of help. Though my book be very tiny, yet you recall that the smallest jewels are sometimes the most precious of all. And indeed, to commend it to you in but few words, it is Plutarch's; and I shall be persuaded that this author has found favour with your lordship if I discover that the little work which I lately dedicated to the king has indeed 20 been well received through your recommendation.

This too will become equally evident if the result of my present preoccupation should correspond to your promises and my own desires. There is no one to whom I could possibly owe more than to a king of all kings the most illustrious, and none to whom I should more willingly be 25 indebted than a prince of all princes the best, particularly since he entertains such a friendly regard for my humble talent, and speaks of it in such complimentary terms. Indeed I stand heavily in his debt already inasmuch

* * * * *

297:20 little work] Cf Ep 272 introduction.

Thomas Wolsey
Unknown sixteenth-century artist
National Portrait Gallery, London

as he honours me frequently with the testimony of his spoken words. Would not any man rejoice at praise from such lips? Yet I should be still 30 more obliged to him did he lend additional conviction to the praise he assigns me by increasing my poor fortune; for there are many men who, as things now stand, refuse to believe that I am equal to his majesty's description of me, since they observe that this position of mine hardly corresponds to his splendid compliments. Farewell, distinguished ornament of court 35 and kingdom.

THE PURCHASING POWER OF COINS AND OF WAGES IN ENGLAND AND THE LOW COUNTRIES FROM 1500 TO 1514

Introduction
A The purchasing power of coinage in the Low Countries
B The purchasing power of the English coinage at Cambridge and Oxford
C The standard of living of the Antwerp mason
D The estimated annual employment and income of an Antwerp mason
E The standard of living of the English mason
F Prices of dyed woollen cloths of Mechlin and Ghent

JOHN H. MUNRO

The following set of tables extends the appendices of CWE I on the purchasing power of the current coinages in the Low Countries from 1500 up to 1514, and considerably enlarges upon them by including a similar table for England, and tables on the purchasing power of masons' wages in both Antwerp and England over this period; the final table continues the prices of luxury woollen cloths to cover the same years. The presentation of tables on coinage, prices, and wages pertaining to Antwerp and neighbouring towns of Brabant (Brussels, Lier, and the seigneurie of Mechlin) is entirely fitting for these volumes of CWE, since Erasmus was a product of the civilization and thus indirectly of the economy of the Burgundian-Hapsburg Low Countries. He spent some early years of his youth studying at s'Hertogenbosch in Noord-Brabant; in his maturity he frequently visited the chief Brabantine towns; and finally he lived four years at Louvain (1517–21) and then briefly at Anderlecht, near Brussels (1521). But particularly appropriate for this second volume, in which Erasmus' Cambridge correspondence looms so prominently, are the two tables B and E on English prices and wages, for they are based almost entirely on data collected from the Cambridge and Oxford regions.

The collector was, of course, the nineteenth-century British economist James E. Thorold Rogers, whose six-volume *History of Agriculture and Prices in England* (Oxford 1866–1901) has been severely criticized for its frequent (and supposed) violations of the canons of statistical sampling. Perhaps some of Rogers' price statistics presented here may suffer from inconsistencies in the actual quantities and qualities recorded; perhaps Rogers did occasionally lapse from unbiased random selection by taking only the highest prices recorded in some years. But beggars of Renaissance statistics cannot always be choosers: except for wheat,[1] there are no comparable sets of English prices for these years. Furthermore, when the purchasing power of the English coinage and of masons' wages in the Cambridge and Antwerp regions are compared, respectively, a reasonably close correspondence is revealed that does much to restore one's faith in Thorold Rogers' statistics. Surely his prices and those for the southern Low Countries, in Herman Van der Wee's *Growth of the Antwerp Market and of the European Economy, Fourteenth to Sixteenth Centuries* (The Hague 1963), cannot both be wrong, and in the same fashion. In any event no such 'statistical crimes' or even misdemeanours have been or can be imputed to Van der Wee's remarkable study, which is based on a thoroughly scrupulous selection from a far broader, more complete range of continuous data, from these four

* * * * *

1 See below, 321, and table E, 342.

Brabantine towns, than is Thorold Rogers' work. It is indeed a model of sophisticated scientific investigation and statistical precision that deserves to be utilized far more fully than it has been so far for the quantitative economic history of this era.[2] Finally the fact that both an English coin, or the equivalent amount of silver, and a mason's daily wage could purchase approximately as much of most of the commodities documented here in the Cambridge region as in the Antwerp region is perhaps surprising in view of the supposed imperfections of the market economy of this period:[3] trade restrictions, labour immobilities, the high cost of transport, import and export duties, guild regulations, the use of 'customary prices,' and the price rigidities found in long-term contractual purchases by institutions, which are the usual sources of historical price statistics. Such a statistical correspondence thus also inspires some confidence in the historical relevance of economic theory, especially concerning the response of supply, of goods and labour, to price and monetary stimuli.

Despite some inflation that became particularly evident in the Antwerp region during the last five years of our period (1510–14),[4] northwestern Europe generally enjoyed at this time a monetary stability that greatly facilitated the construction of these statistical tables. There were no significant wars or market dislocations until the very end of the period; and, above all, there was an unusually long absence of coinage debasements: in France until July 1519; in the Burgundian-Hapsburg Low Countries until February 1521; and in England until August-November 1526. Thus in all the tables prices and the purchasing power of coins and wages have been calculated in terms of a constant money-of-account value[5] for each of the gold and silver coins over the entire fifteen-year period.[6] Nevertheless, despite this apparent monetary stability, one might well challenge the use of the officially proclaimed rates, or indeed any constant money-of-account value, for the gold coins of these tables. It was the market, to be sure, and not the prince's fiat that established the actual exchange value of gold coins.

* * * * *

2 Cf Herman Van der Wee *Growth of the Antwerp Market* (The Hague 1963) I 5–168, for a critical discussion of his statistical sources and methods of computation. Vol I contains the statistics; vol II the historical and economic interpretation.

3 See below, 320–2, for a comparative analysis of these wage and price statistics.

4 See below, 320, for an analysis of the causes of this inflation.

5 Cf CWE I 347 (appendix E).

6 Conversely each coin and each unit of money-of-account contained or represented a specific, constant amount of gold or silver.

Table 1 The market value of gold bullion at Antwerp, compared with the official mint-value of coined gold, in pounds groot Flemish, 1500 to 1515

year (Feb.)	market value of 1 marc[1] of pure gold bullion in pounds groot	percentage of the official mint-value of 1 marc[1] of gold coined = £23.125	year	market value of 1 marc[1] of pure gold bullion in pounds groot	percentage of the official mint-value of 1 marc[1] of gold coined = £23.125
1500	£22.395	96.84	1508	£22.395	96.84
1501	"	"	1509	"	"
1502	"	"	1510	"	"
1503	"	"	1511	"	"
1504	"	"	1512	£22.696	98.14
1505	"	"	1513	"	"
1506	"	"	1514	£23.004	99.48
1507	"	"	1515	"	"

1 1 Marc de Troyes = 8 Paris onces = 244.753 grams (gold at $23^{7}/_{8}$ carats fine)

SOURCE
Calculated from Herman Van der Wee *The Growth of the Antwerp Market* (The Hague 1963) I 133, table XVI

But, as table 1 shows, the market value of gold bullion at Antwerp always remained slightly below the official mint-value of gold coins during this period; and the small differences merely represented the agio or premium that legal-tender coins normally commanded over bullion by virtue of their greater ease of use.[7]

The market value of gold bullion at Antwerp did not in fact rise above the official mint par until 1516–17 (to £23.322 gros Flemish). At about the same time, 27 November 1516, the French government permitted the price of the écu d'or au soleil to rise from 36s 3d tournois to 40s 0d tournois.[8] The market value of gold bullion and coins in England, however, does not appear to have appreciated until the early 1520s.[9]

* * * * *

7 Cf J.H. Munro *Wool, Cloth, and Gold: The Struggle for Bullion in Anglo-Burgundian Trade 1340–1478* (Brussels and Toronto 1973) 25–6.

8 The price of the écu à la couronne similarly rose from 35s 0d tournois to 39s 0d tournois. Denis Richet 'Le cours officiel des monnaies étrangères circulant en France au XVIe siècle' *Revue historique* 225 (1961) 377. Cf Frank Spooner *The International Economy and Monetary Movements in France 1493–1725* (Cambridge, Mass 1972) 121.

9 Albert Feavearyear *The Pound Sterling: A History of English Money* 2nd ed rev E.V. Morgan (Oxford 1963) 47–9

Before particular features of the individual tables can be explained, some general comments on the method of computing the purchasing power of coinage are necessary. First, the prices of the various commodities as given in the printed sources had to be converted, when necessary, into the units employed as common denominators in these tables. They are:

1 the litre (for wine) = 0.21998 Imperial gallon = 0.87992 quarts = 1.75984 pints = approximately 35 oz of wine.
2 the gallon (peas) = 0.125 Imperial bushel = 4.54586 litres
3 the yard (linens, woollens) = 0.9144 metre = 1.3063 Flemish ell
4 the pound avoirdupois (butter, salt beef, loaf sugar, tallow candles) = 453.593 grams
5 the Imperial bushel (wheat) = 8 gallons = 36.36688 litres
6 number = one item of the given commodity (herrings, codfish, eggs, sheets of writing paper).

Second, the quantity of the given commodity that could have been purchased by one penny (1d) of the money-of-account used, Flemish gros (groot) or English sterling, was calculated by taking the reciprocal of the price per unit ($1/x$). Thus, in table A.1, red wine at Lier, priced at 7d gros Flemish per gelte in 1500, cost 2.4648d per litre, and the amount that 1d gros could purchase = 1/2.4648 = 0.4057 litre. That reciprocal multiplied by the money-of-account value of the coins listed in the tables gives us the quantity of the given commodity that each coin could have purchased. Thus the amount of red wine that a gold angel could have purchased in 1500 = 116d × 0.4057 litre = 47.06 litres. These quantities should be taken only as approximations of reality, especially those calculated in terms of foreign coins for the Low Countries in table A. While the gold écus, florins, ducats, and angels were indeed legal tender there, we cannot be absolutely certain – despite the arguments of the preceding paragraph – that they were always accepted at their official values. French and English silver coins, on the other hand, were not officially recognized by the Burgundian-Hapsburg authorities; but these and other silver coins appear to have circulated at values determined approximately by their relative bullion contents.[10] The money-of-account values of these silver coins in table A have been calculated in that fashion; and they have been included in the table chiefly to permit an international comparison of purchasing power, especially a comparison with table B for England. No such problems arise in table B because no foreign coins have been included, on the grounds that such coins were

* * * * *

10 Cf J.H. Munro 'An Aspect of Medieval Public Finance: The Profits of Counterfeiting in the Fifteenth-Century Low Countries' *Revue belge de numismatique* 118 (1972) 127–48; Peter Spufford *Monetary Problems and Policies in the Burgundian Netherlands 1433–1496* (Leyden 1970) 55–73.

not permitted to circulate in England, except at the Calais staple.[11] Even if that ban had been evaded, we could not know precisely what sterling value to ascribe to any of the foreign coins.

Finally, to facilitate comparisons of the degrees of change in purchasing power over this fifteen-year period, quinquennial (five-year) averages of prices, wages, and the quantities of commodities so purchased, and their corresponding index numbers, have been calculated. For all prices and wages the averages and index numbers (price-relatives) were computed by taking the simple *arithmetic* mean.[12] But the quinquennial averages of the quantities of commodities purchased and their corresponding quantity-index numbers (quantity-relatives) had to be computed by the *harmonic* mean, because those quantities are derived, as noted earlier, from the reciprocals of the commodity prices. The harmonic mean, undoubtedly an unfamiliar concept to most readers, is defined as 'the reciprocal of the arithmetic mean of the reciprocals of the individual numbers in a given series.'[13] In tables A and B the relevant harmonic means were in fact easily calculated by multiplying the reciprocals of the average prices for each quinquennium by the corresponding money-of-account values of the coins listed. Thus, for example, the average amount of red wine that a gold angel could have purchased in the years 1500–4 (table A.I) = 1/2.81690 × 116 = 0.355 × 116 = 41.18 litres. Similarly the quantity-index numbers in these tables were calculated by taking the reciprocals of their corresponding price-relatives. The price-index numbers (not given in tables A and B) were calculated by first taking the average of the prices for each commodity in the quinquennium 1500–4 as the base, making it equal to 100; the prices of each

* * * * *

11 Even at Calais, an English outpost on the continent and the official staple for the wool export trade (1347–1558), the crown frequently sought to ban the use of foreign coins. Cf Munro *Wool, Cloth, and Gold* 23–5, 39–40, 59–61, 72–3, 88–9, 175–9. But in 1522 Henry VIII accorded rights of legal tender to Italian and Hapsburg florins and ducats and the French écus d'or (Feavearyear *Pound Sterling* 48).

12 The sum of the prices or wages for the five-year period divided by 5

13 F.C. Mills *Introduction to Statistics* (New York 1956) 108–12, 401. The formula for the harmonic mean (H) is:

$$\frac{1}{H} = \frac{\frac{1}{r_1} + \frac{1}{r_2} + \frac{1}{r_3} + \ldots + \frac{1}{r_n}}{N}$$

where N = the total number of items in the series so averaged.

good for each year and each quinquennial price-average were then computed as percentages of that base. Thus, for example, the price-relative for red wine at Lier in 1507 (A.I) is 112.5, since that price of 3.17d per litre = 112.5 per cent of the average price of 1500–4 (3.169 ÷ 2.817). The corresponding quantity-relative or quantity-index number for 1507 = 1/1.125 = 88.9 per cent. It may be quickly seen that 36.61 litres, the amount that a gold angel could have purchased in 1507, is in fact that same percentage of the average amount purchasable for 1500–4, 41.18 litres. It may also be seen that, had the arithmetic mean been used instead in calculating the quantity-averages and quantity-relatives, the direct relation between commodity prices and quantities purchased would have been destroyed. As a final illustration: table A.IV shows that in, say, 1511 any given coin could have purchased only 76.8 per cent as many smoked red herrings as, on the average, in the years 1500–4; the silver stuiver, for example, would have bought only 8.77 herrings instead of 11.42 herrings as before.

There now follows a more particular analysis of the sources of the statistical data for tables A to F, with descriptions of the types and qualities of the commodities, their provenance if known, the institutions purchasing them, the money-of-account used in recording the purchase, and the units of weight or volume by which the commodities were purchased and their equivalents in the units of these tables. Both Thorold Rogers and Van der Wee have given the 'raw' prices of the various commodities in terms of the money-of-account and units of weight or volume used in the archival records.

TABLE A

The purchasing power of coinage in the Low Countries (Brabant) 1500 to 1514

The prices of all the commodities listed were given in Brabant groots, the duchy's money-of-account (pond groot), which had been tied, since 1435, to the Flemish pond groot by the fixed ratio of £3 Brabant to £2 Flemish.[14] Since the latter is the more familiar unit, and the one used for the notes on the correspondence of Erasmus, the prices have been accordingly converted into Flemish gros (groots) by this ratio.

I Rhine wine: young, good quality red wines, as purchased by various ecclesiastical institutions, hospitals, and the Poor Relief in Lier, by the gelte = 2.840 litres (= 2.50 Imperial quarts). The prices, inclusive of all taxes, centred upon the Easter season.

* * * * *

14 Cf CWE I 322–3, 345, 347 (appendix E).

II butter: fresh, salted local butter, as purchased chiefly by the Béguinage of Brussels, and also by other ecclesiastical institutions, throughout the year, by the 100-pond weight of Brussels = 46.767 kilograms = 103.103 lb avoirdupois.

III salt beef: as purchased by ecclesiastical institutions and hospitals in Mechlin, during the November slaughtering season, by the 100-pond weight of Mechlin = 46.9247 kilograms = 103.451 lb avoirdupois.

IV herrings: dry smoked Flemish red herrings, chiefly from the adjacent North Sea coastal waters, as purchased in Brussels and Mechlin in the Lenten season by various ecclesiastical institutions, hospitals, and the Poor Relief, by the stroo = 500 herrings.

V eggs: probably local fresh eggs, as purchased throughout the year by the Béguinage of Brussels, by the hundred.

VI loaf sugar: fresh cane sugar from the Portuguese islands of Madeira, the Canaries, and the Azores, as sold on the St Bavo market of Antwerp, in October, by the pond of Antwerp = 470.156 grams = 1.03652 lb avoirdupois. The sudden and very large increases in the European sugar supply which the cultivation of these recently colonized islands had produced was responsible for one of the most dramatic price declines over the previous half-century.[15]

VII tallow candles: as purchased by various civic and ecclesiastical institutions in Brussels, Lier, Antwerp, and Mechlin, during the autumn and winter, by the steen (stone) of 8 lb = 3,752.194 grams (as the average of the pound weights of these towns) = 8.2722 lb avoirdupois.

TABLE B

The purchasing power of the English coinage at Cambridge and Oxford 1500 to 1514

The prices were recorded in shillings and pence sterling, and have been given in pence sterling in this table. All references to pounds are to the pound avoirdupois of 453.593 grams.

I red wine: Bordeaux wines, normally 'clarets,' purchased by ecclesiastical institutions and colleges at Cambridge and Oxford, by the dozen gallons = 54.5503 litres.

II herrings: North Sea smoked red herrings, probably supplied by Dutch and Flemish fishermen;[16] purchased at Cambridge and Oxford by the cade or kemp of 500 fish = the Flemish stroo.

* * * * *

15 Cf Van der Wee *Antwerp Market* I 306–7, 318–24.

16 Ibid I 277–8, and below, 323–4

III codfish (mores): from the waters off the Orkney and Shetland Islands and Iceland; purchased at Cambridge by the 'short hundred' = 100.

IV peas: fresh green garden peas, purchased at Cambridge from local producers, by the quarter = 8 bushels = 64 gallons.

V sugar: loaf (cane) sugar, from the Mediterranean, Madeira, the Canaries, and the Azores, purchased at Cambridge and Oxford by the dozen pounds.

VI candles: English and French tallow candles, made from mutton fat, purchased at Cambridge and Oxford by the dozen pounds.

VII paper: good quality writing paper, probably linen paper imported from the Low Countries, averaging 12 inches by 8.5 inches; purchased at Cambridge and Oxford by the ream = 20 quires = 480 sheets.

VIII linen: medium- to good-quality table linen, having a width of 1.0 to 1.5 ells (= yards, not the ell of 45 inches); imported from the Low Countries, Normandy, Ireland, but also from the west of England, and Lancashire, and purchased at Oxford and Cambridge by the dozen ells. It is obvious both from the varying provenance and the variations in price that this is one commodity whose price data lack consistency in quality, and perhaps also in size, if the width varied on occasion. Yet the price averages are remarkably stable.

TABLE C

The standard of living of the Antwerp mason 1500 to 1514

This table offers two complementary measures, but very roughly approximate measures only, of a master mason's real wage at Antwerp, in annual and quinquennial averages from 1500 to 1514. By the first method the purchasing power of his daily summer wage has been calculated by multiplying that wage, expressed here in Flemish gros, by the reciprocal of the unit prices of the eight commodities listed. Thus the amount of butter that a mason earning 8d 8 esterlins a day could have purchased in 1500, when it cost 1.348d a pound avoirdupois, = 8.333 × 1/1.348 = 8.333 × 0.74175 = 6.181 lb. Seven of these series of commodity prices are those given in table A; the eighth is wheat, which has been added here because of the obvious importance of farinaceous foods in the artisan's diet. The wheat price statistics are the arithmetic mean of quarterly wheat prices in the Lier region, in terms of the viertel (quarter) = 86.606 litres = 2.38145 Imperial bushels. One might object that, since rye, a much cheaper grain, was more widely consumed in the Low Countries, its price series should have been selected instead. But to have done so would not have permitted a valid comparison with the real wages of an English mason (who had a greater liking for wheat), since the English rye prices for these years are quite inadequate.[17] Finally, the quinquennial averages of the amounts of these eight commodities that the average daily summer wage could have purchased were again calculated according to the harmonic mean: the quinquennial average of the daily wage multiplied by the reciprocal of the quinquennial average of each of the commodity price series. There are two obvious problems with this method: we have to assume that the mason could purchase these commodities at the same unit price as did the various civic and ecclesiastical institutions; and we have to assume that the entire daily wage was spent on that one commodity.

The second and more comprehensive measure of real wages is a comparison of the index of the mason's money wages over this period with a *weighted* price index based on the commodity prices used in this table. Perhaps the best model for constructing such an index, as a crude indicator of the current cost of living, is the well-known 'basket of consumables' index of Phelps Brown and Hopkins, discussed below for table E. In accordance with their index, the commodity prices of this table would have the following weights:

wheat 23.0%
wine 17.0%
butter 14.0%
salt beef 15.0%
red herrings 14.0%
sugar 8.5%
tallow candles 8.5%
TOTAL 100.0%

Egg prices had to be omitted from this index because they are unavailable for the years 1501–4. Finally, to construct this index annual price-relatives for each of the above seven commodities were calculated, as before, by taking the arithmetic mean of the prices in the quinquennium 1500–4, making that average equal 100 as the index base, and computing the prices for each year and quinquennium as a percentage of that base. Those price-relatives were then multiplied by the corresponding percentage 'weights' of the seven commodities and the results for each year were then summed to produce this weighted price index. The most interesting feature of this table is that the highly organized masons' guild of Antwerp almost immediately responded to the quite considerable inflation of the years

* * * * *

17 Cf James E. Thorold Rogers *History of Agriculture and Prices in England* IV (Oxford 1882) 282–9.

1511–13 by securing an increase in the summer wages from 1513 – their first effective increase since 1442 – and in the winter wage the next year.[18] But it is evident from the table that this wage increase of 20 per cent compensated for only about half of the inflation of those years.[19]

TABLE D
The estimated annual employment and income of an Antwerp mason 1500 to 1514

No measure of an artisan's standard of living can pretend to be adequate without an indication of the wage rates prevailing throughout the year and of the probable number of days worked per year. In this era of daily rather than of hourly wage rates, when the length of the working day was primarily a function of the number of hours of sunlight, and also of the weather conditions, the summer wages were naturally higher than the winter wages. Thanks to Van der Wee's prodigious archival researches, we possess a comprehensive series of wage rates for master masons in both summer and winter seasons, especially from the accounts of Onse Lieve Vrouw church in Antwerp, and estimates of the number of days employment per year in the construction industry there.[20] These statistics are reproduced in table D, and from them I have computed estimated annual wage incomes of the master masons in Antwerp from 1500 to 1514. In accordance with van der Wee's estimates of the average number of days worked in each of the two 'seasons' I have given a weight of 70 per cent to the summer wage (15 March to 30 September) and thus one of 30 per cent to the winter wage (1 October to 15 March).[21] Again using the average of the quinquennium 1500–4 as the base 100, I have calculated annual and quinquennial income-relatives, or an income-index for this period, which may usefully be compared with the weighted price-index reproduced from table C. Employment

* * * * *

18 Van der Wee *Antwerp Market* I 347, 459–61. The wage increase of 1487, necessitated by the severe coinage debasements of the period, was rescinded with the return to a strong coinage in 1490.

19 See below, 320–2.

20 These are pure money wages, without any supplementary payments to the mason in the form of food, drink, lodging, or payments 'in kind.' Cf Van der Wee *Antwerp Market* I 38–51, 333–4.

21 Cf Van der Wee *Antwerp Market* I 44–5; C. Verlinden, J. Craeybeckx, and E. Scholliers 'Price and Wage Movements in Belgium in the Sixteenth Century' in Peter Burke ed *Economy and Society in Early Modern Europe: Essays from Annales* (London 1972) 77–8.

in construction appears to have been quite stable over this period, ranging from a low of 54.8 per cent of the year worked in 1500 and 1505 to a high of 60.2 per cent in 1508–9. The over-all annual average of 213.3 days (58.4 per cent of the year) compares quite favourably with today's employment in construction, still a seasonal industry; and even favourably with an estimate of 236 days employment for someone working continuously a five-day week, except for a three-week vacation and ten statutory holidays. The Antwerp mason probably did not take summer vacations, but he did enjoy many more holy-days in celebration of various saints' feast days than does the modern worker. Finally, the Antwerp mason's estimated annual income of about £7 6s 4d gros Flemish or the equivalent of £5 0s 7d sterling (in 1510–14) puts into better perspective Erasmus' frequent discussions of his pension from Mountjoy and his annuity from Aldington, each valued at approximately £20 0s 0d sterling per year.[22]

TABLE E

The standard of living of the English mason 1500 to 1514

We are by no means blessed with such comprehensive data for the English mason's living standards as we are for the Antwerp artisans. While Thorold Rogers and Phelps Brown and Hopkins have furnished daily wage rates for master masons and others in the construction industry at Oxford and Cambridge, for all the years of our series, they have not stated precisely whether these are summer wage rates or just average annual rates.[23] Their assumption of a ten-hour working day would possibly suggest the former. Nor do they provide any information on the number of days worked per year. But given the daily wage rates, one may at least calculate those two very crude measures of a mason's standard of living, as offered in table C. For the weighted price-index of this table E we are more fortunate, on the other hand, in having readily available the excellent 'basket of consumables' index of Phelps Brown and Hopkins, which requires only a recalculation from their base of 1451–75 to one of 1500–4 to suit the purposes of this table. Despite their disclaimers that their index has too many deficiencies – omitting most fully fabricated goods and house-rents, for example – to be a true guide to the cost of living, it is still far more comprehensive in com-

* * * * *

22 Cf Ep 296:138n.

23 Cf the sources for table E, and E.H. Phelps Brown and Sheila Hopkins 'Seven Centuries of Building Wages' *Economica* 87 (1955), reprinted in E.M. Carus-Wilson ed *Essays in Economic History* II (London 1962) 168–78. They have averaged the daily rate for all building craftsmen, and presented that rate as a constant 6d per day from 1412 to 1532 (177).

Table 2

	commodity classifications, and their components in the Phelps Brown and Hopkins index for the period 1500–1725	percentage weights for each commodity classification in the PB & H index	percentage of total expenditures in the Savernak household spent on each commodity classification (1453–60)
1	farinaceous 1.25 bu. wheat, 1.0 bu. rye, 0.50 bu. barley, 0.67 bu. peas	20.0	20.0
2	meat and fish 1.5 sheep, 15 white herrings, 25 red herrings	25.0	35.0
3	butter and cheese[1]	12.5	2.0
4	drink 4.5 bu. malt	22.5	23.0
	FOOD SUBTOTAL	80.0	80.0
5	fuel and light 4.5 bu. charcoal, 2.75 lb candles, 0.5 pt oil	7.5	7.5
6	textiles and others 0.67 yd canvas, 0.50 yd shirting, 0.33 yd woollen cloth	12.5	12.5
	TOTAL	100.0	100.0

1 Phelps Brown and Hopkins had to omit butter and cheese from their sixteenth-century index (for other periods given a weight of 12.5%) because of serious lacunae in price data. Presumably they compensated for this omission by giving the meat and fish classification that weight, making it 37.5%, in close correspondence with the Savernak budget, in fact.

modities and price data than the mere nine items listed in these tables. Fortunately for us, moreover, their statistical 'basket' received its periodic change in components in 1500, the very year beginning our series. The components of their price index for 1500–1725, and the corresponding weights, are given in table 2, which also compared these weights with the distribution of weekly expenditures in the William Savernak household (Bridport, Dorset) during the mid-fifteenth century.[24]

* * * * *

24 E.H. Phelps Brown and Sheila Hopkins 'Seven Centuries of the Prices of Consumables, Compared with Builders' Wage-Rates' in Carus-Wilson ed *Essays* II 180, 182. They calculated the Savernak household budget from K.L. Wood-Legh *A Small Household of the Fifteenth Century* (London 1956).

A comparison of the price and wage data indices in tables C and E reveals some significant differences. Thus, while the price level at Antwerp in 1510–14 was almost 20 per cent higher than it had been in 1500–4, the English price levels in these two quinquenniums were virtually identical. Most of Antwerp's inflation had occurred in the third quinquennium, during which prices (except wheat prices) had actually soared by 40 per cent. England, to be sure, also experienced some price increases in that same period, but not quite enough in fact to compensate fully for the price decreases of the middle quinquennium. Antwerp's dramatic and peculiar inflation may be attributed in part to a conjunction of factors that did not then significantly affect England: the South German, Fugger-dominated mining boom that was sending a rising tide of silver into the Antwerp mint; Maximilian's wars in nearby Gelderland and northern France, the latter resulting in his conquest of Tournai (1513); the rapid growth in Antwerp's population, with a consequent building boom; and Antwerp's explosive economic expansion as the newly established commercial, banking, and financial capital of early modern Europe.[25] Without equivalent inflationary pressures the money wages of the Oxford and Cambridge masons remained perfectly stable, at 6d sterling per day, over almost all of this period (1503–14), while the Antwerp mason's daily summer wage rose from an equivalent of 5.73d sterling (= 8.33d gros) to one of 6.88d sterling (= 10d gros) during the third quinquennium. Whether or not the 'Oxbridge' masons' *real* wages fared better or worse than those of their Antwerp colleagues over the entire period may be discovered from table 3. It compares the purchasing power of the average daily wage of the two groups of masons in terms of the five commodities common to tables C and E, for the entire period 1500–14 and then for the first and third quinquenniums. The average quantities of these five commodities that could have been so purchased have again been calculated according to the harmonic mean; and the percentages in the last three columns indicate by a plus or minus sign whether the Oxbridge mason could have purchased that much more or less of these goods, respectively, than the Antwerp mason.

A fair comparison of these masons' standards of living cannot really be made, of course, without a great deal more information: the number of days

* * * * *

25 Cf Van der Wee *Antwerp Market* I 546–7; II 113–42; J.U. Nef 'Mining and Metallurgy in Medieval Civilisation' *Cambridge Economic History* (1952) II 469–72; J.H. Munro 'Bruges and the Abortive Staple in English Cloth: An Incident in the Shift of Commerce from Bruges to Antwerp in the Late Fifteenth Century' *Revue belge de philologie et d'histoire* 44 (1966) 1137–59; Etienne Sabbe *Anvers, métropole de l'occident, 1492–1566* (Brussels 1952); Richard Ehrenberg *Capital and Finance in the Age of the Renaissance: A Study of the Fuggers and Their Connections* (New York 1928) 66–72, 234–8, 255–60.

Table 3 A comparison of the purchasing power of the daily summer wages of masons at Cambridge and Oxford and at Antwerp 1500 to 1514

	average quantities of goods purchasable by a mason's daily wage 1500–14		percentage advantage (+) or disadvantage (−) of the English mason in the purchasing power of his wages		
commodity	Cambridge & Oxford	Antwerp	1500–14	1500–4[1]	1510–14[1]
wheat: bushels	0.592	0.568	+4.38	−11.2	+8.7
wine: litres	3.326	2.859	+16.34	+11.8	+18.9
red herrings	43.640	42.350	+3.05	−1.6	+2.6
sugar: pounds	1.55	1.74	−10.97	−13.2	−16.3
candles: pounds	5.35	4.26	+25.56	+15.1	+22.60
average daily summer wage	5.90 d st. = 4.248 grams silver	5.882d st. = 8.555d gr. = 4.233 grams silver[2]	−0.50	−0.31	−3.03

1 For the actual quantities see the averages (harmonic means) for these years in tables C and E.

2 By the silver standard of the double-patard (4d gros); by that of the patard-stuiver, as reduced from May 1499, it would have been just 4.179 grams silver. Cf CWE I 340, and note 2 (in appendix B).

per year worked by the Oxbridge masons; the average number of dependents that each mason had to support (and conversely the incomes of other members of the family); expenditure distributions and popular consumption patterns, with a much broader and more representative list of consumer goods. The statistical comparison itself, moreover, is somewhat vitiated by the frequent lacunae in the English price data, and perhaps also by Thorold Rogers' sampling techniques, so that the harmonic means calculated for the Oxbridge masons' purchasing power may be distorted. Indeed so vociferous have been the objections to Thorold Rogers' wheat price statistics that I have instead substituted in table 3 those of the late Lord William Beveridge, which statistics, although unfortunately coming from a different region (Exeter), command universal respect.[26] The har-

* * * * *

26 The wheat price statistics for Exeter have been converted from the Winchester quarter to the Imperial quarter (of 8 bushels) = 1.0309 Winchester quarters. Cf B.R. Mitchell and P. Deane eds *Abstract of British Historical Statistics* (Cambridge 1962) 484. Thorold Rogers' wheat prices, though taken largely from the Oxford and Cambridge regions, are not based on one consistent source. The quinquennial averages (harmonic means) of the purchasing power of the Oxbridge masons' daily wage in terms of Thorold Rogers' wheat statistics are as follows: 0.560 bu. for 1500–4; 0.882 bu. for 1505–9; and 0.663 bu. for 1510–14.

monic mean calculated from these wheat statistics for the entire period does show a remarkable concordance with that calculated from the Antwerp (Lier) wheat statistics. An even closer and more consistent concordance is revealed in comparing the harmonic means calculated from the two sets of herring statistics. The most surprising divergence is found in the wine statistics, since, as tables A.1 and B.1 show, an English penny in 1500 could have purchased about equal amounts of Rhine and Bordeaux red wines. As those tables also show, the reason for the subsequent divergence is the very sharp rise in the prices of Rhine wines, especially after 1510. One might expect sugar to have been relatively cheaper at Antwerp, since that port had become the European staple for the sale and distribution of the Portuguese-dominated sugar supplies. The continuous gap in the candle statistics cannot be explained, except perhaps by differences in quality, or taxes levied – or by statistical error. Finally, the over-all impression produced by this table is that, thanks chiefly to greater price stability in England, the Oxbridge masons did fare somewhat better in their real wages over this period, especially in the third quinquennium. Indeed if we are to believe the wage and price statistics produced by Thorold Rogers, G.F. Steffen, Lord Beveridge, Phelps Brown and Hopkins, and others, these first fifteen years of the sixteenth century marked the very end of a century-long Golden Age for the English artisan, in terms of low consumer prices and thus of high real wages.[27] Thereafter his real income was supposedly ravaged by the inflations of the so-called Price Revolution, reaching a dismal nadir during the reign of King James I (1603–25), and really not fully recovering until the late nineteenth century.[28] That aged hypothesis still awaits a conclusive test. The statistical researches of Verlinden, Craeybeckx, Scholliers, and Van der Wee on Brabantine wage and price data suggest neither an equivalent Golden Age in the later fifteenth century, nor, during the sixteenth century, such a reduction in real wages. Instead, real wages at the end of that century appear to have been on about the same level as those of 1500. At the same time they conclude that the average artisan's real income was never too far above the margin of subsistence.[29]

* * * * *

27 Cf Phelps Brown and Hopkins 'Seven Centuries of the Prices of Consumables' in Carus-Wilson ed *Essays*, II 183–6, 194–5; G.F. Steffen *Studien zur Geschichte der englischen Lohnarbeiter* I (1901) 112, tables I and II.

28 Cf figure 3 in Phelps Brown and Hopkins ibid 186.

29 Verlinden, Craeybeckx, and Scholliers 'Price and Wage Movements in Belgium' *Economy and Society* 72–81. The one period in which real wages did appear to deteriorate is from 1521 to 1556, but not by as much as the supposed fall in English real wages.

TABLE F

Prices of dyed woollen cloths of Mechlin and Ghent 1500 to 1514

For two reasons it is entirely appropriate that a table on Flemish and Brabantine luxury cloth prices should conclude this series. First, these woollens are by far the most expensive commodity that one could list in these tables; and a contrast of their prices with those for herring, in table A.IV, one of the cheapest of the commodities (just after eggs), highlights a fundamental and far-reaching change that was then occurring in the economy of the Burgundian-Hapsburg Low Countries. Until Erasmus' early youth that economy had been dominated for centuries by the cloth-manufacturing towns of Flanders and Brabant, which had marketed their luxury woollens chiefly at Bruges to foreign merchants who had sold them all across Europe. But by the time that Erasmus entered manhood, the Low Countries' centre of economic gravity was clearly shifting from Bruges to Antwerp, in part because English woollens were, finally, decisively displacing the Flemish-Brabantine cloths from the international luxury markets; in so doing English cloth had found its chief and best outlet at Antwerp.[30] At this great international entrepôt the South German merchants had gained ascendancy by exchanging their large amounts of silver, copper, fustian textiles, Rhenish wines, and other goods with merchants from all over the continent; in return they purchased a goodly share of the English cloths, dyed and dressed mainly at Antwerp itself, which they marketed throughout central and eastern Europe. Then the Portuguese establishment of their spice staple at Antwerp and the development of South German banking completed the pillars of that port's economic hegemony, which would last until the 1560s. But in the meantime the Dutch were building a much more broadly based, more powerful economy which would give them, Amsterdam especially, that hegemony in European commerce and finance from the 1560s to the 1760s, when it was finally undermined by the coming of the English Industrial Revolution. The earliest, perhaps the strongest and longest-lasting, foundation of Dutch economic power was the herring fisheries, which the States-General of 1606 rightly called 'one of the Chiefest Mines of the Netherlands.'[31] The great

* * * * *

30 Munro 'Bruges and the Abortive Staple in English Cloth'; Munro *Wool, Cloth, and Gold*, 181–5; Van der Wee *Antwerp Market* II 119–42.

31 George Masselman *The Cradle of Colonialism* (New Haven 1963) 12, citing the entry of 19 July 1606 in *Groot Placet-boeck van de Staten Generaal*. Cf Thomas Mun *England's Treasure By Forraign Trade* (1664) 75: 'The great Fishing and catching of Herrings is the chiefest trade and principal Gold Mine of the United Provinces ...'; and also Van der Wee *Antwerp Market* I 277–8.

economic importance of herring was that it was a most abundant, very cheap, and highly nutritious foodstuff which, when salted and cured, could be transported over very long distances and stored for considerable periods. It thus served as one of the most important and best supplements to the diet of farinaceous foods for the masses in an age when meat and livestock products were quite expensive and, especially in the winter months, relatively rare commodities. Despite the undue attention that historians have given to the later Dutch spice trade from the East Indies, the other chief components of their commercial and shipping power were Baltic grains, lumber, naval stores, and salt – all at opposite poles from the luxury woollens of Flanders and Brabant.

Thus the second point of significance about this table of woollen cloth prices is that it lifts us dramatically from the world of the building-artisan to those higher and vastly more prosperous levels of society with which Erasmus was wont to consort. These woollen cloths are indeed one of the very few articles of aristocratic consumption that we can currently document and price. The price statistics themselves come from my own researches on the Ghent and Mechlin civic financial accounts, which record the purchases of each town's finest woollens, respectively, to garb the burgermasters and aldermen (schepenen, échevins) on ceremonial occasions. The Mechlin cloth prices are perhaps the better of the two in that the cloths purchased are virtually always of one colour and type – the black Rooslakens – and both the dimensions and the price per ell are always explicitly stated. The Ghent cloths, generally if not always described as Dickedinnen lakens of 30 ells, were of various colours, chiefly blue, black, and green; but at least some measure of quality control was maintained by selecting only those cloths purchased to dress the aldermen in attendance at the annual festival of Onse Lieve Vrouw of Tournai. The fact that, in both the Ghent and Mechlin accounts, the entries record purchases over the year from various, specifically named cloth merchants at slightly differing prices – prices which have been averaged for this table – would suggest that these are market rather than 'contract' prices.

The Ghent accounts in particular also make clear in their *prosenten* entries that these woollens are the very same cloths that the town would on occasion present as gifts to kings, dukes, and archbishops. They were indeed a very special type of woollen cloth, no longer manufactured, made from extremely fine, short-stapled English wools.[32] Unlike today's

* * * * *

32 Munro *Wool, Cloth, and Gold* 1–9; Peter Bowden *The Wool Trade in Tudor and Stuart England* (London 1962) 25–37. Cf also the sources cited in note 33.

worsted-type cloths, they were heavily fulled (felted) after weaving; and the nap was then teasled and shorn several times, so that the weave was quite indistinguishable. Once dyed and dressed, they fully rivalled the better silks in the quality of texture and of workmanship – and indeed also in price. A sixteenth-century ordinance of Ghent stipulated that the town's 'five-seals' Dickedinnen cloths be made according to the following specifications:[33]

1 wools to be used, exclusively: fine 'March' wools of Shropshire and Herefordshire, or Cotswold and Berkshire wools
2 dimensions on the weaving-loom: 42.5 ells by 14.5 quarter-ells = 32.535 yards by 2.775 yards = 90.285 square yards
3 number of warp-threads for the width: 2066 (= 744.5 per yard)
4 weight on the weaving-loom: 88 Ghent lb = 84.2 lb avoirdupois
5 dimensions after fulling: 30 ells by 9.5 quarters = 22.966 yards by 1.818 yards = 41.752 square yards
6 final weight after shearing: 51 Ghent lb = 48.8 lb avoirdupois (= 1.169 lb per square yard).

That such cloths were quite different from and vastly more expensive than the 'Sunday-best' cloths that a well-to-do peasant or master-artisan might purchase as a 'luxury' is demonstrated by columns 5 and 9 of table F. Clearly not many Antwerp masons were going to purchase woollens that would cost them from 12.5 to 15 days' wages, or more, for just one yard – unless, of course, they happened to be guild leaders who served as civic aldermen.[34] These luxury woollens were one commodity whose *real* price

* * * * *

33 M.J. Lameere, H. Simont, et al eds *Recueil des ordonnances des Pays Bas: deuxième série 1506–1700* (Brussels 1910) v 272–83 (ordinance of 1546). Cf also M.G. Willemsen ed 'Le règlement général de la draperie malinoise de 1544' *Bulletin du cercle archéologique de Malines* 20 (1910) 156–90

34 The Mechlin town council purchased each year (from the late fifteenth century) the following amounts of cloth for its leading officials:
1 for each of the four Rentmeesters and eighteen aldermen (schepenen): 10 ells by 2.5 ells of black Rooslakens = 7.535 yds by 1.884 yds = 14.196 square yds, costing £3.544 gros Flemish, on the average, in 1510–14;
2 for each of the two deans of the cloth guilds (dekenen van de wolle werke): half a black Rooslaken, and thus 15 ells each = 11.303 yds by 1.884 yds = 21.295 square yds, costing £5.316 gros Flemish, on the average in 1510–14;
3 for each of the seven jurés of the cloth guilds (ghezwoorenen van de wolle werke): 6 ells of 'zwart lakenen van 5 loyen' (black cloths of 5 seals, at varying prices) = 4.521 yds by 1.884 yds = 8.518 square yds.
Stadsarchief van Mechelen, Stadsrekeningen series I, nos 167, f 146^v (1491–2); no 179, f 177^v (1503–4); no 183, f 177^r (1507–8); no 185, f 177^r (1509–10)

Table 4 Quinquennial averages of the exports of fine woollen cloths from London and by Mechlin 1490–4 to 1510–14

quinquennium	London: broadcloth exports	index 1500–4 = 100	Mechlin: cloth exports	index 1500–4 = 100
1490–4	36,995	77.1	2,108	81.2
1495–9	41,823	87.1	2,410	92.9
1500–4	47,993	100.0	2,595	100.0
1505–9	50,501	105.2	1,905	73.4
1510–4	59,305	123.6	1,842	71.0

SOURCES

1 London: calculated from E.M. Carus-Wilson and Olive Coleman *England's Export Trade, 1275–1547* (Oxford 1963) 110–13 (broadcloths of 24 yards by 7 quarter-yards).

2 Mechlin: calculated from the accounts of 'la clergie de la doyenne de la draperie de Malines' (Mechelen clergie-geld), an export tax, in Algemeen Rijskarchief van België, Rekenkamer nos 11, 613–28. A graph based on these accounts has been published in R. Van Uytven 'De omvang van de Mechelse lakenproduktie vanaf de 14e tot de 16e eeuw' *Noordgouw* 5 (1965) 14, graph 3.

had markedly increased, virtually doubled, over the previous century. Thus in 1410–14 one yard of Ghent Dickedinnen cloths of the type purchased for the Tournai festival, then priced at £5.641 gros Flemish per piece of 30 ells, would have cost the Antwerp mason just 7.85 days' wages – still considerably beyond his reach. By Erasmus' day the luxury woollens of Flanders and Brabant had been clearly priced out of almost all the international markets, especially since the better quality English woollens were then costing only about £3.00 sterling or £4.36 gros Flemish,[35] compared to £13.00 gros Flemish for the Ghent Dickedinnen cloths. To be sure, the Ghent and Mechlin luxury draperies were still in existence, but only as remnants of the former *grande industrie*, surviving rather precariously by catering to a very small, select, most aristocratic clientele that was more conscious of traditional values than of price. The concluding statistics, given in table 4, suggest the nature and degree of the English victory in the European cloth trade that was taking place during these years from Erasmus' young manhood to middle age.

* * * * *

35 Calculated from the 'Particulars' accounts books of the Subsidy of Tunnage and Poundage, King's Rembrancer Exchequer, Customs (port books for London 1509–14, and Southhampton 1500–1): Public Record Office E 122/81/1–3, and 209/2a–2b

TABLE A

THE PURCHASING POWER OF COINAGE IN THE LOW COUNTRIES 1500 TO 1514

The quantities of various commodities that could be purchased by the gold and silver coinages of the Burgundian-Hapsburg Low Countries, France, Italy, and England, at Antwerp and neighbouring towns in Brabant, according to their current prices in Flemish gros, annually and in quinquennial averages†

		relative quantities that could be purchased by							
		silver coins			gold coins				
year	price in Flemish gros	Burgundian stuiver (patard) = 2.000d*	French douzain = 2.066d*	English penny = 1.45d*	Burgundian florin St Philip = 50d*	French écu à la couronne = 71d*	Italian florin or ducat = 79d*	English angel-noble = 116d*	quantity index 1500–4 = 100
1 Red Rhine wine, as sold at Lier (priced in litres = about 35 oz)									
1500	2.46d	0.81	0.84	0.59	20.29	28.80	32.05	47.06	114.3
1501	2.82d	0.71	0.73	0.52	17.75	25.21	28.05	41.18	100.0
1502	3.17d	0.63	0.65	0.46	15.78	22.41	24.93	36.61	88.9
1503	2.82d	0.71	0.73	0.52	17.75	25.21	28.05	41.18	100.0
1504	2.82d	0.71	0.73	0.52	17.75	25.21	28.05	41.18	100.0
average	2.82d	0.71	0.73	0.52	17.75	25.21	28.05	41.18	100.0
1505	2.64d	0.76	0.78	0.55	18.94	26.89	29.92	43.93	106.7
1506	2.99d	0.67	0.69	0.49	16.71	23.72	26.40	38.76	94.1
1507	3.17d	0.63	0.65	0.46	15.78	22.41	24.93	36.61	88.9
1508	2.82d	0.71	0.73	0.52	17.75	25.21	28.05	41.18	100.0
1509	2.82d	0.71	0.73	0.52	17.75	25.21	28.05	41.18	100.0
average	2.89d	0.69	0.72	0.50	17.32	24.59	27.36	40.18	97.6
1510	2.82d	0.71	0.73	0.52	17.75	25.21	28.05	41.18	100.0
1511	2.99d	0.67	0.69	0.49	16.71	23.72	26.40	38.76	94.1
1512	3.52d	0.57	0.59	0.41	14.20	20.16	22.44	32.94	80.0
1513	3.52d	0.57	0.59	0.41	14.20	20.16	22.44	32.94	80.0
1514	3.52d	0.57	0.59	0.41	14.20	20.16	22.44	32.94	80.0
average	3.27d	0.61	0.63	0.44	15.27	21.68	24.13	35.42	86.0

† Averages of prices calculated by the arithmetic mean; averages of quantities and their index numbers calculated by the corresponding harmonic mean. The average of 1500–4 = 100 as the base of the index.

* Value of the coin in Flemish gros

TABLE A (continued)

		relative quantities that could be purchased by							
		silver coins			gold coins				
year	price in Flemish gros	Burgundian stuiver (patard) =2.000d*	French douzain =2.066d*	English penny =1.45d*	Burgundian florin St Philip =50d*	French écu à la couronne =71d*	Italian florin or ducat =79d*	English angel-noble =116d*	quantity index 1500–4 =100
II Butter, as sold at Brussels (priced in pounds avoirdupois)									
1500	1.35d	1.48	1.53	1.08	37.09	52.67	58.60	86.05	109.9
1501	1.51d	1.32	1.37	0.96	33.05	46.92	52.21	76.67	98.0
1502	1.41d	1.42	1.46	1.03	35.43	50.31	55.98	82.20	105.0
1503	1.59d	1.26	1.30	0.91	31.43	44.64	49.67	72.93	93.2
1504	1.55d	1.29	1.34	0.94	32.32	45.89	51.07	74.98	95.8
average	1.48d	1.35	1.39	0.98	33.74	47.91	53.31	78.27	100.0
1505	1.54d	1.30	1.34	0.94	32.42	46.04	51.22	75.21	96.1
1506	1.37d	1.46	1.51	1.06	36.56	51.92	57.76	84.82	108.4
1507	1.71d	1.17	1.21	0.85	29.21	41.48	46.15	67.77	86.6
1508	1.51d	1.32	1.37	0.96	33.05	46.92	52.21	76.66	98.0
1509	1.47d	1.36	1.41	0.99	34.03	48.32	53.77	78.95	100.9
average	1.52d	1.32	1.35	0.96	32.88	46.69	51.95	76.28	97.5
1510	1.75d	1.15	1.18	0.83	28.64	40.67	45.25	66.44	84.9
1511	1.97d	1.02	1.05	0.74	25.40	36.06	40.12	58.92	75.3
1512	2.13d	0.94	0.97	0.68	23.44	33.28	37.03	54.37	69.5
1513	2.21d	0.90	0.93	0.66	22.61	32.11	35.72	52.46	67.0
1514	2.13d	0.94	0.97	0.68	23.44	33.28	37.03	54.37	69.5
average	2.04d	0.98	1.01	0.71	24.53	34.83	38.75	56.90	72.7

* Value of coin in Flemish gros

TABLE A (continued)

		relative quantities that could be purchased by							
		silver coins			gold coins				
year	price in Flemish gros	Burgundian stuiver (patard) = 2.000d*	French douzain = 2.066d*	English penny = 1.45d*	Burgundian florin St Philip = 50d*	French écu à la couronne = 71d*	Italian florin or ducat = 79d*	English angel-noble = 116d*	quantity index 1500–4 = 100
III Salt beef, as sold at Mechlin (priced in pounds avoirdupois)									
1500	0.85d	2.36	2.44	1.72	59.12	83.94	93.40	137.15	95.9
1501	0.72d	2.76	2.85	2.01	68.97	97.93	108.96	160.00	111.9
1502	0.83d	2.41	2.49	1.75	60.32	85.65	95.31	139.94	97.9
1503	0.83d	2.41	2.49	1.75	60.32	85.65	95.31	139.94	97.9
1504	0.83d	2.41	2.49	1.75	60.32	85.65	95.31	139.94	97.9
average	0.81d	2.46	2.55	1.79	61.61	87.49	97.35	142.95	100.0
1505	0.97d	2.07	2.14	1.50	51.73	73.45	81.73	120.00	84.0
1506	0.83d	2.41	2.49	1.75	60.32	85.65	95.31	139.94	97.9
1507	0.82d	2.43	2.52	1.77	60.86	86.41	96.15	141.18	98.8
1508	0.72d	2.76	2.85	2.01	68.97	97.93	108.96	160.00	111.9
1509	0.71d	2.81	2.90	2.04	70.14	99.59	110.81	162.71	113.8
average	0.81d	2.46	2.55	1.79	61.65	87.55	97.41	143.03	100.1
1510	0.69d	2.92	3.02	2.12	72.99	103.64	115.32	169.33	118.5
1511	0.66d	3.04	3.14	2.21	76.07	108.01	120.18	176.47	123.5
1512	0.68d	2.92	3.02	2.12	73.03	103.70	115.39	169.43	118.5
1513	0.75d	2.66	2.75	1.94	66.53	94.47	105.11	154.35	108.0
1514	0.76d	2.62	2.70	1.90	65.39	92.85	103.31	151.69	106.1
average	0.71d	2.82	2.92	2.05	70.56	100.19	111.48	163.69	114.5

* Value of coin in Flemish gros

TABLE A (continued)

		relative quantities that could be purchased by							
		silver coins			gold coins				
year	price in Flemish gros	Burgundian stuiver (patard) =2.000d*	French douzain =2.066d*	English penny =1.45d*	Burgundian florin St Philip =50d*	French écu à la couronne =71d*	Italian florin or ducat =79d*	English angel-noble =116d*	quantity index 1500–4 = 100
IV Flemish smoked red herrings, as sold at Mechlin (priced by the number)									
1500	0.19d	10.42	10.76	7.58	260.4	369.8	411.5	604.2	91.3
1501	0.20d	9.80	10.13	7.13	245.1	348.0	387.3	568.6	85.9
1502	0.19d	10.42	10.76	7.58	260.4	369.8	411.5	604.2	91.3
1503	0.14d	13.89	14.35	10.10	347.2	493.1	548.6	805.6	121.7
1504	0.14d	13.89	14.35	10.10	347.2	493.1	548.6	805.6	121.7
average	0.18d	11.42	11.80	8.30	285.4	405.3	450.9	662.1	100.0
1505	0.18d	11.36	11.74	8.26	284.1	403.4	448.9	659.1	99.6
1506	0.28d	7.25	7.49	5.27	181.2	257.3	286.2	420.3	63.5
1507	0.17d	12.12	12.53	8.82	303.0	430.3	478.8	703.0	106.2
1508	0.23d	8.75	9.04	6.36	218.7	310.5	345.5	507.3	76.6
1509	0.19d	10.73	11.09	7.81	268.3	381.0	424.0	622.5	94.0
average	0.21d	9.69	10.01	7.05	242.2	344.0	382.8	562.0	84.9
1510	0.14d	13.89	14.35	10.10	347.2	493.1	548.6	805.6	121.7
1511	0.23d	8.77	9.06	6.38	219.3	311.4	346.5	508.8	76.8
1512	0.22d	9.09	9.39	6.61	227.3	322.7	359.1	527.3	79.6
1513	0.22d	9.15	9.46	6.66	228.8	325.0	361.6	530.9	80.2
1514	0.31d	6.41	6.62	4.66	160.3	227.6	253.2	371.8	56.2
average	0.22d	8.91	9.21	6.48	222.7	316.3	351.9	516.7	78.0

* Value of coin in Flemish gros

TABLE A (continued)

		relative quantities that could be purchased by							
		silver coins			gold coins				
year	price in Flemish gros	Burgundian stuiver (patard) =2.000d*	French douzain =2.066d*	English penny =1.45d*	Burgundian florin St Philip =50d*	French écu à la couronne =71d*	Italian florin or ducat =79d*	English angel-noble =116d*	quantity index 1500–4 =100
v Eggs, as sold at Brussels (priced by the number)									
1500	0.10d	20.9	21.6	15.2	521.9	741.1	824.6	1210.9	100.0
1501	–	–	–	–	–	–	–	–	
1502	–	–	–	–	–	–	–	–	–
1503	–	–	–	–	–	–	–	–	–
1504	–	–	–	–	–	–	–	–	–
average	[0.10d]	[20.9]	[21.6]	[15.2]	[521.9]	[741.1]	[824.6]	[1210.9]	[100.0]
1505	0.11d	17.5	18.1	12.7	437.8	621.7	691.8	1015.8	83.9
1506	0.10d	20.0	20.7	14.5	500.0	710.0	790.0	1160.0	95.8
1507	0.10d	19.8	20.4	14.4	494.6	702.3	781.4	1147.4	94.8
1508	0.11d	18.2	18.8	13.2	454.6	645.5	718.2	1054.6	87.1
1509	0.11d	17.7	18.2	12.8	441.3	626.7	697.3	1023.8	84.6
average	0.11d	18.6	19.2	13.5	464.2	659.1	733.4	1076.9	88.9
1510	0.12d	17.0	17.6	12.4	425.5	604.3	672.3	987.2	81.5
1511	0.10d	19.6	20.2	14.2	489.2	694.7	773.0	1135.0	93.7
1512	0.11d	17.7	18.2	12.8	441.3	626.7	697.3	1023.8	84.6
1513	0.11d	18.2	18.8	13.2	454.6	645.5	718.2	1054.6	87.1
1514	0.12d	17.4	18.0	12.6	434.8	617.4	687.0	1008.7	83.3
average	0.11d	17.9	18.5	13.0	448.0	636.2	707.9	1039.4	85.8

* Value of coin in Flemish gros

TABLE A (continued)

year	price in Flemish gros	silver coins: Burgundian stuiver (patard) =2.000d*	French douzain =2.066d*	English penny =1.45d*	gold coins: Burgundian florin St Philip =50d*	French écu à la couronne =71d*	Italian florin or ducat =79d*	English angel-noble =116d*	quantity index 1500–4 =100
		relative quantities that could be purchased by							
VI Loaf sugar, as sold at Antwerp (priced in pounds avoirdupois)									
1500	3.86d	0.52	0.54	0.38	12.96	18.40	20.47	30.06	94.6
1501	4.26d	0.47	0.48	0.34	11.73	16.65	18.53	27.20	85.6
1502	3.38d	0.59	0.61	0.43	14.81	21.02	23.39	34.35	108.1
1503	3.38d	0.59	0.61	0.43	14.81	21.02	23.39	34.35	108.1
1504	3.38d	0.59	0.61	0.43	14.81	21.02	23.39	34.35	108.1
average	3.65d	0.55	0.57	0.40	13.70	19.45	21.64	31.77	100.0
1505	4.10d	0.49	0.50	0.35	12.19	17.32	19.27	28.29	89.0
1506	3.62d	0.55	0.57	0.40	13.82	19.62	21.84	32.06	100.9
1507	4.21d	0.48	0.49	0.35	11.89	16.88	18.78	27.58	86.8
1508	4.34d	0.46	0.48	0.34	11.52	16.35	18.20	26.72	84.1
1509	4.34d	0.46	0.48	0.34	11.52	16.35	18.20	26.72	84.1
average	4.12d	0.49	0.50	0.35	12.13	17.23	19.17	28.15	88.6
1510	4.58d	0.44	0.45	0.32	10.91	15.49	17.24	25.31	79.7
1511	4.34d	0.46	0.48	0.34	11.52	16.35	18.19	26.71	84.1
1512	9.65d	0.21	0.21	0.15	5.19	7.36	8.19	12.03	37.8
1513	8.68d	0.23	0.24	0.17	5.76	8.18	9.10	13.36	42.0
1514	7.72d	0.26	0.27	0.19	6.48	9.20	10.24	15.03	47.3
average	6.99d	0.29	0.30	0.21	7.15	10.15	11.29	16.58	52.2

* Value of coin in Flemish gros

TABLE A (continued)

		relative quantities that could be purchased by							
		silver coins			gold coins				
year	price in Flemish gros	Burgundian stuiver (patard) =2.000d*	French douzain =2.066d*	English penny =1.45d*	Burgundian florin St Philip =50d*	French écu à la couronne =71d*	Italian florin or ducat =79d*	English angel-noble =116d*	quantity index 1500–4 =100
VII Tallow candles, as sold at Antwerp, Lier, Mechlin, and Brussels (priced in pounds avoirdupois)									
1500	1.81d	1.10	1.14	0.80	27.58	39.16	43.57	63.97	103.7
1501	1.75d	1.14	1.18	0.83	28.53	40.51	45.07	66.18	107.2
1502	1.90d	1.05	1.09	0.76	26.26	37.29	41.49	60.92	98.7
1503	1.93d	1.03	1.07	0.75	25.85	36.71	40.84	59.97	97.2
1504	1.99d	1.00	1.04	0.73	25.07	35.59	39.60	58.15	94.2
average	1.88d	1.06	1.10	0.77	26.60	37.77	42.03	61.71	100.0
1505	1.99d	1.00	1.04	0.73	25.07	35.59	39.60	58.15	94.2
1506	2.06d	0.97	1.01	0.71	24.33	34.55	38.44	56.45	91.5
1507	2.06d	0.97	1.01	0.71	24.33	34.55	38.44	56.45	91.5
1508	2.16d	0.93	0.96	0.67	23.20	32.94	36.65	53.81	87.2
1509	2.18d	0.92	0.95	0.67	22.98	32.63	36.31	53.31	86.4
average	2.09d	0.96	0.99	0.70	23.96	34.02	37.85	55.58	90.1
1510	2.08d	0.96	1.00	0.70	24.09	34.21	38.06	55.89	90.6
1511	2.04d	0.98	1.01	0.71	24.49	34.78	38.69	56.82	92.1
1512	1.93d	1.03	1.07	0.75	25.85	36.71	40.84	59.97	97.2
1513	2.06d	0.97	1.01	0.71	24.33	34.55	38.44	56.45	91.5
1514	2.18d	0.92	0.95	0.67	22.98	32.63	36.31	53.31	86.4
average	2.06d	0.97	1.01	0.71	24.31	34.52	38.41	56.41	91.4

SOURCES

Coinage values: CWE I 312, 314–18, 327, 331, 336–41 (appendixes A and B)
Prices: calculated from Herman Van der Wee *Growth of the Antwerp Market and the European Economy, Fourteenth to Sixteenth Centuries* I (The Hague 1963) 298, 214, 226, 285, 207, 320, and 252 respectively

* Value of coin in Flemish gros

TABLE B

THE PURCHASING POWER OF THE ENGLISH COINAGE AT CAMBRIDGE AND OXFORD 1500 TO 1514

The quantities of various commodities that could have been purchased by the silver penny and the gold angel-noble (6s 8d ster) in the Cambridge and Oxford regions, according to their current prices in pence sterling, annually and in quinquennial avarages[1]

	I Bordeaux red wine (claret)				II North Sea smoked red herrings			
year	price: pence per litre	litres per penny	litres per gold angel-noble	quantity index 1500–4 = 100	price: pence per herring	number per penny	number per gold angel-noble	quantity index 1500–4 = 100
1500	1.76d	0.57	45.46	97.9	0.096d	10.4	833.3	126.9
1501	–	–	–	–	0.128d	7.8	625.0	95.2
1502	1.76d	0.57	45.46	97.9	0.142d	7.1	565.4	86.1
1503	1.65d	0.61	48.49	104.4	–	–	–	–
1504	–	–	–	–	–	–	–	–
average	1.72d	0.58	46.43	100.0	0.122d	8.2	656.8	100.0
1505	–	–	–	–	–	–	–	–
1506	1.83d	0.55	43.64	94.0	–	–	–	–
1507	1.76d	0.57	45.46	97.9	–	–	–	–
1508	1.71d	0.59	46.93	101.1	0.140d	7.1	571.4	87.9
1509	–	–	–	–	0.136d	7.4	588.2	89.6
average	1.77d	0.57	45.30	97.6	0.138d	7.2	579.7	88.3
1510	1.76d	0.57	45.46	97.9	0.144d	7.0	557.5	84.9
1511	–	–	–	–	0.161d	6.2	498.4	75.9
1512	1.98d	0.51	40.41	87.0	0.130d	7.7	615.4	93.7
1513	–	–	–	–	0.135d	7.4	592.6	90.2
1514	1.76d	0.57	45.46	97.9	0.160d	6.3	500.0	76.1
average	1.83d	0.55	43.64	94.0	0.146d	6.9	548.7	83.6

1 Averages of prices calculated by the arithmetic mean; averages of quantities and their index numbers calculated by the corresponding harmonic mean. The averages of 1500–4 = 100 as the base of the index.

	III codfish (Orkneys & Iceland)				IV green garden peas			
year	price: pence per codfish	number per penny	number per gold angel-noble	quantity index 1500–4 = 100	price: pence per gallon	gallons per penny	gallons per gold angel-noble	quantity index 1500–4 = 100
1500	5.28d	0.19	15.15	83.4	0.71d	1.41	113.15	100.8
1501	2.80d	0.36	28.57	157.2	–	–	–	–
1502	4.89d	0.20	16.36	90.0	–	–	–	–
1503	3.04d	0.33	26.32	144.8	0.72d	1.39	111.30	99.2
1504	6.00d	0.17	13.33	73.4	–	–	–	–
average	4.40d	0.23	18.17	100.0	0.71d	1.40	112.22	100.0
1505	3.00d	0.33	26.67	146.7	0.56d	1.78	142.22	126.7
1506	2.80d	0.36	28.57	157.2	0.75d	1.33	106.67	95.1
1507	2.88d	0.35	27.78	152.8	1.00d	1.00	80.00	71.3
1508	2.80d	0.36	28.57	157.2	0.49d	2.05	163.84	146.0
1509	2.76d	0.36	28.99	159.5	0.73d	1.36	108.94	97.1
average	2.85d	0.35	28.09	154.6	0.71d	1.41	113.15	100.8
1510	2.44d	0.41	32.79	180.4	0.68d	1.47	117.70	104.9
1511	–	–	–	–	0.80d	1.25	100.39	89.5
1512	–	–	–	–	0.97d	1.03	82.58	73.6
1513	5.20d	0.19	15.38	84.7	1.14d	0.88	70.14	62.5
1514	5.80d	0.17	13.79	75.9	1.41d	0.71	56.89	50.7
average	4.48d	0.22	17.86	98.3	1.00d	1.00	80.12	71.4

TABLE B (continued)

	V loaf sugar				VI tallow candles			
year	price: pence per pound	pounds per penny	pounds per gold angel-noble	quantity index 1500–4 = 100	price: pence per pound	pounds per penny	pounds per gold angel-noble	quantity index 1500–4 = 100
1500	–	–	–	–	1.00d	1.00	80.00	111.7
1501	3.00d	0.33	26.67	95.8	1.00d	1.00	80.00	111.7
1502	–	–	–	–	1.23d	0.81	65.08	90.8
1503	2.75d	0.36	29.09	104.5	1.19d	0.84	67.37	94.0
1504	–	–	–	–	1.17d	0.86	68.57	95.7
average	2.88d	0.35	27.83	100.0	1.12d	0.90	71.64	100.0
1505	3.00d	0.33	26.67	95.8	1.00d	1.00	80.00	111.7
1506	–	–	–	–	1.08d	0.92	73.85	103.1
1507	–	–	–	–	1.17d	0.86	68.57	95.7
1508	–	–	–	–	1.13d	0.89	71.11	99.3
1509	–	–	–	–	1.00d	1.00	80.00	111.7
average	[3.00d]	[0.33]	[26.67]	[95.8]	1.08d	0.93	74.42	103.9
1510	4.00d	0.25	20.00	71.9	1.00d	1.00	80.00	111.7
1511	–	–	–	–	1.00d	1.00	80.00	111.7
1512	6.50d	0.15	12.30	44.2	1.00d	1.00	80.00	111.7
1513	6.50d	0.15	12.30	44.2	1.00d	1.00	80.00	111.7
1514	5.25d	0.19	15.24	54.8	1.58d	0.63	50.53	70.5
average	5.56d	0.18	14.38	51.7	1.12d	0.90	71.64	100.0

	VII writing paper (first quality)				VIII table linen (first quality)			
year	price: pence per 100 sheets	sheets per penny	sheets per gold angel-noble	quantity index 1500–4 = 100	price: pence per yard	yards per penny	yards per gold angel-noble	quantity index 1500–4 = 100
1500	6.25d	16	1280	126.7	12.75d	0.08	6.28	59.0
1501	7.29d	14	1097	108.6	–	–	–	–
1502	8.33d	12	960	95.0	5.00d	0.20	16.00	150.6
1503	9.58d	10	835	82.6	4.83d	0.21	16.55	155.7
1504	8.13d	12	985	97.4	–	–	–	–
average	7.92d	12.6	1010.5	100.0	7.53d	0.13	10.63	100.0
1505	8.13d	12	985	97.4	10.00d	0.10	8.00	75.3
1506	8.33d	12	960	95.0	7.58d	0.13	10.55	99.3
1507	6.67d	15	1200	118.8	–	–	–	–
1508	8.33d	12	960	95.0	–	–	–	–
1509	7.03d	14	1138	112.6	5.50	0.18	14.55	136.9
average	7.70d	13.0	1039.0	102.8	7.69d	0.13	10.40	97.8
1510	6.67d	15	1200	118.8	7.50d	0.13	10.67	100.4
1511	6.67d	15	1200	118.8	–	–	–	–
1512	6.46d	15	1239	122.6	6.00d	0.17	13.33	125.5
1513	7.50d	13	1067	105.6	10.00d	0.10	8.00	75.3
1514	5.00d	20	1600	158.3	–	–	–	–
average	6.46d	15.5	1238.8	122.6	7.83d	0.13	10.21	96.1

SOURCE

James E. Thorold Rogers *A History of Agriculture and Prices in England* IV *1401–1582* (Oxford: Clarendon Press 1882) 636–9, 684–6 (red wine); 526–8, 542–3 (red herrings); 533–6, 543–4 (codfish); 275–6, 287–9 (peas); 674–7, 685–7 (sugar); 367–9, 378–9 (tallow candles); 590–4, 605 (writing paper); 552–63, 586 (table linen)

TABLE C

THE STANDARD OF LIVING OF THE ANTWERP MASON 1500 TO 1514

The daily summer wage of a master mason in Antwerp, and its purchasing power, in terms of quantities of various commodities, expressed in annual and quinquennial averages[1]

year	master mason's daily wage in deniers gros Flemish	wheat in bushels (imperial)	red Rhine wine in litres (35 oz)	butter in pounds avoirdupois	salt beef in pounds avoirdupois
1500	8.33	0.690	3.38	6.18	9.85
1501	8.33	0.508	2.96	5.51	11.49
1502	8.33	0.447	2.63	5.90	10.05
1503	8.33	0.583	2.96	5.24	10.05
1504	8.33	0.556	2.96	5.39	10.05
average	8.33	0.546	2.96	5.62	10.27
1505	8.33	0.498	3.16	5.40	8.62
1506	8.33	0.467	2.78	6.09	10.05
1507	8.33	0.529	2.63	4.87	10.14
1508	8.33	0.635	2.96	5.51	11.49
1509	8.33	0.741	2.96	5.67	11.69
average	8.33	0.558	2.89	5.48	10.28
1510	8.33	0.772	2.96	4.77	12.16
1511	8.33	0.635	2.78	4.23	12.68
1512	8.33	0.525	2.37	3.91	12.17
1513	10.00	0.518	2.84	4.52	13.31
1514	10.00	0.627	2.84	4.69	13.08
average	9.00	0.600	2.75	4.41	12.70

smoked red herrings number	eggs number	loaf sugar in pounds avoirdupois	tallow candles in pounds avoirdupois	weighted index of prices 1500–4 = 100[2]	index of the mason's wages 1500–4 = 100
43.40	87.0	2.16	4.60	93.96	100.00
40.85	–	1.95	4.75	103.54	100.00
43.40	–	2.47	4.38	107.65	100.00
57.87	–	2.47	4.31	97.01	100.00
57.87	–	2.47	4.18	97.88	100.00
47.56	[87.0]	2.28	4.43	100.00	100.00
47.35	73.0	2.03	4.18	106.19	100.00
30.19	83.3	2.30	4.05	112.92	100.00
50.50	82.4	1.98	4.05	106.48	100.00
36.44	75.8	1.92	3.87	102.57	100.00
44.72	73.5	1.92	3.83	95.83	100.00
40.37	77.4	2.02	3.99	104.80	100.00
57.87	70.9	1.82	4.01	93.96	100.00
36.55	81.5	1.92	4.08	106.12	100.00
37.88	73.5	0.86	4.31	126.78	100.00
45.77	90.9	1.15	4.87	132.09	120.00
32.05	87.0	1.30	4.60	132.33	120.00
40.09	80.6	1.29	4.38	118.25	108.00

NOTES

1 The averages of wages, price-indices, and wage-indices have been calculated by the arithmetic mean; the averages of the quantities of commodities by the harmonic mean.

2 The weighted price-index has been constructed from the price-relatives of all the commodities in this table, except for that of eggs. For an explanation see above, 316.

SOURCE

Calculated from tables in Herman Van der Wee *The Growth of the Antwerp Market and the European Economy, Fourteenth to Sixteenth Centuries* I (The Hague 1963) 186, 298, 214, 285, 207, 320, 252, and 460 respectively

TOP The écu d'or à la couronne
last struck in 1474
obverse and reverse

CENTRE The Tudor gold angel-noble
as struck from 1485 to 1526
obverse and reverse

BOTTOM The first English shilling (called 'teston' or 'tester')
a silver coin, as struck from 1504 to 1526
obverse and reverse

British Museum, London
The coins on this page are reproduced at 110 per cent of size.

TABLE D

THE ESTIMATED ANNUAL EMPLOYMENT AND INCOME OF AN ANTWERP MASON 1500 TO 1514

The daily summer and winter wages of a master mason at Antwerp, in Flemish gros, the number of days employment per year, and his estimated annual income in pounds gros Flemish and in sterling equivalents, in annual and quinquennial averages

year	daily summer wage (15 Mar.–30 Sept.) in d gr	daily winter wage (1 Oct.–14 Mar.) in d gr	Number of days employment per year	estimated annual income in pounds gros Flemish	equivalent income values in pounds sterling[1]	annual wage-income index 1500–4 = 100	weighted price index[2] 1500–4 = 100
1500	8.33d	6.00d	200	£6.361	£4.373	93.98	93.96
1501	8.33d	6.00d	216	6.870	4.723	101.51	103.54
1502	8.33d	6.00d	216	6.870	4.723	101.51	107.65
1503	8.33d	6.00d	216	6.870	4.723	101.51	97.01
1504	8.33d	6.00d	216	6.870	4.723	101.51	97.88
average	8.33d	6.00d	212.8	£6.768	£4.653	100.00	100.00
1505	8.33d	6.00d	200	£6.361	£4.373	93.98	106.19
1506	8.33d	6.00d	210	6.679	4.592	98.68	112.92
1507	8.33d	6.00d	210	6.679	4.592	98.68	106.48
1508	8.33d	6.00d	220	6.997	4.810	103.38	102.57
1509	8.33d	6.00d	220	6.997	4.810	103.38	95.83
average	8.33d	6.00d	212.0	£6.743	£4.636	99.62	104.80
1510	8.33d	6.00d	216	£6.870	£4.723	101.51	93.96
1511	8.33d	6.00d	211	6.711	4.614	99.16	106.12
1512	8.33d	6.00d	219	6.965	4.788	102.91	126.78
1513	10.00d	6.00d	214	7.847	5.395	115.94	132.09
1514	10.00d	7.00d	216	8.190	5.631	121.01	132.33
average	9.00d	6.20d	215.2	£7.317	£5.030	108.11	118.25

NOTES

1 The amounts in pounds gros Flemish have been converted into equivalent pounds sterling by the ratio of the silver contents of the two moneys-of-account, so that £1 0s 0d gros Flemish = 13s 9d sterling (= £0.6875)

2 For an explanation of the weighted price index, see above, 316.

SOURCE

Calculated from tables in Herman Van der Wee *The Growth of the Antwerp Market* I 347, 460, 541–2; and from table C, above.

TABLE E

THE STANDARD OF LIVING OF THE ENGLISH MASON 1500 TO 1514

The daily wage of a master mason at Cambridge and Oxford, and its purchasing power, in terms of quantities of various commodities, expressed in annual and quinquennial averages[1]

year	master mason's daily wage in pence	wheat (Exeter) in bushels	red Bordeaux wine in litres (35 oz)	smoked red herrings number	codfish number
1500	5.00	0.366	2.84	52.08	0.95
1501	5.75	0.535	–	44.92	2.05
1502	5.75	0.514	3.27	40.64	1.18
1503	6.00	0.517	3.64	–	1.97
1504	6.00	0.517	–	–	1.00
average	5.70	0.485	3.31	46.80	1.29
1505	6.00	0.702	–	–	2.00
1506	6.00	0.634	3.27	–	2.14
1507	6.00	0.578	3.41	–	2.08
1508	6.00	0.678	3.52	42.86	2.14
1509	6.00	0.821	–	44.12	2.17
average	6.00	0.673	3.40	43.48	2.11
1510	6.00	0.704	3.41	41.81	2.46
1511	6.00	0.615	–	37.38	–
1512	6.00	0.604	3.03	46.15	–
1513	6.50	0.669	–	48.15	1.25
1514	5.50	0.679	3.13	34.38	0.95
average	6.00	0.652	3.27	41.15	1.34

SOURCES

James E. Thorold Rogers *A History of Agriculture and Prices in England* IV *1401–1582* (Oxford: Clarendon Press 1882) 684–6, 542–3, 543–4, 287–9, 685–7, 378–9, 605, 586; and 500–6, 518–20 (mason's wages), respectively

B.R. Mitchell and P. Deane eds *Abstract of British Historical Statistics* (Cambridge 1962) 484–5 (Exeter wheat prices)

E.H. Phelps Brown and Sheila Hopkins 'Seven centuries of the prices of consumables, compared with builders' wage-rates' *Economica* 88 (1956), reprinted in E.M. Carus-Wilson ed *Essays in Economic History* II (London 1962) 180, 194

green garden peas in gallons	loaf sugar in pounds	tallow candles in pounds	paper in sheets	table linen in yards	weighted price index[2] 1500–4 = 100	index of the mason's wages 1500–4 = 100
7.07	–	5.00	80.0	0.39	86.40	87.72
–	1.92	5.75	78.8	–	98.45	100.88
–	–	4.68	69.0	1.15	112.13	100.88
8.35	2.18	5.05	62.6	1.24	104.78	105.26
–	–	5.14	73.9	–	98.35	105.26
8.00	1.98	5.10	72.0	0.76	100.00	100.00
10.67	2.00	6.00	73.9	0.60	94.67	105.26
8.00	–	5.54	72.0	0.79	97.43	105.26
6.00	–	5.14	90.0	–	90.07	105.26
12.29	–	5.33	72.0	–	91.91	105.26
8.17	–	6.00	85.3	1.09	84.56	105.26
8.49	[2.00]	5.58	77.9	0.78	91.73	105.26
8.83	1.50	6.00	90.00	0.80	94.67	105.26
7.53	–	6.00	90.0	–	89.15	105.26
6.19	0.92	6.00	92.9	1.00	92.83	105.26
5.70	1.00	6.50	86.6	0.65	110.29	114.04
3.91	1.05	3.47	110.0	–	108.46	96.49
6.01	1.08	5.37	92.9	0.77	99.08	105.26

NOTES

1. The averages of wages, price-indices, and wage-indices have been calculated by the arithmetic mean; the averages of the quantities of commodities by the harmonic mean.
2. The weighted price-index is that of Phelps Brown and Hopkins' 'basket of consumables,' discussed above at 318–19.

TABLE F

PRICES OF DYED WOOLLEN CLOTHS OF MECHLIN AND GHENT 1500 TO 1514

As purchased annually for the burgermasters and aldermen of those cities respectively, in pounds groot Flemish and equivalent pounds sterling English, with quinquennial averages

	black rooslaken cloths, 30 ells long, of Mechlin[1]				dickedinnen cloths of Ghent, 30 ells long, variously dyed in plain colours[2]			
year	price in pounds groot Flemish	equivalent value in English pounds sterling[3]	price relatives 1500–4 = 100	no. of days' labour of an Antwerp mason to buy 1 yd	price in pounds groot Flemish	equivalent value in English pounds sterling[3]	price relatives 1500–4 = 100	no. of days' labour of an Antwerp mason to buy 1 yd
1500	9.521	6.546	97.1	12.13	11.750	8.078	100.4	14.74
1501	10.353	7.118	105.6	13.19	11.500	7.906	98.3	14.42
1502	9.670	6.648	98.6	12.32	11.500	7.906	98.3	14.42
1503	10.355	7.119	105.6	13.19	12.000	8.250	102.6	15.05
1504	9.121[4]	6.271	93.0	11.62	11.750	8.078	100.4	14.74
average	9.804	6.740	100.0	12.49	11.700	8.044	100.0	14.67
1505	10.145	6.975	103.5	12.93	12.100	8.319	103.4	15.17
1506	10.000	6.875	102.0	12.74	12.050	8.284	103.0	15.11
1507	10.000	6.875	102.0	12.74	12.000	8.250	102.6	15.05
1508	10.000	6.875	102.0	12.74	12.250	8.422	104.7	15.36
1509	10.000	6.875	102.0	12.74	12.750	8.766	109.0	16.00
average	10.029	6.895	102.3	12.78	12.230	8.408	104.5	15.34
1510	10.000	6.875	102.0	12.74	13.375	9.195	114.3	16.77
1511	10.000	6.875	102.0	12.74	13.000	8.938	111.1	16.30
1512	10.833	7.448	110.5	13.80	13.000	8.938	111.1	16.30
1513	11.433	7.860	116.6	12.14	13.000	8.938	111.1	13.59
1514	10.889	7.486	111.1	11.56	13.000	8.938	111.1	13.59
average	10.631	7.309	108.4	12.60	13.075	8.989	111.8	15.31

NOTES

1 Black rooslaken cloths of Mechlin: 30 ells long = 20.670 metres = 22.605 yards = 67.816 feet

2 Dyed dickedinnen cloths of Ghent, purchased annually to be worn by the civic aldermen in attendance at the festival of Onse Lieve Vrouw of Tournay: 30 ells long = 21.000 metres = 22.966 yards = 68.898 feet
The woollens of both Mechlin and Ghent had a width, when dyed and finished, that averaged 2.5 ells (10 quarters) = 1.750 metres = 1.914 yards = 5.754 feet.

3 Since the cloths were all priced, in the civic treasurer's accounts, in terms of the silver-based livre gros or the pound groot of Flanders, the corresponding equivalent values in English pounds sterling were calculated according to the current ratio of the silver contents of the Flemish and English moneys-of-account, which was then £1.000 groot Flemish = £0.6875 sterling English.

4 Medley ('mincxel') rooslaken, of variegated colours

SOURCES

Mechlin: Stadsarchief Mechelen, Stadsrekeningen 1499–1500 to 1513–14, nos 175–89; and Algemeen Rijksarchief (België), Rekenkamer nos 41, 280–5

Ghent: Stadsarchief Gent, Stadsrekeningen 1499–1500 to 1513–14, nos 400:34(2)–41(2)

For the daily wages of master masons at Antwerp, see table C.

TABLE OF CORRESPONDENTS

WORKS FREQUENTLY CITED

SHORT TITLE FORMS

INDEX

TABLE OF CORRESPONDENTS

WORKS FREQUENTLY CITED

This list provides full bibliographical information for articles, books, and periodicals referred to in short title form in the headnotes and footnotes to letters 142–297. For Erasmus' writings, see the short title list, pages 354–6.

Allen	P.S. Allen, H.M. Allen, and H.W. Garrod eds *Opus epistolarum Des. Erasmi Roterodami* (Oxford 1906–58) 12 vols
ARG	*Archiv für Reformationsgeschichte*
ASD	*Opera omnia Desiderii Erasmi Roterodami* (Amsterdam 1969–) edition in progress
BHR	*Bibliothèque d'humanisme et renaissance*
Bierlaire	Franz Bierlaire *La Familia d'Erasme: Contribution à l'histoire de l'humanisme* (Paris 1968)
Correspondance	*La correspondance d'Erasme* (Brussels and Quebec 1967–) edition in progress
Creighton	M. Creighton *A History of the Papacy during the Period of the Reformation* (London 1882–94) 5 vols
CWE	The Collected Works of Erasmus
E&C	H.C. Porter ed and D.F.S. Thomson trans *Erasmus and Cambridge: The Cambridge Letters of Erasmus* (Toronto 1963)
EHR	*The English Historical Review*
Emden BRUC	A.B. Emden *A Biographical Register of the University of Cambridge to 1500* (Cambridge 1963)
Emden BRUO	A.B. Emden *A Biographical Register of the University of Oxford to A.D. 1500* (Oxford 1957–9) 3 vols
Geanakoplos	D.J. Geanakoplos *Greek Scholars in Venice* (Cambridge, Mass 1962)
JHI	*Journal of the History of Ideas*
LB	J. Leclerc ed *Desiderii Erasmi Roterodami opera omnia* (Leiden 1703–6) 10 vols
Lupton *Colet*	J.H. Lupton *A Life of John Colet* (London 1887; repr Hamden, Conn 1961)
Mackie	J.D. Mackie *The Earlier Tudors, 1485–1558* (Oxford 1952)
NAKG	*Nederlands Archief voor Kerkgeschiedenis*
Nichols	F.M. Nichols trans *The Epistles of Erasmus* (London 1901–18) 3 vols
NK	W. Nijhoff and M.E. Kronenberg eds *Nederlandsche Bibliographie van 1500 tot 1540* (The Hague 1923, 1962–6) 3 vols
Opuscula	W.K. Ferguson ed *Erasmi opuscula: A Supplement to the Opera Omnia* (The Hague 1933)
Phillips	Margaret Mann Phillips ed and trans *The 'Adages' of Erasmus: A Study with Translations* (Cambridge 1964)
Rashdall	H. Rashdall *The Universities of Europe in the Middle Ages* revised F.M. Powicke and A.B. Emden (Oxford 1936) 3 vols

Reedijk	C. Reedijk ed *The Poems of Desiderius Erasmus* (Leiden 1956)
Renaudet *Erasme et l'Italie*	A. Renaudet *Erasme et l'Italie* (Geneva 1954)
Renaudet *Préréforme*	A. Renaudet *Préréforme et humanisme à Paris pendant les premières guerres d'Italie (1494–1517)* 2nd ed (Paris 1953)
Rossi	V. Rossi *Il Quattrocento* 2nd rev ed (Milan 1933)
Scrinium	*Scrinium Erasmianum* ed J. Coppens (Leiden 1969) 2 vols
SP	*Studies in Philology*
SP Henry VIII	*Calendar of Letters and Papers, Foreign and Domestic, of the Reign of Henry VIII* ed J.S. Brewer, J. Gairdner, and R.H. Brodie (London 1864–1932) 21 vols plus 2 vols addenda
SR	*Studies in the Renaissance*
STC	A.W. Pollard and G.R. Redgrave compilers *A Short-Title Catalogue of Books Printed in England, Scotland, and Ireland and of English Books Printed Abroad, 1475–1640* (London 1926)
Thompson *Colloquies*	Craig R. Thompson ed and trans *The Colloquies of Erasmus* (Chicago 1965)

SHORT TITLE FORMS FOR ERASMUS' WORKS

Acta contra Lutherum: Acta academiae Lovaniensis contra Lutherum
Adagia (Adagiorum Collectanea for the primitive form, when required)
Admonitio adversus mendacium: Admonitio adversus mendacium et obtrectationem
Annotationes de haereticis: Annotationes in leges pontificias et caesareas de haereticis
Annotationes in Novum Testamentum
Antibarbari
Apologia ad Fabrum: Apologia ad Iacobum Fabrum Stapulensem
Apologia ad Carranza: Apologia ad Sanctium Carranza
Apologia adversus Petrum Sutorem: Apologia adversus debacchationes Petri Sutoris
Apologia adversus monachos: Apologia adversus monachos quosdam hispanos
Apologia adversus rhapsodias Alberti Pii
Apologia contra Latomi dialogum: Apologia contra Iacobi Latomi dialogum de tribus linguis
Apologia contra Stunicam: Apologia contra Lopidem Stunicam
Apologia de 'In principio erat sermo'
Apologia de laude matrimonii: Apologia pro declamatione de laude matrimonii
Apologia de loco 'omnes quidem': Apologia de loco 'Omnes quidem resurgemus'
Apologiae duae
Apologiae omnes
Apologia invectivis Lei: Apologia qua respondet duabus invectivis Eduardi Lei
Apologia monasticae religionis
Apophthegmata
Argumenta: Argumenta in omnes epistolas apostolicas nova
Axiomata pro causa Lutheri: Axiomata pro causa Martini Lutheri

Carmina
Catalogus lucubrationum
Cato
Christiani hominis institutum
Ciceronianus: Dialogus Ciceronianus
Colloquia
Compendium rhetorices
Compendium vitae
Conflictus: Conflictus Thaliae et barbariei

De bello turcico: Consultatio de bello turcico
De civilitate: De civilitate morum puerilium
De conscribendis epistolis
De constructione: De constructione octo partium orationis
De contemptu mundi
De copia: De duplici copia verborum ac rerum
Declamatio de morte
Declamationes
Declamatiuncula

Declamatiunculae
Declarationes ad censuras Lutetiae: Declarationes ad censuras Lutetiae vulgates
De concordia: De sarcienda ecclesiae concordia
De immensa Dei misericordia: Concio de immensa Dei misericordia
De libero arbitrio: De libero arbitrio diatribe
De praeparatione: De praeparatione ad mortem
De pronuntiatione: De recta latini graecique sermonis pronuntiatione
De pueris instituendis: De pueris statim ac liberaliter instituendis
De puero Iesu: Concio de puero Iesu
De puritate tabernaculi
De ratione studii
Detectio praestigiarum: Detectio praestigiarum cuiusdam libelli germanice scripti
De tedio Iesu: Disputatiuncula de tedio, pavore, tristicia Iesu
Dilutio: Dilutio eorum quae Iodocus Clichthoueus scripsit adversus declamationem suasoriam matrimonii

Ecclesiastes: Ecclesiastes sive de ratione concionandi
Enchiridion: Enchiridion militis christiani
Encomium matrimonii
Encomium medicinae: Declamatio in laudem artis medicae
Epigrammata
Epistola ad fratres: Epistola ad fratres Inferioris Germaniae
Epistola consolatoria: Epistola consolatoria in adversis
Epistola contra pseudevangelicos: Epistola contra quosdam qui se falso iactant evangelicos
Epistola de apologia Cursii: Epistola de apologia Petri Cursii
Epistola de esu carnium: Epistola apologetica ad Christophorum episcopum Basiliensem de interdicto esu carnium
Epistola de modestia: Epistola de modestia profitendi linguas
Exomologesis: Exomologesis sive modus confitendi
Explanatio symboli: Explanatio symboli apostolorum sive catechismus

Formulae: Conficiendarum epistolarum formulae

Hyperaspistes

Institutio christiani matrimonii
Institutio principis christiani

Julius exclusus: Dialogus Julius exclusus e coelis

Liber quo respondet annotationibus Lei: Liber quo respondet annotationibus Eduardi Lei
Lingua
Liturgia Virginis Matris: Virginis Matris apud Lauretum cultae liturgia
Lucubrationes
Lucubratiunculae

Methodus
Modus orandi Deum
Moria: Moriae encomium, or Moria

Novum instrumentum
Novum Testamentum

Obsecratio ad Virginem Mariam: Obsecratio sive oratio ad Virginem Mariam in rebus adversis
Oratio de pace: Oratio de pace et discordia
Oratio de virtute: Oratio de virtute amplectenda
Oratio funebris: Oratio funebris Berthae de Heyen

Paean Virgini Matri: Paean Virgini Matri dicendus
Panegyricus: Panegyricus ad Philippum Austriae ducem
Parabolae: Parabolae sive similia
Paraclesis
Paraphrasis in Elegantias Vallae: Paraphrasis in Elegantias Laurentii Vallae
Paraphrases in Novum Testamentum
Paraphrasis in Matthaeum: Paraphrasis in Matthaeum, etc.
Peregrinatio apostolorum: Peregrinatio apostolorum Petri et Pauli
Precatio ad Virginis filium Iesum
Precatio dominica
Precationes
Precatio pro pace ecclesiae: Precatio ad Iesum pro pace ecclesiae
Progymnasmata: Progymnasmata quaedam primae adolescentiae Erasmi
Psalmi: Psalmi (Enarrationes sive commentarii in psalmos)
Purgatio adversus epistolam Lutheri: Purgatio adversus epistolam non sobriam Lutheri

Querela pacis

Ratio verae theologiae
Responsio ad annotationes Lei: Responsio ad annotationes Eduardi Lei
Responsio ad annotationem Stunicae: Responsio ad annotationem Iacobi Lopis Stunicae
Responsio ad collationes: Responsio ad collationes cuiusdam iuvenis gerontodidascali
Responsio ad disputationem de diuortio: Responsio ad disputationem cuiusdam Phimostomi de diuortio
Responsio ad epistolam apologeticam: Responsio ad fratres Germaniae Inferioris ad epistolam apologeticam incerto autore proditam
Responsio ad epistolam Pii: Responsio ad epistolam paraeneticam Alberti Pii
Responsio adversus febricitantis libellum: Responsio adversus febricitantis cuiusdam libellum
Responsio contra Egranum: Responsio apologetica contra Sylvium Egranum

Spongia: Spongia adversus aspergines Hutteni
Supputatio: Supputatio calumniarum Natalis Bedae

Vidua christiana
Virginis et martyris comparatio
Vita Hieronymi: Vita diui Hieronymi Stridonensis

Index

Indexes of scriptural and classical allusions will be provided in the final correspondence volume for the entire correspondence series.

This book

was designed by

ALLAN FLEMING

and was printed by

University of

Toronto

Press